BETWEEN GOD AND CAESAR

also published by Paulist Press

other volumes from the WOODSTOCK THEOLOGICAL CENTER

ABOVE EVERY NAME, edited by Thomas E. Clarke
CLAIMS IN CONFLICT, by David Hollenbach
THE FAITH THAT DOES JUSTICE, edited by John C. Haughey
INEQUALITY AND THE AMERICAN CONSCIENCE,
by Christopher F. Mooney
PERSONAL VALUE IN PUBLIC POLICY,
edited by John C. Haughey
RELIGIOUS FREEDOM: 1965 AND 1975,
A SYMPOSIUM ON A HISTORIC DOCUMENT,
edited by Walter Burghardt
TRACING THE SPIRIT, edited by James E. Hug

BETWEEN
GOD AND CAESAR

Priests, Sisters and Political Office
in the United States

MADONNA KOLBENSCHLAG, HM
editor

PAULIST PRESS
New York/Mahwah

Acknowledgement is hereby made of permission to use or excerpt the following publications:

Thomas Gannon, "Reverend Father Congressman," previously published in *America*, November 21, 1970, pp. 424–428.

Joseph A. Komonchak, "Clergy, Laity, and the Church's Mission in the World," previously published in *The Jurist*, 41 (1981), 422–47; and in *Official Ministry in a New Age*, ed. J. H. Provost (Washington: CLSA, 1981), pp. 168–93.

Rosemary Smith, SC, *et al.*, "Political Involvement and the Revised Code," previously published in the *Newsletter of the Leadership Conference of Women Religious*, Vol. 11, No. 2, June 1984, pp. 9–16.

"Religious Life and Human Promotion," a document of the Sacred Congregation for Religious and Secular Institutes, 1980, published by the U.S. Catholic Conference, in *Origins*, February 5, 1981, Vol. 10, No. 34.

Report to the Congregation for Religious, 1978 on "U.S. Religious Orders Today," Conference of Major Superiors of Men and the Leadership Conference of Women Religious (published subsequently in *Origins*, April 20, 1978, Vol. 7, No. 44).

"The Priest and Politics," a publication of the Association of Pittsburgh Priests, June 1983.

Excerpts from the 1983 Code of Canon Law, from *Code of Canon Law, Latin-English Edition* (Canon Law Society of America, 1983) Washington, D.C.

Excerpts from the 1917 Code of Canon Law, from John Abbo and Jerome Hannan, *The Sacred Canons*, Vol. I, 2nd rev. ed., 1960, pp. 198–200, 202–203; and from *Canonical Legislation Concerning Religious*, authorized English translation, Rome, 1919.

Excerpts from "The Ministerial Priesthood," a document of the 1971 Synod of Bishops, in *The Ministerial Priesthood and Justice in the World*, published by the U.S. Catholic Conference, 1982.

Cover art: Kevin F. Novack, C.S.P.

Library of Congress Catalog Card Number: 84-62726

ISBN: 0-8091-2698-2

Published by Paulist Press
997 Macarthur Boulevard
Mahwah, N.J. 07430

Printed and bound in the United States of America

CONTENTS

v

Madonna Kolbenschlag, HM

INTRODUCTION:
THE AMERICAN EXPERIENCE

Religion has never been "the opiate of the masses" in the United States. If the 1984 electoral ferment over religion in politics was not evidence enough, history certainly provides a plethora of examples of the symbiotic relationship between religion and politics in the American culture.

One of the first foreign analysts to comment on the phenomenon was Alexis de Tocqueville, whose observations—recorded during his travels through America in the 1840's—have become something of a cliche:

> In the United States the sovereign authority is religious, and consequently hypocrisy must be common; but there is no country in the world where the Christian religion retains a greater influence over the souls of men than in America.

Nor did the political quality of religion in the U.S. escape de Tocqueville's notice:

> Religious zeal is perpetually warmed in the United States by the fires of patriotism. These men do not act exclusively from a consideration of a future life; eternity is only one motive of their devotion to the cause. If you converse with these missionaries of Christian civilization, you will be surprised to hear them speak so often of the goods of this world, and to meet a politician where you expected to find a priest.[1]

The religious-political alchemy in the American character has been remarkably consistent, although manifested in diverse ways. In

1976, the year of Jimmy Carter's election to the Presidency, a Gallup poll found that 94 percent of the American people believed in God. A variety of other indicators from recent Gallup polls reveals that approximately 68 percent of Americans belong to a church or synagogue; 88 percent say they pray regularly. These percentages are significantly higher than in any other country Gallup has surveyed.[2] This indigenous religious ethos permeates the broad reaches of the American culture, submerged at times by a concern for the things of the world and the distractions of getting and spending, but always ready to rise like an unexpected gusher from a deep underground stream.

While relatively recent and unique, the phenomenon of Catholic priests in Congress and religious sisters in state legislatures has profound cultural as well as ecclesial roots. In cultural terms it is by no means a mutation but in many ways a logical development in a political tradition that began with the colonial period in America when the missionary or minister-politician-overseer was a familiar figure. The social amalgam of sacred and profane pursuits that was the lot of many clergymen was a necessary condition of service in the New World. Moreover, the First Great Awakening spawned a prophetic, evangelical breed of ministers who became the primary catalysts of the Revolution and the emerging Republican consciousness.

In the post-Revolutionary period, many of the clergymen who found their way into the state legislatures neglected to resume their ministry, while others mingled the two careers, generally with the approval of their congregations who regarded politics in the new Republic as an appropriate channel for the expression of religious values and the achievement of evangelical goals. By 1800 there were many in the ranks of the new statesmen who had once served in the ministry. Numerous political addresses, delivered during and immediately after the campaign of 1800, reveal how and why the new political identity appealed so readily to the pious "as a reaffirmation of the evangelical scheme."[3]

The career of men like Stanley Griswold of Connecticut is typical. In the 1790's he preached unceasingly to his parishioners on the glory of the approaching millennium. By 1798, he was promulgating his own vision of the "Republican millennium," and in 1800 he participated in the electoral campaign; thereafter he was frequently featured as a speaker at Connecticut festivals. By 1803 he assumed the editorship of a political journal and soon migrated to Ohio where he was elected to the U.S. Senate and eventually became a Federal judge in the territory of Illinois. His activism exemplified the new spirit of evangelicalism at the onset of the Second Great Awakening.

The odyssey of the minister from pulpit to podium and political office has been a consistent phenomenon ever since. The current Congress numbers four clergymen among its ranks. State and local governments include many more. Thus, when Jesuit Robert Drinan was elected to Congress in 1970 and Norbertine Robert Cornell in 1974, and when Sister Clare Dunn took a seat in the Arizona state legislature in 1974, they were simply the most visible exemplars of an implicit tradition of "vocational democracy" that had finally impacted on the Catholic "minority." They represented, ten years after the Kennedy presidency, another evidence of the "coming-of-age" of the Catholic Church in the United States and the visible affirmation of the American conviction—enshrined in the Constitution—that in no way should one's commitment to the church, at whatever level, be an obstacle to fullest participation in the body politic.

From another point of view, however, the emergence of Catholic clergymen and religious women in political offices was an anomaly, particularly within the Catholic community itself. Since the colonial period and the days of the early Republic, Catholic priests and bishops remained comparatively aloof from politics well into the twentieth century. Catholic churchmen conscientiously abstained from civil offices, and the antagonism many Americans felt for "papist deputies" was a major deterrent until the election of John F. Kennedy in 1960. For many Americans, even after 1970, the prospect of "official" representatives of the Catholic church serving simultaneously as representatives of the people or as functionaries in government was disturbing. This was particularly true among Catholics. Those who saw the church as a separate, sacred enclave with a transcendent purpose were troubled by the new phenomenon. Likewise, those who saw the role of church people as primarily charismatic and prophetic were also troubled, since this phenomenon risked the co-optation of the charismatics and prophets by the very powers and principalities they were called to critique.

Before a decade had passed, conflicts, controversy and disciplinary actions surfaced. Priests bowed obediently to their superiors and to the Holy See; sisters were canonically separated from their communities when they elected to honor their public commitments. Canon Law was revised and the canons affecting clergy and religious in respect to "civil offices" were made more restrictive. Bishops became more wary of granting exemptions, since the Vatican clearly had no hesitation in overriding bishops as well as major superiors on this issue. Catholics, and, indeed, many concerned citizens began to raise new questions about the separation of church and state and about the implications of this phenomenon for the mission of the church.

A 1984 survey conducted by the Leadership Conference of Women Religious and the Conference of Major Superiors of Men at our request revealed a dramatic difference between men and women religious in the degree of participation in civil offices. Community central administrations were questioned about the number of their members who were currently serving or in recent years had served in positions in government—elected or appointed—at the city, county, state and national levels. Approximately half (195) of the total number of religious communities of women in the United States responded, and approximately a third of those (66) indicated the involvement of one or more sisters in such positions. Less than ten were elected officials; most were involved in appointed offices at the state level. An estimated total of 125 sisters in the sample hold political offices. Less than half of the men's communities responded to the survey (49 out of approximately 130 communities of men in the U.S.) Only one indicated the involvement of a member in a political office. We were unable to ascertain or even estimate any figures for secular clergy. The few I did locate were understandably reluctant to make their identity and experience known, but there are some.

The focus of our study, like the subtitle of our volume, necessarily highlights the activity of priests and sisters, since the data reported from the sample of men's religious orders revealed no specific instances of political activity on the part of religious brothers comparable to that of the sisters. Clearly the phenomenon, in terms of numbers, is most visible among religious women. This should in no way be interpreted as an indication that religious brothers are not engaged at all in political ministry—the data simply does not indicate anywhere near the same level of involvement, whether statistically or in terms of specific offices.

In addition, because the political involvement of priests is generally not subject to a communal process and systematic record-keeping, as is the case with most religious women, their political ministry is more difficult to estimate—and probably a phenomenon of lesser magnitude, although similar in kind to that of religious women. On the other hand, our LCWR survey revealed that American religious women were engaged in a broad range of political or quasi-political activity that included the following:

1) Elected offices in legislatures, city councils, county and regional boards and commissions, school boards, etc. The survey identified three sisters who served in the state legislatures of Arizona, North Dakota and Rhode Island. Others have been candidates for the state legislature in Colorado, Pennsylvania, Iowa, Indiana, Minnesota, Wisconsin and South Dakota. Only two or three have been candidates for Congress; fewer than half a dozen have been elected mayors. One was identified as a former candidate for the vice-presidency on the Socialist ticket.

2) By far the greatest number are serving in appointed offices at the state or local level: in state departments of human services, public health, education, environmental protection, on commissions of human rights, economic opportunity, aging. Sisters are also found on local planning commissions, as directors of health, housing, vocational training, in special advocacy offices for the elderly, for children, for minority businesses, for the disabled and handicapped. There are a few who work in federally-funded programs for such things as drug abuse, food and agriculture, geological survey, job training and—increasingly so—in legal aid services.

3) A few sisters have served in government at the national level, either as policy advisors to agencies such as HEW or as legislative aides to members of Congress.

4) A growing number of religious women are involved directly or peripherally in the criminal justice system: in the department of corrections, on parole boards, in the public defender's office, in juvenile court, in prison services. Two women who have recently sought dispensations from their religious orders are a state attorney general and a judge-court master, respectively.

5) While the survey revealed only a few sisters engaged in overt activity in political parties, the number is believed to be somewhat higher, since we have received reports of sisters' involvement as delegates to state and national conventions, as precinct committeewomen, and county party chairpersons and local ward chairs.

6) A final category of activity which is difficult to measure statistically because it is more diffuse is that of lobbyist. It would seem that a few sisters are engaged full or part-time as lobbyists for advocacy organizations or agencies at the state and national level.

Thus it should come as no surprise that in recent years—often for the first time—general chapters of religious communities, particularly of women, are including the discussion of political activity on their chapter agendas. Questions such as "What is considered political activity?", "What should be the limits to that activity in the light of the church's mission, law, and of our own religious charism?", "What about candidacy for office, party politics, civil disobedience?"—are among the questions being asked. What is emerging from the discussion and discernment processes is a range of experienced activities that can form the basis of a kind of taxonomy of political activity relevant to religious professionals. This scheme should be helpful to understanding the subject of our volume:

1) In the strictest sense of the concept political activity is understood as those kinds of activity that are aimed at gaining political power and exercising it through socially constituted forms of government and participation. In a representative democracy, this kind of power is exercised primarily through political parties and the process of being candidates for election—or being appointed to executive, legislative or judicial posts in government and serving in those posts. Such posts, whether at the national, state or local level, involve the exercise of "civil power" as defined by implication in the Revised Code. These kinds of activities are viewed as explicitly political and often categorized as "partisan," but they are predicated on the existence of the most fundamental political act in a representative democratic society, which is the right to vote. The one seems to imply the other.

2) A second level of political activity is often described as "nonpartisan." This kind of activity is overtly political, that is, intended to influence the exercise of power, public policy or the electoral process, but outside the constituted political structures. Examples of such activity include strikes, defense of human rights, demonstrations against public policy, defense of the right of assembly, testimony before legislatures, taking a public stand on controversial issues or impending legislation. Political action committees, ecumenical groups, conferences of bishops and of major superiors, lobbies, women's groups, human rights organizations, labor unions, professional and trade organizations, neighborhood action groups are among those who typically engage in such activity. In a religious context, some of these activities may be seen as fulfilling a "prophetic" imperative; some might be seen as special-interest advocacy. Discerned collaboration and networking is becoming a key element in this kind of political activity.

3) A third level of political activity is generically similar but less focused on specific issues and actions. It involves the presentation of proposals and criticisms that reflect an overall philosophy of socio-political life, a moral vision. Characteristically, it provides a context for

influencing the exercise of social and political power. Many research institutes and "think-tanks" fall into this category. So too the social teachings of the church, the papal encyclicals and bishops' pastorals. (Some would argue that the Peace Pastoral of the American bishops or the Heritage Foundation are exercises of second level politics rather than third level!) Likewise membership in such organizations as the League of Women Voters, Common Cause and other citizens' groups not identified with single issues or specific programs or platforms. The third level of political activity often involves the articulation of an ideology or world view.

4) The fourth level of political activity is both implicit and comprehensive; it involves participation in the socio-political reality as a total system. In this sense no one escapes being involved in political activity. Every action and choice has a political aspect. Thus corporate policies, whether of the Jesuits or General Motors, have political significance. Likewise choices in ministry and lifestyle by religious professionals have a definite political aspect. As a recent Maryknoll policy paper states, "Political significance is determined by factors other than our good intentions and motivations."[4]

The subject of this volume necessarily focuses on the first level: political activity as overt participation in political offices, in political parties, and in the exercise of civil power. The modest survey we conducted would seem to demonstrate the vast spectrum of functions that must be included within the scope of that definition, and suggests the widespread impact that the new canons concerning political activity in the Revised Code could potentially have on religious professionals and on American politics in general. This taxonomy, then, provides a frame of reference for observing and assessing the emergence of "political ministry" among Catholic priests, sisters and brothers.

Inquiring more specifically into the origins of the contemporary U.S. phenomenon, we find that beginning in the 1970's there was a noticeable influx of U.S. religious women—and to a lesser extent, clergy and religious men—into "political ministry," a concept that did not exist until after Vatican Council II. An examination of the representative selection of chronicles in this book reveals a consistent pattern as well as a few variables in the social forces and motivations that brought these men and women to the threshold of political office.

The priests who emerged in the early '70's as candidates for Congressional seats were universally "peace" candidates, running primarily because of their moral outrage over the Vietnam war. Priests who assumed political offices at the local and state level, or in government agencies, were usually identified with disadvantaged constituencies either through urban or rural ministry, or through civil rights activism. Another group seem to have been "reform" candidates, seeking office almost reluctantly because of corruption and incompetence in local situations. Like the ministers of the colonial, revolutionary and republican eras, these clergymen characteristically exhibited an "evangelical" consciousness that at the time seemed to be a zealous response to a need for leadership and reform of public policy.

The sisters, in numbers far exceeding their male clerical and religious peers, emerged into "political ministry" in the 1970's in response to several developments. In terms of remote but definitive influences, one would have to recognize the impact of the Sister Formation Movement and the call to "aggiornamento" ssued by Vatican Council II. The Sister Formation Movement grew out of the NCEA meeting in Kansas City in April, 1952, where the preparation of sisters for the teaching apostolate and the pronouncements of Piux XII on that subject was the major concern on the agenda. The meetings, workshops, programs, publications which the Sister Formation association generated in subsequent years produced a quantum leap in the professional and personal development of Catholic sisters by the late 1960's, just in time for religious congregations to take up the challenge of renewal in the post-Vatican II years. Sociologically, both movements produced in the decade of the 1970's the largest educated, articulate, cohesive and involved group of women in the history of the United States.

More than any other group in the church, the American sisters internalized the theology and ecclesiology of Vatican II; it spurred and inspired their internal congregational renewal and radical changes in the perception of their apostolic ministry. Three issues in particular affected American religious communities' sense of identity and mission: 1) fidelity to their founding charism, 2) collegiality and subsidiarity in internal structures, 3) the option for the poor. Thus the accelerated level of education and professional training along with a new theology of church and religious life led to internal renewal and the expression of it in new ministries. The experience of these new ministries led to a new perception of the structural nature of many social evils and inequities; identification with the disadvantaged and marginated led to a realization that some of these problems had to be addressed through public policy. Direct services were not enough.

Thus the predominant pattern in the emergence of Catholic sisters into "political ministry" is a post-Vatican II transition from primarily middle-class identification to the adoption of a new constituency and priority to be placed on justice and quality-of-life concerns for the disadvantaged and powerless. Most of the first wave of sisters into politics once had an educational ministry. After their chapters of renewal they either changed the base of their ministry in terms of location and/or class (urban ministry, outreach programs, etc.) or the character of the service institution changed. It is significant that the sisters, more often than the priests, cite papal teachings as influential in the development of their call to "politics."

By 1978 the phenomenon was so pronounced that the conferences of major superiors of men and women religious in the United States submitted a report to the Sacred Congregation which described the new consciousness and the "political praxis" that it had generated in American religious. They noted, "In particular it is our belief that the notion of religious assuming certain lay roles in a 'supplementary' capacity is less valuable than at first may appear. The simple fact is that all the political activities we ascribe to religious appear to be not supplementary, but normal."[5]

The cultural concept of "suppleance" has often been invoked to explain and legitimate radical changes in the social role and function of religious groups and individuals. Historically whenever a social need has arisen and the social structures are not mature enough to serve the needs of the population, wherever the state cannot yet "supply" the demands of the new consciousness or social condition, it has often been the case that new forms of religious life have arisen to meet the need. From the earliest centuries of the church secular clergy were accustomed to assume leadership and administrative civil roles for which the lay population was not as adequately prepared. In the post-Renaissance secularization of society, the changing perception of the role of the state outdistanced the capacity of the state to create structures to implement its newly perceived responsibilities. For example after 1500 the secularization of education left a vacuum; in the lag, the Jesuits and the Ursulines came into existence with their special charisms for education. In the late 17th and 18th century, the health and welfare of the masses reached a disastrous stage; a Vincent de Paul and his new concept of Sisters of Charity appeared. Throughout Europe in the 19th and early 20th centuries the rising consciousness of labor, trade unionism and the like produced a variety of phenomena in which religious groups or church persons began to take a more active role in work environments and in politics.

Historically it should be noted that this process of "suppleance" sometimes runs in the opposite direction, namely in the phenomenon by which the accelerating welfare state gradually subsumes many of the social services of the private voluntary sector where so many religious professionals have traditionally functioned. These changed circumstances often precipitate an "emigration" of religious into government-related agencies and services.

In the late 20th century we have the example of "activist" missionaries and clergy in Latin America, most visibly represented by the priest-cabinet ministers in Nicaragua. The theme of "suppleance" runs like a thread through the flowering of apostolic communities down through the centuries. The ethos and motive underlying the phenomenon has been dramatically and cogently expressed by Miguel D'Escoto, priest and Minister of Foreign Affairs for Nicaragua:

> The will of God appears in relationship with history: it arises out of history itself. Many times it leaps out onto our path just when we're on our way to carry out our scheduled work, our programs. God leaps onto our path with unforeseeable things, things that take us by surprise—especially our wounded neighbor. God's wounded people, God's and ours. Suddenly then, I found myself having to dismount, and attend to my people, wounded to the death, and leave the beaten path of my usual missionary activity. I had to follow the example, not of the priest, but of the good Samaritan. I *have* to do this, out of fidelity to Christ and the love of my people—which aren't different things.[6]

The sentiment and rationale expressed by D'Escoto are similar to those expressed by his U.S. counterparts, candidates for somewhat less visible political offices. Father Louis Gigante of Harlem-South Bronx, one of several priests who ran for Congress in the early seventies, but was not elected, justified his candidacy in a heavily black, Puerto Rican and ethnic district ridden with poor housing, crime and drug addiction, in similar terms: "I have to stick my neck out for my people. The politicians have deserted the people. Drugs and crime are destroying our community . . . I want to be a voice for the people . . . I don't have to stand on the fence and make deals."[7] Elizabeth Morancy, who began her term in the Rhode Island state legislature as a Sister of Mercy and a representative of one of New England's poorest districts, has often noted that in her state the mandated salary for serving in the state legislature is only $300 per year, an income which virtually assures the fact that only the rich are likely to be able to afford the luxury of public service. (Fewer than 15 states pay a legislative salary that exceeds

$15,000 per year. In 36 states the average of compensation rates is $7,700.)

Thus it would seem that there is a certain historical continuity in the phenomenon of "political ministry" that clearly connects it with the mission of the church and the special charism of religious men and women, as well as clerics, who for centuries have devoted themselves to the spiritual and corporal works of mercy, the works of education, healing, social service and justice. "Political ministry" emerged organically out of the tradition. The divergence of religious persons into secular "politics" seems to be related to three possible conditions: 1) a social need that is not being met, or 2) a function that has been corrupted and needs corrective influence, or 3) the changed locus of support for social services and access to the constituent population. The question being asked now is whether the emergence of U.S. clergy and religious into politics is related to and justified by the impairment of political and social structures in the present era; for example, by the effect of bureaucracy, changes in social policy, the impact of affluence, the power of single-interest groups to capture the political process, the apathy of the electorate, economic fluctuations, etc.

Apart from the questions of social and historical context and the justification of political ministry are the more crucial questions of how this phenomenon affects the church's understanding of itself and of the American perception of the proper relationship of church and state.

The essays and reflections in this volume touch in a variety of ways on the question of our understanding of the church's mission and the extent to which it should be identified with "human promotion" in general. One school of thought would make the distinction between sacred and secular clear and essential, and would appeal to the traditional concept of the church as "societas perfecta." Another point of view would insist that Vatican II erased such dualism and would appeal to Paul VI's Evangelii Nuntiandi which proclaimed the mission of the church as a call to "transform every sphere of the human . . . to evangelize not from the outside, as though it were a matter of adding an ornament or a coat of paint, but from within, at the core of life."[8] Paul VI's exhortation as well as many other documents of the magisterium have clearly established the integral relationship between evangelization and human promotion.

The same line of argument points to the clear identification of the mission of the church with the work of justice as articulated by the contemporary church. When the 1971 International Synod of Bishops affirmed that "Action on behalf of justice and participation in the

transformation of the world fully appear to us as a constitutive dimension of the preaching of the Gospel,"9 theologians claim that the
church was articulating a third essential element in the understanding
of its mission, adding a new emphasis on the "ministry of justice" to
the traditional role of the preaching of the Gospel and the celebration
of the sacraments. This perspective raises a further question: if the
ministry of justice is "constitutive" of holiness and the church's mission, then to what extent can one postulate engagement in "politics" as
constitutive of the Christian life?

Another set of questions related to the issue of clergy and religious in politics concerns the distinction between roles within the
church. It is clear that there is ambiguity in respect to this issue, both
in church teaching as well as in practice. One question deals with the
role of the priest as gatherer and unifier of the people of God and to
what extent this is compatible with formal political activity. One school
of thought insists that the priest should be restricted to "those things
which only a priest can do." At the other end of the spectrum is the
view that regards such opinions as elitist and not coherent with the
post-Vatican II theology of church and ministry. Still another point of
view, currently a preferred one in the higher circles of church authority, maintains that "politics" is a prerogative of popes and pro-
nuncios, but not of ordinary clergy and religious.

Perhaps the most conflictive question deals with the role of religious women in the church. Are they laity, as the canonical structure
and power of the church clearly implies; or are they quasi-clerical, as
the minds of the faithful often suppose? To what extent do the prophetic and ministerial charisms of their religious congregations demand and promote greater engagement with the political process?
Finally, there is the question of whether, in the minds of the public,
and of the Catholic laity in particular, the influx of church "professionals" into formal political roles will be seen as a kind of "neo-clericalism" justified in the name of democracy.

It has been said that "Enculturation is an exigency of incarnation."
The phenomenon of clergy and religious persons in political roles can
only be examined and assessed within a particular cultural context: the
way we are church is inevitably more significant than the theory of
church. The historical ecclesiological experience of American Catholics has been affected by the same factors which have affected all believing Americans. American Catholics' perceptions of ecclesial
identity, roles and structures have been influenced by the following
factors to greater or lesser degree: pluralism, the principle of free association (voluntaryism), the concept of separation of church and

state, political democracy, congregationalism, and pragmatic millen-
nialism.

Thus while the issue of involvement in "partisan politics" means
one thing in Italy and France, another in Canada and Great Britain, it
has an entirely different significance in the United States where the
party system becomes an instrument for national consensus, compromise and coalition rather than a doctrinaire and ideological force.
Nevertheless the question of whether ecclesial integrity or the political
process itself may be compromised by the involvement of clergy and
religious in politics is a real one.

In addition to the ordinary exigencies of representative government, examples of extremist groups and politicians by-passing the
electoral process and eliciting the intervention of the Vatican abound.
Bishops have also been implicated in the "pollution" of the electoral
process by forcing the resignation of ecclesial persons from public offices and by influencing the voters in regard to their candidacy. For
Americans, these interventions raise many questions about the wisdom
and prudence of Catholic clergy and religious seeking or accepting political offices. Likewise there is the question of to what extent a priest
or religious serving in a government post or in the judiciary engages
in an act of complicity with a system that is inherently coercive and
potentially violent to persons, or that might involve implementation of
policies that some would judge to be immoral or contrary to the teaching of the magisterium. In which case the question must be asked, does
the risk of complicity or "scandal" weigh more heavily on religious
professionals than on lay persons?

Another set of questions concerns ecclesial power and authority
specifically. Here there is much confusion in the current United States
experience. The 1983 Code categorically forbids priests and religious
to seek political office; at the same time it does not rule out exceptions
to the law. On the other hand, the Vatican has chosen to disallow any
exceptions among the cases that have been brought to its attention.
Jurisdictional conflicts have arisen when a superior, acting with the informed consent of her community and legitimate canonical autonomy,
grants a permission for a ministry that is later rescinded by a local ordinary when the authority of the community is by-passed. Or, we have
situations similar to the cases in Michigan and Minnesota in 1983-84:
one bishop in Michigan revokes his permission to a religious sister to
serve in a state government post for human services and suspends a
priest for attending the Democratic party convention as a delegate.
Another bishop in Minnesota allows a religious sister to occupy a human services post very similar to the one sought by the sister in Mich-

igan and approves of one of his priests attending the Democratic convention as a delegate. Similarly, a sister in New England is forced to leave her community in order to continue her service in the state legislature; a priest in a Western state is allowed to continue in the same post. Or we have a situation such as the Canadian instance in which the decision of the local ordinary granting permission to a priest to serve in Parliament was suddenly overruled by the Vatican. Confusions abound.

Canon Law itself adds to the confusion since the 1983 Code implies that a priest or religious may not work "actively" for a political party but might be an advisor to a president. If the prohibitions are directed at involvement in partisan politics as well as the exercise of civil power, this would seem to create serious ambiguities in the interpretation of those prohibitions in different cultural contexts.

Finally, there remain some sociological and psychological aspects of the phenomenon that raise other questions. The migration of significantly greater numbers of religious women into political activity by comparison with clerics and religious men is no doubt related to their socialization in the post-Vatican II period of renewal and other factors already described. Nevertheless we should not underestimate those factors which impacted most directly on the individual sister's sense of identity and personal autonomy. For example, since Vatican II U.S. religious women—more so than religious men—have experienced a radical change in social identity, from a conventional "sign" to that of dynamic "public witness." The removal of the habit no doubt had much to do with this changed perception—no longer are most religious women comfortable being objectified as "sacred, vowed objects" by the church. This changed identity and role has rearranged values and priorities. In particular, it has upgraded values related to the "common good" and the function of citizenship, values ranging all the way from participation in the political process to civil disobedience. The prophetic and risk-taking aspects of the evangelical life have been enhanced by their identification with authentic political action.

The impact of the women's liberation movement in the United States coincided with many of these developments and should not be underestimated in terms of its widespread effect on American sisters' self-understanding, sense of mission and theological perspective.

Moreover, at the same time as they were becoming more aware of their authentic power in the larger social community, they were becoming even more aware of their disempowerment within the church structure. Thomas O'Meara has described their situation in terms of ministry:

In the United States perhaps seventy percent of the ministry is and has been performed by religious women all of
whom are officially not in the ministry and who, because
real ministry through jurisdiction is tied to ordination to
one or two orders, have no real public life in the church . . .
Certainly their vast accomplishments since the nineteenth
century show that they are major ministers in the American
church. Religious women present the most dramatic
phenomenological "non-compute" in the world of clerical
and lay states; for in their "non-ministry" lie great services, and in their non-sacral spirituality are perduring
charism and ministry.[10]

Sisters have grown in a painful awareness of their "non-compute"
status in the church. For those who are gifted and experienced, the
avenues to legitimate service and power are blocked. My own non-sci-
entific survey of religious women who are making lateral moves into
non-church ministries suggests another, more unconscious motivation: what I call the p-factor, or "patriarchal flight."

O'Meara's analysis of the persistence of clericalism among Jesuits,
Dominicans, and others who are not usually leaders of local communities constitutes a complementary anomaly to the situation of women
religious, and leads him to conclude that "Religious life challenges the
separateness of clergy and laity . . . For these various reasons, the social
framework given by the clergy-laity distinction cannot survive."[11]

Perhaps the most edifying fact that emerges from the record of
experience presented in this book is the "teleology" that this phenomenon represents—a continuity within a tradition and a certain sense of
analogical, inevitable development, a kind of fidelity to a sense of mission. By this I mean that there is a clear and dynamic coherence between a Geno Baroni's ministry as a young priest in Altoona, speaking
out for workers' causes or organizing a parish credit union and his role
in HUD as a policy adviser or as supporter of the Consumer Cooperative Bank. Likewise, the same coherence is visible in the ministry to
the disadvantaged of a former teacher like Sr. Ardeth Platte in an inner-city school in Saginaw and her advocacy of their cause and other
important social issues in her subsequent role as city councilwoman.

In the final analysis, the phenomenon of American sisters and
priests serving in public offices might perhaps be seen as one aspect of
the coming-of-age of the U.S. church: no longer marked by Jefferson-
ian reticence and "political celibacy," nor by the defensive, self-conscious immigrant status, but a church rising to its full stature as an

articulate, pragmatic and pluralistic manifestation of the Catholic tradition incarnated in a distinctly American milieu. In her most recent sociological study of Catholic sisters in the United States, Sister Mary Augusta Neal identifies this transition: "Before 1965 we were major culture carriers; now we are becoming culture-makers." Her observation echoes a passage in Gaudium et Spes: "In each nation and social group there is a growing number of men and women who are conscious that they themselves are the crafters and molders of their community's culture."[12]

This book records the experience of some of those men and women.

ACKNOWLEDGEMENTS

I wish to offer a special word of thanks to my faithful collaborators, Thomas Gannon, S.J., the director of the Woodstock Theological Center, senior fellow John Langan, S.J., Woodstock librarians Thomas Marshall, S.J. and William Sheehan, C.S.B., as well as other colleagues who were helpful in the production of this volume; also to Jude Howard, Eileen Phillips and the office staff who assisted in the preparation of the text, and to Sr. Lora Ann Quinonez, the LCWR staff, and Keith Brennan, SDS, of the CMSM staff who assisted us in the collection of survey data.

NOTES

1. Alexis de Tocqueville, *Democracy in America*, 2 vols., ed. Phillips Bradley, Vintage Books (New York: Random House, 1945) I, 314,317.

2. The Gallup Poll of 1974-76 surveyed the U.S., Canada, Italy, Australia, Benelux, United Kingdom, France, West Germany, and Scandinavia.

3. Alan Heimert, *Religion and the American Mind: From the Great Awakening to the Revolution* (Cambridge, Mass.: Harvard University Press, 1966) 541.

4. I am indebted to the chapter policy papers of several religious communities for the substance which I used to develop this taxonomy, and in particular to a Maryknoll reflection paper #15 on "Mission" from the Maryknoll General Assembly, 1984, and to J.B. Libanio, *Spir-*

itual Discernment and Politics: Guidelines for Religious Communities (Orbis, 1983).

5. "Report to the Vatican: Religious Orders Today," a joint report of the Leadership Conference of Women Religious and the Conference of Major Superiors of Men of the United States, presented to the Vatican Congregation for Religious, April 1978, published in *Origins*, April 20, 1978.

6. Miguel d'Escoto in *Ministers of God, Ministers of the People*, ed. Teofilo Cabestrero (Maryknoll, NY: Orbis Press, 1982), pp. 114-15.

7. Fr. Louis R. Gigante in *National Catholic Reporter*, June 19, 1970, p. 8.

8. Evangelii Nuntiandi, 20.

9. "Justice in the World," Third International Synod of Bishops, November 30, 1971, 6.

10. Thomas F. O'Meara, OP, *Theology of Ministry* (New York, Ramsey, NJ: Paulist Press, 1983), p. 166.

11. Ibid., 167.

12. Sister Mary Augusta Neal, SNDN in "Current Forms of Religious Life in the United States Church," an address to a conference of bishops and major superiors on Religious Life in the United States, Boston College, June 22, 1984. Gaudium et Spes, 55.

Part 1
BACKGROUND AND ANALYSIS

The phenomenon of Catholic priests and sisters serving in political offices is best viewed from a variety of perspectives. In this section Gerald Fogarty records the generally distanced relationship of U.S. Catholic clergy to political governance and partisan politics since the colonial period. Mary Ewens and Nancy Sylvester reveal the gradual but accelerating engagement of American religious sisters in political ministries, particularly in the twentieth century. James Provost offers a comprehensive analysis of the origins and development of Canon Law affecting priests and religious vis-à-vis politics. Rosemary Smith and an LCWR panel of canonists complement this with a commentary and discussion of the provisions in the Revised Code. Paul Weber delineates the Constitutional aspects of the involvement of religious professionals in political office; John Langan looks at the phenomenon of politics itself and estimates the degree to which involvement may compromise ecclesial mission and identity. Joseph Komonchak provides an interpretation of the distinction between clerical and lay roles in the church that has crucial implications for our subject. Finally, Agnes Cunningham suggests a series of theological issues that must be considered in any effort to assess the validity of political ministries.

19

Gerald P. Fogarty, SJ

PRIESTS IN PUBLIC OFFICE: AN HISTORICAL OVERVIEW

On January 25, 1638, the assembly of the colony of Maryland met for the first time. The minutes for the session list all the members in attendance and then noted that there "were summoned to appear by vertue of writts to them directed: mr. Thomas Copley, Esq., of St. Maries hundred mr. Andrew White mr. John Altham of the same hundred." The three men were Jesuit priests and also landowners. In the latter capacity, they were eligible, if not obliged, to sit in the assembly. Their agent in the assembly, a layman, "excused their absence by reason of sickness."[1] The following day, the Jesuits were again summoned, but their agent stated "that they desired to be excused from giving voices in this Assembly."[2] The reasons for the priests refusing to sit in a legislative assembly and thus hold civil office were complex and now partially buried in the obscurity of seventeenth-century Maryland history. First of all, the assembly also acted as a law court, empowered to impose the death penalty—an action forbidden to priests in canon law.[3] Second, the Jesuits were then embroiled in a quarrel with the colony's proprietor, Cecil Calvert, the second Lord Baltimore, over whether, in fact, he recognized their right to own property and, if so, whether they could own it in their own names or as representatives of the Catholic Church in Maryland.

Whatever were the motives of Copley (*alias* Philip Fisher), White, and Altham (*alias* Gravenor), they established a precedent in American Catholic history that priests were to remain out of politics. They took this stance within the context of working out the practice of the separation of Church and State, in accordance with which "Church" came to mean clergy, who, in turn, were not to be involved formally in the affairs of state. This is not to say that the priests failed to speak out when civil and ecclesiastical matters became intertwined. In 1718, for example, the assembly of Maryland, then under a Protestant pro-

21

prietor, enacted a law disenfranchising Catholics. Father Peter Attwood, then the superior of the Maryland Jesuit Mission, wrote a pamphlet outlining his arguments that such a law violated the civil and property rights of Catholics simply because of the religion they espoused.[4] The act was passed and Catholics were forbidden to vote or hold office, but other aspects of the act, notably the rights of Catholics to inherit, buy or sell property, were known more for being ignored than for being enforced.

The anti-Catholic laws of Maryland added a new dimension to the developing Maryland Catholic tradition. Not only had Church come to mean clergy, who, of their own volition, from the colony's beginning had refused to take part in civil matters; but religion had also come to be a private affair. The stance which the laity took on political matters was indistinguishable from that taken by their Protestant counterparts. There is perhaps no better example of this mentality than Charles Carroll of Carrollton, the sole Catholic signer of the Declaration of Independence.

In the spring of 1773, Carroll was emerging as a leader of the patriotic party arguing against some of the actions taken by the British governor of Maryland. Using the pen-name "First Citizen", Carroll presented his arguments in the *Maryland Gazette* in answer to Daniel Dulany, who used the name "Antillon." At one point, Dulany stated that Carroll's "patriotism is entirely feigned" and that his reasons should be dismissed "because his religious principles are not to be trusted." For Carroll, this was an *ad hominem* argument with no bearing on the issue at hand. In his refutation of Dulany, however, he came dangerously close to asserting that for him at least his religious beliefs played no role in the formation of his views. "What my speculative notions on religion may be," he wrote,

> this is neither the place nor time to declare; my political principles ought only to be questioned on the present occasion; surely they are constitutional, and have met, I hope, with the approbation of my countrymen; if so Antillon's aspersions will give me no uneasiness. He asks, who is this Citizen? A man, Antillon, of an independent fortune, one deeply interested in the prosperity of his country: A friend to liberty, a settled enemy to lawless prerogative.[5]

As the debate progressed toward American independence, Carroll consistently argued for liberty, but eschewed any identity with or influence by "Catholic principles."

The American movement for independence occasioned the first participation of a priest in a directly political issue. In 1773, Pope Clement XIV suppressed the Society of Jesus; the priests in the English colonies—all of whom had been Jesuits—became secular priests subject to the Vicar Apostolic of the London District. John Carroll, a cousin of Charles, was then in Europe but returned to Maryland. The following year, the British parliament passed the Quebec Act, guaranteeing religious toleration to the inhabitants of the recently conquered Canadian territory. The Continental Congress included this as one of the "intolerable acts" justifying American independence from Great Britain. The Congress, like many of the American governments which followed it, was not always consistent. On September 17, 1774, it adopted as its own, the resolutions of Suffolk County, Massachusetts, that the act was "dangerous in an extreme degree to the Protestant religion and to the civil rights and liberties of all America." On October 21, 1774, it included these sentiments in its address to the People of Great Britain. Four days later, however, it addressed the inhabitants of the province of Quebec, urging them to join the American cause and suggesting Switzerland as an example of where Protestants and Catholics lived in harmony.[6] Congress followed this overture with an armed invasion of Canada the following summer. But the Bishop of Quebec, Jean-Olivier Briand, would have none of this. He threatened with excommunication any of his subjects who collaborated with the rebel forces. Into this charged atmosphere, Congress decided to dispatch an embassy, composed of Benjamin Franklin, Samuel Chase, a Maryland delegate, and Charles Carroll. To these politicians was added Father John Carroll.[7]

John Carroll was chary of accepting "the distinguished & unexpected honour" conferred on him by Congress. For one thing, he did not think the Canadians intended to be anything more than neutral toward the rebellion to their south and had not suffered from the injustices and made the remonstrances and petitions prerequisite to the last resort of taking up arms. More to the point, however, not only did he think "the nature & functions" of his priesthood rendered him " a very unfit person to be employed in negotiations, of so new a kind to me, of which I have neither experience of (*sic*) systematical knowledge," but he also hoped to

> be allowed to add, that tho I have little regard to my personal safety amidst the present distress of my country, yet I cannot help feeling some for my character: and I have observed that when the ministers of Religion leave their duties

of their profession to take a busy part in political matters, they generally fall into contempt & sometimes even bring discredit to the cause, in whose service they are engaged.[8]

Carroll's reservations about taking the assignment, then, flowed from his feeling that the mission was fruitless and from his conviction that, as a priest, political involvement would jeopardize his religious credibility.

Despite Carroll's reservations, he set out on this mission in April, 1776. John Adams, who wrote out his instructions, envisioned that he would baptize Canadian children and administer "Absolution on such as have been refused it by the torified Priests in Canada."[9] But this mission was a failure. For allowing Carroll to use a chapel and for dining with him once in Montreal, Father Pierre Floquet, another ex-Jesuit, was suspended by Bishop Briand. Franklin fell ill and had to return early to Philadelphia. Carroll eagerly agreed to go along as his travelling companion and thus cut short his sortie into diplomacy.[10]

It would be easy to construe Charles Carroll's reticence about his "speculative notions on religion" in terms of the anti-Catholicism prevailing in 18th-century Maryland. But his cousin John's reservations were expressed within another context. Despite the inconsistent response of the Continental Congress to the Quebec Act, anti-Catholicism was beginning to decline. John Carroll was respected and accepted both as a Catholic and as a priest.[11] His reservations were derived from his strong conviction that those in spiritual authority should not be involved in civil affairs. He believed that the papacy's involvement with politics had led to the suppression of the Society of Jesus.[12] In his private correspondence, however, he manifested his strong support for the Revolution.[13] Yet, once independence was won, he resented the Congregation of Propaganda negotiating directly with the new American government about the appointment of a bishop.[14] Carroll's attitude toward priests in politics, therefore, was shaped by his own experience of seeing his religious order suppressed by a pope acting under political pressure and by his developing notion of the separation of Church and State, which provided for the freedom of the Church, but which identified Church with clergy. As first Bishop and Archbishop of Baltimore, Carroll consistently maintained this position.[15]

In Carroll's view, then, politics was the proper sphere of laymen, several of whom held elective office on the national level in the early republic. Charles Carroll was elected to the Continental Congress, signed the Declaration of Independence, and was then elected to the first United States Senate from Maryland (1789–1792). Daniel Carroll, the brother of John, was elected to the Continental Congress and to the Constitutional Convention; from 1789 to 1791, he represented Maryland in Congress. Thomas Fitzsimons, an Irish-born merchant in Philadelphia, was elected to the Constitutional Convention and to the first United States Congress. But as immigration changed the composition of the American Church, anti-Catholicism again broke out. Few Catholic laymen, much less priests, would even be considered for elective office.

A notable exception to this tradition was Father Gabriel Richard, S.S., a chaplain to the French militia fighting for the Americans in Michigan during the War of 1812, pastor in Detroit, co-founder and vice-president of and professor at the University of Michigan. While he was visiting the Ottawa Indians in the summer of 1823, two colonels in the French militia approached him about running for delegate to Congress from the Michigan territory. The colonels said they were speaking on behalf of several "Americans," that is English-speaking settlers, as well. Richard's own bishop, Edward Fenwick, O.P., of Cincinnati, was then on his way to Europe, so Richard wrote for approval to Bishop William Louis Dubourg, S.S., then resident in St. Louis. For some time the priest had been seeking to counter the Protestant missionaries among the Indians by procuring a Jesuit. He was, moreover, concerned about corruption among the government Indian agents who entered into a collusion with their friends to deprive the Indians of their land and to pay low prices for furs. As the delegate in Washington, Richard would have a strong influence with the government to procure a Jesuit missionary for the Indians and to obtain justice for them.

Bishop Dubourg encouraged Richard to run for the office. "Everything considered," he wrote,

> I do not think you need hesitate to accept the nomination proposed to you. Providence wishes this extraordinary means to come to your help and to the help of the Church in your area. I hope that you will decide in the affirmative and I will rejoice if my letter gets to you in time to destroy the fears that you had about accepting and will inspire you with the confidence such a position demands.[16]

With Dubourg's letter in hand, Richard returned to Detroit and declared his candidacy. He won the election handily against five contenders.

Once in Washington, Richard obtained faculties from his fellow Sulpician, Ambrose Marechal, Archbishop of Baltimore. There is no evidence that either Marechal or the people of Michigan thought Richard's holding office was unseemly for a priest. The French-born Marechal and the French-speaking people of Detroit were more used to seeing the spiritual and temporal spheres intertwined than John Carroll who reflected an Anglo-American tradition. Richard had also complied with canon law by obtaining the permission of Dubourg and of his superior in France.[17] Finally, one of his principal reasons for accepting the nomination was to put forth to the government the Indians' request for a Jesuit missionary.[18]

Richard served one term as delegate (1823–1825), but then was defeated in his bid for re-election. In retrospect, his service in Congress was as much that of a Church lobbyist as of a politician. The people he represented in Michigan were a population composed of original French settlers, English-speaking Americans, and Indians. His decision to run for office and the support he received from Dubourg was based on his recognition of the need for a strong voice in Washington in behalf of Indian and Church interests. Anti-Catholicism, moreover, was not a factor in Michigan politics as it was in the east.

Anti-Catholicism was a prime factor in the forming of the short-lived "Catholic" party in New York City. In 1840, the fiery Bishop John Hughes of New York began battling the Public School Society, which distributed funds for public education and which was dedicated to the inculcation of the religious and moral values contained in the Bible. In short, the Public School Society used education to promote Protestantism. Hughes argued for a share in the public funds for Catholic schools or to make the public schools religiously neutral. In this he had the support of governor William Seward. Though a Whig, Seward urged the legislature to abolish the Public School Society, because its intolerant attitude kept 20,000 city children from attending the schools. The legislature referred the matter to the Secretary of State, John C. Spencer, who prepared a report fundamentally backing up Seward, calling for an end to the Public School Society, and recommending the election of a school commissioner in each ward.

The Spencer report was the principal issue in the fall election of New York City for the state legislature. The Whigs nominated a ticket rejecting the Spencer report and opposing any change in the educational system. The Democrats, already the party of the immigrants, attempted to straddle the fence—a majority of its candidates opposed any change in the system, but the party had taken no position. Hughes tried a desperate maneuver. On October 30, only four days before the election, he summoned a meeting at Carroll Hall and called for an independent ticket. Hughes may have intended only to threaten the Democrats and force them into line. The Democratic candidates, however, now came out unanimously against the Spencer report. In the election, the Whigs won, but the Catholic ticket received 2,200 votes— a number sufficient to have given the victory to the Democrats.[19] Hughes failed to win his point, but he did show the power of the Catholic vote. The Carroll Hall ticket, however, was the only example of a Catholic party in American politics and it was dedicated to a single issue—the right of Catholic children not to be indoctrinated in Protestantism in public education. The ticket was not intended and did not become a permanent party.

As American Church leaders devoted more of their efforts to assimilating the immigrants into American culture while protecting their faith, the notion of a Catholic layman or priest in political life receded farther from the mainstream of the tradition. Such was not the case, however, in the newly conquered territories of the southwest. In 1855, Father Jose Manuel Gallegos won election as delegate from the New Mexico Territory. He spoke in Congress against the "new French bishop," John B. Lamy and the French clergy he brought with him. He met an immediate rebuttal on the floor from his defeated opponent in the election, Miguel A. Otero, who defended Lamy and charged Gallegos with fraud in the election. Congress found in Otero's favor and dismissed Gallegos, who had already been suspended from the active ministry.[20] Gallegos is a bad example from which to draw any positive conclusions. He was already somewhat of a renegade and had not obtained his superior's permission to run for office. On the other hand, though he was later ousted from Congress, it is important to note that he, like Richard, came from a region in which the non-Anglo population had not yet absorbed the developing American Catholic tradition of the separation of Church and State.

The Catholic interpretation of the separation of Church and State developed within the context of anti-Catholicism and it led to a separation of religion and public policy. With the persistence of the identification of Church with the clergy, priests and bishops took no part in what were seen as political matters. They thus remained aloof from the controversy over abolition. In 1859, the Ninth Provincial Council of Baltimore stated that "our clergy are to be prudently on guard not to interpose themselves in the faithful's judgments; for it is necessary that these (judgments) be truly free on all questions pertaining to civil and social reason, within the limits of Christian doctrine and law." The clergy were to leave "to worldly men the cares and solicitudes of civil factions, the contentions of power, the sickness of deluded ambition."[21] The council was, of course, addressing the clergy of a region which would soon be divided by the Civil War.

During the Civil War, bishops and priests tended to reflect the values of their regions and supported their respective governments. Some went further and used their influence for their government's cause. In 1862, John Hughes, who had become the first Archbishop of New York in 1850, went to Rome at the request of Abraham Lincoln and Secretary of State William Seward to persuade Pope Pius IX not to recognize the Confederacy. In the Eternal City, he learned that several American prelates had protested against his undertaking of a mission for the government.[22] In 1864, Bishop Patrick N. Lynch of Charleston took up residence in Rome in an effort to win the pope to the Confederacy's cause. He found himself exiled there and his return to the United States was arranged only through the intervention with the government of several northern prelates.[23] The missions of Hughes and Lynch could be construed as more patriotic than political forays into the affairs of government, but they seem identical with precisely the type of activity on the part of clergy which John Carroll eschewed.

In 1884, the bishops of the nation met for the Third and last Plenary Council. They cited the Ninth Provincial Council's statement on clergy in politics and went on to say "priests are zealously to abstain from publicly discussing political or merely secular affairs, both outside the church and all the more so inside it." But the bishops wished their decree not to be understood, "as if there must be absolute silence about the gravest obligation, by which citizens are bound, even in public affairs, to labor always and everywhere according to the dictate of conscience, before God, for the greater good both of religion and of their republic and country."[24] In short, then, the bishops by 1884 were beginning to recognize that some "political" issues might demand that the clergy speak out.

One such issue was the social question in the United States and the rights of labor. In the fall of 1886, Father Edward McGlynn, pastor of St. Stephen's Church in New York City, spoke in favor of the candidacy of Henry George for Mayor of New York. McGlynn, already a thorn in the side of Archbishop Michael A. Corrigan for espousing a number of controversial social causes and George's modified socialism, had spoken in the campaign against the expressed command of the archbishop. For his disobedience, he was suspended from the priesthood for two weeks. On election day, he toured the city in an open carriage with George and Terrence Powderly, Grand Master Workman of the Knights of Labor. After refusing a summons to Rome to explain his social theories, McGlynn was excommunicated in the summer of 1887. His reconciliation to the Church in December, 1892, became a *cause celebre* in the growing antagonism between Corrigan and the more liberal bishops, notably John Ireland, Archbishop of St. Paul.[25]

Ireland himself was not in the least averse to entering into politics. In October, 1894, he was in New York, where he studiously avoided Archbishop Corrigan but publicly met with former President Benjamin Harrison and other prominent Republican leaders. They invited him to give an address at a banquet and he took the opportunity to state that the Church was not identified with either of the two political parties. Well aware of the strong New York Catholic identification with the Democratic Party, he chastised those New York priests who used their pulpits to urge their people to vote Democratic. Finally, he supported the candidacy of Father Sylvester Malone of Brooklyn for the New York State Board of Regents, which supervised education throughout the state. Unfortunately, he did not seem to know that one of Malone's opponents was Bishop Bernard McQuaid of Rochester.

Strong in the camp of Corrigan and the conservatives, McQuaid took to his pulpit against Ireland on November 24. He denounced Ireland for travelling in the entourage of politicians and for meddling in affairs outside his own diocese. For himself, he said that he could not be classified as either a Republican or a Democrat and in fact "for twenty-seven years I have never cast a vote, out of anxiety not to put it in any man's power to say that I had voted for one party or the other." He acknowledged that

> while it may have been a duty to exercise the privilege of a citizen and vote, I have felt that a more sacred duty devolved on me of preserving unsullied the high and holy office of bishop by keeping clear of entanglements with any political party. It has been traditional in the church of the United States for Bishops to hold aloof from politics. This tradition has been handed down to us by Bishops, whose greatness was real, and not newspaper greatness, pandering to the sensational popularity of the day.

McQuaid made it clear that he would have thought Ireland equally "blameworthy," had he "made himself conspicuous in favor of the Democratic party." In short, the bishop was articulating the tradition which had begun with John Carroll and which had been repeated as recently as the Third Plenary Council in 1884.[26]

McQuaid was perfectly correct in interpreting the American tradition, but he made a mistake in choosing his pulpit as his forum. With his characteristic flamboyance, Ireland fired off a lengthy defense to Rome. His speech, he said, was all part of his program to defeat anti-Catholicism, especially the American Protective Association, by showing that Catholics belonged to both parties. He made it clear, he continued, "that I do not seek to thrust myself into the political arena, that I raise my voice in the interests of the truth and of the Church." As for McQuaid's boast that he had never cast a vote, Ireland could only retort: "I go to the electoral polls, and I believe I would be remiss in my duties as a citizen if I did not go. Our priests and our bishops, at least the greater number, are proud of those rights as citizens, and exercise them, and our fellow countrymen would have little esteem for us, if we acted otherwise. The Americans hold as a maxim that he who does not exercise his right to vote deserves public opprobrium, or exile."[27]

Ireland's defense was successful, so successful in fact that he won an apology from the Cardinal Secretary of State and McQuaid received a strong rebuke. McQuaid apologized to the Cardinal for any pain he had caused the Holy See, but still recommended a reprimand for Ireland.[28] Ireland received no reprimand from Rome and continued his association with the Republican Party. In the presidential election of 1896, he publicly repudiated the Democratic candidate, William Jennings Bryan, and supported the Republican, William McKinley. This brought queries about his action to Rome and the request that Archbishop Sebastian Martinelli, the second apostolic delegate to the United States, investigate. Martinelli's report was a complete vindication of Ireland. The archbishop, he said, had "expressed his opinion not as Archbishop nor as reflecting the views of the Catholic Church, or of the Holy See . . . but simply as a private citizen." Martinelli then took the opportunity to explain the two-party system to his Roman superiors. The parties differed, he wrote, in regard to economic policies and their conceptions of the central government, but "Catholics belong indistinguishably to both parties; and it is good."[29]

In retrospect, Martinelli's understanding of the American political system and his defense of Ireland marked a watershed. Ireland's public espousal of the Republican Party was part of his general program of aggressive Americanization. As his program took shape and was exported to Europe, it became known as Americanism, the movement which proclaimed the advantages to the Church of such American notions as the separation of Church and State. In 1899, Leo XIII condemned Americanism. With that condemnation, American priests and bishops not only retreated from attempting to explain to Europe the meaning of religious liberty but also refrained for another generation from giving any appearance of taking sides on political issues. Not all were by any means happy with this situation. In July, 1900, Father John R. Slattery, first Superior General of the Josephites, was in Paris where he was appalled to find the French Church ignoring Bastille Day. His comments were caustic and reflected a tortured mind. "When shall we clergy, French or American," he wrote, "learn to be one with our country? Is the woman's gown we wear ever to make us not only the neuter sex but the hermaphrodites of nations as well?"[30] In a few years, Slattery would leave the Church over Modernism.

Slattery's remarks were extreme, but the retreat of the American clergy from taking political stands was exacerbated by growing anti-Catholicism. Catholics, whether clergy or lay, kept a low profile. Woodrow Wilson's anti-Catholicism was only thinly veiled, though he did have a Catholic adviser. The presidential campaign of Alfred E. Smith brought forth still more anti-Catholic feeling. The campaign had as at least one of its foci Smith's religion. Smith did seek the advice on Church-State matters of Father Francis P. Duffy, former chaplain of the Sixty-Ninth New York Regiment and a former seminary professor and editor of the liberal *New York Review*, which met its demise with the condemnation of Modernism. Duffy's role was strictly that of providing information on Catholic teaching.[31]

The circumstances leading to the defeat of Al Smith made it seem unlikely that a Catholic would ever occupy the White House. It was difficult enough for a member of the Catholic laity, much less a priest or religious, to hold elective office.

The silence of Catholics *qua* Catholics began to change during the next four years. In the election of 1932, the major issue was the Depression. No bishop spoke out on the candidates and even leading Catholic spokesman on the social question, like Father John A. Ryan, remained neutral. Not so Father Charles Coughlin, Pastor of the Shrine of the Little Flower in Royal Oak, Michigan. By 1931, Coughlin was broadcasting from his church a radio program which reached several million people. In April, 1932, he openly endorsed Franklin D. Roosevelt. For half of Roosevelt's first administration, his plea to his listeners was "Roosevelt or Ruin." His speeches were sprinkled with quotations from papal social encyclicals, but he was neither a theologian nor an economist. Whether from personal pique at not being an adviser to Roosevelt or from real fear of the New Deal programs, he launched an assault on the president. In 1934, he founded the National Union of Social Justice to promote his legislative causes in Washington. Though the majority of the hierarchy were opposed to his attacks on Roosevelt and other leaders his own ordinary, Bishop Michael J. Gallagher of Detroit, continued to support him. The only restriction placed on him was that the apostolic delegate, Archbishop Amleto Cicognani, ordered him not to broadcast his radio program from his church.[32]

The hierarchy was caught in a dilemma now familiar to the American Church. If the bishops issued a statement against Coughlin, the Church would be accused of denying freedom of speech. If they remained silent, the Church would be charged with agreeing with him. While Coughlin remained a problem for the Church and for Roosevelt, the latter was gaining important Catholic support. In 1935, the president received an honorary degree from the University of Notre Dame and he and Cardinal George Mundelein of Chicago exchanged warm praise.[33] The following year, Coughlin announced the formation of a third party with Congressman William Lemke as its presidential candidate.[34] The priest had now formally entered into the political arena. In September, however, Mundelein took the opportunity of registering to vote to give a newspaper interview. Roosevelt was "his friend," said the paper, and the American people should feel gratitude "for the prosperity, the happiness, and the freedom now abroad in our land."[35] Mundelein did not positively endorse Roosevelt, but his message was clear. Leaders of the Democratic Party, however, were concerned that Coughlin's third party might drain off voters. They enlisted the aid of John A. Ryan, then a monsignor, who made one radio broadcast defending Roosevelt's legislative programs against Coughlin's charges. Ryan received a rebuke from the ordinary of Washington, to whom he was subject, Archbishop Michael J. Curley of Baltimore.[36]

Lemke's campaign, of course, failed, but it represented the first time in the American Church that a priest had formed a party. From that aspect, Coughlin differed from McGlynn, who supported a third-party candidate for mayor, but had not actually been an organizer of the party. But, most of all, Coughlin differed from McGlynn in having the total support of his ordinary. That support ended with the death of Bishop Gallagher early in 1937. The Holy See elevated Detroit to the status of an archdiocese and appointed Edward Mooney as the ordinary. For some time, Mooney had already been involved with the Coughlin case. He found himself attempting to steer a middle course between having the Church accused of stifling freedom of speech and

allowing Coughlin to appear to represent the Catholic position. Ultimately, it was the National Association of Broadcasters which brought
the end to Coughlin's radio series in the fall of 1940 and the Justice
Department, perhaps with Mooney's advice and support, which
caused the demise of Coughlin's crusade waged in the pages of *Social
Justice*.[37]

The Coughlin case must be seen within the context of a Catholic
community still uncertain about its status within American society. To
the bishops who opposed him, including his ordinary after 1937, it was
imperative to make clear that he did not represent the Church's views
on the social issue. His anti-communism, which led to his anti-Semitism, induced secular authorities to discipline him. But his medium of
communication presented to the bishops a difficulty not foreseen in
the *Code of Canon Law* of 1917; they had no effective way of censoring
the air-waves as long as his ordinary authorized his speaking within his
own diocese.

Coughlin's final assault on Roosevelt's policy was the charge that
the United States was being led into World War II by British propaganda. He urged American isolationism. The declaration of war, however, brought several bishops into close contact with the government
and consequent involvement with political affairs. Archbishop Francis
Spellman of New York was the primary, but not the sole, example.
Early in 1943, he undertook as military ordinary to visit American
troops abroad. Pius XII also asked him to come to Rome to discuss
certain matters which the Archbishop never divulged. Roosevelt then
added his own commission. Since Spellman was to pass through Spain,
the president requested that he see General Francisco Franco, explain
that the American and British alliance with Russia was not an alliance
with communism, and convince Spain to remain neutral. Although
Pius XII may have supported this intercession with Franco, it was essentially the same type of mission which John Carroll had so hesitantly
undertaken and later repudiated; it was also like the missions of
Hughes and Lynch during the Civil War. In Rome, Spellman may also
have met with some Italian political figures eager to negotiate a separate Italian surrender.[38]

Despite Spellman's involvement in politics and diplomacy, there
were no protests such as accompanied Hughes' mission. There were
numerous reasons for this change in attitude. First, the necessity to
prove Catholic patriotism led other Catholics to turn a benevolent eye
upon Spellman's foray. Second, he was a known friend of Pius XII,
who valued his mediation with Roosevelt. Third, American participation in World War II did not create widespread dissent; there were,

therefore, no political factions with which to take sides. Fourth, the American Church was becoming a major force in American society; it had to enter into "political" matters if its influence was to be effective. In the final analysis, however, Spellman did represent a departure from a strict interpretation of the tradition inherited from John Carroll.

The end of the war brought another up-surge of anti-Catholicism, which finally caused Spellman to abandon a two-decade attempt to have the United States establish diplomatic relations with the Holy See[39]—an issue resolved only by President Ronald Reagan in 1984. In the 1950s, however, anti-Catholicism was gradually cancelled by anti-communism, especially by the crusade launched by leading Catholics, such as Senator Joseph McCarthy, who gained considerable clerical support.[40] But this clerical support did not take the form of partisan politics. An important legacy of the anti-communist crusade was that it made possible a Catholic running for president. John Kennedy openly espoused his Catholicism, but made it clear that he was not subject to clerical domination. In fact, he seems not to have sought any direct clerical advice. Only after he had prepared his speech for the Houston Ministerial Association did an aide discuss the text over the phone with John Courtney Murray, S.J.[41]

The election of Kennedy was a symbolic, but important victory for American Catholics. They were no longer to be viewed as second-class citizens. This assimilation to American society, moreover, coincided with the Second Vatican Council's call for the Church to be more actively involved in the modern world. The Council called on citizens to exercise their rights and duties to vote and stated that "the Church praises and esteems those who devote themselves to the public good for the service of men and take upon themselves the burdens of public office."[42] It also stated that the Church might have "to pass moral judgments even in matters relating to politics, whenever the fundamental rights of man or the salvation of souls requires it."[43]

American Catholics were soon confronted with a situation demanding an application of their new-found assimilation and the Council's teaching. The Vietnam War produced a new Catholic expression of patriotism. While the majority of Catholics probably supported the war, as their predecessors had done in the past, others protested and demonstrated against it. More importantly, several priests became convinced that vocal opposition to government policy was insufficient. In order to change that policy, they believed they would have to participate in government itself.

By the spring of 1970, four priests had declared themselves candidates for Congress. Three were running for the House of Representatives: Louis R. Gigante of New York, Joseph R. Lucas of Ohio, and Robert Drinan, S.J. of Massachusetts. John J. McLoughlin, S.J. was the Republican candidate for Senator from Rhode Island. All were running in opposition to the war. Although there were twelve clergymen altogether running for office and there were already three Protestant ministers in the Congress, only the Catholic clergy seemed to provoke the Church-State question. Drinan, then the dean of the Boston College Law School, saw no conflict and predicted that the voters of Massachusetts, which had sent the first Catholic to the White House, would have no difficulty in electing a priest to Congress. The sudden appearance of priests running for office led the American bishops at their annual meeting in 1970 to ask each bishop to discourage priests from holding elective office. Gigante may have spoken for the others when he said that he agreed with the bishops in principle, but that the war demanded a more direct involvement in the political process.[44] Despite the reservations of the hierarchy, each of the priest-candidates had obtained his ecclesiastical superior's permission to run for office, in accord with the Code of Canon Law.

In the election of 1970, only Drinan won. Lucas and Gigante remained in their previous ministries. Drinan's fellow New England Jesuit, McLoughlin, accepted a post as a speech-writer for President Richard M. Nixon, shifted his position on the war, and publicly acknowledged his political differences with Drinan.[45] It should have been clear to the American public that priests in politics did not mean a monolithic presentation of the Church's values and concerns.

In 1972, Drinan was joined in Congress by Father Robert J. Cornell, O.Praem., of Wisconsin. Cornell served two terms before he was defeated in 1978. Drinan was making a bid for a sixth term in 1980 when he received an order from Pope John Paul II through Father Pedro Arrupe, S.J., the Superior General of the Jesuits, to withdraw from the race. The issue was raised that a priest-congressman could not faithfully serve both his constituents and his religious superiors. Although the papal command seemed at first to apply only to Drinan, a few days later Father Cornell, making a bid for re-election, was ordered by Bishop Aloysius Wycislo of Green Bay to withdraw.[46] There were at that time other priests and religious holding elective office on the state or local level. Did the directive apply to them as well? Sister Carolyn Farrell, the Mayor of Dubuque, said she was unaffected.[47] Nor was there any mention made of those who held appointed office.

Monsignor Geno Baroni was appointed assistant secretary of Housing and Urban Development during the administration of President Jimmy Carter. Whether Baroni's appointed position was merely tolerated or whether it was acceptable because it did not involve controversial issues was left an open question. Three years later the papal command that Sister Agnes Mary Mansour resign from an appointed office in Michigan shed no light on his position. It remains unclear whether the pope excludes religious from holding appointed office altogether or only from holding an appointed office, such as Sister Agnes Mansour's which required her to supervise programs that provided funding for abortions.

Until the Vatican and other ecclesiastical archives are open for research, it is impossible accurately to assess the motives behind the papal directive affecting Drinan. The conclusions drawn here are, therefore, necessarily only tentative. First of all, there was a long-standing American Catholic tradition that priests should not be involved in politics. This tradition was rooted in the colonial Maryland experience and expressed by John Carroll. When taken together with Charles Carroll's statement, however, the tradition was in danger of making the separation of Church and state mean a divorce between religion and public policy and of equating the Church with clergy. In the early national period, the only priest to hold public office was Richard, but his role as a delegate in Congress was an extension of his work among the Indians and he represented a territory not yet imbued with an established American Catholic tradition. There was later, in addition to canon law which required a priest to have his superiors' permission to run for office, American ecclesiastical legislation which prohibited the clergy from discussing politics outside or inside the church.

The first major alteration of Carroll's tradition occurred during the Civil War with the missions to Rome of Lynch and Hughes. Yet, these missions can be construed as expressions of patriotism within a society which was still suspicious of the political loyalties of Catholics. John Ireland altered the tradition still further by publicly proclaiming his adherence to the Republican Party as part of his aggressive program of Americanization. For him, it was essential that Catholics not be exclusively identified with either of the two parties. Archbishop Martinelli, the apostolic delegate, probably better understood the American political system than many Europeans of today. For all practical purposes, to hold office means to be a member of one of the two principal parties. Unlike European political parties, however, American ones, as Martinelli explained in 1896, are not based on different ideologies.

Membership in an American political party, nevertheless, raises the question of ethical pluralism. To be either a Republican or a Democrat does not necessarily mean that each party member accepts the party's entire platform; there is room for personal dissent. In a pluralistic society, it is impossible to have the law accurately reflect any one ethical viewpoint. For a priest to belong to a party which actively advocates what the Church condemns, abortion for example, is confusing to many Europeans as well as Americans. Drinan had voted against various forms of the Hyde Amendment cutting off public funds for poor women to have abortions on the grounds that, while he opposed abortion, the Constitution guaranteed all citizens, rich and poor, equal access to such services.

But Drinan's voting record does not seem to have been the major factor in the papal decison, for Cornell, who had voted the opposite way, was also told not to run for office. Pope John Paul II's primary motive seems to have been that he does not think a priest or religious, male or female, should hold political office. In this, he may have in mind the statement of the Council that it is necessary "to distinguish clearly between the activities of Christians, acting individually or collectively in their own name as citizens guided by the dictates of a Christian conscience, and their activity acting along with their pastors in the name of the Church."[48] For him, the Church might mean clergy and religious, men and women committed full time to making the Church visible in the world. If this is correct, then he reflects what has been in fact an American tradition, but one which had undergone modifications as situations necessitated.

NOTES

1. *Archives of Maryland* (71 vols.; Baltimore: Maryland Historical Society, 1883-1970), I, 2.

2. *Ibid.*, 5.

3. Thomas J. Hughes, S.J., *History of the Society of Jesus in North America: Colonial and Federal* (London: Longmans, Green, and Co., 1908), *Text*, I, 380–384.

4. (Peter Attwood), "Liberty and Property or the Beauty of Maryland Displayed" *United States Catholic Historical Society*, III (1889–1890), 237–263.

5. John Tracy Ellis (ed.), *Documents of American Catholic History* (Chicago: Henry Regnery Company, 1967), I, 129.

6. *Ibid.*, 134–135.

7. James J. Hennesey, *American Catholics: A History of the Roman Catholic Community in the United States* (New York: Oxford University Press, 1981), pp. 63–64.

8. Thomas O. Hanley (ed.), *The John Carroll Papers* (3 vols.; Notre Dame: University of Notre Dame Press, 1976), I, 46.

9. Hennesey, p. 64.

10. *Ibid.*, 65.

11. See *The Book of Abigail and John: Selected Letters of the Adams Family* (Cambridge: Harvard University Press, 1975), p. 116.

12. See for example *The John Carroll Papers*, I, 31–32.

13. Carroll to Plowden, April 27, 1780, in *ibid.*, I, 55–56.

14. Carroll to Plowden, April 10, 1784, *ibid.*, I, 146.

15. Carroll seemed to contradict his opposition to government involvement in Church matters when he consulted James Madison about the appointment of a bishop for the newly-purchased Louisiana Territory. Carroll, however, was concerned about having a French bishop for the French-speaking populace and queried Madison only to find out if such an appointment of a non-American would be obnoxious to the government; he was not inviting government intrusion. See Carroll to Madison, Nov. 17, 1806, in *ibid.*, II, 534–536.

16. Quoted in Dorita Mast, *Always the Priest: The Life of Gabriel Richard* (Baltimore: Helicon, 1965), p. 197.

17. In 1658, Alexander VII prohibited priests from involvement in politics. The Congregation of Propaganda reiterated this prohibition in regard to the missions in 1659. Fundamentally, the prohibition developed out of a similar medieval prohibition of priests from engaging in business and later from practicing law or medicine. The issue of priests holding political office became of greater concern after the French Revolution. Exempt from the prohibition were prelates whose offices brought with them civil obligations, such as sitting in legislative assemblies, and priests who had their ordinary's permission to hold office. Cardinal Hergenrother summarized the 19th-century developments and noted that there were two views of the propriety of clerics holding office. The one argued that the priest should have no role in politics on the grounds that his office is strictly spiritual. The other argued that the priest had not only a spiritual office in the Church, but was also a citizen. While both views could be supported from the Fathers and medieval canonists, a political function had always to be an expression of the spiritual office of the priest. See "Ueber

die Betheiligung des Klerus an politischen Fragen," *Archiv für katholisches Kirchenrecht*, 15 (1865), 67–84; see especially p. 82. Richard seems to have been as much concerned with fulfilling the prescriptions of canon law as obtaining the permission of his superior to take on an obligation which would take him away from his mission.

18. Mast, p. 194.

19. Ray Allen Billington, *The Protestant Crusade: 1820–1860* (Chicago: Quadrangle Press, 1964), pp. 150-152.

20. Hennesey, p. 136.

21. Quoted in *Acta et Decreta Concilii Plenarii Baltimorensis Tertii* (Baltimore: John Murphy & Sons, 1886), p. 44.

22. Richard Shaw, *Dagger John: The Unquiet Life and Times of Archbishop John Hughes of New York*: Paulist Press, 1977), pp. 350–351.

23. Hennesey, p. 156.

24. *Acta et Decreta Concilii Plenarii Baltimorensis*, p. 44.

25. Robert Emmett Curran, *Michael Augustine Corrigan and the Shaping of Conservative Catholicism in America, 1878–1902* (New York: Arno Press, 1978), pp. 390–393.

26. Frederick J. Zwierlein, *The Life and Letters of Bishop McQuaid* (3 vols.; Rochester, NY: Art Print Shop, 1926), III, 207-210.

27. Archivio Segreto Vaticano, SS 280 (1897), fasc. 3, 44ʳ-52ᵛ, Ireland to Rampolla, St. Paul, Dec. 13, 1894.

28. Gerald P. Fogarty, *The Vatican and the American Hierarchy from 1870 to 1965*, Vol. 21 of *Päpste und Papsttum* (Stuttgart: Anton Hiersemann Verlag, 1982), p. 138.

29. Archivio Segreto Vaticano, SS, 280 (1898), fasc. 2, 58ʳ-ᵛ, Martinelli to Rampolla, Washington, Dec. 20, 1896.

30. Archives of the Diocese of Richmond, Slattery to O'Connell, Paris, July 14, 1900.

31. Hennesey, p. 252.

32. Charles J. Tull, *Father Coughlin and the New Deal* (Syracuse: Syracuse University Press, 1965), pp. 1–58; Fogarty, p. 243.

33. George Q. Flynn, *American Catholics and the Roosevelt Presidency, 1932–1936* (Lexington: University of Kentucky Press, 1968), pp. 184–185.

34. Tull, pp. 143-144.

35. *The Times* (Chicago), Sept. 15, 1936.

36. Francis L. Broderick, *Right Reverend New Dealer: John A. Ryan* (New York: Macmillan,1963) pp. 225-228.

37. Tull, pp. 173–185, 188–227; Fogarty, pp. 251–252, 277–278.

38. Fogarty, pp. 291–293.

39. Ibid., 321-332.

40. See Donald Crosby, *God, Church, and Flag: Senator Joseph R. McCarthy and the Catholic Church* (Chapel Hill: University of North Carolina Press, 1978).

41. Donald E. Pelotte, *John Courtney Murray: Theologian in Conflict* (New York: Paulist Press, 1975), p. 76.

42. Austin Flannery (ed.) *Vatican II: Conciliar and Postconciliar Documents* (Collegeville: Liturgical Press, 1975), p. 982.

43. Ibid., p. 984.

44. *New York Times*, Feb. 23, Apr. 26, 1970.

45. Ibid., May 5, Oct. 15,1971.

46. Ibid., May 5, 6, 7, 1980.

47. Ibid., May 6, 1980.

48. *Vatican II*, p. 984.

Mary Ewens, OP

POLITICAL ACTIVITY OF AMERICAN SISTERS BEFORE 1970

INTRODUCTION

In 1803, after President Thomas Jefferson bought Louisiana from France, the Ursuline Sisters in New Orleans wrote to him, requesting a guarantee that their good works and property would be untouched by this change in government. In his response he assured them that the American government encouraged groups such as theirs which promoted the "furtherance of the wholesome purposes of society, by training up its younger members in the way they should go."[1]

This cordial exchange was probably the first of the many contacts with important political figures which would enliven the history of American sisterhoods. Within a decade, these same sisters would be nursing General Jackson's soldiers after the Battle of New Orleans. The Georgetown Visitation Sisters began in 1799 their long tradition of educating the daughters of prominent Washington politicians.

Thus, from their early beginnings, American sisters have interacted with political figures and been aware of the political process. Some have been very actively engaged in this process, particularly when this became necessary for the furtherance of the ministry. Within the limits of a few pages, one cannot hope to paint the total picture of all of the political activities engaged in by the approximately 220,000 sisters who have lived in America from the arrival of the Ursulines in New Orleans in 1727 until the 1970's.[2] One can, however, sketch in the background those aspects of their milieu which would affect their participation in political life, and with broad brush strokes delineate some figures in the foreground whose lives are representative. We will examine the ways in which some individuals, institutions, and whole congregations participated in political life, despite cultural norms that stressed aloofness from "the world."

THE CANONICAL AND CULTURAL CONTEXT

During the period we are studying, sisters' lives were shaped by canon law regulations and the Church's expectations for religious women. Through the centuries the Church had formulated precepts regarding enclosure that were based on the notion that women were weak, emotional beings who were incapable of serious thought or of controlling their own lives. Enclosure regulations were aimed at keeping religious women behind convent walls and limiting their contact with the world beyond them so as to protect nuns from the evils which lurked there.[3] In practice this could mean that sisters did not attend Mass in their parish church; that playground supervision was carried out from a convent window; that sister-nurses were not allowed to work on maternity cases; that sister-teachers could not teach boys older than ten years of age; that sisters did not go out at night; that access to newspapers, magazines, books, movies, radio, and television was strictly controlled.

The bull "*Conditae a Christo*" of 1900 finally gave official recognition to the hundreds of active congregations that had sprung up in the nineteenth century in response to the need for works of charity outside cloister walls. No longer was strict enclosure a requirement for Church approval, but many of the practices that were related to it continued in force. With the codification of canon law in 1917, the application of these prescriptions to the minute details of daily life became a science engaging a whole corps of priest-experts. The very different approaches of English common law and Roman law led Americans in some instances to interpret general rules more stringently than was intended by Roman lawmakers. Every five years major superiors had to fill out a long questionnaire regarding their community's adherence to canon law and submit it to Rome.

A few excerpts from Mother Mary Gerald Barry's letters to the Adrian Dominican congregation which she headed from 1933 until her death in 1961 will indicate ways in which cloistral regulations affected sisters' daily lives. In her letter of May 25, 1934, we read:

> The sisters assigned to Chicago, or those visiting in Chicago during the summer, may not visit the World's Fair. The scenes there are not necessary for your education . . . Familiarity with anyone outside the Community or of your own family leads to destruction.[4]

On June 7, 1935, she advised:

> Walking in unknown places tends to lead one into devious paths and often evil ways. For this reason, walks outside the convent grounds are to be discouraged.[5]

In the thirties, Mother Gerald warned against "radioism," and in the fifties, sisters were reminded that television could only be used to watch Bishop Sheen, the President, or other educational or religious programs approved by the superior.

Such were the Church's expectations for religious women up to the time of the Second Vatican Council. Such negative attitudes towards the world outside convent walls, and such strict control over all contact would not seem to facilitate participation in the political arena. For many sisters a sheltered life of prayer and good works sufficed. But for others, particularly those who were the administrators of hospitals, schools, orphanages, etc., contact with the sick, the poor, the immigrant, the families of their neighborhoods brought an understanding of social problems and a desire to remedy them. Intelligence and common sense often triumphed over legalism.

In the eighteenth and nineteenth centuries, there was less knowledge of canon law, and America's status until 1908 as a mission territory made the adherence to it less important. Bishops who were hard-pressed to care for their people encouraged religious communities to do whatever was necessary to establish the schools and other institutions that were so desperately needed. There was a constant interaction with governmental agencies, whether for legal incorporation or payment for the care of indigents and sick soldiers. Legislation that affected schools or dictated building codes or zoning ordinances affected them, and they kept an eye on public policies.

Whether one was an immigrant from a foreign land, a resident in newly-Americanized territories, or American born, one could not fail to be aware of the principles of American democracy and the hurly-burly of American politics. Sisters taught the children of leading citizens and politicians, nursed in military hospitals in times of war, and watched their graduates marry into influential families. They prepared themselves to vote intelligently, and prepared others for citizenship. In periods when anti-Catholic sentiment characterized one political party or another, they could not remain indifferent.

Though tradition dictated that sisters should remain apart from the everyday world, there was another thrust in the Church which drew them out to an active concern for the well-being of others. Enlightened popes and bishops had become aware of the dire straits of many of their flock who lived and worked under impossible conditions, and had tried to arouse their fellow Catholics to address the situation.

Pope Leo XIII, in his encyclical *"Rerum Novarum"* of 1891 and the *"Quadragesimo Anno"* of Pope Pius XI (1931) called attention to the rights of workers and studied problems of property and capitalism and questions of social justice. Cardinal Gibbons established himself as the champion of the worker when he defended the Knights of Labor in Rome in 1887 and succeeded in persuading the Vatican to lift its condemnation of the American branch of that organization, which was the forerunner of the American Federation of Labor.

The National Catholic Welfare Conference, which was founded in 1919 as a national office to coordinate various projects of the American Church, was a catalyst for the promotion of social justice and the application of the social teachings of the Church. The "Bishops' Program of Social Reconstruction" which was issued that same year examined current social problems and suggested legislation that would solve them. It is significant that ten of its eleven proposals would later be part of Franklin Roosevelt's New Deal.[6]

Pope Pius XII began in 1939 to address women regarding their obligation to work for the improvement of society through civic and political action. Particularly in his addresses to teaching sisters in 1951 and to contemplative nuns in 1958 did he direct religious women to be aware of problems of the contemporary world. Pope Paul VI expressed similar ideas in a talk entitled "New Horizons for the Woman Religious" in 1964.[7] Religious communities which kept abreast of the latest developments in Church teaching, and which saw the effects of social injustices in their daily work among the poor, certainly had the impetus to search for some solutions.

This is the context in which American religious women lived out their lives up to the time of the Second Vatican Council. Now let us examine the ways in which some individual sisters and communities interpreted their roles as sisters within the American political system.

INDIVIDUAL AND COMMUNITY INTERACTION

The chief ways in which Americans participate in the political process are through the ballot box and through various methods of influencing those who hold public office. Office holders themselves may seem to have the greatest political power, but they will not keep it for long if they are unresponsive to their constituencies. Though I have not found examples of sisters holding legislative office in the period under study, there are many instances in which they exerted influence in the political arena. Let us examine some of them.

Sister Blandina Segale had come from Italy to America with her family at the age of four and joined the Sisters of Charity of Cincinnati in 1866 when she was sixteen. In 1872 she began her twenty-one years of service in Colorado and New Mexico, where she was a part of the development of the primitive frontier settlements into thriving towns and cities. Sister Blandina's congregation was a branch of the first indigenous religious community of women founded in America. Its rules were adapted from those formulated by St. Vincent de Paul for the French Daughters of Charity. He had been aware that cloister regulations could limit the good works of his sisters, so warned them not to call themselves "religious," because, "Who say 'religious' say 'cloistered,' and the Daughters of Charity must go everywhere."[8] Sister Blandina seems to have gone everywhere and known everyone. She built schools and hospitals and introduced the "American method" of building with bricks and mortar in putting up the tallest building in the Territory of New Mexico. She confronted murderers, championed the rights of Indians and Mexicans, and tamed Billy the Kid. A journal in which she described her experiences for her sister has been published, and gives ample illustration of her intelligence, common sense, and knowledge of human nature.[9]

Most interesting for our purposes are those incidents which illustrate the ways in which she influenced legislators and other political groups. Here is how she obtained a grant from the legislature to support her hospital:

> During the legislative session which took place the early part of the year, a thought came to me: "Why not invite the law-makers to visit the hospital?" Knowing the Speaker of the House made it easy to address a note of invitation, which I did. . . . Punctually at the time appointed, every member of the House and Senate . . . was here . . . The visitors had noticed how few were the facilities we have to care for the sick. A gentleman representing the sympathy of all asked, "Sister, what can we do to assist in ameliorating the present condition of your hospital? . . .
> "Pass a Relief Bill allowing the hospital $400 per month," I answered. . . .
> The "Relief Bill" was passed, but it will be some months before we receive any benefit from it.[10]

Her influence in Santa Fe was such that aspirants to political office sought her good will and made a promise of support for her projects a part of their campaign. When she needed to increase the amount paid by the County for the burial of indigents from $8 to $15, she reminded the new County Commissioner of his promises, but had to put on pressure of her own before she could accomplish her purposes.[11]

She was very much aware of local politics, though she usually made it a practice "not to speak of politics or the acts of politicians."[12] She explained the local situation to her sister thus:

> There are two political parties here, Republicans and Democrats. The first party goes by the name of the "Santa Fe Ring." This party has been doing things to suit themselves, so the Democrats say. . . . Among the powers that be, there is graft. County warrants are issued for debts assumed by County Commissioners. These warrants are depreciated to fifty per cent of their face value. The graft comes in when those who have the power to depreciate, purchase, and turn in at face value.[13]

The sisters taught in the public schools in Albuquerque, and were paid with warrants payable when taxes would come in. They had to pay interest on borrowed money for school expenses. When the face value on the warrants amounted to $6,000, Sister Blandina decided to try to have them legalized by the legislature, so they and other teachers would receive full face value for them. She did not trust the young lawyer who represented her district in the Territorial Legislature, so went to a trusted legal advisor. This angered the representative, who vowed to kill the bill aimed at legalizing the warrants. While she was in Santa Fe getting support for the bill, a legislator approached one of the sisters in Albuquerque, asking her to get Sister Blandina to support an omnibus bill that would include her claims but also unauthorized expenses for furniture and other items. He then approached Sister Blandina and said,

> "I cannot understand, Sister, why you are coming to draft a bill that will be tabled. Do listen to a lawyer who has your interest in mind as well as the cause he represents here. Do let me persuade you agree to an 'Omnibus Bill.' "[14]

She responded that she was satisfied with the way the bill was drafted. When she met the governor, he remarked to her, "I understand you are doing some lobbying." She explained the situation, and he responded, "Fear not Sister. Your claim is just, and you shall have the pleasure of seeing me sign the bill."[15] She scouted out people whose signature would be needed for the warrants, and remained in Santa Fe until the governor signed the bill. Bonds were then issued, with coupons bearing 6% interest. Thus did Sister Blandina successfully lobby for a bill which would ensure that all public school teachers would receive their just due from the government.

When the father of one of her pupils was about to be lynched by townsmen who were accustomed to taking the law into their own hands, Sister Blandina insisted that the sheriff accompany the man and herself through the streets past the angry mob. Thus did she bring an end to lynch law in Trinidad, Colorado.[16] The prisoner remained in jail until it was time for the Circuit Court to convene. It is no wonder that she could comment, "From the time Judge Hallett became judge of the Circuit Court, he and his court members have regularly made a visit to the Convent."[17]

For the last thirty-five years of her life, Sister Blandina ran a settlement house for Italian immigrants in Cincinnati. Among many other activities centered there was that of handling juvenile court cases. When the juvenile court was being organized in Cincinnati, Sister Blandina was invited to the first meeting. Later the court appointed her a probation officer, and her center had its own juvenile court. In an attempt to end white slavery in the city, she brought a case to court, with the hearty approval of the city's leading lawyers. Upon her death in 1941, at the age of 91, the whole city of Cincinnati mourned this sister who had taught, by word and example, the responsibilities of citizenship and the American way of using the legislative and judicial processes to ensure that justice is done.

OTHER CONGREGATIONS

Sisters, like other citizens, used the judicial and legislative systems to right wrongs and promote the common good. The Little Sisters of the Poor in Washington, D.C., caused motions to be introduced in Congress in 1874 and 1884 which resulted in grants of money for the construction of a home for the aged poor.[18] The Sisters of the Holy Names of Jesus and Mary successfully challenged before the Supreme Court an Oregon law which said that all children between the ages of eight and sixteen had to attend public schools. The decision in their favor in 1925 in *Pierce* vs. *Society of Sisters* has been called the Magna Carta for Catholic Education.[19]

MOTHER KATHERINE DREXEL

Mother Katherine Drexel, foundress of the Sisters of the Blessed Sacrament for work among Blacks and Indians, was one who was well aware of the power of the ballot box, and the obligations and privileges of citizenship. When she read in the newspaper in 1934 of an anti-lynching bill before Congress, and of the opposition of some Southern Congressmen to its passage, she said, "We must help put this bill through if we can,"[20] and sent off letters to the superiors of all of her houses. She asked them to get in touch with their Congressmen and urge them to vote for the bill and to write to President Franklin Roosevelt as well.

Many congregations of sisters worked in schools and hospitals on Indian reservations, and this work was often threatened when changes in policy emanated from Washington. At certain periods government money helped to support Catholic Indian schools, and at other times these subsidies were rescinded. Mother Katherine Drexel and other church leaders monitored developments such as these and lobbied for solutions which would protect the Indians' right to religious freedom.

In her Christmas letter of 1897 Mother Drexel informed her sisters that one of these crises was pending:

> Even now there is in Congress a petition of Cardinal Gibbons for reopening the matter of the contracts for Indian schools. The salvation of many Indians may depend on the government's keeping up the Catholic Indian schools. The Sisters must pray for this.[21]

The Rev. Joseph Stephan, official liaison between Church and government in matters affecting the Indian missions, was in Europe. The Catholic Indian Bureau and members of congregations whose sisters worked among the Indians urged Mother Drexel to speak before the Senate and explain the need for school subsidies and the excellent work which they supported. She, however, deferred to Archbishop Patrick Ryan of Philadelphia, saying he could do a much better job. Meanwhile the sisters would pray for his success.[22]

THE MARYKNOLL SISTERS

American sisters who went as missionaries to foreign lands were in a special position, facing different cultural and political traditions when they embarked upon their work. Maryknoll, the first American Catholic foreign mission society, chose South China as its first mission field, and sent four priests there in 1918. In 1921, the first Maryknoll sisters arrived in Hong Kong, where they prepared themselves for their work on the mainland. In 1922 six of them began their mission work at Yeungkong.

The sisters worked with and followed the advice of the Maryknoll Fathers. Their policies regarding political activity were very clear:

> Maryknoll's policy in China, as in other foreign countries, was to keep aloof from anything political. The missionaries did not discuss or participate in politics. In the midst of the Nationalist Revolution in 1928, Maryknoll's *The Field Afar* explained that "the political is none of our affair. . . ." The Sisters reported that they were forbidden by their superiors to discuss politics. In addition, the Sisters dealt with the peasant women and children of China who apparently had little political knowledge or interest in national affairs and were interested in peace and the routine of their daily lives.[23]

Their practice was to encourage Chinese Catholics to promote civic and social reform. Maryknoll's approach differed from that of other missionaries, who aimed at planting seeds of an institutional Church, and built churches, schools, and orphanages with that goal in mind. Maryknoll sought to develop a spiritual edifice, a native church guided by native sisters and priests. Any buildings that might be erected should be put up by Chinese Catholics, when and if they felt the need for them. The Maryknoll Sisters went out among the people, making friendly overtures and instructing those who showed an interest in the faith. They visited people in their homes and taught in the villages, living and eating with Chinese families. They moderated sodalities and other groups aimed at social and apostolic action.

The Maryknoll Sisters who developed these techniques in the 1930s were ahead of other communities, which continued to frown on contact with the world beyond convent walls. This idea of a direct apostolate for sisters was picked up by Cardinal Leon Joseph Suenens in the 1950s. He corresponded with Sister Marcelline of Maryknoll and told her in 1957 that he was experimenting using the same techniques among sisters and brothers in Belgium.[24] In 1962 he disseminated these ideas in a book entitled *The Nun in the World*, which had a tremendous influence on American sisters, and opened to them a vision of a new apostolate serving the Church in the world rather than apart from it.[25]

In recent decades, particularly in Latin America, Maryknoll sisters have sometimes become involved in political actions against structures that they consider to be unjust and oppressive. Some have died because their championing of the poor was seen as a threat to the established political order. Others have been expelled from the countries in which they were working. Many have had to ponder the choice between speaking out and remaining silent, and the possible consequences of each course of action.

CATHOLIC COLLEGES

Catholics who were inspired by the papal encyclicals on social justice, the Bishops' Program of Social Reconstruction, and the vigorous leadership which Monsignor John A. Ryan gave to the Social Action Department of the National Catholic Welfare Conference, helped to create a number of social action organizations in the 1920s, '30s, and '40s. Catholic colleges, particularly those for women, were centers where an awareness of national and international affairs was fostered and problems studied. There were also opportunities for students to participate in activities aimed at correcting or alleviating social ills. (It is not mere happenstance that many of the women in top political positions in the 1980s are graduates of Catholic women's colleges.)

A case in point is that of Rosary College in the Chicago suburb of River Forest, where a remarkable group of Sinsinawa Dominican Sisters animated the faculty and administration. Sister Thomas Aquinas O'Neill, in her capacities as philosophy teacher and president, placed the college in the forefront of the movements for social betterment in Chicago, and encouraged faculty members to participate in these movements.

Her letters, often written on postcards, to public figures became legendary; they extended both her influence and her friendships. In 1934 she started an "Education for Leisure" program of free noncredit evening and Saturday courses, a new idea at the time which brought the college national attention. When the Catholic Worker movement began in 1933, she and Sister Madeleva of St. Mary's, Notre

Dame, co-sponsored a series of lectures by Dorothy Day, Peter Maurin and others to make the movement known.

Lecture series such as this on national and international problems and events were common at Rosary College from the time of its foundation in 1922. According to one who was there at the time, the aim was:

> to make students, faculty and hundreds of people who attended the sessions mindful of their responsibilities to influence legislation and administration by proper use of the prerogative of citizenship.[26]

This was one of the chief ways in which sisters influenced political life. The same writer continues:

> As college students and their associates could play an important part in the development of internationalism as a preliminary to achievement of world peace, our college made many efforts to cultivate in students an intelligent interest in world affairs.[27]

The caliber of these efforts is indicated by the fact that the most prominent speaker at the first regional conference of the Catholic Association for International Peace, which was held at Rosary College in 1937, was Mrs. Franklin Delano Roosevelt. This organization espoused many proposals that were eventually carried out, such as a federated Europe and a world Bill of Rights.

Rosary College students and alumni were given many opportunities to help in settlement houses, inner-city parishes, and projects for the poor and needy. Nor did the faculty lag behind. Sister Mary Ellen O'Hanlon lectured and wrote on race relations. Sister Vincent Ferrer Bradford, economics and political science teacher, devoted a great deal of time and energy to social justice issues and consciousness-raising to stimulate people to promote legislation that would solve national and world problems. This descendent of Governor William Bradford of Plymouth Colony worked tirelessly for social justice, concentrating on labor problems in the 1920's and 1930's and on peace and internationalism in the 1940s.

She was an early lecturer for and participant in the Catholic Conference on Industrial Problems, which was founded in Chicago in 1922. She spoke at both local and national meetings of this group, in cities all over the country. This afforded her the opportunity to meet major authorities on labor problems and to show that "women wearing the religious habit and 'living behind convent walls' need not be isolated from but deeply concerned with the society in which they work."[28] Wide publicity was given to these conferences and Sister Vincent Ferrer's talks were quoted in the Atlanta *Constitution* and the *New York Times*. When she spoke in San Francisco, which was becoming highly unionized, a barber pleaded with her to stay a few days longer so she could explain to the local sisters why they should not cross a picket line.

This sister, who taught workers about their right to organize and to have a just wage, went down into the copper mines in Anaconda and attended Senate hearings during a U.S. Steel strike in 1937. When the C.I.O. was organizing workers in the thirties, and the Communists were trying to infiltrate the union, Earl Browder, head of the American Communist Party, quoted Sister Vincent Ferrer in his publication, "A Message to Catholics."

For ten years beginning in 1937, she was a teacher in the staff of the Summer Institutes for Women Workers sponsored by the National Council of Catholic Women. At these institutions she came to know many women active in the labor movement, including Agnes Nestor of the Women's Trade Union League of Chicago, who had successfully promoted minimum wage legislation for women in Illinois. One evening the guest speaker was Frances Perkins, the Secretary of Labor.

Sister Vincent Ferrer was long active in the Catholic Association for International Peace, which had been founded in 1927 to promote world peace through justice and charity. She was a vice president of this organization and represented it at the 18th International Congress of Pax Romana in 1939. This meeting broke up when Hitler invaded Poland and Britain and France declared war on Germany.

In 1943 Sister Vincent Ferrer began eight years of teaching evening and Saturday classes in current economic problems, social reconstruction, international affairs, the Dunbarton Oaks plan, programs for peace, and the social encyclicals, at the newly-opened Sheil School of Social Studies in Chicago, a school which aimed to present the Church's social teachings and apply them to modern problems. The classes, which were free, attracted people of all ages and creeds. Guest speakers included Father John Courtney Murray, Barbara Ward Jackson, and Saul Alinsky.

In the 1940's Bishop Sheil urged Sister to give two lectures scheduled at Hull House even though she had received many letters protesting the Communist influence there. When a man in the audience asked her about a current national problem, she responded, "If I were a member of the Senate today, I would vote 'yes' on the bill." He replied, "That is just where you belong."[29]

In an article in *America* for December 12, 1970 entitled "Catholic Social Action: Where Do We Go From Here", Ed Marciniak included Sister Vincent Ferrer in a list of people who

> crystallized a body of Catholic social thought, characteristically American, ecumenical in outreach, and attractive to the laity. Nourished by the social encyclicals of Leo XIII and Pius XI, this troupe of writers, speech-makers and activists laid the philosophical footing for a social movement that was to flourish for three decades . . . until the middle 1960's.[30]

The combination of a body of social thought with the American genius for organization had dynamic results in organizations that were open to ecumenical activity, able to adapt earlier principles to new practice, and adjust educational approaches to new demands. Tens of thousands of Catholics, Marciniak says, launched organizations and undertook programs as a result of the impetus they received from those social thinkers.

Thus the political activity of sisters in the nineteenth and twentieth century was both individual and institutional. If individual sisters in a particular place and time sometimes exerted a powerful influence over political or legislative affairs, the impact of some Catholic institutions, particularly high schools and colleges, was extraordinary. In imparting Catholic social thought and responsibility for citizenship, in sensitizing their students to political issues, and in the influence on public affairs in the surrounding community, these institutions prepared many Catholics for a visible and articulate role in the public life of the nation.

THE WINDS OF CHANGE

Education seems to have been a key factor which influenced sisters' openness to and awareness of contemporary trends. The sisters on college faculties were generally the most highly-educated members of their congregations. After the First World War, accrediting agencies and state licensing departments began to insist on college degrees for teachers. Sisters who did not possess degrees took classes after school, on Saturdays, and in the summer while teaching full time. This expedient did not allow for leisurely study or the acquisition of that love of learning that becomes a life-long pursuit.

This changed in the 1950s, when the promptings of Pope Pius XII and the founding of the Sister Formation Movement led to a more solid and continuous educational experience that prepared sisters to become qualified professionals before undertaking the duties of their ministry.[31]

Other milestones of the 1950's were the two international meetings of major superiors of women's communities in Rome in 1950 and 1952, and the formation of the American Conference of Major Superiors of Women in 1952. At the urging of the Pope, superiors who had been grappling with community problems alone now joined forces to seek common solutions. As this organization developed and changed in succeeding decades, major superiors were brought up to date on new theological and scriptural insights and were inspired to new understandings of their mission. These they shared with the members of their communities.

When the Second Vatican Council convened in 1962 and asked sisters to re-examine their lives in the light of the Gospel and the needs of the contemporary world, both the young sisters who were the products of the Sister Formation Movement and their superiors general had already been prepared for new responses to changed conditions. Sisters of all ages became aware of contemporary scriptural and theological thought and avid students of the documents and discussions of the Council. Their response to these insights took many forms.

In the decade that followed the Vatican Council, sisters participated in civil rights marches and voter registration drives. They protested the Viet Nam War and the nuclear build-up. They boycotted grapes and Nestles' products, defended tenants against unjust landlords, and organized the Grey Panthers to lobby for more benefits for the elderly. Everywhere they worked to improve the lot of the poor and the oppressed. Some ultimately decided that they could best carry out the Gospel message by working as legislators in government agencies for the promotion of social justice.

SISTER MARY LUKE TOBIN

Sister Mary Luke Tobin, who was president of the Sisters of Loretto in the 1960's and one of fifteen female auditors at the Second Vatican Council, has likened the new understanding of that period to the opening of successive doors, as the Gospel message was "revisioned" in the light of change in Church and society. In a memoir describing what she and other sisters experienced during the Council and after she tells how Cardinal Suenens' book *The Nun in the World* "stunned" sisters with his assertion that they

> were too separated from the present currents of life that are moving among the peoples of the world and should be acting as "animators" for groups of men and women whose everyday lives need evangelization.[32]

In 1964 Sister Mary Luke was elected president of the Conference of Major Superiors of Women. The position of national leadership enabled her to share her insights from observing Council sessions and from her discussions with Council *periti*, with non-Catholic observers and others, and with all of the congregations in the country. These insights led her and other sisters to become more involved in the political and economic spheres. Thus does she describe the ways in which different individuals responded to this call:

> Although action for social justice that flows from the imperatives of the gospel has many modes of implementation, all members are learning to respect the choices of others. Some elect to teach social responsibility and others elect to support it . . . Some have chosen to express their concern in more publicly involved ways, . . . in confrontative rallies and demonstrations and by joining coalitions for wider political action in the struggle for justice. Some have felt that only examples of nonviolent civil disobedience will draw attention to critical problems . . . and they have been willing to be arrested. . . .[33]

Sister Mary Luke became more actively involved in anti-war protests after a visit to Viet Nam, where she represented the Catholic Peace Fellowship on a fact-finding mission. In 1972 she held a prayer service at the stockholders' meeting of Honeywell, Inc., a firm which manufactured anti-personnel weapons for use in Viet Nam. New insights impelled her to more active protests:

> It was increasingly evident to me that words and actions intended to persuade politicians to modify their stands were ineluctably connected with the gospel of love and life. Once this connection had become clear, each decision to partici-

pate in an anti-war action did not need to be separately ag-
onized over, but was a link in the chain of resistance and
protest.[34]

In an attempt to spur on House and Senate action, she participated in 1972 in lobbying efforts on Capitol Hill with other members
of Clergy and Laity Concerned. After they were told that there would
be no antiwar legislation until after Nixon's visit to Moscow, they gathered in the rotunda for prayer. They continued to sing and pray, despite announcements that the rotunda was closing, and ended up
being arrested and spending the night in jail.

In 1973, after the bombing of Hanoi, she went on a peace pilgrimage to seek the help of European religious leaders. Upon their
return, her group submitted a statement to the Sub-committee on Europe of the House Committee on Foreign Affairs. Other approaches
were also used, as she writes,

At all times during these missions, we were constantly writing to the President and to Congress, urging the cessation
of the bombing of Viet Nam. Did such appeals and appearances further the cause of peace? There is little evidence
that they did. However, one can only resort to the conviction that all anti-war efforts were useful in helping to bring
about an end to the war.[35]

Could it have been the seeming futility of lobbying members of Congress on urgent matters such as war and the nuclear buildup that finally convinced some religious that they could be more effective if they
became members of Congress themselves?

Sister Mary Luke is an exceptional example of the pattern of
awareness and involvement that is characteristic of many American sisters whose spiritual journey has brought them from the personal experience of renewal and concern for local issues to a global vision and
ministry. The doors and windows which Vatican Council II opened for
her and so many others will never again be closed.

CONCLUSION

Thomas Jefferson was uttering prophetic words when he noted
that groups of religious women like the Ursulines of New Orleans
would serve America by furthering "the wholesome purposes of so-

ciety." He certainly would have applauded their participation in all aspects of American civil life, their promotion of the rights and duties of good citizenship, and their participation in protests and civil disobedience against a government that was seen to be trampling on human rights.

American sisters have been involved in exercising and safeguarding both their own civil and political rights and those of others, Indians, Blacks, Vietnamese, American workers. They have taught people what their rights were, and made them aware of problems that needed to be addressed. They have joined with others to lobby for needed legislation. Although enclosure regulations inhibited social and political interaction, unusual situations which required a fresh look at the implementation of the gospel message brought new approaches that flowed from American pragmatism and common sense. Thus Sister Blandina and the Maryknoll Sisters were open to the needs of their people in frontier and missionary settings. And the Maryknoll example influenced Cardinal Suenens, whose book *The Nun in the World* stunned American sisters made complacent and lethargic by too much enclosure and too little challenge.

The education given to sisters and students in Catholic colleges, the insights gleaned from papal conciliar and episcopal documents, the spur to internal renewal, and contact with many Catholic and ecumenical groups which focused on a myriad of problems, all helped to burst the walls of their cocoon. The Sister Formation Movement, the sharing among major superiors, and finally the Second Vatican Council impelled sisters to take a fresh view of the Gospel imperative, and to explore, like butterflies, a world of new ideas and changed realities. When they began to study the problems of their world, the gross injustices of racism and the Viet Nam War, plus a nuclear build-up that threatened world destruction, it became clear that this new world needed their total attention. They have attacked the problems of peace and justice with a vigor born of gospel urgency, and never again will the butterflies return to their cocoons.

NOTES

1. Henry C. Semple (ed.) *The Ursulines in New Orleans, A Record of Two Centuries, 1729–1925* (New York: Kenedy, 1925), p. 62.
2. This number is a rough estimate, based on the total numbers of sisters reported in official Catholic directories for 1850 (l,344), 1900 (40,340), and 1963 (177,354).

3. I have treated the matters of enclosure and canon law regulations for religious women in far greater detail in: Mary Ewens, O.P., *The Role of the Nun in Nineteenth-Century America* in the series "The American Catholic Tradition" (N.Y.: Arno Press, 1978).

4. *The Charity of Christ Presses Us*, ed. Sister Mary Philip, O.P., (Milwaukee: Catholic Life Publications, Bruce Press, 1962), p. 20-21.

5. Ibid., p. 36.

6. *The Catholic Church U.S.A.*, Louis J. Putz, C.S.C., ed., (Chicago: Fides, 1956), p. 140-141.

7. Sister M. Charles Borromeo Muckenhirn, *The Changing Sister*, (Notre Dame, IN: Fides, 1965), p. 263-65.

8. Henri Levedan, *The Heroic Life of Saint Vincent de Paul*, trans. Helen Younger Chase (New York: Longmans, 1929), p. 209.

9. Sister Blandina Segale, *At the End of the Santa Fe Trail*, (Milwaukee: Bruce, 1948), passim.

10. Ibid., p. 143-44.

11. Ibid., p. 150-52.

12. Ibid., p. 149.

13. Ibid., p. 158.

14. Ibid., p. 260-61.

15. Ibid., p. 201.

16. Ibid., p. 59-62.

17. Ibid.

18. Rev. John F. McShane, *Little Beggars of Christ*, (Paterson, N.J.: St. Anthony Guild Press, 1954), p. 44.

19. Mark D. Howe, *The Garden and the Wilderness* (Chicago: University of Chicago Press, 1967), p. 238, 368.

20. Katherine Burton, *The Golden Door*, (N.Y.: P.J. Kenedy & Sons, 1957), p. 268.

21. Ibid., p. 160.

22. Ibid.

23. Sister Mary Ann Schintz, O.P., "An Investigation of the Modernizing role of the Maryknoll Sisters in China," unpublished Doctoral Diss. UW-Madison, 1978, p. 129.

24. Ibid., p. 131 ff. 369 f.

25. Newman, Westminster, Md., 1962.

26. Sister Vincent Ferrer Bradford, "Aspects of Catholic Thought and Action in the Thirties and Forties," Unpublished typescript, Saint Clara Convent Archives, Sinsinawa, Wisconsin, n.d., p. 14.

27. Ibid., p. 15.

28. Ibid., p.1.

29. Ibid., p. 26.

30. Ibid., p. 511-512.

31. These matters are discussed at some length in Sister Bertrande Meyers, D.C., *Sisters for the 21st Century*, (New York: Sheed & Ward, 1965).

32. Mary Luke Tobin, S.L., *Hope is an Open Door*, (Nashville: Abingdon, 1981), p. 15.

33. Ibid., p. 65-66.

34. Ibid., p. 100.

35. Ibid., p. 105.

Nancy Sylvester, IHM

POST-VATICAN II SISTERS AND POLITICAL MINISTRY

On December 17-19, 1971, forty-seven Roman Catholic sisters met at Trinity College in Washington, DC, in response to an invitation "to plan a network of sisters to deal with social policy questions."[1] Marge Tuite, OP, Josephine Dunne, SNCJ, and Mary Hayes, SND, solicited supporters from the newly-formed National Assembly of Women Religious; others were invited from the Leadership Conference of Women Religious lists or simply by word of mouth. Through the auspices of the National Center for Urban Ethnic Affairs (NCUEA) Msgr. Geno Baroni officially convened the meeting and put at the women's disposal the NCUEA administrative talent of Rita Mudd, Sister of Providence of Spokane, WA, and Jerry Ernst, field service director. The weekend meeting was filled with issue input and community organizing techniques. By the end of the meeting Audrey Miller, a sister of Providence of Pittsburgh, assumed the leadership role after raising a question as to why men should lead the task of organizing women religious. Motivated by their deep belief that women religious could affect real change in public policy, the sisters voted by an overwhelming majority to accept the motion presented by Adrian Dominican, Carol Coston, that the sisters present "form a political action network of information and communication."[2]

These women founded NETWORK, the first registered Catholic social justice lobby. Since sisters arrived in the United States there have always been individuals who were politically active influencing passage of local and state laws, emphasizing citizenship responsibility, organizing for just wages, etc.; but until NETWORK there was not one organization to link the various individuals and congregations who began to understand the necessary and demanding connection between faith and public policy. NETWORK provided the outreach necessary. It was and continues to be an empowering network of participation to counteract the network of vested interests and power described by the bishops in their *Call to Action*.[3] From its beginnings NETWORK was to work for just legislation on a whole range of issues but with a primary focus on how U.S. policy affects the economically poor. Its advocacy positions continue to be informed by the Gospel, the Church's social justice teachings and personal faith reflections on injustice. NETWORK's ministry, now shared by both lay and religious, continues as a tribute to the founding mothers' instinct for integrating faith and politics in working for social justice.

The women of NETWORK eventually called this integration of faith and political involvement, "political ministry." Alan Geyer, Director of the Center for Theology and Public Policy, in an article for *Christianity and Crisis* in 1983, spoke about the importance of this term: "For the shocking and marvelous term 'political ministry' we are especially indebted to our Roman Catholic sisters and their apostolate through NETWORK."[4a] The ensuing involvement in political ministry by hundreds of women religious and their congregations is both the culmination of certain developments within religious life, society and the Church, and a legitimation for individual sisters who choose to run for public office or who accept political appointments.

Many forces converged to affirm this ministerial call to political involvement. I will focus on three major areas: first, on the experiences of the women who began NETWORK; second, on significant developments during renewal of religious congregations; finally, on the theological self-understandings of Church and mission that emerged from Vatican II and later Synod statements.

During the 1960's and 70's some religious women began to leave the institutionalized forms of ministry for new forms of service. Sisters who worked in urban ministry, community organizing and the civil rights movement experienced a new and different challenge from the people they served.

Among the 47 women who gathered in Washington in 1971 were some who administered low-income housing programs in Washington, DC; served as special services directors for housing projects within the black community in Ft. Lauderdale, FL; counselled dropouts in St. Louis; organized tenants on the Hill in Pittsburgh as part of the Catholic Interracial Council; worked on women's issues as staff with the United Church of Christ. They had already begun to live the 'option for the poor.' They experienced the racism of our society, the economic inequities and the oppression of sexism. Working on a day-to-day basis with the effects of unjust structures they began to feel the powerlessness and the frustration that existed in the lives of the poor.

They came to realize that alleviating the effects of injustice was not sufficient. They saw the necessity to complement direct services with a ministry of structural change.

Maureen Kelleher, RSHM, an early NETWORK staff member, wrote in the first NETWORK Quarterly in 1972 about the sisters' emerging awareness: "Sisters began to feel that they were running around stamping out brush fires as they tried to prevent gang wars or counsel drug addicts. After reflecting on the causes of gang wars and the availability of drugs, they recognized the need to address themselves to action on the causes of these problems, causes related to unemployment, substandard housing and corruption in high places. And so this combination of study and experience has brought them to a new consciousness leading to a new response—organizing for social impact."

Another woman among the 47 who also articulated this growing interest in structural change was Marge Tuite, OP. She understood the Gospel call to transform unjust structures and often articulated this aspect of ministry. "Never is the Gospel dimension of ministry negotiable. It is a listening ministry to the signs of the times; it is a ministry of risk that demands both an individual and corporate stance in lifestyle and issue response within the framework of the gospel message."[4] Marge worked twelve years in Harlem and five years at the national Urban Training Center in Chicago where she prepared southern organizers to return South to continue the struggle for racial justice. She used her skills in organizing, group development and social analysis in service to many congregations who wanted to take seriously the role of empowerment within their ministerial commitments.

Tuite was also a founder and first chairwoman of the National Assembly of Women Religious' Social Concerns Committee and served on the Catholic Committee on Urban Ministry's (CCUM) Board. It was during the 1971 CCUM meeting that Tuite and Geno Baroni shared their visions. Baroni was at that time the Executive Director of NCUEA after having previously served as director of the Washington Archdiocesan Office for Urban Affairs and as program director of the Urban Taskforce of the United States Catholic Conference (USCC).[5] Baroni consistently prodded the American Catholic Church to respond to the plight of the disadvantaged in urban America. He was convinced that influencing public policy through the legislative process was critical in achieving social justice. In addition he felt women religious were far more ready to respond to the justice imperative than the priests. Tuite also firmly believed that sisters were a potential force as agents of social change and that they were indeed ready. These two energizing leaders joined together in their belief that Catholic sisters could be agents for social change by organizing to influence the legislative process. They planned the meeting from which NETWORK was born.

Carol Coston, OP, a founding mother and NETWORK's Executive Director for eleven years, recalls that first meeting and the energy she experienced that strengthened her for the unique organization she was going to lead. "In 1971 I was working in Florida where religious women were just starting to get organized. So this was a unique experience for me to be in a room full of 47 activist sisters - many of whom had already shared my own experiences in working with the poor. They, too, knew about inadequate medical care, inaccessible food distribution systems, unfair voting practices and racist resistance to open housing ordinances. Many of us felt that we were just patching up bad public policy at the local level and saw the need to help create better policy at the national level. I really felt the energy in those women to do this new kind of ministry."

The ministerial experiences of these sisters convinced them that structural change was necessary to transform injustice; this new consciousness was not an aberration in religious life but had roots in significant developments that occurred prior to and during the renewal of religious congregations.

One early development within certain religious congregations contributed significantly to the readiness of sisters to engage in the public policy arena. Under the leadership of Mary Emil Penet, a Monroe IHM, and Sister Ritamary Bradley, CHM, editor of the Sister Formation Bulletin, the Sister Formation Movement began in 1952. Its purpose was to integrate the intellectual, cultural and professional aspects of a sister's life with her spiritual and apostolic growth. In the late 50's this was accomplished by withdrawing sisters from the parochial schools where they taught so that they might complete either their bachelor's or master's degree and through a nationwide program of workshops and resource facilitation for formation personnel. Although not foreseen by the founders, this process—with its specific orientation toward integration—"enabled sisters to develop a heightened understanding of themselves, their vocations, their church and its relationship to the world,and to pursue with confidence their role as leaders. . . (It) facilitated the evolution of an educated mass of women, open to diversity, to the promptings of conscience and to a critical awareness of the social changes occurring in the Church and in the world."[6]

Through the Sister Formation Movement, sisters emerged in the 60's as the largest educated class of women within the Catholic church. They assumed leadership roles in their various institutions, and many sisters began to risk new forms of ministry which brought them into direct contact with the poor and into the social arena.

As early as 1961 an inter-community group organized the Urban Apostolate of Sisters in Chicago. These sisters initiated home visiting programs, set up adult education programs and worked in public housing projects in an attempt to create alternatives that could respond to the needs of the children and their families that were not being addressed through the traditional classroom. These types of inter-community projects proliferated throughout the country after 1963. By 1965, in the programs of the Urban Apostolate alone, over 400 sisters participated. After Lyndon Johnson's Economic Opportunity Act of 1964, sisters were found working in Head Start, Upward Bound and in summer programs sponsored jointly by archdioceses and by the US Office of Economic Opportunity.[7] What these experiences provided for the sisters involved was an expansion of traditional ministries, a hands-on involvement with the poor of their cities, and experiences of injustice which challenged them to analyze its causes as well as its symptoms.

As sisters began to work outside of the traditional institutions they became part of the broader societal movements. In the early years of the civil rights movement sisters joined with Martin Luther King, Jr. in his march on Washington on August 28, 1963, participated in the voter registration drives of '64 and '65, and marched in protest in Selma and Cicero. *The Other America* written in 1962 by Michael Harrington was a popular book among many women religious. Its clear presentation of the invisible poor within our own country provided the beginnings of social analysis for sisters who had experienced the effects of poverty and its twin evil, discrimination, and now desired to address its root causes.

Out of the experience of social sin there also emerged a new sense of hope. Marching with King in the '60's and witnessing the subsequent civil rights victories stirred hope for political and social change. This feeling was heightened by the Kennedy presidency. It renewed "a fundamental twentieth-century American faith in government's commitment to serve all its citizens and to mediate a reasoned discussion leading to enlightened public policy, particularly in the area of racial justice."[8] In addition, the election of a Catholic to the presidency in 1960 challenged the residual anti-Catholic sentiment in the U.S. and freed Catholics to look anew at their roles as both responsible citizens and as persons of faith. It was no longer necessary to remain silent in the face of injustice perpetrated by U.S. policy in order to be considered a loyal citizen. Catholics could even be trusted with public office at the national level.

Sisters soon joined the ranks of those who understood the growing abyss between the American ideal and American life. Public policy needed to be challenged and critiqued as it kept Black people from their rightful claim to equality and as it maintained the gap between rich and poor, skewing the distribution of our resources so as not to provide for the basic human needs of its citizens. By the late '60's many sisters also became involved in the anti-war movement. They challenged a foreign policy that wasted our young men in an undeclared war and that continued funding the war without any opportunity for citizen participation in those decisions. They assisted conscientious objectors who saw alternative service to their country as an imperative of their faith commitment.

This willingness to challenge policy and structures on the outside was focused just as vigorously on religious life's internal structures as sisters took seriously the call to adaptation and renewal of *Perfectae Caritatis*. The task was two-fold:

> The appropriate renewal of religious life involves two si-
> multaneous processes: (1) a continuous return to the source
> of all Christian life and to the original inspiration behind a
> given community and (2) an adjustment of the community
> to the changed conditions of the times.
>
> *(Perfectae Caritatis #2)*

The renewal chapters of 1967 and '68 took place under the aegis of the Church's new self-understanding as articulated in the Vatican Council. There was to be an attentiveness to the world in which women religious lived and to the longings and specific needs of this historical time. Many sisters who had experienced powerlessness with the poor were now chapter delegates and took seriously the Council's emphasis on collegiality and subsidiarity. They challenged the authoritarian structures of governance and set about transforming the process of decision making within their own congregations. This experience of changing their own structures to be more responsive to the needs of those for whom they exist became a key factor in maintaining the hope for change within the political order. Sisters experienced the reality and the power of participating in the decisions that affected their lives—a right which is central to political ministry.

During the renewal years three national organizations were formed to respond to specific needs not being addressed within the Church or individual congregations. They were the National Black Sisters Conference (NBSC) 1968, the National Coalition of American Nuns (NCAN) 1969, and the National Association of Women Religious (NAWR) 1970. Each addressed the right to self-determination and participation in the decision-making structures of both the Catholic Church and society.[9]

These grassroots organizations complemented the leadership being provided by the Conference of Major Superiors of Women (CMSW, later renamed Leadership Conference of Women Religious, LCWR). Women in congregational leadership during renewal read, studied and prayed over the theological and pastoral insights developed during this time. Cardinal Suenens' book *Nun in the World*, published in 1962, had widespread influence on congregational renewal. In 1971 CMSW's Atlanta Assembly had as its theme "The Church is for the World," and its program addressed the need to equip sisters to become active participants in working for social justice within their ministries. One of the Assembly's resolutions was to sponsor regional workshops that would expand the sisters' awareness, orient them to social needs, and prepare them to assume leadership roles in community development.[10] Geno Baroni participated in these follow-up regional workshops and challenged sisters to translate their influence into constructive initiatives for social change.

These workshops addressed social issues, provided tools of analysis, explained the political processes, urged both corporate and individual involvement of women religious in combating poverty, racism and other kinds of dehumanization. Sisters attended these workshops throughout the fall of 1971 and spring of 1972. For many sisters there was a growing readiness for active engagement in political ministry.

Opportunities to minister directly with the poor and experiences with the social movements and developments in renewal were for the sisters directly related to their understanding of religious life. In addition, these realizations were complemented by simultaneous developments within the teaching Church which contributed to the growing understanding that to be a woman religious "in the world" demanded working for justice.

One of the most influential documents of Vatican II was the Pastoral Constitution on the *Church in the Modern World (Gaudium et Spes)*. In this document the bishops expressed the consensus that to be Church is to live and act within the world. The Church understood itself to have an explicit role to make the human family more truly human, in fact it has a responsibility to further the values of human dignity. An important aspect of the mission of the Church is to proclaim and foster human rights, to establish and build up the human community and to initiate action for the service of all, especially of the poor.[11] *Gaudium et Spes* firmly links peace to justice. The inequities of the current economic order must be addressed as well as the putting right of "political grievances." Justice is central to the Church's mission.[12]

> God destined the earth and all that it contains for the use of all men and all peoples. . . Furthermore, the right to have a share of earthly goods sufficient for oneself and one's family belongs to everyone.
> . . . If a person is in extreme necessity, he has the right to take from the riches of others what he himself needs. . . According to their ability, let all individuals and governments undertake a genuine sharing of the goods. . . (*Gaudium et Spes*, 69.1)

While the spirit of Vatican II was gradually being integrated into the life of the Church, the Latin American bishops met in Medellin in 1968. Their meeting had a profound impact on the Church's further understanding of the centrality of justice in achieving peace. The Bishops of Latin America chose to begin their reflection with their experience and the experience of the people they served. In doing that the bishops articulated their role as Church in a suffering world with a new boldness and clarity. The bishops named the causes of injustice and poverty as structural, as institutionalized violence. The bishops articulated a "preferential option for the poor" and accepted the call to be in solidarity with the materially poor. This identification with the poor brought a responsibility for action. They favored a process of organizing the popular sectors which are capable of pressing public officials who are often impotent in their social projects without popular support.[13] The bishops realized the power of grassroots action for justice and saw their role in assisting the poor and oppressed to attain liberation.

Medellin impacted on the Church's self-understanding, especially in the Western hemisphere. The "option for the poor" and the struggle for liberation from oppressive structures took on a new significance. Pope Paul VI addressed the need for the Church to become involved in political activity as a way to participate in the economic decisions which affect the lives of the poor. In his encyclical *Octogesima*

Adveniens (the Call to Action) written in 1971, Paul focuses on the shift from being involved with the economic questions to the underlying political ones.

> Economic activity is necessary and, if it is at the service of humanity, it can be 'a . . . sign of Providence.' It is the occasion of concrete exchanges between persons, of rights recognized, of services rendered and of dignity affirmed in work. . . Yet it runs the risk of taking up too much strength and freedom. This is why the need is felt to pass from economics to politics. It is true that in the term 'politics' many confusions are possible and must be clarified, but each one feels that in the social and economic field, both national and international, the ultimate decisions rest with political power. (*Octogesima Adveniens*, #46)

This desire to address the political questions was fueled by a respect for the importance of the economic order in shaping human lives; the belief that human freedom must intervene to render economic distribution more just; the conviction regarding the right of persons to participate in decisions, including economic policies, that affect their lives.[14]

Participation in decision making and engagement in political activity became key concepts in the work of justice. Later in 1971 the Synod of Bishops issued their statement *Justice in the World* which placed the ministry for justice at the center of the Church's mission.

> Action on behalf of justice and participation in the transformation of the world fully appear to us as a constitutive dimension of the preaching of the Gospel, or, in other words, of the church's mission for the redemption of the human race and its liberation from every oppressive situation. (Justice in the World, #6)

Donal Dorr in his book, *Option for the Poor,* articulates how this synod understood the key injustice. "According to (this document) there is one central issue which lies at the heart of the structural injustices of today's world: lack of participation by people in determining their own destiny. . . To be in a marginal situation is not simply to be economically deprived but perhaps more basically to be deprived of the political power to change one's situation."[15]

This articulation of the key injustice being a lack of participation in political decision making provided a theological framework for women religious' reflection on political action as an appropriate response for transforming unjust structures. It was a legitimizing as well as motivating source for the women who began NETWORK. Thus, at the end of the December '71 weekend, a steering committee was formed and they assigned themselves as their first task: the reading and studying of the *Call to Action* and *Justice in the World*.[16] They were authorized to establish a basic model of NETWORK and to compose a rationale based on the principles contained within those two documents.

In the months that followed, the steering committee, together with Carol Coston, OP, NETWORK's first Executive Director and Margaret Hohman, SCN, the second staff member, created the basic organization, programs and financial basis for NETWORK. They worked closely with the Leadership Conference of Women Religious.

At its annual Assembly in 1972 Carol Coston presented the NETWORK idea and organization to 100 major superiors, after which the entire assembly passed the following resolution.

> The members of LCWR support the NETWORK in its efforts for social justice by letters of support, by financial contributions, and by encouraging other sisters to become active members.

The rationale which accompanied this resolution stated that NETWORK was a clear response to challenges put forth in congregational chapter enactments, to the LCWR by-laws, to specific objectives of the Commission on Pastoral Concerns as well as Pope Paul VI's *Call to Action* and the Synod statement on justice.[17]

This resolution achieved a legitimacy for NETWORK. Many congregations encouraged their sisters to join this organization, to read its newsletter, to respond to its legislative action, to attend its annual legislative seminar in Washington, even to consider being an intern with the staff in order to learn the skills of lobbying and organizing. Political Ministry became an option for women religious, an option that was in keeping with the Gospel call to action on behalf of justice.

Through NETWORK's outreach and particularly through the yearly seminar, hundreds of sisters and communities became involved in political action. On the average 125 sisters attended the annual week-long seminar beginning in 1972. A review of the participants' lists shows the names of a number of women religious who would become involved in staffing diocesan peace and justice centers and intercommunity offices; in working with other justice-oriented organizations; and in seeking public office. Membership growth went from 47 in 1971 to over 500 by the end of 1972 to 2500 in 1973. In 1984 the paying membership is at 7600, of which approximately 60 percent are religious. It is significant to note that because of the unique nature of NETWORK's original membership many of these single memberships are really group ones. A survey done in 1983 indicated that on the average 13 people belonged to NETWORK on the one paid subscription/membership. This outreach provided a network of support at the same time that the organization's publications provided a theological framework for the individual's call to follow the Gospel in political ministry. Although NETWORK was certainly not the motivating factor for all women religious who entered the political arena, it created a supportive milieu and a legitimacy for many of the women who would seek political office or accept government appointments as a way of living out their call to political ministry.

The decision to run for political office is of course a complex process; however, the influence of NETWORK and its educational significance is reflected in the experience of several women religious office holders.

The first sister elected to a State House of Representatives was Clare Dunn, CSJ. She was a longtime NETWORK friend, participating in the first seminars and publications. In 1974 Clare made the decision to run for the Arizona state legislature where she served from 1975 until her untimely death in 1981. She saw the NETWORK seminar experience as a real education for what sisters could do in political ministry. "Our experiences this week have reinforced our convictions that the Church is as much at home on Capitol Hill as it is in St. Peter's Basilica. We need not apologize for what some will fearfully term as an activist orientation. If it is true that 'action on behalf of justice is a constitutive dimension in the preaching of the Good News', and if, as St. Paul says, 'it is God who puts both the will and the action into you', we must not worry if we find ourselves, like Paul, 'slaving day and night proclaiming God's Good News.' NETWORK provides us with a clear and viable avenue for action. I think it also gives us a superb model that can be applied to all levels of government."[18]

A Grand Rapids Dominican, Ardeth Platte, ran for the Saginaw city council in 1973 and continues to serve the poverty community which she represents in that same capacity today. Ardeth addressed the NETWORK Board in May, 1983 and shared with them the influence NETWORK had on her decision to run for office. "In the summer of 1973 I had the privilege of attending my first NETWORK Legislative Seminar in Washington, DC. It culminated in a decision to say 'yes' to the commitment to peace and justice through the legislative process. The seminar taught me the relationship of social, economic and political patterns and what good public policies involved. There was a possibility that a preferred world could be patterned through the legislative process."

Elizabeth Morancy, RSM, is seeking her fourth term as a state legislator in the Rhode Island General Assembly. Liz was one of the founding mothers of NETWORK and recalls the impact the December '71 meeting had on her. "I already had the instinct that political involvement was a way to serve people and respond to the Gospel. But that December meeting brought all the various strands together for me. It confirmed my instinct, the seed that was growing inside, and added the theological framework of Gospel, Vatican II, and *Call to Action* to my interpretation of what was happening in our local area. It legitimized my decision to run for office."[19] Liz took seriously the challenge to think globally and act locally and became involved in her local neighborhood. Although she lost her run for the State Senate in 1976, she was successful in her bid for a seat in the General Assembly in 1978.

Arlene Violet, a sister of Mercy and former NETWORK Board member, is currently running for Attorney General in Rhode Island.[19a] Victoria Mongiardo, another founding mother of NETWORK, accepted an appointment to serve in the Carter Administration on his "ethnic desk" while she was still a sister. Although not holders of public office, NETWORK staff members offer these reflections on the meaning of political ministry in their lives.

> I see political ministry as an extension of the Church's mission, a viable form of service. It is especially important in this historical moment when decisions are being made that affect us all.

> I am in political ministry because the political process is where power resides, power to create just structures more responsive to the people, especially marginalized people.

> I believe it is essential to change social structures in order to ensure just relationships among people and nations, to

facilitate equitable systems of interaction and decision making. My political ministry allows me to do that.[20]

These women see their political involvement as an extension of their ministry for justice. For these women and others, NETWORK's founding provided a rich convergence of energy, insight and experience. The 47 women in 1971 drew on each other's expertise, supported each other's intuitions that political involvement was ministry, articulated the theological underpinnings of their response to the Gospel call to change unjust structures, and organized a vehicle to carry this message to others. The NETWORK seminars continue to be opportunities for meeting other women of similar conviction, for learning the skills of lobbying, organizing and impacting the political process.

NETWORK is a focus for political ministry within the American sisterhood and serves as a catalyst for many sisters' further involvement in political life. In a special way the women who choose to minister in public office testify to the truth of Pope Paul VI's statement in the *Call to Action*: "Politics are a demanding manner of living the Christian commitment to the service of others."

NOTES

1. NETWORK archives. Minutes of first meeting, December 17-19, 1971.

2. Ibid.

3. *Justice in the World*, 1971, Introduction.

4. Marge Tuite, OP, "Gospel Ministry", *Gospel Dimensions of Ministry*, NAWR Publications, Chicago, 1973, p. 22.

4a. Alan Geyer, "Political Ministry in the Real World," *Christianity and Crisis*, vol. 43, no. 3, March 7, 1983, p. 61.

5. Geno Baroni came to Washington in 1960 from the diocese of Altoona-Johnstown, PA. He founded the NCUEA and later served in the Carter Administration as Assistant Secretary of HUD.

6. Mary Hayes, SND, unpublished manuscript on NETWORK's history, 1981. Mary Hayes attended the December 1971 meeting and is a history professor at Trinity College, Washington, DC.

7. Ibid.

8. Ibid.

9. See Hayes, op. cit., for a fuller explanation of the origins and purposes of these organizations.

10. Hayes, op. cit.

11. Donal Dorr, *Option for the Poor, a Hundred Years of Vatican Social Teaching*. Orbis Books, Maryknoll, NY, 1983, p. 137.

12. Ibid., pp. 121-122.

13. Ibid., p. 303.

14. Francine Cardman and Margaret Farley, RSM, "Testing the Vision", NETWORK Publications, Vol. 9, no. 1, January-February, 1981, p. 24.

15. Dorr, op cit., p. 182.

16. Carol Coston, Staff reflections on NETWORK's 10th Anniversary.

17. Hayes op. cit.

18. Clare Dunn, CSJ, "The Challenge of Political Ministry", NETWORK Quarterly, Vol. III, No. 3, Summer 1975.

19. Elizabeth Morancy, RSM, Phone interview with Nancy Sylvester, Spring 1984. Subsequent to this writing, Morancy's bishop refused to grant her permission to hold public office and she was forced to seek dispensation from her religious vows in order to remain a candidate for the Rhode Island Legislature.

19a. Subsequent to this writing, Violet was also refused permission to stand as a candidate for public office and she sought dispensation from her religious vows.

20. "NETWORK on Political Ministry", NETWORK Quarterly, Vol. 7, No. 3, Summer 1979, p. Bl.

James H. Provost

PRIESTS AND RELIGIOUS IN POLITICAL OFFICE IN THE U.S.: A CANONICAL PERSPECTIVE

On the surface of it, the canon law governing the holding of political offices by priests and religious seems quite simple. According to the 1983 Code of Canon Law they are forbidden to hold any public office which entails participation in civil power (c. 285, #3), and may take an active role in political parties only if the competent ecclesiastical authority considers this necessary to defend the Church or to promote the common good (c. 287, #2). But things are seldom quite that simple when the Church's law is examined in detail, even on this issue. This study proposes to do such an examination, exploring the Church's law in its historical sources and analyzing the present legislation in its text and textual context.

Here is a preview of what will emerge. In the tradition of church legislation clergy and, from an early stage of their existence, religious were forbidden to hold public office. However, early in the tradition there were also exceptions to this prohibition. The most common exceptions have been to hold a public office which is attached to an ecclesiastical office, or is necessary to defend the rights of the Church, or is required to protect those who are defenseless in society. As political life expanded to include more of the populace in the political process, the Church's law applied the same prohibition and similar exceptions to political activity by priests and religious.

There are some limitations to this study which need to be acknowledged from the outset. First, the provisions of church law do not necessarily reflect actual practice. Repeated legislation on a given issue usually means that what it prohibits was still going on; why else the need to repeat the law so forcefully?

Second, church law is comfortable with prohibiting something in general, and then permitting exceptions to be made for individual cases. It often specifies who can make the exceptions through dispensation or interpretation. The canon law system admits of further interpretation by commentators who can extend the exceptions by careful analysis, comparison with other canons, and applications to new situations. The system of canon law, in other words, is more flexible than a surface reading of the canons themselves might indicate.

Third, the Church is not run solely by canon law. The canons provide a framework, but the inner politics of the Church are much more complex and are subject to greater personal influences than the law would seem to imply. For example, even where the law permits a bishop to exercise his own discretion in permitting an exception to some prohibition, pressure from higher authorities can in practice close the door left open by the law.

Finally, this study does not attempt a systematic analysis of the rationale for the Church's law on this question. However, the reasons for the law do emerge from time to time in the texts, and these will be noted in passing.

This study looks first to the sources which form the foundation for the current law, examining their historical evolution. Then it analyzes the current legislation in terms of the prohibitions and exceptions it contains. A brief explanation will also be attempted of the special rules governing religious on this issue in the Church today.

CANONICAL SOURCES[1]

Early Church

The canonical stance of the early church in regard to clergy and political office was part of the overall problem of Christians and public office prior to Constantine. In general, all were advised to avoid civil offices because of the implications for idolatry (Emperor worship being required as a sort of loyalty test) and the temptations to immorality that were so common to office holders.[2] For clergy there was in addition a Scriptural reason cited to keep them from such offices, 2 Timothy 2:4.[3] One dedicated to the Lord should focus on spiritual matters and not become ensnared in the cares of this world.

Under Constantine civil offices became open to Christians and early canons even provided for letters of recommendation to be given by bishops for those who were taking high office within the Empire.[4] This resolved the general question of Christian participation in public office; the condition of clergy and, later, monks, however, began to receive special attention.

Initially this was an attention in civil law which granted them exemptions from certain civil burdens.[5] However, church legislation began to exclude clergy from secular offices, particularly when these seem to have been sought for the cleric's own personal gain. These early prohibitions were imposed on the grounds either that the cleric could not at the same time perform adequately both his ecclesiastical functions and the secular office,[6] or that the clergy and monks were leaving their vocations and entering into public life full time.[7] It should be remembered that the rule of relative ordination was not only the general practice but also the canonical requirement, and clergy were considered bound to their church offices in a special manner.[8] To take up a civil office would impede them from giving full attention to church concerns and might eventually require them to move to another post. Religious (monks) were subject to the same restrictions as clergy because they had given up the world for a higher life and were not to turn back.

Legislation in the East for the sixth through the twelfth centuries continued in the same vein. Picking up on existing ecclesiastical law, imperial legislation prohibited clergy and monks from holding specific public offices,[9] and the Second Council of Nicea established a rule for the universal Church that clergy were not to take up mundane and secular cares for civil officials.[10] Attention was focused primarily on secular activities by clerics, especially their involvement in business affairs; the public offices listed here relate primarily to either business concerns or acting as lawyers.

Medieval Western Legislation

Western legislation reflects the same mixing of concern over business and public offices. The primary interest of the early compilers of canonical sources was the involvement of clergy in business unbecoming to the clerical state. Such activity gave the impression of avarice among the clergy.[11] Priests, however, were specifically permitted to serve as civil judges in Spain by the Fourth Council of Toledo,[12] and frequently in the West church officials, including but not limited to bishops, exercised civil as well as ecclesiastical jurisdiction. With the settlement of the lay investiture controversy by the Concordat of Worms in 1122,[13] Western church legislation adopted the position of excluding clergy from public offices in principle because clerics should devote themselves full time to the service of God; however various exceptions were allowed in practice.

Gratian, for example, expressed concern over clerical avarice and combined prohibitions from the past concerning business activities and public offices to build an impressive array of citations so that Hoffman comments, "there is no doubt that as a general rule clerics were to be forbidden civil offices."[14] Yet Gratian also admits of exceptions. Clerics were permitted to serve as guardian or protector for a minor. They could engage in litigation if this was directed by the bishop in order to safeguard church concerns, to care for defenseless orphans or widows, or for other persons who needed the help of the Church. Clerics could serve as judges in civil courts provided no death penalty would be involved.[15]

Besides drawing on the past through the new compilations of canons, the Church in the West during this period also issued new legislation which, partly because of the literary style of councils at the time, tended to be expressed in severe terms. The Third Lateran Council reversed the precedent set by the Fourth Council of Toledo and prohibited clerics from serving as secular judges, and the Fourth Lateran Council enjoined clerics not to hold secular offices.[16] Religious were subject to more severe penalties than clergy if they violated the law.[17] The Decretals of Gregory IX and Boniface VIII collected these and other sources to reinforce the position that "clergy and monks were not to mix themselves in the business of the world."[18]

However, exceptions and specific cases appear throughout these laws,[19] giving at least the impression that clergy and monks were quite involved in various secular pursuits, including public office, and that the legislation was in effect trying to regulate their involvement so as to avoid avarice, a clerical role in the "shedding of blood" (the death penalty), and the neglect of clerical office. In regard to this last concern, absolute ordination replaced relative ordination at the beginning of the thirteenth century in the West, freeing those in sacred orders to move about and, in some respects, follow a political career within the exceptions permitted in the law. Indeed, the prohibitions continued to regulate primarily their business interests and such civil offices as were incompatible with the clerical state. Other activities, including serving as chancellor to kings, were readily accepted; for example, it was not until Thomas More's appointment in 1529 that a non-cleric was Chancellor of England.[20]

Developments Prior to 1917 Code

The Council of Trent did not enact any new legislation concerning clergy and religious in politics but referred to existing norms and called for their careful observance.[21] The council considered those who dedicated themselves to divine ministry to have left the world behind in favor of a higher place; their lives should provide a mirror of heavenly life for everyone else to see and imitate.

At the level of Roman Curia the Congregation for the Propagation of the Faith had a two-fold purpose for instructing its missionaries not to become involved in secular, and especially political, affairs. One was the witness to a higher life and the wholehearted ommitment they were to have to the gospel; the other was more pragmatic, not to turn local officials against the missionaries. This position was stated in 1622 in one of the earliest circulars put out by the Congregation, and was made more explicit in instructions sent in 1659 to the Vicars Apostolic of foreign missionary societies.[22]

The consensus among canonical authors of the period was that clerics were generally prohibited from accepting public office, and that priests were subject to an excommunication if they accepted secular jurisdiction. Other clerics, whether bishops or lesser clerics, were not subject to such a penalty. The prohibition, moreover, was not considered to apply to a situation where the civil office was tied to the ecclesiastical one, or where a prelate held temporal authority on some other title.[23]

Service as an advocate or a judge in a civil court was viewed as a civil office in this period. The various exceptions developed in earlier legislation continued to be repeated and expanded by the commentators.[24] Attention was beginning to shift, however, from the concern over avarice to the question of how the Church should relate to modern governments, and indeed how it would be perceived and dealt with by civil authorities if its clergy were actively engaged in various political offices or activities.

During the reunification of Italy in the nineteenth century several practical questions arose from Italian bishops outside the Papal States concerning cooperation by Catholics with the new government. In particular, the question arose as to priests serving in various public offices (including mayor of the town), and the oath of office required by the secular government. In a fairly nuanced series of responses which opened the way for Catholics to participate in the Italian government under certain safeguards, the Apostolic Penitentiary responded that clerics were not permitted to assume or exercise civil or lay offices without permission from proper church authorities, and they were never permitted to take the oath required by the government. Permission to accept the offices, therefore, could be given; but since ecclesiastics were never to take an oath before a lay authority, the requirement of a civil oath proved to be a new obstacle.[25]

The political offices we have considered in the legal sources so far could be appointive, and many of them were. The development of elections and democratic systems posed a new situation for church authorities. Concern surfaced, for example, in the seventeenth century over the involvement of priests in political activities in Goa. Alexander VII and Clement IX warned against priests proposing candidates for public office or getting involved in political gatherings.[26]

In the United States, the bishops adopted a cautious approach to the role of clergy in politics. At the Ninth Provincial Council of Baltimore in 1858 the bishops included a warning in their pastoral letter that clergy stay out of political matters.[27] The context for the warning was the gathering storm that erupted in the American civil war, and the provincial meeting brought together all the bishops of what would be the Confederacy with important bishops from the North. Although this political situation had changed by 1884, the Third Plenary Council of Baltimore adopted this same pre-war caution as legislation for the entire Church in the United States: priests were to abstain from public discussions on political matters, whether outside church buildings or even moreso within them.[28] No specific regulation was made about political offices, however.

Leo XIII, faced with growing anti-Catholic legislation in Hungary, urged the bishops there to take action together, holding meetings to discuss the situation and promoting legislative candidates favorable to the Church's position. Yet he also warned against priests becoming too involved in politics in line with Paul's advice to Timothy noted earlier (2 Tim. 2:4). However, in line with the advice of Gregory the Great, he did permit clerical involvement for the sake of safeguarding religion or promoting the common good.[29] A more open approach to priests' involvement in political elections is evident in Pius X's dealing with France in 1906, where they were allowed to run for the Chamber of Deputies provided they obtained the permission of their own ordinary and the ordinary of the place where they were running for office.[30]

To sum up, on the eve of the codification of the Church's law these elements of the tradition were recognized:[31]

1. Clerics were, in general, forbidden to hold political office; they were to devote themselves full-time to religious concerns.

2. The same was true of religious, and on an even stronger basis because of their religious commitment to concerns beyond this world.

3. In addition to various exceptions for clerics and religious to act as advocates in civil courts, some clerics were permitted to hold what we would term today strictly political office. These varied from political positions attached to the ecclesiastical office they held (e.g., certain bishops in virtue of their see were senators or held similar civil offices), to indults granted on a standing basis, to special pontifical permission for bishops. Other clergy could serve in legislatures with the permission of the appropriate ordinaries.

4. While the overriding concern for the religious dimension of clerical life weighed in favor of seldom holding political office, and the welfare of the Church in dealing with modern governments sometimes counseled that clergy avoid any political involvement, nevertheless the conditions of the times led some to recommend that clergy may indeed have to seek political office; but then it should be only a few, and these ought to be outstanding.[32]

1917 Code of Canon Law[33]

The first code of Canon Law, issued in 1917, was based on this centuries-old legal tradition. Canons 138 and 140 listed a variety of activities unbefitting the clerical state; canons 139, 141 and 142 prohibited clergy from engaging in other activities which, even though they were not "indecorous," were still considered to be alien to the clerical state. Included among these latter were business activities and secular involvements which had been prohibited in the past.

With regard to political office, the code distinguished between legislative offices and other public offices. For non-legislative offices, clergy were forbidden to assume public offices which included the exercise of lay jurisdiction or administration (c. 139, #2); any exception required permission from the Apostolic See. To serve in a legislative capacity as senator or deputy (equivalent to a member of the House of Representatives in this country), a further distinction was made. If the Holy See had issued a pontifical prohibition against clergy serving in such capacities in the area, the permission of the Holy See was required to make an exception. In other parts of the world clergy could run for election to these positions provided they had the permission of their own ordinary and the ordinary of the place where the election was being held (c. 139, #4).[33]

In virtue of canon 592 religious, whether clergy or not, were bound by the same prohibitions. To fulfill the conditions of canon 139, #4 for legislative elections, permission of their own superior would be required in addition to that of the local ordinary where the election was taking place.[34]

The commentators on the 1917 code were generally in agreement on the meaning of canon 139 when it dealt with the issue of clergy and religious in political office.[35] They developed lists of what was prohibited and discussed what exceptions might exist within the terms of the canon.

With regard to non-legislative offices (c. 139, #2) clergy were excluded from exercising two types of lay authority. The first was administration, the ordinary direction of one's subjects for the common good and in the regular observance of laws; the other was jurisdiction, which can be defined as the power to govern through laws, decrees, etc.[36] An apostolic indult would therefore be required to serve as mayor, commissioner, judge, sheriff, attorney general, prosecuting attorney, governor, tax commissioner, state superintendent of schools, head of a department in a municipal or state government, etc. For certain non-political public offices, the permission of one's ordinary would also be required, primarily because these positions involved the obligation to render an account for one's administration (c. 139, #3). Examples would be to serve as president, moderator, secretary or treasurer of public institutions or charitable organizations.[37]

In regard to legislative offices, at the time the code took effect in 1918 there was a pontifical prohibition against clergy in Italy serving in the legislature.[38] In 1957 secular and religious clergy in Hungary were forbidden to run for the parliament, and those who may have been serving at the time were to quit within one month.[39] Otherwise, no other pontifical prohibition is reported so that in all other places the requisite permissions under the 1917 code were to be given by the appropriate ordinaries.

One major exception affected bishops and other prelates of the same or higher grade. They could not grant this permission to themselves, so for one of them to accept a public office or a legislative post the permission had to be sought from the Holy See. This requirement did not bind, however, if according to the constitution they held the position ex officio and the Holy See had in any way approved the arrangement. When a bishop did hold such an office, he was to provide for the proper care of the diocese through a vicar general.[40]

A question was raised as to how the rule on permission to run for the legislature (c. 139, #4) was to be implemented when an electoral district included more than one diocese. For example, from which ordinary, or ordinaries, would a priest or religious have to obtain permission in order to run for U.S. Senator in a state with several dioceses? The European commentators were of the opinion that permission was needed only from the ordinary of the place which was the legal center of the election.[41] This might have worked well in a European situation where a principal town and surrounding country areas formed the electoral district, but in the United States there seemed to be no legal center for a state-wide election. Brunini was of the opinion that a majority of the ordinaries would have to give their permission, although it need not be unanimous.[42]

In the United States there are some agencies which were not covered by either the prohibition of holding non-legislative offices which exercise lay jurisdiction or administration (c. 139, #2), or the restrictions on running for a legislative office (c. 139, #4). For example, a local school board is elective, but not legislative; it depended on the authority of the board relative to the superintendent or other administrator whether the board itself exercised jurisdiction or administration, and the extent to which members of the board were held to render an account in the sense of canon 139, #3. Therefore, it is not clear whether clergy were excluded by the 1917 code from running for this or similar positions. There was no problem, however, in clergy serving on non-legislative study commissions or public bodies promoting civic life if these did not involve jurisdiction or administration.[43]

There was a centralizing tendency in the 1917 code, evident in the requirement of an apostolic indult to hold non-legislative offices. The fact that the local ordinary rather than the Holy See could give permission to run for the legislature would seem to be an exception to this centralization, and to indicate some openness toward the involvement of clergy in keeping with the decisions taken prior to the code concerning clergy in France. However, bishops were soon told to be restrictive in granting such permissions,[44] and the Holy See began to make it clear that any political involvement by clergy was undesirable.

This position was not evident immediately after the promulgation of the code, for no objection was raised when the bishops of Central Africa asked if priests could serve on civil tribunals judging cases concerning natives, provided no grave personal penalty was at stake,[45] and

Benedict XV, who issued the 1917 code, was not opposed to peaceful and legitimate political involvement by French Canadian clergy seeking to amend the school laws there. However, it was not long before he wrote to discourage political activity by clergy in Hungary, Belgium and Poland.[46] Later, when the Church was subject to open persecution in Mexico, Pius XI protested the government's attacks but warned against clergy being involved in political partisanship.[47]

Catholic Action developed during this period as a formally recognized movement. In some European countries it tended to take on a political tone and warnings were issued to priests to support Catholic Action and give it a proper direction, but at the same time to avoid involvement in partisan politics.[48]

The involvement of clergy and religious in Italy was a special concern to the Holy See prior to the signing of the Lateran Pact. The Holy See had been accused of meddling in Italian politics, particularly on behalf of the "Partito Popolare," because of the support local clergy were showing to this conservative political movement. A special warning was sent to the Italian bishops that clergy must abstain from forming or favoring political parties,[49] and this was repeated two years later to religious superiors in Italy.[50] Both letters went to pains to emphasize the personal rights of individual priests and religious, but due to their public position in the Church they were to remain neutral in all political questions. In response to an inquiry in 1927, the Italian bishops were assured they could impose this stance by issuing precepts and punishing disobedient clerics and religious.[51]

In the United States the issue of clergy and politics was posed rather forcefully by Father Coughlin. The combination of his outspoken views on a variety of political issues and his popularity made him a genuine political force, even though he did not hold political office. A lively debate from a canon law standpoint took place in the pages of the *American Ecclesiastical Review* in 1935, Edward V. Dargin arguing that such activity was forbidden by canon 139, the Third Plenary Council of Baltimore, and various statements of recent popes. William F. Murphy of Detroit came to his fellow diocesan's defense with a scholarly refutation based not only on the text of the law but on a variety of commentators on the code.[52] As is known, Coughlin obeyed his archbishop when told to cease his political activities, and particular law in at least one diocese was eventually issued to forbid clergy from active leadership in political organizations.[53]

During and after the Second World War, a new tone enters the official statements of the hierarchy or semi-official church spokesmen relative to politics. Respecting the prohibitions of canon 139, they nevertheless became increasingly involved in directly political questions, especially the question of voting for candidates of specific political parties. This was done in virtue of the teaching authority of the Church, and the threat to faith and morals that they judged certain political parties posed.[54] At the same time, the involvement of some clergy in political activities called into question the "Priest-Worker" experiment in France and eventually led to its disapproval by the Vatican.[55]

The issue of priests and religious in political office was not a major question at Vatican II. There was an effort made to clarify the distinction between clergy and laity on the basis of the lay person's typical involvement in secular concerns, but even here it was admitted that at times clergy are legitimately engaged in secular activities.[56] In the time after the council a number of priests began to apply in their ministry the spirit of openness to the world and concern for justice which marked the teaching of the council. For example, the priest-worker movement was again authorized in France, although the members were prohibited from taking on responsibilities in political parties or labor unions.[57]

The increasing activism of priests in various parts of the world led to a more direct reflection on the issue at the 1971 Synod of Bishops. Although the synodal documents are not law, they do represent statements of policy and as such are intended to guide the application of the law in contemporary circumstances. Acknowledging the contingency of political options, the synod recognized the right to personal opinions by priests but at the same time called for them to "keep a certain distance from any political office or involvement."[58] Priests should rely instead on the mature involvement of lay persons to provide a Christian influence in the political world.

The requirement found in canon 139, #4 that a priest obtain permission from his ordinary to run for legislative office, seems to have been extended by the synod to any active political involvement by priests. "Leadership or active militancy on behalf of any political party is to be excluded by every priest unless, in concrete and exceptional circumstances, this is truly required by the good of the community, and receives the consent of the bishop after consultation with the priests' council and, if circumstances call for it, with the episcopal conference."[59]

It should be noted that two canonical structures which did not exist when the 1917 code was promulgated were now included in presenting the process of obtaining permission from one's ordinary. The priests' council was to be consulted by the bishop before giving his consent. If circumstances called for it, the bishop was also to consult with the conference of bishops before giving his permission. The synod did not specify what those circumstances might be, but it also clearly left the granting of the permission in the hands of the local ordinary and did not restrict it to the Apostolic See.

Despite the caution expressed by the synod, some clergy and religious began to speak publicly about their political rights and even their duty to run for office.[60] Some went on to obtain the necessary permissions and seek election.[61] What becomes significant from a canon law point of view is the response to these candidacies by officials at the Vatican. While the code clearly permitted clergy to seek election to legislative offices if they had the required permissions of the appropriate ordinaries, and while those ordinaries could grant that permission provided it was done sparingly (in light of the 1922 response mentioned above and in keeping with the guidelines from the synod), nevertheless the candidacy of these clergy was clearly frowned upon.[62]

Thus we have the somewhat more complicated context in which the 1983 code was developed and is to be understood.

CURRENT LAW

The 1983 Code of Canon Law simplifies the detailed prescriptions of the 1917 code on the obligations of clergy, but in keeping with the developments that preceded it the new canons also make more extended provisions with regard to clerics engaging in political activities. In another change from the 1917 canons, the new code reflects the broader dispensing powers of bishops which resulted from the Second Vatican Council.

Prohibitions in the Code

Canon 285 calls on clerics to refrain from whatever is unbecoming and to avoid whatever is alien to the clerical state. The canon then goes on to make this specific prohibition:

> #3. Clerics are forbidden to assume public offices which entail a participation in the exercise of civil power.[63]

Note that while the canon states a prohibition similar to the one in the 1917 code, it does not reserve exceptions to it to the Apostolic See the way the earlier code did.

There is no provision concerning running for legislative office comparable to the one found in the 1917 code, but there is a new canon dealing with political and labor union activities. After encouraging clerics to foster peace and harmony based on justice, canon 287 stipulates:

> #2. Clerics are not to have an active role in political parties and in the direction of labor unions unless the need to protect the rights of the Church or to promote the common good requires it in the judgment of the competent ecclesiastical authority.

The restrictions of canons 285 and 287 are applied to members of religious institutes by canon 672, and to members of societies of apostolic life by canon 739. By definition, lay members of secular institutes are not bound by these restrictions (cc. 710, 713), and even though they are clergy, permanent deacons are specifically exempted from them (c. 288).

What is involved here? First, it is clear that certain activities are forbidden by the law. The prohibition in canon 285, #3 is much stronger than earlier versions of that canon. The first text proposed in 1977 was similar to the 1917 code, focusing on the permissions needed to assume such public offices rather than on the absolute prohibition. It read as follows:

> Bishops are not to assume public offices, especially those which entail a participation in the exercise of civil power, without the permission of the Holy See, nor other clerics unless they have obtained permission from the the same Holy See in places where the pontifical prohibition is in effect, or in other places from both their own ordinary and the ordinary of the place in which they intended to exercise the power or administration.[64]

The same text appeared in subsequent drafts, only the "especially those" being dropped in the final version submitted to the pope in 1982.[65] The text as it now reads is the result of the review conducted by John Paul II with six advisors, and has changed the focus from permission needed to obtain such offices to a straight prohibition. This, however, is a disciplinary law and as we shall see later, it is subject to dispensation (a relaxation of the law in particular cases) rather than the granting of a permission specified in the law itself. The practical difference is not that great, in that in case of either dispensation the action of a higher authority is needed. The new text, however, has a more chilling effect on the willingness of higher authority to act; it is usually easier to obtain a permission than a dispensation.

The forbidden activities are specified as relating to a public office which entails participation in the exercise of civil power. This would include all those offices forbidden under the terms of the old code when it spoke of civil administration or jurisdiction. Insofar as a member of a legislative body "participates" in the exercise of civil power, priests and religious are restricted from holding these offices as well.[66] It would also seem that members of zoning boards, school boards, and similar bodies may participate in the exercise of civil power, and if so these would also be forbidden offices.

Second, priests and religious are ordinarily not to hold leadership positions in political parties and labor unions (c. 287). Whether an "active role" in a political party would even include holding party membership probably depends on local political circumstances. For example, in certain parts of Africa the very fact of belonging to a political party is itself to take an active role in politics. The bishops there have already told their clergy not even to enroll in a political party. In the United States, however, registering according to one political party or another does not make one a party activist and constitutes only a "passive voice" rather than an active role.

The code therefore prohibits clergy and religious from the following political activities in the United States: serving as party workers, committee members, delegates to conventions, candidates for elected office, or spokespersons for the party.[67] It also excludes clergy and religious from holding office in labor unions. However, the canons do not exclude clergy and religious from being members of labor unions, or from having membership in non-partisan political action committees, participating in non-partisan special interest organizations, or carrying on a lobbying effort. Thus it would be permissible for priests and religious to be members of a Right to Life group, Network, a peace movement, organizations for moral legislation, etc., but they could not be party workers for the Republican, Democratic, or other political parties.

Exceptions

The law itself provides for exceptions to the above prohibitions. The first relates to holding public office, for only those which entail a participation in the exercise of civil power are forbidden.[68] Thus a priest or religious may serve on a non-partisan citizens' advisory com-mmittee, or could be a personal advisor to the president, governor, mayor or other government official.

Second, if in the judgment of the competent authority it is needed to protect the rights of the Church or to promote the common good, a priest or religious could take an active role in a political party or in the direction of a labor union. This is a significant legal shift from the "permissions" required in the 1917 code to run for legislative office. Now the exception to the prohibition is given by the law itself, rather than through a permission granted by the authorities involved. That is, the competent ecclesiastical authorities make a judgment about the conditions; if the judgment finds these conditions are present, then the law itself permits the priest or religious to become involved in ac-tivities which are otherwise forbidden by the same law.

Requiring permission for clergy to engage in political action and leadership of labor organizations can be traced back to the restoration of the priest-worker movement in France, where a similar restriction was imposed on the priests involved.[69] The cautions of the 1971 Synod are also evident in the canons. But when it comes to determining who are the "competent ecclesiastical authorities" in this situation the code does not repeat the provisions of the 1917 code or the added details of the synodal statements, although earlier versions of the canons had done so.[70] So who are they?

In keeping with the general norm that later laws are to be related to earlier ones (c. 21) and that canons of the 1983 code "insofar as they refer to the old law are to be assessed also in accord with canonical tradition" (c. 6), it would seem that the authorities who could grant permission to run for legislative office under the 1917 code may pro-vide the judgment required by canon 287, #2 for the law to make the exception concerning political activity or leadership in a labor union.

For secular priests the competent authority is at least their own diocesan bishop. They are bound by a special obligation to obey their own ordinary (c. 273), are to undertake duties entrusted to them by their ordinary (c. 274, #2), and need his at least presumed permission to be absent from the diocese for a notable period of time (c. 283, #1). Their diocesan bishop has a special bond of authority over them in virtue of the priests' incardination (c. 265). So clearly, as in the 1917 code, a priest's own ordinary would be a competent authority in this situation.

Moreover, a diocesan bishop has a special reponsibility to see to the enforcement of church discipline (c. 392), and this is applied with particular reference to the priests of the diocese (c. 384). He possesses all the power necessary to exercise his pastoral office (c. 381, #1). He is the one who must determine what is for the common good of the people entrusted to his care (c. 391, #1). If anyone is a "competent authority" to determine what is needed to promote the common good or to protect the rights of the Church, it should be the diocesan bishop.

Secular clergy outside their own diocese are subject to the determination of the diocesan bishop in the place where they are staying in matters pertaining to the common good (c. 13, #2, 2°). Therefore, in addition to their own ordinary, the authority competent to determine for them whether the conditions permit political activity would also be the diocesan bishop of the place where they are staying.

Religious engage in apostolic works according to the procedures of their own constitutions and statutes (cc. 586-587); these should determine the appropriate authorities whose intervention may be required to engage in political activities. As with secular clergy outside their own diocese, so with religious the bishop of the place where they are staying is the competent authority to determine whether the conditions required in canon 287, #2 are present, so that the law itself would permit them to engage in political activities.

Note that such activity does not include holding public office but it could include running for office on a partisan ticket. Similarly, if a priest or religious decided to run in an election on a non-partisan ticket, as is sometimes done in various jurisdictions in this country, the canons do not strictly prohibit this.[71] If the priest or religious wins the election, however, a new problem arises; given the prohibition of canon 285, #3, how could they assume the office?

Here is where another major exception contained in the code comes into consideration, namely the power of the diocesan bishop to dispense from the general law of the Church. Reversing the restrictions of canon 81 in the 1917 code, Vatican II stated the right of a diocesan bishop to dispense from general church law.[72] Paul VI specified this applies to disciplinary laws which have not been explicitly reserved to the Apostolic See.[73] Retaining this development in canon 87, #1, the new code in effect authorizes a diocesan bishop to dispense a priest or religious from the restrictions of canon 285, #3 in individual cases, for unlike the 1917 code there is no reservation of this matter to the Apostolic See in the 1983 code.

A dispensation is a favor granted at the discretion of the bishop; it is not a right to which a priest or religious could lay claim. The bishop cannot grant such a dispensation unless he has a just and reasonable cause (c. 90, #1), specifically in this case that the dispensation would contribute to the spiritual good of the faithful (c. 87, #1). However, if the bishop decides to give the dispensation, he can dispense anyone within his territory, as well as his own subjects outside his territory, and the dispensation is valid not only in his diocese but even in other areas where a priest or religious subject to him may be working (c. 91).[74]

To sum up, the law prohibits priests and religious from holding public offices which entail participation in the exercise of civil power, but the diocesan bishop can dispense them from this prohibition in individual cases if there is sufficient cause to do so. It is left to the bishop's discretion to determine whether there is sufficient cause, and whether to exercise his power of dispensing in a given case.

The law also prohibits priests and religious from taking an active role in political parties unless the competent authority judges that this would be necessary for the defense of the Church or is required in order to promote the common good. The competent authority to make such a judgment is the ordinary of the priest or religious, as well as the local ordinary of the place where this activity is to take place. In effect, the 1917 code provision seems to remain in effect so that in order to run for office on a partisan ticket, priests or religious would need a determination from their own ordinary and the ordinary of the place where the election is being held. Under the new code, however, this determination is not a permission but a judgment that the conditions are verified for the law itself to permit them to run.

While this is what a careful analysis of the text has to say, it must also be admitted frankly that pressures within the Church from various sources are seeking to limit the application of the dispensing power of bishops, and desire that a narrow determination be given by competent authorities concerning the conditions for active political involvement. This goes beyond the question of canon law, however, and relates more directly to politics internal to the Church—that art of the possible which is where law and life interact.[75]

Religious

As mentioned earlier, canon 672 applies the restrictions on clerics to members of religious institutes and canon 739 makes the same application to members of societies of apostolic life. This application to religious has to be seen especially in light of the provisions of the new code on religious institutes.[76]

A religious institute is characterized in the law by the public vows its members take, their life in common, and a "separation from the world proper to the character and purpose of each institute" (c. 607, #2 and 3). It differs from the other form of consecrated life, secular institutes, particularly by the aspect of separation from the world precisely as part of the public witness religious give to Christ and the Church (c. 607, #3). How all this is to be lived is spelled out for each institute in its "proper law," consisting in the constitutions and statutes adopted by the institute and approved by competent ecclesiastical authority (c. 587). The proper law should also determine how members become involved in various apostolates and the authorities responsible for them.

Underlying the law is the general presumption that individual religious will participate in a corporate apostolate of the institute rather than follow an individual apostolate. However, actual practice among contemporary religious does not always conform to this presumption and shows various approaches to selecting apostolates. Some institutes maintain clearly identified corporate apostolates; others have been accommodating their approach in the spirit of their founders and in accord with the charism of the institute (c. 578), and have adopted individual apostolates within the community's spirit. All this does appear to be within the letter of the law (c.677, #1).

Yet even individual apostolates are to be carried on in the name and by the mandate of the Church (c.675, #3). Combined with the emphasis on separation from the world, this would appear to be an added restriction on religious becoming involved in political activities or holding public political office. However, true to canonical tradition, exceptions are possible even according to the wording of the canons.

For example, canon 677,#1 calls for an accommodation of the apostolate of institutes themselves "prudently to the needs of times and places, including the use of new and appropriate means." The accommodation of the apostolate can even be such that if a religious undertakes an apostolate in the name of the institute which requires living where there is no community of that institute, the individual may be exempted from the requirement of community life (c. 665, #1). So if out of a deep commitment to social justice, for example, a religious institute were to determine that some political involvement has become necessary to carry out its mission in particular times and places, a religious who took up that involvement could be considered to be carrying out an apostolate of the institute even if it appears to others as an individual apostolate. As discussed earlier, the code also requires the intervention of appropriate ecclesiastical authorities outside the institute in order to implement this kind of apostolate, whether it is considered to be that of an individual or of the institute.

In carrying out their apostolate, religious are subject to the local diocesan bishops (c. 678, #1). They are also subject to their own superiors (c. 678, #2), and the law calls on bishops and religious superiors to consult about the works of the apostolate (c. 678, #3) in an effort to avoid conflicting signals to individual religious. In some situations the law itself attempts to preclude such conflict situations.

For example, religious must have the bishop's permission to open a house in his diocese (c. 609, #1). Such a house, it should be noted, is more than just where individual religious live in common; it is a juridic person in the Church and constitutes a distinct legal entity (c.634, #1). While in many institutes only the Motherhouse is so constituted, in others individual religious houses are erected wherever members live in community. Unless the bishop places restrictions when he gives his permission, the erection of a house brings with it the right to carry on all the apostolates proper to the religious institute (c. 611, 2°). Religious assigned to that house therefore have the implicit authorization from the bishop to carry out the works proper to the institute.

On the other hand, a bishop may request a religious institute to undertake an apostolate in his diocese, or even ask for a specific member of the institute to carry on a particular work in the diocese. Under these circumstances, a contract is to be signed which clarifies the various responsibilities and thus attempts to avoid mixed signals later on (c. 681, #2).

The law does not provide advance norms for situations where religious are carrying on a specialized apostolate apart from a house of the institute and which is also not a diocesan work. These might include, for example, religious who teach in secular institutions, provide health care in hospitals not run by the institute or in public health facilities, or who are involved with various movements not connected with the institute. These persons may be carrying out works in the spirit of the institute, but not as a commitment of the institute itself; if this individual religious were to cease working in the particular position, the institute has no commitment to provide a replacement. A number of religious communities in the United States have adopted this style of ministry. The relationship with the local bishop has to be worked out in each situation by the institute involved.

In exercising a specialized apostolate of this type, an individual religious could seek for various reasons to take an active role in a political party, to run for election on a partisan ticket, or to take a public office which entails the exercise of civil power. In such a situation a diocesan bishop must be included in the decision along with the proper authorities of the religious institute. Only a diocesan bishop is competent to interpret whether the conditions required in canon 287, #2 are present and only he can dispense from the general law of canon

285, #3 prohibiting public office with civil power. But which diocesan bishop is to be involved?

By attachment to a house, a member of a religous institute acquires a domicile (c. 103) and with it a proper bishop (c. 107, #1). This bishop can dispense a person domiciled in his diocese even though the person is outside the diocese at the time (c. 91), so he could be the bishop involved at least for dispensing from canon 285, #3. The dispensation could also be given by the bishop of the place where the religious sought to take the office. As discussed earlier, the bishop of a diocese is the one charged with determining if the conditions of canon 297, #2 are present so that a religious could take an active role in a political party.

What happens if the bishop refuses to dispense or judges the conditions for active involvement in a political party are not present? If the religious superior is of the same opinion as the bishop and refuses permission, the vow of obedience leaves little choice for the individual religious to pursue this proposed work. If the religious superior is of a different mind from the bishop, the resulting conflict situation could theoretically be resolved in one of several ways.

First, the bishop has the final authority for political activity and public office for a religious as religious. This does not deny the civil rights of the individual religious, but based in the separation from the world which characterizes religious life it closes the option of exercising those civil rights while at the same time retaining full status as a religious.

Legally there are two choices open to the religious. One is to seek dispensation from the vows and to pursue the apostolate personally, perhaps through consecrated life in a secular institute. The other is to seek exclaustration by which the individual remains attached to the religious institute but suspended from its life for a time.

Exclaustration has been used increasingly in recent years in place of dismissal from a community or dispensation from the vows.[77] Canon 687 describes the effects of exclaustration:

> Exclaustrated members are free from obligations which are incompatible with their new condition of life and at the same time remain dependent on and subject to the care of their superiors and also the local ordinary, especially if the member is a cleric. The members may wear the habit of the institute unless it is determined otherwise in the indult. However they lack active and passive voice.

Under the new code an indult of exclaustration for three years can be granted by the supreme moderator with the consent of the council, although outside authorities must intervene if it is to be extended (c. 686, #1). It is theoretically possible that a religious community might exclaustrate a member whose desire to seek political office was approved by the community but not by the bishop, thus freeing the member of the obligations incompatible with the new condition of life, although how the exclaustrated member will relate to the local bishop could be a problem.

CONCLUDING REFLECTIONS

The canonical tradition of the Church clearly prohibits clergy and religious from taking on political office, but at the same time clearly permits it under certain circumstances. The provisions of the 1983 code are in keeping with this tradition, although the current expression of the law has nuances of its own.

Aside from permanent deacons, who are the only clergy specifically exempted from these restrictions, clergy and religious are forbidden to take public offices which entail the exercise of civil power, and are not to take an active role in political parties unless certain grave reasons, as judged by competent ecclesiastical authority, permit otherwise. Yet exceptions are possible under the law, ranging from the competent authority's judgment to a dispensation by a diocesan bishop in particular cases. These exceptions do not negate the law, but provide for the adjustment of law to varying circumstances of time and place.

The application of the law in the United States, as elsewhere, is a primary responsibility of the bishops. They are charged with seeing to its adaptation to local conditions, to enforcing the law for the sake of the common good, and to making the determinations and granting the dispensations authorized under the law.

But the bishops are not alone. The law is given for the whole people of God. The application of the law is not only a matter of official interpretation, but also of custom, which is the best interpreter of law (c. 27). The implementation of the code must not be done at the expense of the mission of the Church, for it is designed specifically to promote and support that mission.[78] Given the responsibility of all the people of God for the mission of the Church (c. 211), their right to apostolic initiatives (c. 216), and their duty to promote social justice (c. 222, #2), the involvement of clergy and religious in political office is a more complex issue than before, and one which requires the careful discernment of the church community together with its leaders.

One of the values law secures in the Church is that despite momentary pressures or specific situations, the principles of Catholic life are safeguarded for future generations. So it is with the issue of clergy and religious in political office; the canonical tradition continues to safeguard the insights that such offices are not usually the proper concern of priests and religious, yet at times the welfare of God's people and the witness of the Church may call for exceptions. Beyond this the law itself does not go. The rest is left for politics, the art of the possible even within the Christian community.

NOTES

1. See Richard J. Stack, "Clerics and Civil Offices: A Historical Synopsis," JCL Dissertation, The Catholic University of America, Washington, DC, 1962, who provides a general contextual perspective; a careful textual analysis appears in James R. Hoffman, "Civil Offices for Clerics: A Historical Study," JCL Dissertation, The Catholic University of America, Washington, DC, 1966.

2. See Tertullian, *De corona*, ch. 11: *PL* 2, col. 91-93; trans. "The Chaplet," *The Fathers of the Church* 40: 255-258. Note that this was written after Tertullian had become a Montanist. Synod of Elvira (305 or 306 AD), cc. 1, 3, 4, 56: Ioannes Mansi, *Sacrorum Conciliorum Nova et Amplissima Collectio* (Paris, 1901-1927) 2:6, 15.

3. "No soldier becomes entangled in the affairs of civilian life; he avoids this in order to please his commanding officer." Cyprian seems to be the first to cite what became a standard Scriptural warrant in later canonical legislation; see his *Letter 66*: *PL* 4, col. 397-399; trans. "Letter 1," *The Fathers of The Church* 51: 3-4.

4. For example, the Synod of Arles (314 AD), c. 7, provided that Christians accepting the position of governor in another area were to obtain letters of recommendation from their own bishop to the bishop of the new area; Mansi 2: 471.

5. *Codex Theodosianus* XIV, 2: 1, 2. Hoffman distinguishes these burdens (munera) from public dignities or offices (magistratus), the latter not being closed off to clergy by civil legislation; Hoffman, pp. 10-11.

6. Council of Sardica (343 AD), c. 8, censuring the North African bishops for spending so much time at the imperial court; Mansi 3: 25. Apostolic Canons (341 to 381 AD), cc. 6, 80, 82: Mansi 1: 30, 46.

7. Council of Chalcedon (451 AD), cc. 3 and 7: *Conciliorum Oecumenicorum Decreta (COE)* (Freiburg: Herder, 2nd ed. 1962), pp. 64, 66.

8. Council of Nicea (325 AD), c. 16: *COE* 12-13; Chalcedon, cc. 5 and 6: *COE* 66.

9. Justinian, *Novellae* 123, c. 6: clergy are not to receive or collect taxes, be recorders of deeds, superintend households, act as attorneys in litigation, or serve as surety for any of these activities; Leo VI The Wise, *Novellae* 86: clergy are not to defend lawsuits, arrange marriages, redeem slaves, or carry on similar activities.

10. Nicea II (878 AD), c. 10: *COE* 122-123.

11. Both Burchard of Worms and Ivo of Chartres cite Chalcedon, c. 3, for example, but emphasize the prohibition of business activities it contains; they do not cite c. 7 which focuses more on public office. See Burchard, *Decretum* II, c. 145; Ivo of Chartres, *Decretum* VI, cc. 218, 242, 393-396.

12. Toledo IV (633 AD), c. 31: Mansi 10: 628.

13. For an analysis of the controversy and its setting in medieval Church-State relations, see Brian Tierney, *The Crisis of Church & State 1050-1300* (Englewood Cliffs, NJ: Prentice-Hall, 1964).

14. Hoffman, p. 33. In Gratian, see c. 3, D. XXIII; c. 26, D. LXXXVI; cc. 1 and 3, D. LXXXVIII; c. 3, C. XX, q. 3; c. 1, C. XXI, q. 3.

15. C. 1, C. XXI, q. 3.

16. Lateran III (1179 AD), c. 12: *COE* 194; Lateran IV (1215 AD), cc. 16, 18: *COE* 219-220.

17. Lateran III, c. 12: *COE* 194.

18. C. 4, 5, 8, 9, X, *ne clerici vel monachi saecularibus negotiis se immisceant*, 50; c. 3, *ne clerici vel monachi. . .* , III, 24, in VI°.

19. The glossators were quick to point out various exceptions. For example, the prohibition of Lateran III, c. 12, applied to clerics in major orders (ordained to a title, hence assured of income from the Church), and to those in minor orders who were supported by church revenues. The glossator points out that those in minor orders without church income could handle civil cases, but excluded them from criminal cases. See the *Glossa ordinaria* at c. 1, X, *de postulando*, I, 37.

20. Alphonsus reports that tacit pontifical concession or even custom permitted clerics to be chancellors in secular curias even into the eighteenth century; see *Theologia Moralis*, nova editio, ed. Leonard Gaude, IV (Rome: Typis Polyglottis Vaticanis, 1912), p. 508.

21. Trent, Sessio XXII (1562 AD), *de reformatione*, c. 1: *COE* 713-714.

22. S. Congregatio de Propaganda Fide, encyclical letter, January 15, 1622: *Collectanea S.C. de Prop. Fide* I (Rome: Typographia Polyglotta, 1907), n . 2, pp. 1-2. Idem, instruction of 1659 to Vicars Apostolic of foreign mission societies: ibid., no. 135, pp. 42-43 (also in *CIC Fontes* 7: 20-21).

23. Stack, "Clerics and Civil Offices," p. 51.

24. Ibid., pp. 54-57.

25. "Ex S. Apostolica Poenitentiaria," *Acta Sanctae Sedis* (*ASS*) 2 (1867) 675-679, especially n . 7 at p. 678.

26. Alexander VII, constitution *Sacrosancti*, January 18, 1658: *Collectanea* I, n. 129, pp. 39-41 (*CIC Fontes* 1:451); Clement IX, constitution *In excelsa*, September 13, 1669: *Collectanea* I, no. 187, pp. 62-63 (*CIC Fontes* 1: 469).

27. *Pastoral Letter of the Archbishop and Bishops of the Province of Baltimore*, May 9, 1858 (Baltimore: John Murphy & Co., 1858), pp. 12-13.

28. *Acta et Decreta Concilii Plenarii Baltimorensis Tertii*, no. 83 (Baltimore: John Murphy & Co., 1886), p. 44.

29. Leo XIII, encyclical letter *Constanti Hungarorum*, September 2, 1893, n. 9: *ASS* 26 (1893-1894) 124-135 (*CIC Fontes* 3: 409).

30. Congregation for Extraordinary Ecclesiastical Affairs, response of April 2, 1906: *ASS* 39 (1906) 192. This provision was repeated for France after a change in the civil law again permitted clergy to be elected to the Chamber of Deputies; see Consistorial Congregation, decree of May 9, 1913: *Acta Apostolicae Sedis* (*AAS*) 5 (1913) 238.

31. See Prof. Dr. Hergenrother, "Ueber die Betheiligung des Klerus an politischen Fragen," *Archiv für katholisches Kirchenrecht* 15 (1866) 67-84; Francis X. Wernz, *Ius Decretalium*, II (Rome: Typographia Polyglotta, 1899), pp. 324-329.

32. Prof. Dr. Heiner, "Anschluss der Geistlichen von den politischen Wahlen," *Archiv für katholisches Kirchenrecht* 84 (1904) 107-116; see also Wernz, *Ius Decretalium*, II, 3rd ed. revised and enlarged (Prati: Libraria Giachetti, 1915), p. 345.

33. The most extensive commentary on this aspect of the 1917 code is found in Joseph Brunini, *The Clerical Obligations of Canons 139 and 142*, Canon Law Studies 103 (Washington, DC: Catholic University of America, 1937).

34. Ibid., p. 60.

35. See John A. Abbo and Jerome D. Hannan, *The Sacred Canons*, vol. 1 (St. Louis: B. Herder Book Company, 1952), pp. 198-200; T. Lincoln Bouscaren, Adam C. Ellis and Francis N. Korth, *Canon Law: A Text and Commentary* (Milwaukee: Bruce, 4th ed. rev. 1963), pp. 118-

119; Felix M. Capello, *Summa Iuris Canonici*, vol. 1 (Rome: Pont. Univ. Gregorianae, 6th ed. rev. 1961), p. 231; Ioannes Chelodi, *Ius Canonicum de Personis* (Vincenza: S.A. Tipografica, 3rd ed. 1942), pp. 198-199; Ferdinand Claeys-Bouuaert and G. Simenon, *Manuale Juris Canonici*, vol. 1 (Wetteren: DeMeester et fils, 5th ed. 1939), pp. 181-182; Eduard Eichmann and Klaus Mörsdorf, *Lehrbuch des Kirchenrechts*, vol. 1 (Munich: F. Schöningh, 10th ed. 1959), pp. 279-280; Carl Holbock, *Handbuch des Kirchenrechts*, vol. 1 (Innsbruck: Tyrolia, 1951), p. 251; Heribert Jone, *Commentarium in Codicem Iuris Canonici*, vol. 1 (Paderborn: F. Schöningh, 1950), pp. 147-148; Philippo Maroto, *Institutiones Iuris Canonici* (Rome: Commentarium pro Religiosis, 3rd ed. rev., 1921), pp. 649-651; Stephanus Sipos and Ladislaus Galos, *Enchiridion Iuris Canonici* (Rome: Herder, 7th ed. rev. 1960), pp. 111-112; Francis X. Wernz and Peter Vidal, *Ius Canonicum*, vol. 2 (Rome: Univ. Gregorianae, 1923), pp. 149-153; Stanislaus Woywod and Callistus Smith, *A Practical Commentary on the Code of Canon Law* (New York: Joseph Wagner, rev. and enlarged ed. 1962), pp. 72-74.

36. Brunini, pp. 22-23.

37. Ibid., p. 23. Jerome Hannan observed that prior to the 1917 code the permission of the Holy See was required for such positions in virtue of a decree from the Consistorial Congregation, *Docente Apostolo*, November 11, 1910: *AAS* 2 (1910) 910; however, a reply from the Code Commission on June 3, 1918 indicated this was now up to the local ordinary: *AAS* 10 (1918) 344. See Hannan, "Cases and Studies: Priest as Financial Secretary," *The Jurist* 7 (1947) 417-418.

38. Capello, p. 232, explains this was because of the special circumstances there at the time. The prohibition was lifted with the Lateran Pact in 1929; see art. IV of the Lateran Pact, *AAS* 21 (1929) 277-278. The concordat contained a provision, however, that under Italian law a cleric would need a nihil obstat from his ordinary in order to hold public office.

39. Congregation of the Council, decree of July 16, 1957: *AAS* 49 (1957) 637.

40. Commission for the Interpretation of the Code, response of April 25, 1922: *AAS* 14 (1922) 313; trans. *Canon Law Digest (CLD)* 1: 127.

41. See, for example, Capello, pp. 232-233; Chelodi, p. 199, n. 1; Sipos, p. 112.

42. Brunini, pp. 61-62.

43. See Jerome D. Hannan, "Elaborate or Simple Method to Eliminate Divorce?" *The Jurist* 9 (1949) 396-407; P. Feeney, "The Priest in Local Politics," *The Furrow* 30 (1979) 71-79.

44. Commission for the Interpretation of the Code, response of April 25, 1922: *AAS* 14 (1922) 313; *CLD* 1: 127.

45. Commission for the Interpretation of the Code, response of May 14, 1919 (private): *CLD* 2: 55-56.

46. Benedict XV, letter to Cardinal Begin and the other bishops of Canada, June 7, 1918: *AAS* 10 (1918) 440-442; *CLD* 1: 126. Idem, letter to Cardinal Csernoch (Hungary), March 12, 1919: *AAS* 11 (1919) 122-123; *CLD* 1: 126. Idem, letter to Cardinal Mercier and the other Belgian bishops, February 10, 1921: *AAS* 13 (1921) 127-130; *CLD* 1: 127. Idem, letter to Cardinals Kakowski and Dalhor and the other bishops of Poland, July 16, 1921: *AAS* 13 (1921) 424-426; *CLD* 1: 127.

47. Pius XI, letter to Archbishop Mora y Del Rio and the other archbishops and bishops of Mexico, February 2, 1926: *AAS* 18 (1926) 175-179; *CLD* 1: 127.

48. On Catholic Action, see especially Pius XI, letter to Cardinal Bertram of Warsaw, November 13, 1928: *AAS* 20 (1928) 384-387; *CLD* 1: 128-132. Idem, letter to Cardinal Segura y Saenz of Toledo, November 6, 1929: *AAS* 21 (1929) 664-668; *CLD* 1: 132-136. Idem, encyclical *Non abbiamo bisogno*, June 29, 1931: *AAS* 23 (1931) 285-312. It was in Italy that Catholic Action was most accused of political involvement, but similar complaints were voiced elsewhere occasioning cautions, for example, to the French clergy by the Holy Office in its decree of July 5, 1939 on *L'Action Francaise*: *AAS* 31 (1939) 303-304; *CLD* 2: 397-399.

49. Secretary of State, letter to ordinaries of Italy, October 2, 1922: Xaverius Ochoa, ed., *Leges Ecclesiae post Codicem iuris canonici editae (LE)*, vol. 1 (Rome: Commentarium pro Religiosis, 1966), col. 499.

50. Congregation for Religious, letter to religious superiors in Italy, February 10, 1924: *LE* 1, col. 652.

51. Congregation for the Council, response of March 15, 1927: *AAS* 19 (1927) 138; *CLD* 1: 128.

52. See Edward V. Dargin, "Father Coughlin and Canon Law," *AER* 93 (1935) 29-35; William F. Murphy, "Priests in Politics," *AER* 93 (1935) 269-279, with rejoinder by Dargin, pp. 279-288.

53. See the report of the norm adopted by the Archdiocese of Cincinnati, "Political Implications Prohibited," *The Jurist* 12 (1952) 111.

54. In addition to the question of voting for Communist candidates, condemned in the decree of the Holy Office of July 1, 1949 (*AAS* 41 (1949) 334; *CLD* 3: 658-659), there was a notable editorial in *L'Osservatore Romano* on May 18, 1960, which asserted the right of the Church to direct Catholics how to vote. This was written in the context

of the Italian political situation, but had serious repercussions in the United States where John F. Kennedy was running for President. See comments in *Commonweal* 72 (1960) 244-245, 317-318. There was a pastoral letter issued in Puerto Rico that same year directing Catholics not to vote for the Popular Democratic Party, which caused similar concern in the United States; see comments in *America* 104 (1960) 163-165. The *Tablet* reports pastoral letters in light of elections were issued by the bishops in Malta (*Tablet* 215 [1961] 236, 368), Uganda (ibid., p. 1160), Peru (ibid., p. 1242), Kerala, India (ibid. 216 [1962] 189), Germany (ibid., p. 244), and Rhodesia (ibid., p. 317).

55. See documentation in *CLD* 4: 97-102; 5: 200-205.

56. Constitution on the Church *Lumen gentium*, no. 31. See discussion in Joseph A. Komonchak, "Clergy, Laity, and the Church's Mission in the World," *The Jurist* 41 (1981) 422-447. An edited version is reprinted in this volume.

57. *CLD* 6: 168-169.

58. 1971 Synod of Bishops, *The Ministerial Priesthood*, Part Two, I, 2, b (Washington, DC: USCC Publications, 1982), p. 17.

59. Ibid.

60. See reports and analysis in René Coste, "Le prêtre et la politique," *Nouvelle revue théologique* 94 (1972) 912-932.

61. An example of one who did not obtain this permission, a fact publicized by his bishop, is a priest who ran for a municipal election in Avignon, France, on the Communist ticket; see Eugene Polge, "A propos de la candidature des prêtres aux elections municipales," *La Documentation Catholique* 68 (1971) 423-425. Father Drinan and others in the United States did obtain the appropriate permissions.

62. This disapproval was expressed informally but quite publicly through the secretary to Cardinal Wright, who at the time was prefect of the Congregation for Clergy. See, for example, Donald Wuerl, "Pulpit and podium: The problem of the priest-politician," *Homiletic and Pastoral Review* 73, no. 6 (March, 1973) 60-66; also his articles in the English language version of *L'Osservatore Romano* 138 (1970) 10-11 and 201 (1972) 8-10; *The Priest* 28 (1972) 52-59; and *AER* 166 (1972) 520-536.

63. *Code of Canon Law, Latin-English Edition* (Washington: CLSA, 1983). All subsequent translations of canons from the 1983 code are taken from this source.

64. *Schema Codicis Iuris Canonici* (Vatican City: Typis Polyglottis, 1977), c. 146, #2.

65. See *Schema Codicis Iuris Canonici* (Vatican City: Libreria Vaticana, 1980), c. 260, #2; *Codex Iuris Canonici: Schema novissimum iuxta*

placita Patrum commissionis emendatum atque Summo Pontifici praesentatum (Vatican City: Typis Polyglottis, 1982), c. 289, #2.

66. One of the members of the Code Commission suggested spelling this out, but the secretariat responded that legislative, administrative and judicial civil power are all understood by the words of the canon; see Pontificia Commissio Codici Iuris Canonici Recognoscendo, "Relatio," *Communicationes* 14 (1982) 173.

67. In discussing an earlier draft of this canon the working group which was preparing it considered a proposal to restrict the prohibition to having a directive role in political parties (similar to the prohibition from having a directive role in labor unions), but decided against this because even participating in making propaganda for a political party could cause dissension in the Christian community; see report in *Communicationes* 14 (1982) 83.

68. As remarked above, the 1977 and 1980 versions of c. 285 prohibited any public offices, although those which involved a participation in the exercise of civil power were singled out: "Officia publica, ea praesertim quae participationem in exercitio civilis potestatis secumferunt. . . ," *Schema Codicis Iuris Canonici*, c. 260, #2. In the 1982 version submitted to the pope, the "ea praesertim" had been deleted.

69. See *CLD* 6: 168.

70. As reported above, the earlier versions of c. 285 had spelled out various authorities to give permission for clergy to hold public office, and the earlier versions of c. 287 on political parties and labor unions had referred back to these same authorities. Thus, as under the 1917 code and subsequent decrees, a bishop would have needed the permission of the Holy See, clerics in a place where the pontifical prohibition was in effect would also have needed the permission of the Holy See, and other clergy would have been required to obtain the permission of their own ordinary as well as the ordinary of the place "in which the power and administration were intended to be exercised." One member of the Code Commission objected to this last provision as unworkable in cases of national elections, and proposed instead that the norm of the 1917 code be retained; see "Relatio," p. 173.

71. Such an interpretation is based on the fact that since priests or religious do not lose their civil rights when they are ordained or make religious profession, a restriction on the free exercise of their rights must be interpreted strictly (canon 18); that is, there is no restriction in the law unless it clearly says so.

72. Decree on the Pastoral Ministry of Bishops *Christus Dominus*, n. 8b.

73. Paul VI, motu proprio *De episcoporum muneribus*, June 15, 1966: *AAS* 58 (1966) 467-471; *CLD* 6: 394-400.

74. Conceivably the bishop of diocese A could determine the conditions to be present for a priest or religious to run for office (c.287, #2), and if the person won, could dispense from the prohibition against holding a public office (c. 285, #3) even though the place where the office was physically located was in diocese B. However, to engage in any active role in a political party while on the job, the priest or religious would need the permission of the bishop of diocese B in whose territory the person was now working. On the other hand, if elected in diocese A the priest or religious could be dispensed from canon 285, #3 by the bishop of diocese B where the office is to be exercised. At the national level in the United States, this means a bishop could determine that the conditions were such as to warrant a priest or religious taking an active role in a political party by seeking election to Congress, and if the election were successful, could dispense the person from the limitation of canon 285, #3. However, the archbishop of Washington would have to determine if the conditions warranted continued active participation in party activities by the new member of Congress. Clearly, the situation could become very complex!

75. See Peter Huizing and Knut Walf, *May Church Ministers be Politicians?* Concilium 157 (New York: Seabury Press, 1982).

76. Religious institutes are governed by the general canons on institutes of consecrated life (cc. 573-606) as well as the special canons on religious institutes themselves (cc. 607-709). This section of the law underwent considerable modification in the course of drafting the new code. It will take some time for competent commentaries to appear on it. For an initial attempt, see Domingo J. Andres, *El derecho de los religiosos: Comentario al codigo* (Rome: Comentarium pro Religiosis, 1984).

77. While earlier practice limited exclaustration to a limited time and for specific purposes, recent responses from the Apostolic See indicate a preference for exclaustration over forced dismissal from an institute with dispensation from the vows except in certain limited circumstances. See the developments reflected in the various replies reported in *Roman Replies*, ed. William A. Schumacher, 1981 (Washington: CLSA, 1981), pp. 38-39; ibid., 1982 (Washington: CLSA, 1982), pp. 38-40; ibid., 1983 (Washington, CLSA, 1983), pp. 21-23. Informal communications indicate the Apostolic See has directly suggested exclaustration rather than forced dismissal with dispensation from the vows for problem religious, but has insisted on dismissal rather than exclaustration for religious who desire to remain

attached to the institute while exercising a public office entailing civil power.

78. John Paul II, apostolic constitution *Sacrae disciplinae leges*, January 25, 1983: *AAS* 75 Part II (1983) xii-xiii; *Code of Canon Law, Latin-English Edition*, p. xv.

Rosemary Smith, SC

POLITICAL INVOLVEMENT
AND THE REVISED CODE*

I have organized my comments on political involvement into three parts 1) context; 2) the content of the law; 3) and comments, mainly in the form of questions. Political involvement is a broad category of activities including such things as voting, peace marches, lobbying, civil disobedience, the formation of public opinion by issuing statements or testifying before government commissions, or choosing not to, as USCC has done recently on a few crucial issues. It is important to acknowledge that we all participate in political activity as citizens, and even most church groups, most religious communities, most organizations within the church including USCC participate in political activity in a variety of ways. Having mentioned these aspects of political involvement, I will now focus on public office which presents many questions today.

Webster defines public office as a special duty, charge or position, conferred by an exercise of authority for a public purpose. This includes again a broad spectrum of possibilities: full and part time, appointed or elected, participation in any one of the three classical branches of government—executive, legislative, judicial—on the local, state or federal level. Obviously we are talking about a broad range of activities when we talk about public office. Political parties are more or less permanent organizations promoting specific principles and candidates for public office. Labor unions are another part of this con-

---

*This contribution was one of several brief papers presented at the Secretariat of the Leadership Conference of Women Religious in Silver Spring, Maryland, in April 1984. After the presentation there was further discussion and reflection by a panel of canonists. What follows is an edited version of the article that appeared in the June 1984 LCWR Newsletter.

troversial subject. They are organizations formed to serve their members' interests, usually around wages, working conditions or things of that nature. Having defined my terms, I am going to be talking primarily about public office.

The next statement under this context is an historical note, for I think it is helpful to know the roots of the question, and to see that the law has taken different forms and has been applied differently in its long history. I will say a few words about the law with regard to clerics in public office, but I will not pursue this aspect in depth. By way of example, in the first few centuries of Christianity there was no general church law about clerics in public office. What warnings there were, were directed to all Christians, clerics and laity alike. The concern was idolatry, because associated with public office was the obligation to offer worship to the Roman gods. So, too, throughout history the concerns that have shaped the law and its applications have varied.

There are some relevant conclusions from this history of the law. First, although there were practical cautions, being a cleric and holding public office has never, in the history of the church, been considered intrinsically incompatible. A second conclusion that I have observed within the history of the law is that general legislation on clerics holding public office has consistently envisioned and provided for exceptions. That has been true even in later centuries when there was general legislation. A third conclusion: the question of non-clerical religious holding public office has not been an issue until recently and therefore there is little reference to such in the law until this century. It simply wasn't an issue for all kinds of sociological reasons.

I would like to speak now about the content of the law. The previous law, i.e., the 1917 code, has four canons I'd like to mention as a base from which to compare what we have now and then to try to sort out the differences. Again I will talk about the law governing clerics, and then its connection, such as it is, to religious. The three canons I am going to mention from the section on clerics are #121, #138, and #139 in the 1917 code. #121 is a claim of the church, not a disciplinary law. It is a claim to immunity for clerics from what is alien to the clerical state such as military duties. It includes offices that would be alien to that state as well. It doesn't define alien. The next canon #138 is a disciplinary law. Clerics are to abstain from anything unbecoming to the clerical state (that is understood to be different from alien) unless circumstances or the local ordinary provide otherwise—so there is recognition that exceptions are possible. The next canon #139 is the heart of the matter in the 1917 code. It begins by repeating that clerics are to avoid what is alien. The second paragraph in summary states that among other things clerics shall not assume public offices which involve the exercise of lay jurisdiction or administration. The fourth paragraph of this same canon in the 1917 code goes on to say that clerics shall neither solicit, that is stand for election, nor accept appointments to the office of senator or deputy without the permission of the Holy See in areas where there is a pontifical prohibition. It goes on to say that in other areas where there is no such prohibition the permission of one's ordinary and the ordinary of the place where the elections will take place is needed. That is the content of the law regarding clerics and the public office in the 1917 code.

How are religious tied into these regulations for clerics? In the 1917 code, canon #592 makes the general statement that common obligations of clerics also bind religious unless, from the context of the words or the nature of the thing it is determined otherwise. So there is vagueness, and the application to religious is variously interpreted. The question of religious and public office was not an issue in the church in the United States until recently for a number of reasons. One is the general forbidding tone of the law, another is the social tenor, and another has to do with the fact that the church was a missionary church until this century and there were strong prohibitions from the Congregation for the Propagation of the Faith against missionaries being involved in the political activity of a country. These prohibitions for missionaries originated in concordats with some of the countries that were colonizing and exploring.

Since the 1917 code was promulgated, there have been a number of developments in the life of the church. First there were several authentic interpretations of this law, all interpreting the law strictly in relation to clerics. There was never an authentic interpretation that applied specifically to religious. Another development in the life of the church was the Second Vatican Council in which the church by and large defined itself in relation to the world, rather than in isolation from it. And I think that is an important element in the whole process. It was a stance of engagement, basically.

The third development I will mention is a document having to do with dispensating power; this is also crucial to the general understanding of how the law was to be interpreted. This interim legislation issued in 1966 reserves to the Holy See a list of dispensing powers, one of which was the dispensation to allow clerics to assume public office. This is therefore a precedent for the Holy See being involved in decisions in this matter as recently as 1966. A fourth pertinent development is the 1971 Synod of Bishops which dealt with the question of clerics in political office in the document *Ministerial Priesthood*. This is not law. However it is a consensus of the understandings of the bishops in the light of which future law should be formed and it allowed for the possibility of holding political office in extraordinary circumstances and for the good of the community, with appropriate consent. It did not rule it out.

Much more recently, the document *Religious Life and Human Promotion* (1980) addressed the question of religious specifically in political office. There are two sections, eleven and twelve, which deal directly with the question of political office. In summary it speaks of the risks involved and expresses reservations, but it does affirm the possibility. This possibility is very clear, and I quote: "Active involvement in politics remains an exception then, to be engaged in only by way of exception, and under exceptional circumstances."

As you know the revision process was a long one. However by October 1981 the Pontifical Commission for the Revision of the Code had finished its work, and sent the schema to the pope with the recommendation that it be promulgated as written. In that schema, the law regarding political office was phrased substantially the same as in the 1917 code. Keep in mind that this formulation had been approved by worldwide consultation of bishops and was not seen as a question needing discussion. It was decided that this was an appropriate way of regulating it. However when the revised code came out a year or so later, it was changed. There were some notable word changes, and in my opinion, an important deletion. The canons in the new code which I will discuss in relation to the 1917 code are canons #285, #287 and #672 in the section on religious. #285 in the first and second paragraphs talks about what is unbecoming to clerics and what is alien to them. In the third paragraph however the canon adds, "clerics are forbidden to assume public offices which entail a participation in the exercise of civil power." There are three differences that I would note from the prior rendition in the 1917 code. First of all the verb "vetantur" is used, which means they are forbidden. In the prior code it said: "they are not to assume." In my interpretation, this is a more emphatic prohibition than in the prior code. The second change that I would like to note is that the 1917 code spoke of the exercise of lay jurisdiction or administration while the revised code uses the general term "civil power." "Civilis potestas" appears to be a more encompassing term, and I suspect that that is the intent. The third difference in the law is the excising of the provisions for exception. There still are possibilities of exceptions, but the law does not include how one goes about applying for those exceptions. All of these changes were a surprise; none of them were expected. It seems that the changes were intentionally more restrictive.

The other pertinent canon in the section on clerics is #287. It has two paragraphs. The first paragraph is basically an exhortation. "Clerics shall foster peace and harmony based on justice . . . " The second, also not in the prior code, is a disciplinary law, and it says that clerics are not to have an active role in political parties or in the direction of labor unions, unless the need to protect the rights of the church or to promote the common good requires it, and this requirement must be in the judgment of the competent ecclesiastical authorities. I call your attention to a few words. The canon does not talk about membership in political parties or membership in labor unions. It talks about their direction, generally speaking. It provides within the law itself the kinds of exceptions which will be countenanced, e.g., the protection of the rights of the church. I believe that the intent there is focused on the church as institution, that if the property of the church is endangered, clerics may somehow get involved in an active role. Another word I call your attention to is the necessity that this involvement be required. Not just that it is warranted, but that it is required. This is a relatively strong word. It also does not say explicitly who makes the judgment. It simply states, a competent ecclesiastical authority. These are just a few observations, and there is nothing against which to compare. Since this is a new inclusion we don't have prior jurisprudence to draw on for a better understanding.

The final canon I want to talk about is #672 which refers to religious. It is clearly the intent that religious be included here. Whether it is wise is another, separate question. The intention is made clear when it is stated, "religious are bound by the prescriptions," and five canons are listed, including #285 and #287 about which we have just spoken. There is no question about whether it is intended. The canons are named specifically.

I would like to conclude my comments by identifying what to me are a few concerns or anomalies in the law, and then raise four questions which I think identify the underlying issues. The first concern has to do with the exception of permanent deacons from the prohibitions. Canon #287 is the canon in question. Although permanent deacons are clerics, they are not bound by either the canon on public office or the canon which has to do with political parties and labor unions, unless particular law determines otherwise. This gives recognition to the fact that regulations could vary from culture to culture, or from locale to locale. What are we to infer from this? Certainly that public office and participation in civic life are not inherently incompatible with being a cleric is already evident in the history of the law, but what else? On what is the disciplinary distinction based? Is it economic? Is it public visibility? How are these distinctions made?

The second anomaly or concern that I have has to do with the Holy See itself and public office. Canons #362-367 speak about legates of the Holy See. Despite the generally forbidding tone of the law regarding clerics and religious in public office, the present practice of the church and the intent of the law reserves to clerics offices in the papal diplomatic corps. Granted these are in fact ecclesiastical offices, but they are also public offices, entailing participation in the exercise of civil power. In many countries clerics are the heads of the diplomatic corps. Although their first responsibility is said to be coordination of the church in that area, their duties extend beyond that. To say that they are not holding public offices and that they do not have civil power is difficult. I see that as an anomaly in the law.

The third concern that I would like to mention is the oversight responsibility of bishops indirectly for the charism, and more directly for the works of religious institutes. There are principles stated in the law which are as yet unclear in practice. The law speaks of just autonomy in the internal life of religious congregations, it speaks of fidelity to mission and work, accommodating this tradition prudently to the times. Another canon (#678) states that authority regarding the apostolate lies with the bishop and also with the major superior. The final paragraph says that bishops and superiors should "proceed after consultation," an attempt to deal with the practical issues. In principle I see this as a possible conflict of interest. In practice I see confusion and a potential for injustice.

My concluding questions:

The first is related to the principle of enculturation. In a country which holds the free exercise of civil rights in very high esteem, as we do in the United States, how is the principle and the necessity of enculturation to be honored in regard to this aspect of the law?

The second question has to do with what model of the church prevails in the writing of the law and in the interpretation of the law? Are different criteria to be used in determining what is appropriate service to the church as institution, as opposed to what is appropriate service to the church as the people of God? Who establishes these criteria? They are not written down anywhere.

My third concern was mentioned earlier. In the absence of an accessible and responsive system of recourse how are these issues to be settled in peace and harmony with justice?

And the last question has to do with religious life itself. What is religious life called to today? How can both its ecclesial dimensions and charismatic dimensions be respected?

DISCUSSION

Following the presentation by Rosemary Smith, SC, the discussion was joined by:

James Coriden, a presbyter of the Diocese of Gary, Indiana, and Academic Dean at the Washington Theological Union. A professor of Canon Law, he has been engaged in several research projects of the Canon Law Society of America, and is the author of many journal articles on canonical matters.

Sharon Holland, IHM, a canonist in the Detroit Metropolitan Marriage Tribunal and in the Office of the Delegate for Religious. She teaches Canon Law at St. John's Provincial Seminary.

Margret Mary Modde, OSF, director of the Department of Canon Law for the Catholic Health Association in St. Louis, Missouri. She has consulted and lectured widely on canonical matters.

Rosemary Ronk, RSM, at the time of the discussion a member of the central administration of the Sisters of Mercy of the Union. She died in August 1984 after a brief illness.

(Coriden)—I am grateful for the historical context because we tend not to think of the many clerics who have occupied public office in past centuries, with the complete approval of the church. In fact, there were bishops in the early centuries who were the defenders of the walls of the city and exercised other public functions. This was expected of them, to some extent thrust upon them, and quite commonplace. In our own country historically it is commonplace, both in the past and in the present, to have ministerial figures occupying public office. Jesse Jackson is simply the latest in a long, long line. How many people on Capitol Hill are ordained ministers? At any given time there are many. In our pluralistic tradition in the United States ministerial background, even ordination, is not disqualifying for public office.

What I would like to pose to you is a distinction which I have heard and wonder if you agree with. On the one hand it is inappropriate for priests in pastoral offices, with parish responsibilities to take part in partisan involvement. As part of their pastoral office they are called to be ministers of peace and harmony and really should be trying to bring together, bridge over, or unify their people and should not engage in things which are explicitly partisan in a political sense. On the other hand religious have as one of their primary functions, the call to be prophetic. When not engaged in pastoral work narrowly defined (for example, heading a parish community, leading people), that same preoccupation with unifying is not primary. Indeed there are times when public or political roles can be given by public service of various kinds. Do you think that is a reasonable distinction?

(Smith)—Yes, I do. In the 1971 Document on Ministerial Priesthood the Synod of Bishops stated that priests should be a sign of unity. That is one of the arguments for their not getting involved. However I believe there are even exceptions in those situations. What is the unity to which one is witnessing? Is it the status quo? That is what not getting involved amounts to at times. But I think basically your distinction is one I would agree with. Religious would be more frequently, more appropriately involved. Even then, however, I see it as a valid but exceptional ministry. I don't think it is the primary work that any community would be involved in, and even some communities not at all. It simply wouldn't fit their charism as I see it.

(Modde)—In a country where we talk about separation of church and state a great deal, and where we insist upon it, how do you see the life of a person totally committed to a church organization functioning within the state situation?

(Smith)—There would be situations in which it would be difficult. I think that in making such a decision the charism of the community, the skills and gifts of the individual, and also the particular situation in which the individual religious is looking to function would have to be weighed. I believe there would be situations in which an individual would not be able to function well, making it pointless to try serving in that kind of position. In theory, however, I don't think it is a problem.

(Holland)—I think that touches something that I want to explore. Jim mentioned that it might be more appropriate for religious than for priests to be involved in what might be called a prophetic stance. I have to question to what extent one can be involved in public office in our country in a political or civic position, and retain the prophetic witness, speaking Gospel over against some of what is going on in society. Isn't that another part of the total picture that one has to look at in discerning when it is appropriate and when it is not?

(Smith)—Again that is one of the risks that *Religious Life and Human Promotion* lists.

(Ronk)—Is there anything in the law that allows a period of time for exploration of ministries that we do not have much experience with? We do not have an adequate body of experience to determine whether or not the participation of women religious in elective office is indeed supportive of Gospel values. Is there some way to provide a period of time in which we could explore as groups of people whether or not in effect the religious community supports the person in that ministry? In other areas we have allowed people to try new ministries and then we have studied the data.

(Smith)—Something we were talking about before comes to mind here. When someone moves into the area of public office, that individual is moving into the public arena, and so it becomes more visible and more subject to scrutiny. It isn't a private experiment as our prayer horarium was.

(Ronk)—The hospital system in this country is not private. I think ministerially we have been public ministers in the past.

(Smith)—Yes, I am just saying that it becomes more controversial as it becomes more public.

(Modde)—I believe the church does owe us further explanation. In our various documents and throughout the documents of Vatican II, we are taken as church to the brink of total involvement in the world. These are beautifully stated documents, but when we get to the brink and we meet barriers, we cannot totally participate as church. Somehow we need a better explanation on why barriers are there. The barriers are hard to understand especially because of the way we say we are to participate as church in the world. We have developed a concept of the church and world which no longer says the church is here and the world is there, but one that encourages a unity of the two as we work toward the furthering of the Kingdom. Then we are told: But don't do this. I challenge us as church to give ourselves a better explanation of why.

(Coriden)—That is well taken, but also if you had to choose between the two I wish they would give dispensations rather than explanations. It should be made quite clear that this is a dispensable law and that that is the Roman way of saying: "Adapt it to your culture." The bishops should be enlightened enough to see the kinds of exceptions desirable, or to see a need to experiment with ministries, permitting it, unless there is some overwhelming reason not to. Unless there is going to be countersign to Gospel values in a particular instance, the dispensation should be given.

(Modde)—I agree with the dispensation being given now, but I would like to carry this discussion a bit further and say that we don't live well with dispensations as we well know. So I would like to see dispensations given, but also I would like to see the question of why-the-barriers explored and dialogue fostered. It is quite evident that the dialogue has almost been cut off relative to this question.

(Smith)—I would like to suggest a way of moving that forward. It seems to me that the people who are drawing the fire shouldn't be the ones who have to ask for the explanation. Some other body that is in the position of getting a hearing might seek an explanation, or explore the dimensions of the question, or request another group—such as the Canon Law Society of America—to take it as a study question. The individuals who are already risking a great deal should be relieved of this further burden.

(Modde)—I would agree with that, but I would also like to see the individuals who have participated in political activity brought together to share and reflect on the reasons they feel this is a viable ministry within the church. It is important that they participate in that evaluation. Very often we do much of our evaluation in isolation from the individuals who have been involved.

(Ronk)—I think that is something that many religious communities have done in the last 15 to 20 years when we moved into new areas. Groups involved in new ministries have come together and reflected on their experience.

(Coriden)—We need to examine the ministry. What has been the result? What was the acceptance? What was the fallout? I believe there is enough of a track record to begin some analysis of it in our experience.

(Ronk)—There was a time when religious could not be doctors or lawyers, so we do have some parallel experiences that could be looked at.

(Ronk)—What about the particular law of an individual congregation in relation to the new code? If the particular law could be interpreted to include the possibility of political life, would that take precedence over this interpretation of the code?

(Smith)—There was a recent statement from SCRIS that anything that is opposed to the common law of the church should be brought into line with that law.

(Holland)—It is a common principle that a part of the whole cannot be in contradiction to the whole. That was stated explicitly in the 1917 code. It was not stated explicitly in the new code for some reason, but has been subsequently reiterated.

(Modde)—One way that this is being taken care of is in the critiquing of constitutions by the Holy See.

(Holland)—Is the point of your question whether a congregation can provide space for something like political ministry?

(Ronk)—Well, I was trying to determine the flexibility allowed to a congregation in relation to this question. Can a religious congregation say, "in the following situations," or "within these parameters we would see that political ministry is an acceptable type of ministry?" Is the law so strong at this point within the code that you could not even conceive of a community being able to make Chapter statements like that?

(Holland)—It seems to me that a congregation probably wouldn't make that explicit a statement in constitutions. If the Chapter were to make that kind of a statement, it seems it would assume the pursuit of the necessary permission. I can conceive of the Chapter looking at the question, making a study of it, thinking about that kind of direction, but an individual seeking political office still would have to seek the necessary permission.

(Ronk)—It seems that through the past 15 years our membership has moved toward this kind of involvement, where there is gift and talent, and so in a sense the Chapter is now in a position to either abort that movement or to come back and say something stronger about it. I believe it has to do with the relationship of ourselves to the world and how we function.

(Coriden)—I think you may be reading too much into the law in regard to political involvement. The law is bad enough without it being interpreted as setting back that whole direction. It doesn't say anything about lobbying, it doesn't say anything about a lot of things. It really is a very narrowly drawn law and there are a thousand involvements for every one that requires the bishop's dispensation for involvement. The law is certainly not against public involvement, encounter with the world, witness in a thousand kinds of ministries. This one the Pope himself changed, because I assume it is the Pope's own personal view about this narrow area of partisan politics. I really think it would not be fair to the law to say that it is against all the other kinds of involvements in the same direction.

(Smith)—But even on that one issue where some communities are hurting I think it is important to keep in mind that we are at the point of potential conflict in some isolated instances, not because of failure but because of growth.

Paul J. Weber

CLERGY IN POLITICS: THE CONSTITUTIONAL QUESTION

For good or ill, few contemporary Catholics are aware of the long history of bigotry, prejudice, and hostility that dogged our ancestors. Gone are organizations such as the Order of the Star-Spangled Banner, a secret society whose political component was the American Party, popularly called the "Know-Nothings." Formed in 1849, only white Protestants without Catholic relatives could join. Their political philosophy is well summarized by Professor Ahlstrom:

> . . . Upon joining, they swore to oppose the election of foreigners and Roman Catholics and to renounce other political ties. If a member advanced to the exalted second degree of the order he . . . had to swear that he would not appoint foreigners or Roman Catholics to public office and that he would remove them wherever it was legally possible.[1]

Gone also are the days less than a century ago, when hundreds of Republican party candidates for public office found anti-Catholicism a potent rallying cry, when the Democrats would be tarred as the party of "Rum, Romanism and Rebellion," and when the American Protective Association, whose members swore never to hire or strike with a Catholic and never to vote for one, would be an ominous political force.

But the legacy remains. On the one hand, there is lingering suspicion about the motives of priests and sisters running for or accepting political office. On the other hand, there is a hesitation within the Catholic community to see politics as a legitimate vocation. Throughout, there is the odor of something faintly unAmerican, with a vague hint that a noble principle called "separation" has been violated. Fortunately, the constitutional status of clergy in politics is not nearly so clouded. Neither the constitution, nor the principles of separation—correctly understood—are violated by priests and sisters serving in political offices.

CONSTITUTIONAL HISTORY

During the first century and a half the American colonies were governed under English Common Law. One practice for the most part carried over from England was the exclusion of ordained ministers from public office. This exclusion was justified on several grounds: since there was an established church, and the clergy were paid government employees, this prevented dual office holding; since clergy benefices were under the control of the Crown, it was feared that their presence in the House of Commons would increase the power of the monarchy in that body and that political affairs would distract them from attention to their "sacred duties." Finally, political philosopher John Locke argued in the name of political liberty for keeping clergy walled "within the bounds of the church, nor can it. . . (clerical authority). . . in any manner be extended to civil affairs; because the church itself is a thing absolutely separate and distinct from the commonwealth."[2]

In the first days of the Republic, it was the influence of Locke and the attempt to work out the meaning of separation of church and state that led thirteen of the first twenty-six states to exclude clergy from political office. The New York constitutional provision of 1777 was fairly typical:

> And whereas the ministers of the gospel are, by their profession, dedicated to the service of God and the cure of souls, and ought not to be diverted from the great duties of their functions; therefore, no minister of the gospel or priest of any denomination whatsoever, shall at any time hereafter, under any pretense or description whatever, be eligible to, or capable of holding, any civil or military office or place within this state.[3]

Other state constitutional provisions were almost identical, although Louisiana's had an interesting twist:

> No person *while he continues to exercise the functions* of a clergyman, priest or teacher of any religious persuasion, society

or sect, shall be eligible to the general assembly or to any
office of profit or trust under this State.[4]

Canon Stokes speculates that the underlying provision was added
under the influence of one Eligius Fromentin, a lawyer and former
Jesuit priest who was a Louisiana senator from 1813 to 1819.[5] As states
became more sophisticated in their ability to govern, such restrictions
gradually disappeared, although as we shall see shortly, Tennessee's
restriction did not disappear until 1978, and then only as a result of a
Supreme Court decision.

On the national level, there has never been any constitutional restriction on clergypersons holding elective or appointive office. The
matter was discussed at the time of the writing of the constitution and
there was some powerful opposition to allowing clergy to run for office. In 1783, Jefferson drafted a constitution for Virginia which specifically excluded military officers, felons and clergy from being
elected to public office. Madison objected strenuously, however, and
a year after he guided the drafting of the U.S. Constitution, he spelled
out his reasoning in an argument that still rings true:

> Does not the exclusion of Ministers of the Gospel as such
> violate a fundamental principle of liberty by punishing a re-
> ligious profession with the privation of a civil right? Does it
> (not) violate another article of the plan itself which exempts
> religion from the cognizance of Civil power? Does it not vi-
> olate justice by at once taking away a right and prohibiting
> a compensation for it? Does it not in fine violate impartiality
> by shutting the door (against) the Ministers of one Religion
> and leaving it open for those of every other?[6]

Jefferson was persuaded by Madison's argument and changed
that part of the draft. A letter written to an acquaintance in 1800 explaining his change of mind is interesting because it shows that his opposition was not based on any problem with "separation," but with
putting clergy in positions of privilege. As he wrote then:

> [I]n the same scheme of a constitution [for Virginia which
> I prepared in 1783, I observe] an abridgment of the right
> of being elected, which after 17 years more of experience
> and reflection, I do not approve. It is the incapacitation of
> a clergyman from being elected. . . . Even in 1783 we
> doubted the stability of our recent measures for reducing

them [the clergy] to the footing of other useful callings. It now appears that our means were effectual. The clergy here seem to have relinquished all pretensions to privilege, and to stand on a footing with lawyers, physicians, etc. They ought therefore to possess the same rights.[7]

When the federal Constitution itself was written, the Madisonian view had prevailed and the document contained only a single relevant statement in Article VI: ". . . no religious test shall ever be required as a qualification to any office or public trust under the United States." While the original intent was clearly to prohibit any attempt to limit office holding to those professing a religious belief, the words can equally well be read to thwart prohibitions against ministers, priests and sisters serving in public office.

Two years after the constitution was written, Congress passed the First Amendment which reads in part, "Congress shall make no law respecting an establishment of Religion or prohibiting the free exercise there of" . . . While these religious clauses, as they are called; have given rise to an enormous number of cases, only once has the U.S. Supreme Court applied them to the issue of a minister running for public office, a case titled *McDaniel v Paty, et al.* Throughout American history, professional religious have run for federal office without serious constitutional challenge.[8]

McDANIEL v PATY

The constitutional issue for both federal and state levels was finally settled when the Court decided a case from Tennessee in the spring of 1978.[9]

Rev. McDaniel, an ordained Baptist minister with a church in Chattanooga, filed to become a candidate for membership in a convention called to reform Tennessee's constitution. One of his three opponents in the election, Ms. Selma Paty, sought a court order to have his name struck from the ballot. According to Tennessee law, Paty had a valid point. When it established the ground rules for a constitutional convention in 1976, the state legislature passed a series of laws among which was the statement that "Any citizen of the state who can qualify to membership in the House of Representatives of the General Assembly may become a candidate for delegate to the convention. . ."[10] Unfortunately for McDaniel, the Tennessee constitution was also extraordinarily clear on the point ". . . no Minister of the Gospel, or priest of any denominations whatever, shall be eligible to a seat in either House of the Legislature."[11] In his defense McDaniel's lawyer argued that this provision of the Tennessee constitution violated the first and fourteenth amendments to the federal constitution and therefore should be declared null and void. A lower state court agreed and McDaniel was allowed to run for the delegate spot. After he won the election, the state Supreme Court overruled the first verdict and held that McDaniel was illegally elected. He appealed to the United States Supreme Court.

About the only thing the justices agreed on in the case was that excluding a professional religious from running for public office is unconstitutional. No majority opinion was written because no five justices could agree on a single reason for finding the Tennessee provision contrary to the Federal Constitution. Chief Justice Burger, writing for himself and Justices Powell, Rehnquist and Stevens, reasoned that McDaniel's First Amendment right to the free exercise of religion was violated because the freedom to practice as he sees fit, i.e., as a minister, is conditioned on his surrendering his right to seek political office.

Tennessee had argued that if it allowed clergy to be elected "they will necessarily exercise their powers and influence to promote the interests of one sect or thwart the interests of another, thus pitting one against the others."[12] The court wasn't persuaded, however claiming that history didn't bear out that contention. Burger concluded that "To condition the availability of benefits. . .upon this appellant's willingness to violate a cardinal principle of his religious faith (by surrendering his religiously impelled ministry) effectively penalizes the free exercise of his constitutional liberties."[13]

Justice Brennan, who rarely agrees with the Chief Justice in any event, wrote a concurring opinion for himself and Justice Marshall. Brennan argued that the Tennessee constitution violates *both* the free exercise and the establishment clauses. Tennessee argued that the exclusion of ministers and priests did not interfere with religious belief or even the practice of their ministry in any way. Only candidacy for legislative office was prohibited. But, writes Brennan, "The purpose of the Tennessee provision is. . .to bar from political office persons regarded as deeply committed to religious participation because of that participation—participation itself not regarded as harmful by the State." Therefore, the right to run for office in this case must be absolutely protected under the free exercise clause.

The usual standard against which state laws are measured to determine if they violate the establishment clause is three-pronged: (1)

Whether the law has a secular legislative purpose; (2) whether the law has a primary effect of either advancing or inhibiting religion; and (3) whether the law results in excessive entanglement between government and religious institutions. According to Brennan and Marshall, there could hardly be a clearer example of a provision which inhibits religion. Therefore Tennessee's constitution also violates the Establishment clause.

Neither Burger nor Brennan could persuade Justices Stewart or White with their reasoning. Stewart wrote a concurring opinion to make the point that whatever else it is, the Tennessee prohibition is a religious test, "penalizing an individual for his religious status—for what he is and what he believes in. . . ." Therefore it violates Article VI of the federal constitution.[14]

Justice White, on the other hand, relied on the Equal Protection clause of the fourteenth amendment to the federal constitution. The Tennessee statute uses a religious classification, which like a racial or sexual classification, can only be used if there's a compelling reason. Since all the other states manage without such an exclusion, Tennessee's reasoning is not persuasive. White also observes that on the one hand the statute only limits candidates for the legislature, and not for executive or judicial offices and therefore is too narrowly drawn. On the other hand, some ministers will not be divisive and will discharge their official duties properly, so the regulation is overinclusive.

McDaniel v Paty leaves a lot of unanswered questions. The constitutionality of ordained or professional religious in political office, however, is not one of them. The 8-0 vote (Justice Blackmun did not participate in the decision) provides a very solid precedent not likely to be reversed in the forseeable future. While the reasoning is not as clearcut and focused as constitutional scholars would like, the variety of grounds— free exercise, establishment, Article VI (the religious test), and equal protection— underlines the constitutional protection provided to those clergy who seek public office.

THE ISSUE OF SEPARATION

If the constitutionality of clergy taking political office is so overwhelmingly affirmed by the Supreme Court, why are there constitutional questions raised by otherwise well-informed citizens? One reason is that there is a great deal of confusion around the meaning of the term "separation of church and state." Contrary to popular opinion, the phrase nowhere appears in the constitution and it means different things to people who use the term. At this point, it may be useful to look at the "separation of church and state" concept to understand the different ways it may apply to the issue of clergy in politics. For the popularization of the separation concept we are indebted to Thomas Jefferson's letter to the Danbury Baptists, in which he wrote:

> Believing with you that religion is a matter which lies solely between man and his God, that he owes account to none other for his faith or his worship, that the legitimate powers of government reach actions only, and not opinions, I contemplate with sovereign reverence that act of the whole American people which declared that their legislature should "make no laws respecting an establishment of religion, or prohibiting the free exercise thereof" *thus building a wall of separation between church and state.*[15]

The difficulty with the "separation" interpretation of the religion clauses is not that it is wrong, but that it is inadequate. It is a *generic* term susceptible to several specific meanings, not all of which are equally valid interpretations of the Amendment. It is this vague understanding of the type of separation required by the First Amendment which leads to some opposition to participation of clergy in the political process. An exploration of the specific types of separation may be valuable as a means of clarifying this point.

Structural Separation involves formal legal and systemic ties between religion and the polity. This is a fundamental type of separation and is distinguished from organic types of social organization which do not differentiate between church and state as such. The establishment of an Islamic Republic in Iran is a recent example of an organic church-state relationship. The characteristics of structural separation are independent clerical and civil offices, separate organizations, personnel performing different functions and paid from different sources, separate systems of law and independent ownership of property. It does not exclude the special protections, privileges and economic supports commonly included in the term "established church." With few exceptions, Western Christian churches and nations have had a structural separation of church and state since the third century. It is clear that Jefferson and Madison and many other founders accepted the need for this type of separation, and where they found vestiges of organic relationships, as in the religious elements of the common law, they vigorously sought to end them. At the same time, they found structural separation an inadequate safeguard for governmental independence and religious liberty.

Absolute separation is a term itself susceptible to several meanings. Professor Leo Pfeffer in his still influential book, *Church, State and Freedom*, for example, defines his meaning of absolute separation by quoting nineteenth century jurist, Jeremiah S. Black:

> The manifest object of the men who framed the institutions of this country was to have a State without religion and a church without politics—that is to say, they meant that one should never be used as an engine for the purposes of the other. . . For that reason they built up a wall of complete and perfect partition between the two.[16]

Probably the most well-known statement of an absolute separationist view is that of Justice Hugo Black when he defined the Establishment Clause in *Everson v Board of Education of Ewing Township*:

> The "Establishment of religion" means at least this: Neither a state nor the Federal Government can set up a church. Neither can pass laws which aid one religion, aid all religions, or prefer one religion over another. . . *Neither a state nor the Federal Government can, openly or secretly, participate in the affairs of any religious organizations or groups and vice versa. . .*[17]

Justice Black's definition certainly was not applied to Rev. McDaniel; indeed it was not even quoted. But it does raise an interesting question: does a clergyperson running for or accepting a political office run as an individual or as the representative of a religious group? The answer is not as simple as it may seem. In the American political system, an individual is almost invariably identified with a particular group, usually a political party, but also racial, sexual, ideological, ethnic, religious and age groupings. In one sense, the individual is expected to "represent" these groups. On the other hand, a person in office is held solely responsible for his or her actions, whether representative or not. This is a distinction absolute separationists sometimes have difficulty making.

Transvaluing separation is that type in which it is one objective of government to secularize the political culture of the nation, that is, to reject as politically illegitimate the use of all religious symbols or the appeal to religious values and motivations in the political arena. It would deny all aid to religious organizations under any circumstances. In its extreme form, this type of separation denies to church organizations the right to legal existence, to form corporations, to hold property, to operate schools, businesses or charitable institutions, or to publish religious tracts. It denies to individuals the right to meet for religious discussion, to proselytize or to make a public display of their faith. The basic rationale of transvaluing separation is that religion is a private matter, not only in the sense of being nongovernmental, but in the sense of being something intensely, even exclusively personal. Even in a milder form, those who believe in transvaluing separation would emphatically reject any claim that a religiously identified person could hold political office. Unfortunately, even where transvaluing separation is public policy as in the Soviet Union, the language used is the more generic term, separation of Church and State.

Supportive separation acknowledges the need for structural separation, but within that framework takes as normative Justice Douglas's dictum that,

> We are a religious people whose institutions presuppose a Supreme Being. We guarantee the freedom to worship as one chooses. We make room for as wide a variety of beliefs and creeds as the spiritual needs of man deem necessary. We sponsor an attitude on the part of government that shows no partiality to any one group and that lets each flourish according to the zeal of its adherents and the appeals of its dogma. When the state encourages religious instruction or cooperates with religious authorities by adjusting the schedule of public events to sectarian needs, it follows the best of our traditions. For it then respects the religious nature of our people and accommodates the public service to their spiritual needs.[18]

Supportive separation is a more accurate name for what has traditionally been called "accommodation" of church and state. The linchpin of this type is that it would allow appropriate aids and privileges to all religions so long as there was no discrimination between religions. Accommodationists would have no constitutional objections to clergy in public office, although like many others, they may have theological, political, or moral objections.

Equal Separation rejects all political or legal privilege, coercion or disability based on religious affiliation, belief or practice, or lack thereof but guarantees to religiously motivated or affiliated individuals and organizations the same rights and privileges extended equally to other similarly situated individuals and groups. It is consciously based on an equal protection interpretation of the First Amendment and requires government neutrality both between religions and between religion and non- or even anti-religious beliefs, values, and practices. It provides protection without privilege.[19]

Unfortunately the equal separation concept is not palatable to either those who would put religion on a pedestal or those who relegate it to the sanctuary, the former because religious institutions and individuals could lose their privileges, the latter because religion would retain its protections. It is one thesis of this essay that the founders intended to form a nation based on the principles of structural and equal separation, and that any interpretations of the First Amendment which rely on absolute, transvaluing or supportive separation will lead to erroneous views of what religious groups or individuals may or may not do within the confines of the constitution. What the original founders (in this case, that means primarily the members of the First Congress who voted for the First Amendment and the members of the state legislatures who ratified it) intended is not the last word on the meaning of the religion clauses, but their intent is certainly a major component in determining the meaning of that clause. Certainly in dealing with clergy in public office the Supreme Court has followed an equal separation interpretation of the constitution.

CONCLUSION

In this brief essay I have addressed the constitutional issue of priests and sisters holding political office. Clearly, there are few constitutional rights more fully protected, and claims that the practice violates the separation of church and state are based on an erroneous understanding of that concept. This does not mean that exercising that right is good pastoral practice or good public relations. Anti-Catholicism is never far below the surface in American politics. That is an issue far more potent than any constitutional limitations.

NOTES

1. Sidney E. Ahlstrom, *A Religious History of the American People*, vol. I, p. 677-78.
2. C. Baldwin (ed), *Words of John Locke*, vol. 5, p. 21.

3. Francis Newton Thorpe, *The Federal and State Constitutions*, vol. 5, p.2637.

4. Ibid., p. 1374, emphasis added.

5. Anson Phelps Stokes, *Church and State in the United States*, p. 160.

6. G. Hunt (ed), *The Writings of James Madison*, vol. 5, p. 288.

7. P. Ford, *The Works of Jefferson*, vol. 9, p. 143.

8. Indeed there are numerous examples of ordained ministers and priests serving in the United States Congress. They include Rev. Manasseh Cutler (Congregationalist) 1801-1805; Rev. Gabriel Richard (Catholic) 1823-1825; Rev. Henry Augustus Muhlenberg (Lutheran) 1829-1839; Rev. Adam Clayton Powell (Baptist) 1945-1971; Mr. Elbert Thomas (Mormon) 1933-1951; Rev. Robert Drinan (Catholic) 1971-1980; and John Buchanan (Baptist) 1965-1980. Interestingly enough, both Richard and Drinan, the Catholics, were forced out by opposition from within the Catholic Church.

9. For those not versed in constitutional law, some explanation might be helpful. As originally written, the Bill of Rights limited only the national government. "Congress shall make no law . . . ." States could both establish religion and limit it at their discretion. (The last state to abolish its establishment of religion was Massachusetts in 1833.) However, the Supreme Court, beginning in 1925 began to apply the Bill of Rights, one phrase at a time, to state actions. The Court's basic argument for doing so was that the due process clause of the fourteenth amendment was meant to incorporate the various protections of the Bill of Rights. The free exercise clause was incorporated by the Court in *Cantwell v Connecticut* (1940), and the establishment clause was incorporated in *Everson v Board of Education* (1947). What that has meant is that the same standards which apply to the federal government now apply to the states.

10. Cn. 848, #4, 1976 Tenn. Pub. Acts.

11. Tennessee Constitution, Art. IX, No. 1.

12. *McDaniel v Paty* 435 U.S. 618 at 628-29.

13. Ibid. at 626.

14. More specifically, Stewart argued that the case, *Torcaso v Watkins* 367 U.S. 488 (1961), which struck down a Maryland requirement that a Notary public declare his belief in the existence of God, as violation of Article VI, was the controlling precedent.

15. Saul Padover, *The Complete Jefferson* (1943) pp. 518-519. (Emphasis added).

16. Leo Pfeffer, *Church, State and Freedom* (1967) p. 179. The quotation is from Jeremiah Black, *Essays and Speeches* (1885) p. 53. Inter-

estingly, Pfeffer wrote an *Amicus Curiae* brief in *McDaniel v Paty* supporting the right of clergy to run for public office!

17. 330 U.S. 1 at 182 (1947). Emphasis added.

18. *Zorach v Clausen* 343 U.S. 306 at 310 (1952).

19. Probably the best, although by no means perfect, example of equal separation is found in the treatment of religious groups on a par with other not-for-profit groups such as literary, scientific, fraternal and charitable organizations in section 501(c)3 of the Internal Revenue Code.

John Langan, SJ

POLITICS—GOOD, BAD, OR INDIFFERENT? A PHILOSOPHICAL ASSESSMENT

I. A QUESTION, AMERICAN AND UNIVERSAL

A great deal of current debate over the question of whether priests and religious should hold political office or should be actively and visibly involved in politics centers on the subject side of the question, that is, on the priests and religious themselves. The argument is most often about their experience and the effect of that experience on their character and vocation, or it is about their special responsibilities as officials of the church and members of religious communities, or it is about their distinctive mission and ministry as contrasted with that of the laity. These are all themes well worth reflection and discussion.

But in this paper I would like to focus on assessments of politics and the political dimension of life. These assessments may rest on philosophical or theological foundations, more or less clearly perceived; but they also depend on our experiences and beliefs about politics in this culture and this polity. For the question we are reflecting on in this volume is about the distribution of roles within complex, interlocking societies. Answering the question may push us back to deeper beliefs about human nature and destiny, about God and sin and salvation, about the nature of the state and the state of nature. This way of approaching the question opens up vast, indeed eternal perspectives, which are relevant and may even be decisive. But we also need to recall that the question about the political activity of priests and religious arises within a particular historical context within a particular culture. It concerns the legitimate scope of activity for Roman Catholic priests and religious in the United States of America in the period after 1960. This is the time when American Catholicism, with the election of John F. Kennedy in 1960, achieved full political acceptability and in which

Catholicism, both American and non-American, underwent extensive changes in the aftermath of Vatican II.

On the other hand, while the question we are considering in this collection of essays arises within an American and Catholic context, it also, because of the universalizing element that is so fundamental in our moral and legal reasoning, is bound up with many parallel questions which can be asked about other combinations of political and religious roles both within the American political system and within other political systems. Thus, negative answers about clerical or religious participation in politics in the United States are often thought to imply negative conclusions about similar participation in the politics of Nicaragua or Poland or the Philippines. The argument is also run in the reverse direction: if it is legitimate for priests to serve in the revolutionary government of Nicaragua, how can it not be legitimate for priests and religious to serve in the democratic legislatures of North America? It should be observed, however, that practical arguments of this general type fall far short of strict implication. For they involve large and disputable assumptions about "other things being equal," say, as between revolutionary movements and partisan politics or between the United States and Nicaragua. Even within a framework of universal principles such as the Code of Canon Law proposes to offer, cases need to be addressed on an individual basis which takes account of the diversity of particular situations. This, of course, is a point which Aristotle recognized long ago in his analysis of law and justice and which was extended by Aquinas in a notable argument about the essential incompleteness of legal systems. The parallel questions about other, comparable situations rarely deliver a knock out punch to the opponent; but they do serve two important functions. They extend and deepen our search for the rational basis (if any) for policy decisions, and they serve to remind us of other contexts which may influence or be influenced by the decisions taken in our own context.

In addition to the questions about other situations within the transnational reality that is contemporary Roman Catholicism, there are several other interesting sets of questions about the activity of religious persons in other political systems. The first set, the most unpredictable, and possibly the most perplexing in the short run, arises from perceived resemblances to very different political and religious systems, for instance, the political role of the mullahs in post-revolutionary Iran. Not much can be settled, but a lot of heat can be generated by comparing the Ayatollah Khomeini and Father Drinan as religious figures in politics. It is unwise to overlook the possibility that a visceral dislike for the one might be transferred to the other. People can be swayed in their judgments by parallels which are less than exact but which can be put forward with plausible rhetoric.

The second set of questions comes out of the prior historical development of the actual social context under consideraton, namely the United States. Should Father Gabriel Richard have served in Congress as a delegate for the territory of Michigan? Should U.S. Catholics have formed a political party or caucus of their own comparable to the Catholic parties of Germany and Italy? Were church authorities right to silence Father Coughlin? Should Catholic clergy and religious have been more or less concerned about opposing the U.S. war in Vietnam? Would altering any of these outcomes make any difference for the legitimacy of religious engagement in politics? The decisions actually taken in *our* past constitute a body of positive and negative precedents which can be endorsed or rejected. They serve as important orientation points for contemporary discussion; they partly determine the accepted boundaries of the various roles, they articulate some standard concerns such as not preaching politics from the pulpit, obeying one's hierarchical superior, protecting the interests and reputation of one's ethnic group or clients.

A third important set of questions, too often neglected in internal Catholic discussions, has to do with the results for other Christian churches of the political activity of their ministers. Assessments of the political-religious careers of Jesse Jackson, Martin Luther King, and members of Congress and other government officials who have been ministers or who have exercised religious authority in different church structures (such as John Danforth of Missouri, Robert Edgar of Pennsylvania, and Walter Fauntroy of the District of Columbia, in the present Congress or Ezra Taft Benson of Utah and John Foster Dulles of New York in the Eisenhower cabinet) does not settle matters within the quite different institutional and theological pattern of Roman Catholicism. But reflection on this different but parallel experience of Protestant America is valuable for understanding both the religious traditions and the differences in role-identification and social perception.

II. ONE QUESTION, MANY ACTIVITIES

Interesting as these questions are, they should not prevent us from turning our attention from the subject side of the question to the object side; from the religious personages themselves who may carry on a certain kind of activity to the activity that is being carried on. For it is obvious that an important aspect of resolving any dispute about whether priests or religious should do X is achieving clarity about what X is, why it is important, and how it should be evaluated. This does not require that we achieve the definitive truth about the nature of X or that such a truth even if we got it would settle the issue once and for all. For X may also be Y, and X may over time change in some ways that require us to alter our evaluation of it. This rather abstract and algebraic point can be seen more clearly if we consider some of the actual questions that can arise about possible combinations of activities.

First, should religious provide health care for the sick? Christian tradition has generally regarded this as both a good and praiseworthy thing to do, and religious institutes of various sorts (not only in the Catholic tradition) have been set up with this as a primary and distinctive task. But consider the further question: should religious go into business? Should there be Benedictine copying machines or Jesuit banks or Sacred Heart boutiques? Should there be Dominican stock-brokers or Mercy automobile dealers? (One can even imagine an argument that religious would be the best sales persons for used cars, since they would be more honest and more credible than other groups and since they would be providing inexpensive transportation for the needy.) By and large, church tradition has rejected these possibilities; not because the activities involved are inherently wrong, but mainly because they pose serious problems for the observance of religious poverty, both individually and collectively. But there have traditionally been exceptions for certain agricultural and food products, for items intended for ceremonial purposes, and for the internal needs of the religious community. But suppose that providing health care (doing X) is also at the same time entering into business (doing Y)? This gives rise to a new set of questions about what should be done, since church tradition and norms now point to contradictory conclusions, depending on whether running a hospital is to be seen as performing a corporal work of mercy or as conducting a business. The crucial point here is not to answer this new set of questions but to acknowledge that one activity may be described in a number of different ways and that this diversity of descriptions is closely linked with a diversity of assessments and policies.

Second, should religious continue to do a normally praiseworthy activity if important circumstances or conditions change and so produce a significant alteration in our assessment of the activity? For instance, it has been agreed that it is appropriate for religious to operate schools. It is also agreed that religious (like everyone else) may not do what is morally wrong and that the practice of racial discrimination is morally wrong. If we suppose that a school operated by religious, say in South Africa, comes under a government order to exclude black students, should the religious carry on the activity of operating the school? Or imagine a Catholic hospital that might be required by a change in the laws to provide abortion as a medical service. The point again is not to say what should be done but to indicate the possibility that our evaluation of an activity may need to change over time as a result of changed circumstances and that abstract acceptance of a certain kind of activity does not entail approval of it in all possible circumstances.

A final preliminary observation that needs to be made before we examine the main question of this essay arises naturally from a very common temptation that confronts all the participants in the current debate. That temptation is to try to settle the issue once and for all by a straightforward appeal to principle. This has the attraction of offering a basis for a definitive "yes" or "no" and thus avoiding explicit consideration of all the contextual factors that may have influenced a decision in a particular case. For just this reason it is likely to be especially attractive to those in authority who bear the burden of decision and who, when challenged to offer a public defense of what they have decided, find that they may not be free or competent to lay out the various relevant considerations. Appealing to a single principle for the resolution of complex cases may, in the pressures of the moment, be an understandable shortcut and may protect confidentiality and other important values. But when we shift the venue of discussion from the press conference to the seminar room, we can see two main reasons why the simple appeal to principle is inadequate one way or the other.

It is not possible to settle the complex issues of political participation and involvement by a purely moral judgment of the type found in traditional moral theology. Political action or participation is not one homogeneous kind of activity about which it makes sense to offer one comprehensive moral judgment of the type we can make about lying or taking another's property or taking innocent life. Participating in politics includes campaigning for office, making policy decisions, organizing support for programs and movements, exercising the powers of office. It includes actions that are performed by individuals and by groups, actions that may be defined and even constituted by law and actions that may be in defiance of law (which, we should recall, may itself be unjust). These different actions have positive and negative aspects to them, opportunities for good and evil. This range of activities, which is interwoven with some of the most important and characteristic human concerns, cannot be brought under one moral rubric which would enable us to assess all political activity as good or bad, right or wrong. This holds true even if we allow that a universal judgment about a certain type of action (e.g. taking another's property) may have some legitimate exceptions. Certain kinds of activities such as offering or taking bribes, which are primarily but not exclusively political, can indeed be condemned. But to use this judgment to show that Christians or religious may not engage in political life, one would need to show a strong connection between such proscribed activities and the holding of political office. This is unlikely to be the case in contemporary Western democracies. But it is worth recalling that certain societies have put morally or religiously unacceptable conditions on serving in political office, conditions which would make it impossible not merely for priests and religious but for Catholics or Christians or theists to hold political office. But whether we are thinking about the Roman demand for emperor worship or an oath recognizing the King of England as supreme head of the Church or the refusal of communist regimes to allow religious believers to hold positions of trust, the salient point is not that these are sound restrictions which indicate appropriate limits for the involvement of religious persons in politics, but that they are objectionable violations of human dignity and freedom aimed at either excluding certain classes of people from sharing in the rights and benefits of political life or at ensuring the domination of a particular ideology or system of religious belief.

III. COMPROMISE IN POLITICS

The situation is somewhat trickier when the connection between political office and the morally or religiously unacceptable actions is not a matter of explicit legal requirement but is instead a matter of common expectations and practices that no one defends publicly but that no one expects to see challenged or altered. Bribes, kickbacks, mingling of personal and official assets, the intentional overlooking of serious violations of the law, favoritism in awarding contracts, are all thought to be standard practice in certain corners of government, even in prosperous and highly developed societies. These practices, when they are carried on in parts of the Third World, are sometimes presented as evidence of cultural differences and as an argument for a relativistic approach. But this indulgent line can't apply in our own country, where such things are clearly regarded as both legally and ethically unacceptable. Sometimes there is merely an aura of corruption about a particular municipality or government agency or political campaign; but sometimes there can be a long and detailed history of criminal investigations and convictions. Shrewd observers may, in either situation, have good reason to think that a person could not hold a political office without engaging in or at least winking at various corrupt practices. In these circumstances, the point of encouraging a priest or religious to run for the office or to accept appointment to it may be to bring about a reform in the situation by bringing in a person who will not be affected by existing patterns of crime and corruption. One may well be sceptical about the ability of a priest or religious to accomplish reforms under such conditions. The priest or religious will encounter, as almost anyone would, considerable difficulties in finding ways of transforming a corrupt situation. For these ways must be effective in a world too often run by burly sinners and must not cancel or obscure the religious character of his or her motivation and objectives.

We often speak of the danger that a religiously-identified political figure would compromise his or her ideals. This is a misleading way of conceiving the task of religious approaches to political action. Compromise is no evil in a democratic and pluralistic society in which political actors have a great variety of motives and acknowledge different standards of judgment for their actions. Compromise in such a situation is both necessary and desirable as a mode of realizing (even if imperfectly) the common good in a way which respects the autonomy and dignity of other persons. Compromise has to be an essential element in a Christian realist understanding of political life. Acceptance of the necessity of compromise rescues a realistic Christian involvement in politics, whether by the clergy or the laity, from fanatical or utopian delusions. But compromise is not and cannot be a value in itself; and our experience gives us reason to be concerned over its negative aspects. It can involve a splitting of the difference between justice and injustice in a given situation; it can lead us to treat two poles of opinion or two sides of a dispute on an artificially equal basis; it can signal a comfortable acceptance of evils that really could be changed; it can mask or manifest weaknesses in both commitment and analysis. Whether compromise actually does these things in any particular case is not a matter that can be settled by a priori considerations. Rather, it requires a careful appraisal of the possibilities present in the situation and a measure of clear and humble self-knowledge and self-confidence.

There are, however, I would argue, three specific limits to compromise which Christians in politics should observe. The first of these is the most stringent. Christians should not enter into compromises which require them to be actively involved in doing evils which are not justifiable. Just war theory and significant elements in the Catholic moral tradition affirm that inflicting evils on other persons can at times be justified. Regrettably, there is no general limit which can be applied in a fashion which eliminates the need for a personal judgment about the justifiability of the evil in a given case. It may at times be necessary to allow others to do evils which they either do not recognize or which they are willing to inflict for the sake of other gains. Christians have to look both at the need for justification and at the limits of their power to prevent evil. Without undertaking to banish evil from the realm of political decisions, they are not free to do evils for which reasonable justification cannot be provided. This point has to be understood narrowly. Silence or non-resistance in the face of evils, cooperation with others who do or advocate evil things are not to be equated with the doing of unjustifiable evils. This is not to endorse a passive attitude of forbearance or a policy of civil cooperation for all cases. Some evils are so monstrous and so manifest that cooperation on other matters or silence are not adequate responses. But political life in the earthly city requires us to coexist in at least some imperfect social harmony with people who knowingly and willingly do wrong things and even while God's law, which is the norm of the heavenly city and the norm for our conduct as Christians, forbids us to do these evils ourselves or to approve their being done. The tensions of this situation affect not merely priests and religious but also Christians in general and indeed all women and men of good will. The real necessity that we are under to collaborate in a sinful society does not set any of us free from the demands of morality.

The second consideration that should limit compromise for morally concerned persons in public life is more variable and subjective. It has to do with the psychic burdens of compromise, which can include a sense of defeat, frustration, anger, regret, even revulsion. Even when a particular political compromise is not open to a decisive moral objection, it may stir up feelings which disrupt the peace and the sense of moral integrity of the persons involved. A person who enters political life for the sake of a cause or a moral value may have profound regrets at the imperfections and the costs of what he or she is able to accomplish. These regrets are likely to have a morally significant content and to be interwoven with moral feelings. Some sense of regret and anger is a justifiable and appropriate response to the pettiness and selfishness that shape so much of political life. Such an emotional response is something to be borne and to be worked out. Two dangers that can seriously harm the political actor are the loss of peace and satisfaction in the political struggle itself and the loss of the sense of personal integrity. These dangers are often not clearly seen by the individual, who can, however, usually benefit from the advice of friends.

The third limit to the practice of compromise in political life bears in a special way on priests and religious. Its applicability depends on the social context rather on the psyche of the political actor. It is the danger of scandal. The problem of scandal arises not merely from the doing of evil, but also from the appearance of evil. We do not want to limit our possibilities for creative and beneficial action by deferring to the prejudices of narrow-minded or censorious people. We do not want to worry about "what the neighbors will say," about all the possible negative inferences that people will draw about our actions, our agreements, even our silences. Political life, especially as it is conducted in the United States with its open culture and its independent media, subjects those who are actively involved in it, both to great pressure and to the possibility of pitiless exposure. Aside from blemishes on the record of one's previous conduct of personal affairs, there can often be political compromises which, for one reason or another, it is not feasible to explain or to justify in public even when they may have seemed justifiable to the person making the decision at the time. A political actor may not be able to distance himself or herself from the appearance of abetting or endorsing or subsidizing some evil. A serious argument can be made that even if some situations of scandal are in truth unavoidable, religious should not voluntarily expose themselves to a greater likelihood of such situations.

IV. A POSITIVE VIEW OF POLITICS

These reflections on compromise as a characteristic feature of political life, on the dangers it presents, and on the limits that should be put on it, have actually brought us to the main topic of this chapter, which is the bearing of fundamentally divergent evaluations of political life on the argument about whether priests and religious should seek and hold political office. There are four major positions that need to be considered. First, politics is an important, appropriate and good human activity, in which there are occasional moral failures. Second, politics is a corrupt and degrading activity, the offspring of conflict and greed and the source of oppression and deceit. Third, politics is inescapable so that a person has no real choice about whether or not to participate in political life, (though he or she may have some room for choice about the mode of participation). Fourth, politics is an indifferent activity, of itself, neither good nor bad, to be engaged in or abstained from according to one's circumstances and preferences.

To illustrate the first position, we can recall the principles and the aspirations of Catholicism at the time of Vatican II, particularly as these are presented in the encyclical of John XXIII, *Pacem in terris* (1963), and the Council's pastoral constitution on the church in the modern world, *Gaudium et spes* (1965). In this position participation in political life accords with human dignity and the social character of the human person. A political order which enables people to exercise their rights and duties actually contributes to their religious understanding and their practical life of faith. These are points that John XXIII clearly affirms:

"The dignity of the human person involves, moreover, the right to take an active part in public affairs and to contribute one's part to the common good of the citizens." (*Pacem in terris*, par. 26)

"Since men are social by nature, they are meant to live with others and to work for one another's welfare. Hence a well-ordered human society requires that men recognize and observe their mutual rights and duties. It also demands that each contribute generously to the establishment of a civic order in which rights and duties are progressively more sincerely and effectively acknowledged and fulfilled." (*Pacem in terris*, par. 31)

"When the relations of human society are expressed in terms of rights and duties, men become conscious of spiritual values and understand the meaning and significance of truth, justice, charity, and freedom. Moreover, when moved by such concerns, they are brought to a better knowledge of the true God, who is personal and transcendent." (*Pacem in terris*, par. 45)

In a broadly similar fashion, Vatican II offers a friendly and favorable appraisal of Christian involvement in the tasks of the modern world, including its political life: "All that men do to obtain greater justice, wider brotherhood, and a more humane ordering of social relationships has greater worth than technical advances." (*Gaudium et spes*, par. 35)

"Earthly progress must be carefully distinguished from the growth of Christ's kingdom. Nevertheless, to the extent that the former can contribute to the better ordering of human society, it is of vital concern to the kingdom of God." (*Gaudium et spes*, par. 39)

"They are mistaken who, knowing that we have here no abiding city but seek one that is to come, think that they may therefore shirk their earthly responsibilities." (*Gaudium et spes*, par. 43)

The Council affirms the classical Catholic teaching that "the political community and public authority are based on human nature and hence belong to an order of things divinely foreordained" (par. 74), while acknowledging that there is no definitive religious or philosophical resolution to disputes about the right form of government. The Council goes on to encourage political activity in what has to be conceived of as some form of constitutional democracy when it says: "It is in full accord with human nature that juridical-political structures should with ever better success and without any discrimination, afford all their citizens the chance to participate freely and actively in establishing the constitutional bases of a political community, governing the state, determining the scope and purpose of various institutions, and choosing leaders." (*Gaudium et spes*, par. 75) The council speaks of "a right and duty to vote freely in the interest of advancing the common good" and of "the special and personal vocation" of all Christians in the political community. At the same time it recognizes the place of "legitimate but conflicting views" about temporal affairs. It both encourages political parties to "foster whatever they judge necessary for the common good" and warns against preferring partisan advantage to the common good (par. 75).

These two fundamental documents of contemporary Catholicism strongly affirm the moral worth of the political community. This affirmation has roots both in the Aristotelian and Thomistic appraisal of political life as a natural aspect of human fulfillment and in the generally positive experience of the church in preaching the gospel and ministering to its members in constitutional democracies. These societies encourage an active role for citizens, protect rights of freedom of conscience and expression, and are prepared to allow non-violent forms of social and political conflict to come to the surface. Because of the generality so characteristic of church statements on political matters and because of the general desire of the leaders of the council to shed the old image of censorious triumphalism and defensiveness in the church's relations with the world, there is less of a tendency to dwell on the warts on the face of the modern world than would be appropriate in a realistic and critical assessment of modern society. Neither John XXIII nor Vatican II was naively ignorant of the serious problems confronting the world in the early 60's, as the council's treatment of the "supreme crisis" presented by issues of peace and war in the nuclear age makes manifest. But in those more optimistic days the church wished to present itself in the vanguard of the party of hope and to insist on the "close links between earthly affairs and those aspects of man's condition which transcend this world". (*Gaudium et spes*, par. 76) The modern world had been fashioned to a large extent in defiance of the church's authority, and it was profoundly important for the church to express its approval of the possibilities for Christian expression and action that are present in this world, among which the moral choices involved in a free political life are particularly significant. A detailed denunciation of the dangers and evils of political life was inappropriate for the wider pastoral task. In fact, the church wishes to stress the beneficial prospects for independent collaboration. So the council writes:

"In their proper sphere, the political community and the church are mutually independent and self-governing. Yet, by a different title, each serves the personal and social vocation of the same human beings. This service can be more effectively rendered for the good of all, if each works better for wholesome mutual cooperation, depending on the circumstances of time and place." (*Gaudium et spes*, par. 76)

Both the pope and the Council see the political realm as not merely one of opportunities to contribute to the good, but also as a realm of obligation, marked by duties as well as by rights (as we have already seen in the Council's statement about voting). Thus the Council speaks of the political vocation of Christians as requiring "that they give conspicuous example of devotion to the sense of duty and of service to the advancement of the common good." (*Gaudium et spes*, par. 75) Serving in political office, of course, is not normally something that falls within the scope of moral obligation. But the Council echoes Pius XII in saying: "Let those who are suited for it, or can become so, prepare themselves for the difficult but most honorable art of politics. . . . Let them devote themselves to the welfare of all sincerely and fairly indeed with charity and political courage." (*Gaudium et spes*, par. 75)

In reflecting on the implications of this strongly favorable assessment of the moral and religious possibilities of democratic political life, we should not forget what the Council says elsewhere in the same document about the separate responsibilities of laity, clergy, and bishops. One of the particular concerns of the Council is, in fact, to affirm the independent competence of the laity and to set them free from detailed political tutelage and from the crippling effects of clerical domination. So the Council says:

"Secular duties and activities belong properly although not exclusively to laymen. . . .Laymen should also know that it

is generally the function of the well-formed Christian conscience to see that the divine law is inscribed in the life of
the earthly city: From priests they may look for spiritual
light and nourishment. Let the layman not imagine that his
pastors are always such experts that to every problem which
arises, however complicated, they can readily give him a
concrete solution, or even that such is their mission. Rather,
enlightened by Christian wisdom and giving close attention
to the teaching authority of the Church, let the layman take
on his own distinctive role." (*Gaudium et spes*, par. 43).

In an advanced industrial society, we may be inclined to regard
the acknowledgment of the inability of the clergy to solve complex secular problems as a concession to the obvious. But we should bear in
mind that clericalism in politics is likely to be a recurring temptation
especially in those societies where the body of persons trained in secular social disciplines and the practices of modern economics is either
very small or is restricted in its freedom to apply its skills to the shaping
of society (e.g., Nicaragua or Poland). In our own society some persons
involved in political disputes try to resolve them by appeals to religious
authority. The secularizing of the values and attitudes of priests and
religious is not the only danger to be feared when they enter the political arena; imparting an inappropriately clerical or religious tinge to
what should be a religiously neutral or secular activity has historically
been an equally serious danger.

So the council should not be read as endorsing a general incorporation by Christians of the world into a new kingdom run on religious principles. But the positive evaluation the Council gives of the
world and of the possibilities of political action, its willingness to use
the language of vocation and to stress the value of cooperation between church and political order, and the readiness of both John
XXIII and the Council to affirm the human rights of all persons,
among which they clearly include rights of political expression and
participation all combine to foster the aspiration that some priests and
religious have had to enter into political life as active exponents of
Christian values. This, of course, is not the explicit teaching or advice
of the Council. But it is important to recognize that much of what Vatican II said in *Gaudium et spes* could lead priests and religious to look
on political action and political office as a form or an extension of their
religious ministry. If all people have rights and duties of political participation, and if political action creates important possibilities for the
realization of fundamental moral and religious values, then there has

to be a presumption that priests and religious have a right to enter into political life and may even at times have a duty to do so. Clearly, this is not the last word on the matter. But only if we see that this view is a plausible way of developing the position of Vatican II, can we understand the readiness of some highly dedicated priests and religious to see their political careers in religious terms as well as the nature of the subsequent conflict about whether they were right in doing so. Their move into politics has to be seen both as crossing a well-established boundary and as a plausible extension of the values and attitudes of Vatican II, which in its turn was expressing some contemporary implications of the positive appraisal of political participation given by Aristotle and Aquinas as well as by modern democratic theorists.

V. A NEGATIVE VIEW OF POLITICS

This is far from being the only fundamental appraisal of political life that has been offered by reflective observers and concerned Christians. Whether one looks at the intrigue of the Nixon White House or the billing practices of defense contractors, at the fall of Saigon or the covert operations on the borders of Nicaragua, at the deceptions used by law enforcement agencies or the hollow promises of politicians seeking election, one finds abundant evidence for the view that political life, far from being a forum for the exercise of civic virtue, is really an arena for factional combat and a marketplace where favors are for sale and justice is denied to those who are unable to pay for it. One can regard these things as temporary aberrations in American society or as sicknesses in the public body which require more or less drastic treatment. But the continuing power of self-interest and the recurrent lack of vision that, as Reinhold Niebuhr insisted, affect social groups even more decisively than they confine individuals, do not seem to be the kinds of things that will yield to revolutionary transformations, much less to modest measures of reform. One can grant that the constitutional democracy of the United States with its federal system of checks and balances and its independent judiciary avoids the worst abuses of political power and that it is capable of doing some wise and generous things along with many necessary things which present no great moral difficulty even to a sensitive conscience. But at the same time one can believe that the corrupting effects of power are so pervasive that persons with a primary responsibility to the church should not subject themselves to such temptations and pressures.

This line of reflection can serve as a sobering corrective to some of the more naive and optimistic forms of collaboration with the world which emerged after Vatican II. It can remind us of unpalatable truths whose bitterness we often attempt to conceal with soothing ideological narcotics. It can enable us to deal with the disappointment of revolutionary expectations and with the unexpected collapse of established pillars of righteousness. It can be an astringent and invigorating restorative after periods of utopian naivete or torpid conformity. It can draw upon an ever renewed supply of episodes of fraud, oppression, selfishness, and cruelty for contemporary confirmation. At the same time it looks back to Scripture and to the line of realistic political theorists from Thucydides, Tacitus, and Machiavelli onwards for deeper patterns of interpretation.

But this negative view of political life runs into four major difficulties when it is asserted in isolation as the truth about politics. First, it suffers from the logical difficulty that attends virtually any sweeping generalization, namely, the problem of making a fallacious move from undeniable instances of evil in political life to a universal conclusion about political life as such. Episodes of corruption, even periods of pervasive corruption, do not tell the whole story. Second, when the view is stated in a very strong form, it establishes more than its users normally want to claim. For if the evils of political life are so great and so inescapable, then the church should forbid the laity as well as clergy and religious to engage in politics. Third, if there is some significant possibility of reducing or alleviating the evils of political life, then adopting a totally pessimistic view is defeatist and encourages passivity and irresponsibility in the face of avoidable evils. Indeed, the more serious and harmful the evils of political life are, the more urgent is the need to respond to them in a way that overcomes evil with good. This point can be seen as a moral difficulty, a failure to struggle against evil when it is really possible to do so. But it may also be connected with a restricted view of the effectiveness of Christ's redemption of humanity in the task of transforming the world. Fourth, the pessimistic view may involve an implicit comparison with a social realm which is free from the contending passions and interests of political life. This realm may be monastic, or it may be taken to be the church as a whole. Even a cursory reading of church history should dispel the illusion that a religious environment and religious commitment preclude the possibilities of political temptations and evil. These can arise in the course of efforts to gain control of the religious institution itself or as part of an effort to use the religious institution to alter or to draw benefits from the larger political world. The likelihood, the extent, the heinousness of these evils varied with the church's proximity to political power. But even when the church was a persecuted or despised minority, there could be ferocious factionalism, painful conflicts of loyalties, and abuses of authority. A praiseworthy desire to keep the church from excessive political entanglement and from the moral dangers so commonly found in the political realm should not blind us to the presence of similar dangers and temptations that are inescapably present in the internal workings of the church.

For these four reasons as well as because of its incompatibility with the position adopted by Vatican II and John XXIII, the starkly negative appraisal of political life should not be adopted. But neither should it be forgotten, for it derives its plausibility from events which are only too real and from considerations which are a necessary part of a mature political awareness.

VI. THE INEVITABILITY OF POLITICS

Comparison of the goods and evils in political life seems to be undercut in a particularly drastic way if one takes the view that political involvement is inevitable. In this view, we can no more remove ourselves from political conflict and its moral challenges than fish can leap out of the ocean and survive. We are tied to a political system by our habits of consumption, by our compliance with laws, by our avoidance of conflict, by our membership in certain classes and groups. In varying degrees, according to this line of thought, we are all implicated in the follies and crimes of those who govern us. The task is not to avoid moral condemnation by withdrawal from political life and by passive avoidance of ambiguous action. Rather, our duty is to bring about a new and better order of things. In one of the favored maxims of this approach, "not to decide is to decide." Putting the matter off, refusing to have an opinion, letting abuses go on when one could intervene are all so many votes in favor of the existing system. Our social life is inescapably political; and we cannot expect to insulate or protect the church from that, whether priests and religious seek political office or not. Even the sacral activities of the church have a political dimension to them. Historically, they have inculcated patience, submission and acceptance of authority; they have dulled impulses to radical change and our readiness to hear the demands of the Lord for peace and for justice on behalf of the poor and the oppressed.

All this may sound like echoes of the discordant fusion of bourgeois radicalism, vulgar Marxism, and pop existentialism which

formed the shifting and unstable ideological tonality of academic protest in the late '60's and early '70's and which has continued to be
sounded in the churches since then. In one sense, it assimilates our
political orientation to our fundamental religious condition of belief
or unbelief, both as this has been interpreted by William James in his
view of religious faith as a forced option and as it has been presented
in certain Scriptural texts, particularly the saying of Christ in Lk.
11:23—"He who is not with me is against me." For this reason, the position that political involvement is inevitable both for the church and
for its individual members has the attraction of a familiar pattern of
thought and runs the risk of seeming to invest our political stance with
a false ultimacy. This position also exhibits a wobbling between liberty
and determinism which is only too characteristic of moralistic forms of
Marxism which attempt to combine large-scale historical inevitability
and an affirmation of the crucial importance of individual conversion
and commitment.

Banal and vulnerable as much of this line of argument has become, it can serve to remind us of several important considerations.

First, the church and its members are often not free to pick or
choose the form and content of their political involvements. A crisis in
the political community may very well present religious persons and
groups with a forced option. Sometimes the crisis can be massive and
all-absorbing, as in the rise and suppression of Solidarity in Poland or
in the civil wars in Nicaragua and El Salvador or in the aftermath of
the Pinochet coup in Chile. On a smaller scale, the presence of a Salvadoran refugee in the sanctuary, the burning of a cross in the neighborhood, the closing of a local factory, the establishment of an
abortion clinic may impel congregations or church members or leaders
to take politically significant stands. These actions are likely to have the
incompleteness, the partiality that are inherent in particular actions.
They are responses to need or to evil present in situations, sometimes
in acute form. Political action is often not a matter of applying a principle or an ideology, or of optional activity. While choice in voting or
in executive, legislative, judicial, and regulatory decision making is a
central feature of political life, the actors in political conflict are usually
not able to choose the ground on which they will struggle, nor are they
able to redefine at will the terms or the context of their struggle. There
are indeed forced options in political life. But in ordinary circumstances the decision to participate in political life by seeking or holding
political office is not one of them. Nor should it be. In our culture this
decision is normally a personal matter. It is as a step in the person's
career or life plan and it is an expression of personal inclinations and

aspirations. In a religious context, the decision to seek or hold political office is often spoken of as an extension of the person's previous work and of the value commitments expressed in the religious or priestly role or in the language of personal discernment and search.

Second, this line of argument on the inevitability of political involvement draws part of its plausibility and importance from the fact that in any given society the church has a history and a social location which are not alterable at will and which can have very important political implications. These do not always fall into one pattern, nor are they necessarily fixed forever. Thus, the intertwining of the work of the church with the objectives of colonial administration in French, Spanish, and Portuguese colonies creates a different matrix for the working out of the social demands of Christian faith than does the ministry of the church to immigrants in a society that was simultaneously pluralistic and racist such as the late nineteenth century United States. The tensions between any given polity with its culture and its unresolved problems and the mission of the church to proclaim the values of the Gospel and to maintain a presence in an often hostile world will in many cases produce politically significant conflict. The religious aspects of the church's mission cannot be neatly separated from more partisan concerns, for instance when the church is linked with immigrant groups or racial minorities that are regarded with suspicion or hostility. Totalitarian regimes often define membership or active participation in the church as itself a politically significant act. So even a minimalist interpretation of the social mission of the church cannot escape this problem altogether. Nor is it possible or appropriate to handle political conflicts or the political implications of internal church decisions on doctrine and discipline by pretending that they do not exist or by holding that because such consequences are not deliberately or clearly intended they are therefore trivial. The church, like the secular intelligentsia and the media and the academy, needs to ask itself critical questions about the possibility of ideological taint in its presentation of human and evangelical values, even while it rejects reductionist views which would see in every presentation of values and in every program for the realization of values in society merely an extension of the claims of personal or class interest. The social location and the historical direction of a particular local or national church need to be grasped as centrally important facts about that church, facts which cannot be transcended in a voluntaristic fashion but which must be critically examined and taken as a point of departure (positive or negative) for action. Church policies, even those calling for abstention from various kinds of political involvement, cannot themselves be offered as totally devoid of political content. This point is compatible with our recognizing that particular decisions by church leaders constitute a sincere and earnest effort to keep a distance between the church and the arena of political combat or to lower the church's political profile.

Third, given the political character of many of the church's positions and policies, the seeking or holding of political office by individual members of the church, even those whose state of life involves a close identification with the church and some share in pastoral responsibility, should be understood in the context of the church's entire range of political involvements. The holding of political office by priests and religious is neither a totally independent question from the church's general political stance nor, on the other hand, should it be decisive for that stance. For Father A or Sister B to hold political office as the candidate or appointee of a party should not be interpreted as commitment of the church to the views of either the individual or the party. It should not be thought that forbidding priests and religious to hold political office effectively cancels the political involvement of the church or that allowing them to hold political office would enable them to articulate the whole range of the church's social concern in a particular time and place. The possibility that priests and religious holding public office would function as the effective shapers of the church's political stance is presumably one reason why Pope John Paul II and the American Catholic bishops are not keen to have priests and religious serving as independent political actors.

VII. AN ANSWER

The pessimistic view of political life can be used as one factor leading us in the direction of the conclusion that participating in political life is neither good nor bad in itself but is essentially indifferent. This allows for particular political acts and roles to be assessed on an individual basis, which recognizes the diversity of social and cultural contexts. It also allows ecclesiastical authorities the leeway to forbid priests and religious to serve in political office and to allow for occasional exceptions, a combination of possibilities which is not easy to reconcile with either the optimistic or the pessimistic views in their strongest form. It allows priests and religious to think about the pursuit and holding of political office as neither a call amounting in some cases to an obligation nor a fall from grace into a world that is beyond redemption. This middle position gives up the strong sense of political life contributing to human fulfillment and moral growth which one finds in Vatican II and in celebrations of the Aristotelian ideal of citizenship, and which is so prominent in the optimistic view. It also gives up the acute sense of moral danger which is commonly associated with the negative view. It seems to be a *juste milieu*; an unexciting resting place in the middle of the argument. But it becomes a bland and unilluminating compromise position if it simply displaces the first two positions which insist more vehemently on the goods and on the evils that are to be found in political life. The middle position cannot be taken as obviously true without robbing the debate of all point; it is to be reaffirmed only after the strengths and weaknesses of the other positions are explored and tested. For the character of political life is such that the permanent renunciation of participation in it would leave us truncated in our social humanity and in our response to the needs and challenges of others and that careless engagement in it can expose us to unfaithfulness, to self-centered careerism, and to a misuse of the church and its authority for partisan or personal ends.

If something like this view is correct, we need to keep three points in mind. First, in holding that various forms of active involvement in politics are indifferent, we are pointing to a balance of possibilities for good and evil; we are not asserting the triviality or the lack of value of political activity. The balance of goods and evils in undertaking various forms of political activity and specifically in pursuing and holding political office is not decisively set in one direction or the other in a way that permanently settles the general issue. This allows for the matter ceasing to be indifferent when we move to the level of particular cases; that is, when we can reflect on the extent and the likelihood of goods and evils that can result from an individual's decision in a given social and historical context. Second, even before we get to the level of particular cases, it is possible to discern certain historical trends or elements of social structure which are likely to have a decisive effect on the balance. For instance, there is probably no one who would defend clerical participation in the Nazi-sponsored government of Slovakia during World War II. The enormity of the evils in which that government was involved as a tool of the Nazis, was not simply the result of particular wrong decisions by individuals but could have been anticipated by anyone who understood the character and aspirations of the Nazi regime. On the other hand, there can be times when the active involvement of the clergy in politics offers the prospect of stability and improvement for groups and causes that they represent without jeopardizing fundamental moral and religious values. The political service of Gabriel Richard in the Michigan territory, the political clout of immigrant pastors in the United States, Don Luigi Sturzo's organization of the Popular Party in pre-Fascist Italy, fit this pattern, a pattern with which the priests who have been serving in the Nicaraguan government would like to identify themselves. The presence and the variability of such historical and structural factors is a major reason why we should not expect to arrive at a resolution of the question of active participation by priests and religious in the exercise of political power which will hold for cultures and societies of all times. The third point that needs attention is the connection between indifference and liberty. In traditional moral theology, what was indifferent was taken to fall within the realm of freedom and so neither to be forbidden nor commanded (except, of course, as the matter became determined by specific circumstances). It is also obvious that the obedience of religious to their superiors and of priests to their bishops is not restricted to doing what is morally obligatory and to refraining from doing what is morally wrong but extends to many matters which are in themselves indifferent. At this point the locus of the argument must shift from assessments of the worth and moral character of political activity to a theology and discipline of authority and obedience within the church. The practical side of that theology should recognize the goods to be achieved in and through the various forms of political participation, their contribution to the development of free persons, and the worth of political and moral community. At the same time it should include a recognition of the morally imperfect character of most political activity and of the temptations that the exercise of political power brings with it. It also has to recognize the need in our time to protect the church's commitment to give an open and honest public witness to moral and religious values. This witness can be badly damaged by factionalism and by struggles for power. There is also a need to protect the integrity and fidelity of the person who has freely undertaken to devote his or her life primarily to the service of the church. There is here what I would call a kind of ecclesial jealousy, which may not be totally unlike the ambivalence or even disapproval which one spouse feels for another spouse's political career. This "jealousy" needs critical scrutiny, since it can sometimes take petty and shortsighted forms; but it is an important indicator about possible threats to the integrity and clarity of a deep commitment. The presence of these diverse and conflicting considerations suggests the need for a resolution of the problem which would not invoke a single decisive principle but which would balance distinct values in a flexible and discreet way, which is sensitive both to the aspirations and needs of individuals who may be considering the possibility of political office and to the social and ecclesial contexts within which the decision is to be made.

My personal surmise is that with rare exceptions the balance of considerations would be against priests and religious seeking and holding public office.

Joseph A. Komonchak

CLERGY, LAITY, AND THE CHURCH'S MISSION IN THE WORLD*

Since he became Pope, John Paul II has made the Church's right to promote social justice and peace a prominent part of his ministry and message. The social, political, and economic conditions of the many countries he has visited have regularly been brought under the judgment of the Christian gospel. But in his many addresses the Pope has also warned several times of the danger of confusing the respective roles of the clergy, religious, and laity with regard to the Church's social mission. The Pope's speeches in Mexico in 1979 are typical. He reminded the bishops at Puebla that, according to the council, "secular duties and activities belong properly, although not exclusively, to laymen." He went on:

> It is necessary to avoid supplanting the laity, and to study seriously just when certain ways of substituting for them retain their *raison d'etre*. Is it not the laity who are called, by virtue of their vocation in the Church, to make their contribution in the political and economic areas, and to be effectively present in the safeguarding and advancing of human rights?[1]

Similar remarks were addressed to priests:

> You are not social directors, political leaders or functionaries of a temporal power. So I repeat to you: Let us not

*This essay is a slightly revised and shortened version of an article that first appeared in *The Jurist*, 41 (1981), 422–47, and in *Official Ministry in a New Age,* ed. J.H. Provost (Washington, D.C.: CLSA, 1981), 168–93.

149

pretend to serve the gospel if we try to "dilute" our charism
through an exaggerated interest in the broad field of temporal problems. . . . Do not forget that temporal leadership
can easily become a source of division, while the priest
should be a sign and factor of unity, of brotherhood. The
secular functions are the proper field of action of the laity,
who ought to perfect temporal matters with a Christian
spirit.[2]

Pope John Paul has repeated these positions on several occasions
since 1979[3] and he has taken steps to discourage and ban direct political activity by priests and religious, the best known cases being those
of Jesuit Fr. Robert Drinan, the priests holding government positions
in Nicaragua, three Sisters of Mercy—Agnes Mary Mansour, Elizabeth
Morancy, and Arlene Violet—as well as a priest in the Canadian Parliament, Fr. Robert Ogle. The Pope's motivation for these disciplinary
interventions is apparently complex, aimed at avoiding several dangers: the possibility of scandal involved in the support of controversial
legislation or public policies; the confusion of Christian principles of
social action with political ideologies and their reduction to political
programs; the compromising of the unifying role of the priest and the
loss to both the Church and world of the witness to the transcendent
given by religious. He does not entirely preclude the possibility of
clergy and religious engaging in social and political activities; but it is
clear that for him these activities are typically the role of the laity.
    Several issues are involved. First, there is the canonical and the-
ological distinction between clergy and laity. Second, there are the customary assumptions about their respective roles, which need not be
what the canonical and theological definitions would lead one to expect. Third, there is the Church-world relationship as defined theologically. And, finally, there is the Church-world relationship as in fact
realized in the remote and proximate past and in the contemporary
situation. This essay will address these issues in the course of an ex-
position and critique of Vatican II's teaching on the laity and on the
Church's mission in the world.

VATICAN II ON THE LAITY

    Two different approaches to the clergy-laity distinction and re-
lationship are visible in the conciliar documents. The first of these is

canonical, reflecting "the divine and hierarchical structure of the Church" (LG 43). From this perspective there is a twofold differentiation among the members of the Church, that between the ordained clergy and all others. Thus, the religious life is not "an intermediate state between the clerical and lay condition; rather some Christians from both groups are called by God to enjoy a special gift of grace in the life of the Church" (LG 43). Canonically and hierarchically, then, there are only two conditions of Christian life, the clerical and the lay.

A second approach is visible when the Council goes on to say of the religious state that, "while it does not enter into the hierarchical structure of the Church, it belongs undeniably to her life and holiness" (LG 44).[4] The concrete self-realization of the Church is not adequately described solely in terms of its hierarchical differentiation. The neat twofold distinction is disturbed by the presence of religious who may be either clergy or laity in the canonical sense.

But there is a further complication when the life of all three groups, clergy, religious, and laity, is looked at more concretely. Now again there is a twofold differentiation, but now it is between clergy and religious on the one hand and the laity on the other. This distinction appears in *Lumen Gentium* 31, where the Council explained at length what it understood by the term, "the laity."[5]

The term is first explained by means of a negative qualification: "The term 'the laity' is here understood to mean all the faithful except the members of a holy order or of a religious state approved by the Church." This is immediately followed by a positive description: the laity are "the faithful who, incorporated into Christ by baptism, established in the People of God, and made in their own way sharers in the priestly, prophetical, and kingly office of Christ, exercise their own role in the mission of the whole Christian people in the Church and in the world." While this description is a fine statement of the dignity and responsibility of all Christians, laity included, it also clearly applies equally well to the clergy and religious. It was necessary, then for the council to state more precisely the distinctive character of the laity:

> A secular character is proper and peculiar to the laity. For members of a sacred order, although they can sometimes engage in secular affairs, even by practicing a secular profession, still by reason of their particular vocation are principally and expressly ordained to a sacred ministry. At the same time, religious by their state give outstanding and striking witness that the world cannot be transfigured and offered to God without the spirit of the beatitudes. As for

the laity, it is their proper vocation to seek the Kingdom of God by engaging in temporal affairs and ordering them according to God's will. They live in the world, that is, they are engaged in each and every work and business of the earth and in the ordinary circumstances of social and family life which provide, as it were, the texture of their existence. There, in the world, they are called by God so that, led by the spirit of the gospel as they carry out their role, they may, like a leaven, contribute to the sanctification of the world as if from within and thus, resplendent especially by the witness of their life, by faith, hope and love, they may manifest Christ to others. It belongs to the laity in a peculiar way to illuminate and to order all temporal things, with which they are so closely associated, in such a way that they may be realized and grow according to Christ and may be for the glory of the Creator and Redeemer (LG 31).

This secular charter of the lay Christian life is presupposed in the remainder of this chapter where the council explains how the laity have roles in the twofold task of establishing and building up the Church and of ordering the world according to God's will. So, for example, the lay apostolate is "a participation in the very saving mission of the Church," and it is their "special vocation . . . to make the Church present in those places and situations in which only through them can the Church be the salt of the earth" (LG 33). The laity exercise their share in Christ's threefold office in the ordinary circumstances of the world, where in fact it is they who have "the principal role" in bringing the world to its goal in justice, love and peace (LG 36).

This teaching is echoed in the Decree on the Apostolate of the Laity, which beings with a programmatic statement:

In the Church there is a diversity of ministry but a unity of mission. To the apostles and their successors Christ entrusted the office of teaching, sanctifying and governing in his name and by his power. But the laity, made sharers in Christ's priestly, prophetical, and kingly office, carry out their roles in the mission of the whole People of God in the Church and in the world. In reality, they exercise their apostolate by their work for the evangelization and sanctification of people and by their efforts to make the spirit of the gospel permeate and perfect the temporal order, so that their efforts in this area may bear clear witness to Christ and serve the salvation of people. But, since it is proper to the lay state that they lead their lives in the midst of the world and of secular affairs, laypeople are called by God in their Christian fervor to exercise their apostolate as a leaven in the world (AA 2).

Chapter II of this Decree, which is devoted to the objectives of the lay apostolate, begins by distinguishing two goals of Christ's redemption and of the Church's mission: salvation and the renewal of the whole temporal order (AA 5). The next two paragraphs vindicate the right of the laity to participate in this twofold purpose. The task of evangelization and sanctification, while "committed in a special way to the clergy," also is borne by the laity (AA 6). The whole Church is to work to renew the world, with pastors offering the principles and moral and spiritual assistance.

As for the laity, they have the proper responsibility to take on the restoration of the temporal order and, guided by the light of the gospel and the mind of the Church and prompted by Christian love, to act within that order directly and definitely. As citizens among other citizens, they cooperate with their specific competence and by their own responsibility; everywhere and always they are to seek the justice of the Kingdom of God (AA7).

Later, the Decree states that "the apostolate in the social environment, that is, the effort to inform with the Christian spirit the mentality and behavior, laws and structures of the community in which one lives, is so much the duty and responsibility of the laity that it can never be properly fulfilled by others" (AA 13).

These descriptions of the laity's proper role in secular affairs should be seen against the background of the three basic concerns of these two conciliar documents.[6] The first was to vindicate the laity's right to share in the building up of the church and in its central saving mission. They were to be shown to be more than the passive objects of the clergy's ministrations.

The second concern was to clarify the nature and basis of the lay apostolate. The council asserted the sacramental and charismatic basis of that role. Christians were deputed by God himself, in virtue of their baptismal incorporation into Christ, to carry out their own role in the Church. Several possible types of relationship with the hierarchy were envisaged, of which Catholic Action and its "mandate" is only the strictest.[7] Essentially, a genuine initiative and autonomy was granted the lay apostolate.

Thirdly, the council wished to affirm the truly Christian and ecclesial character of the laity's daily secular activity. Laypeople are to act in the world as Christians; it is as workers, as married, as parents, that they serve Christ, and this activity, prior to any official ecclesiastical authorization, constitutes their ecclesial role. In turn, this involvement in the world grounds their contribution to the self-constitution of the Church. In the world they are to act as Christians. In the Church they are to speak and act as *laypeople*; i.e., as persons whose secular involvement itself qualifies them to make a unique and irreplaceable contribution to the Church. As Schillebeeckx puts it:

> The layman's Christian relationship with the world colours his whole (active) being as a Christian—his life of prayer, his forms of faith, love and hope, his contribution as a non-office-bearer to the primary, religious mission of the Church and even his specifically lay collaboration with the hierarchy in their apostolate (either in an organized form or not).[8]

On the whole, then, the council sought to establish the Christian and ecclesial significance of the everyday life of the layperson as in itself a real share in Christ's and the Church's mission and to establish also that the Church itself, in its primary task of self-realization, needs from the laity precisely those insights, perceptions, orientations, which only the life in the world makes likely or even possible.[9]

Before a theological critique of the council's statement on the laity can be offered, it is necessary to examine what precisely the council intented to do in the fundamental paragraph (LG31) in which it explained the term "laity." In the *Relatio* which introduced Chapter IV of *Lumen Gentium*, the council fathers were asked to note that "this chapter does not offer an '*ontological*' *definition* of the layperson, but rather a '*typological*' *description*," which was only to be taken "in the context of the matter and purpose of this schema."[10] A similar explanation introduced paragraph 31:

> The council does not intend to give a definition that would settle discussions in the schools, as, for example, whether religious and, *a fortiori*, members of a secular institute are to be considered laypersons and in what sense. Furthermore, the council is not proposing an "ontological"

definition of the layperson, but rather a "typological" description.[11]

The statements on the secular character of the laity simply offered "a *typology of the layperson* in the world, as compared with clerics and religious."[12]

Because these clarifications of the council's intent are not always kept in mind in discussions since the council about clergy and laity, it is worthwhile pointing up some of their features. First, the council does not proceed from a definition of the "essence" of the lay condition (I take this to be what an "ontological" definition might offer). Instead, the council presents a "typological description." This appears to be a terminological innovation in church documents, and the *Relator* offered no help in explaining it. We are, it is clear, offered a description, and, it seems, a description of a type, that is, of what typifies a layperson's situation and activity. A layperson typically is married, has a job, lives in the world, etc.

Second, the source of this typification is clearly not metaphysical. It also seems not to be theological, at least not in the sense of some biblically, traditionally, or dogmatically required notion of the layperson. Not only does such a notion not exist, but the *Relator* made it clear that the text offered only a description and one which was not intended to settle disputed theological points, as, for example, whether the theological notion of a layperson coincides with the canonical. It remains, then, that the council offered simply a description that reflects typical differentiations among the members of the Church that have become customary. As such, it would seem the description need not necessarily apply to every previous age of the Church nor be considered to preclude future developments which might alter the customary typical differentiations of roles.

Third, like ideal-types in the social sciences, the council's descriptions admit exceptions. Laypeople can be quite closely involved, even in full-time occupations, in church-internal activities; in exceptional circumstances, they may even be entrusted with offices normally reserved to the clergy.[13] Similarly, the clergy may occasionally be involved in secular affairs or have a secular occupation.[14]

Fourth, it can be asked whether, if the description of the lay person is only "typological," the same might not be true also of the descriptions of the clergy and religious, at least with regard to their secular involvement. If so, the council's typifications of the latter as *not* having a "secular character" could be regarded as having the force only of descriptions of customary role-distributions.

Acceptance of this suggestion is perhaps impeded by the council's use of the language of "states of life." The *Relator* explained that the phrase, "the state of those Christians called laypeople" (LG 30), was used rather than "condition and mission," so that "the laity would be acknowledged to have the honor of constituting a *state* in the Church, at least in a broad sense."[15] Neither here nor anywhere else did the council specify what it meant by a "state," a question on which both theologians and canonists have disagreed.[16]

But a perhaps unintended sociological consequence of conceiving clergy, religious, and laity as distinct "states of life" can be noted. The phrase can, of course, be used purely descriptively, to refer simply to different typical situations or conditions. But it can also easily become prescriptive, so that the typical or customary becomes normative. "States" then take on almost ontological status, and this can serve the useful purpose of legitimating the taken-for-granted and ensuring the continuance of the customary. "Ontological" definitions of the priesthood and religious life are not uncommon at all.[17]

It is not within the scope of this essay to study the development and implications of an "ontologizing" of the "states of life"; but in passing I should mention how it affects an understanding of the relationship between the various "states" and secular activity. Particular historical forms, say, of the priesthood are canonized and then provided with a theological legitimation which sees in them the very "essence" of the priesthood. The essence, determined prior to any set of concrete situations, on theological or canonical grounds, is then examined to determine the legitimacy of priests' involving themselves in particular types of behavior. Typical forms and characteristic behavior, which arose historically in response to particular conditions, now are removed from history, ontologized, and made normative for any conceivable set of circumstances, even ones quite different from those in which the typical forms and behavior first arose.

But if the *Relator's* remarks about the merely typological character of the description of the laity can be extended also to the clergy and religious, then it would seem that the council's remarks about the latter need not be assigned prescriptive force. Certainly the council was at least describing typical relations between all three conditions and secular activities. It was probably also intending to be prescriptive at least in the sense that the typifications were not considered to be inappropriate in the past and, probably, for the future as the council saw it. It is legitimate at least to ask whether the council's typifications continue to be appropriate; and an answer to that question will very much depend on an evaluation of the council's understanding of the relationship betweeen the Church and the world.

VATICAN II ON CHURCH AND WORLD

It is by now a commonplace that the Second Vatican Council expressed a far more positive attitude towards the modern world than had been reflected in many earlier official statements and actions by Catholic authorities. This went beyond a mere acceptance that, after all, the Church was living in the twentieth century and ought finally to give up all hope of the return of a vanished era. The council acknowledged a legitimate and proper secularization of the world and used the word "autonomy" to refer to its effect.[18] It regularly sought to avoid any suggestion that it wished to see the world and its affairs again under the control of the Church or the clergy.[19] It acknowledged the benefits the Church could receive from the world, many of which have resulted from the very developments which have given the modern world its distinctive character (GS 44). In this positive description of the modern world it is not unjust to see a conciliar equivalent of the "theology of secularization" which had its brief moment of glory around the time the council was meeting.

The council's understanding of the relationship of the Church to the world may be studied in its statements about what the Church is to do in and for the world. Thus, according to *Lumen Gentium*, the laity are to engage in temporal affairs in order to direct them in accordance with the sanctification of the world; their efforts are so to illumine and order temporal matters that these may be realized and grow according to Christ and for the glory of God (LG 31). By their everyday activities, the laity "consecrate the world itself to God" (LG 34). They work "so that the world may be filled with the spirit of Christ and may the more effectively attain its destiny in justice, love, and peace," Christ himself by their efforts "illumining the whole of human society with his saving light" (LG 36).

Gaudium et Spes begins with the statement that the Church "feels itself to be intimately linked with the human race and its history" (GS 1) and then offers its own description of the world the Church wishes to serve:

> The world which the council has in mind is the whole human family with the totality of realities among which it lives,

the world as the theatre of human history, marked by human labor, failures, and triumphs, the world which Christians believe to have been established and sustained by the Creator's love, reduced to slavery and to sin yet freed by the crucified and risen Christ who has broken the power of the Evil One, so that it might be transformed according to God's plan and attain to its perfection (GS 2).

Such a world the Church now addresses, offering to clarify its problems in the gospel's light and to supply the Spirit's saving help. For "the human person must be saved and human society restored. The hinge of our discussion will be the human person, one and whole, body and soul, heart and conscience, mind and will" (GS 3).

Progress in bringing societies better to promote the good of persons, the council says, reveals the presence of the Spirit, and the gospel is like a yeast which arouses an unbreakable demand for human dignity (GS 26). People may not be content with a purely individualistic morality (GS 30). Human activity in the world has, by God's own will, an inherent dignity and value (GS34-36). If history shows that the greatest accomplishments have been threatened by sin, Christians preach the possibility of the purification and perfecting in Christ. Recognizing the divine author of the goods they possess, people will learn how truly to possess them (GS 37).

Against this background, the council considers the relationship between Church and world. The Church knows itself to be a society of divine origin, nature, and purpose. Still it exists here on earth, sharing the world's lot, and called to be "a leaven and, as it were, the soul of human society, which is to be renewed in Christ and transformed into the family of God." This leads to a programmatic statement of the Church's role:

> In pursuing its own saving purpose, the Church does not only communicate the divine life to the person, it also casts its reflected light in some way over the whole world, especially by healing and elevating the dignity of the human person, by strengthening the cohesion of human society, and by endowing the daily activity of people with a deeper sense and meaning. The Church thus believes that through each of its members and its whole community it can contribute much to make the human family and its history more human (GS 40).

The following paragraphs explicate this statement. Paragraph 41 discusses the Church's defense of human dignity. The Church's role in strengthening society is the subject of paragraph 42: although "the proper mission, which Christ entrusted to his Church, is not of the political, economic, or social order—the purpose he gave it is of the religious order," still the Church can contribute to the making of society, but by faith and love and not "by some external dominion exercised by purely human means." Paragraph 43 attributes Christian significance to daily activity in the world, which it is one of the great errors of the day to think can be separated from faith. "Secular duties and activity belong properly, even if not exclusively, to the laity." While they may look to their pastors for guidance and spiritual support, they must assume their own responsibility in and for the world. "The laity, who have an active role to play in the whole life of the Church, must not only imbue the world with a Christian spirit; they are also called to be witnesses to Christ in all circumstances, in the very heart of the human community." Bishops and presbyters are to preach the gospel so that it illumines all the earthly activities of the faithful and, with the religious and the laity, to "demonstrate that the Church with all its gifts by its presence alone is an inexhaustible source of all those resources of which the modern world is in so great a need" (GS 43).

In turn, the Church receives from the world. Past experience, scientific progress, and cultural diversity cast great light on human nature and open new avenues to truth. The Church has used and will use the language and thought of various peoples to articulate its own message. Its own social structure "can be enriched by the development of human social life, not of course as if anything were lacking in the constitution Christ gave it, but in order to understand it more deeply, to express it better, and to adapt it more successfully to our times." In general,

> whatever contributes to the development of the community of humanity on the level of family, culture, economic and social life, and national and international politics, by God's plan also contributes in no small measure to the community of the Church insofar as it depends on things outside itself. Indeed, the Church admits that it has benefitted and still benefits from the very opposition of its enemies and persecutors (GS 44).

Overall, the documents of Vatican II do not clearly offer a single and coherent view of the relationship between Church and world. This is perhaps no surprise, given that they were drawn up by different groups of bishops and theologians and that each of them was often the fruit of considerable compromise.

Moreover, many of the statements are on such an abstract theological level that it is difficult to give them specific enough content to make them subject to theological evaluation. As in other teachings, we often find different statements set alongside one another, like beads on a rosary, with little internal connection. The great question which a concrete theology would ask, for example, is how the vindication of the world's autonomy is to be reconciled with the statements about its need to be "sanctified," "consecrated," or "infused with a Christian spirit,"—and all this without a new clerical or ecclesial domination. How does one relate again what the council accepts as now distinct orders: the religious and the political, economic and social, the spiritual and temporal, the divine life and its reflected light? At least one group of critics maintains that the council has not succeeded in overcoming the old distinction between a natural and a supernatural destiny.[20] The world's "autonomy" can sound a great deal like the *finis naturalis* which the council seems to have repudiated with regard to the individual. But can the individual have a single, supernatural destiny and the world and society only a natural one?

In two respects the council's statements reflect the theology of the years in which they were composed. The first of these is the confident acknowledgment of the world's autonomy. This effect of secularization is presented as legitimate development, in accord with God's creation and not threatened by the need for Christ's redemption or by the Church's mission. It is not hard to recognize here the "theology of secularization" and the confident optimism of the early 1960's of which it was only a reflection. The Church's role in society, for example, is presented as that of strengthening social cohesion; little attention is given to social conflict, and the atmosphere is quite different from that of later documents such as *Octagesima adveniens* or the 1971 Synod's "Justice in the World," not to mention the theologies of revolution and liberation which soon succeeded the theology of secularization.

The second of these reflections of the state of contemporary theology is visible in the council's tendency to present the Church's mission as directly and immediately affecting individuals. The council appears to have no difficulty in articulating the meaning of the faith in terms of the situation, needs and desires of individuals, but its discussion of its significance for the social, economic, and political realm is, theologically, quite tentative and even hesitant. The council fathers were not able to agree upon a clear and strong statement on the relationship between the central Christian message and mission and the social realm.[21]

One wonders also if there is not some correlation between this hesitation before the social implications of the gospel and the fact that, in its typologies of Christian activity, the clergy and religious typically see to the Church-internal affairs while the laity have as their primary and typical role the mission of the Church to the world. One must be careful here, for the council certainly affirmed the right and duty of the laity to be involved in the immediate self-constitution of the Church and it did not exclude entirely the worldly activity of clergy and religious. Still, typologies do count for something, as, for example, when the word "also" must be introduced into the descriptions of roles.[22] The primary means by which the Church is present and active in the world is the laity. The growing autonomy of the world has meant the banishment of clergy and religious from the secular world, where, however, the laity still reside.[23] Having one foot in both realms, the religious and the political, economic and social, they are uniquely placed to make Christianity effective in the larger world. It would probably be an exaggeration to say that in its insistence on the autonomy of the secular and in its role-typologies, the council is simply making a virtue out of necessity and coping as best it can; but one is entitled at least to some reservations about a view of the Church-world relationship that bears so great a resemblance to modern Western society's notions about the appropriate social role of religion.[24] One suspects that political and economic liberals would have far less difficulty with the conciliar teaching than, for example, with the Church-world understanding of many liberation-theologians.

This correlation between the Church-world relationship and the clergy-laity relationship is confirmed by an unexpected paragraph of Yves Congar. In a discussion of the ecclesiological problem raised by the new question of the relation between the spiritual and the temporal, Congar notes that the single mission of the Church, precisely because it includes both orders, raises the question whether "the full exercise of the Church's mission does not surpass the structures and means of the Church insofar as it is an original society of divine right." In the world that mission is exercised by the clergy through their prophetical preaching, but only the laity can make it truly effective. He goes on:

> The laity are, in their very life, the living link between the Church and the world. Once again they are then acting in-

sofar as they are Christians. The distinction will not so
much be between "acting as a Christian" and "acting insofar
as they are Christians," that is, as the Church. It will rather
be between the Church as a positive institution of divine
right (with its hierarchy and sacraments) and the Church as
the People of God immersed in human history and marching on the same journey. In the end, there will no longer be
a distinction between "laity" and the "apostolate of the laity." The distinction will be between what derives from the
jurisdiction of the Church and what derives solely from its
prophetical element. . . .[25]

After repeating that "it is the person, the *Christian* person, *i.e.*, a member of the messianic people, who is the link between 'the Church' and
the temporal order," Congar suggests the need for another distinction
in the meaning of the word "Church":

Between the Church in the strongest and most dogmatic
sense of the word, engaging the whole body by the voice of
its public authority, and the faithful considered individually, there exist either in fact or, in varying degrees, in law,
concrete communities of whom the word "Church" can be
used in a lesser and relative, but still real, sense.[26]

It is surprising to find that Congar, who more than anyone else
was responsible for recovering the general reference of the word
"Church," should here use it in a sense which appears to exclude the
laity, whose task, he says, is to be a link between *Church* and world. Congar certainly has stressed often enough that the laity *are* the Church in
the world; but his slip is perhaps an indication that the view that the
Church really is integrally constituted before it faces the world in the
persons of the laity is still very powerful and is easily taken for granted.
Congar's suggested distinction of another sense of the word "Church,"
to cover small communities of Christians actively involved in the world,
may be an attempt to face the difficulty raised by that view's tendency
to restrict, at least typically, the Church's temporal mission to individual lay people. Those small communities seem to mediate between the
two senses of "Church" which he had already proposed, the hierarchical and sacramental Church of divine institution and the Church as
the People of God on pilgrimage in and with the world. It is clear that
the difficulties in conceiving the relationship between Church and

world or between the two missions of the Church directly relate to the clergy-laity relationship and vice-versa.[27]

CHURCH AND WORLD RECONSIDERED

The obscurities and difficulties in the council's view of the Church-world and clergy-laity distinctions derive, it will here be argued, from an incomplete reflection on the Church's new situation in a secularized world and from a consequently ineffective pastoral response. "Church" and "world" have come in the modern era to mean different things than before, in part precisely because their mutual relationship has so remarkably changed. Some may find it easier to admit that the meaning of "world" has changed than to say that "Church" has also changed in meaning. But there is a sense in which these are correlative terms, each defined by the other, and, if that is so, then "World" cannot change in meaning without "Church" also changing.

This becomes clearest if one makes the "political turn" in theological method. Political theologians claim that they are engaged in something quite different from a "theology of politics."[28] The latter is another "regional" theology, another "theology of. . . ," adding another topic to the already long list of possible objects of theological inquiry. A "theology of politics" is represented by one of the questions asked by Gustavo Gutierrez: "What is the meaning of the struggle against an unjust society and the creation of a new man in the light of the Word?"[29] The form of the question is familiar: What, in the light of revelation, is the meaning of X, Y, or Z? Most of the council's statements about the world reflect this sort of "theology of . . ."; they respond to the question, What, in the light of the Word, should the Church say or do about the modern world?

The political theologians claim to be doing something quite different, to be asking quite different questions. They are illustrated by another question which Gutierrez poses: "What is the *meaning of the faith* in a life committed to the struggle against injustice and alienation?"[30] This sort of question does not concern faith's implications for some particular aspect of human life, but the significance of a prior commitment *for the interpretation of faith itself*. Now the form of the question is: What, in the light of this commitment, is the meaning of X, Y, or Z, where these letters represent various constituents of Christian faith. Faith is not being asked to illumine an endless series of particular problems; faith itself is being illumined by the prior commitment. Since the commitment stands prior to all theological questions, a political theology is not merely regional, but foundational and comprehensive.[31]

The necessity of this "political turn" appears in the very anthropocentric "turn to the subject" of which it is a critical corrective and extension. For an anthropocentric theology, existence as a human problem and project has central hermeneutical significance. Revelation is not an arbitrary intervention by God, surprising and challenging an inexpectant humanity. It is a fulfilment of desires which the Creator has inscribed in every human heart and mind, a response to needs experienced by every sinner's heart. For such a theology, faith can only be rendered intelligible by reference to the problems involved in the free self-realizations of concrete men and women. While there are many council statements which do not employ this hermeneutical stance and simply use biblical, traditional, or dogmatic language, it is safe to say that this language need not be incompatible with an anthropocentric approach and that the latter is even in evidence in certain documents, particularly in *Gaudium et Spes*. It is in fact this sort of approach that determines the council's definition of the Church in distinction from the world. The council has asked, "What, in the light of the problem of human existence, is the Church?"

But the political theologians object to such an anthropocentric theology that it does not really deal with human existence in its full concreteness. It ignores the fact that concretely existence is a political problem,[32] and so works with an abstract individual. The "incarnate subjectivity" which it acknowledges and to which it refers the gospel's message is incarnate in the human body, but its political, social and cultural embodiments are overlooked. As Dorothee Sölle remarked of Bultmann's theology, this interpretation "neglects the conditions of its own preunderstanding."[33] It takes for granted the validity and even universality of its analysis of the problems of human existence which serves as its *Vorverständnis*. But the existential problems are not (or at least are not merely) universal problems; they are concrete problems, politically, socially, and culturally conditioned if not determined; and, if they are universal, it is only because they are concrete problems everywhere.

If the political character of human existence is neglected, an anthropocentric theology will attempt to interpret the meaning of the faith or of one of its constituents (the Church, for example) by reference to an imaginary and abstract individual. Such a theology will not, of course, consider that its reference-point is abstract or imaginary, but that is because it takes for granted and universalizes the specific political conditions in which human existence is a concrete problem. That human existence poses the concrete problems that it does pose in part at least because the political, social and cultural order is what it is, is neglected or trivialized. A truly concrete and self-critical anthropocentric theology can only be a political theology, for which existence is known to be a political problem and project.

It is neglect of this political dimension of human existence that permitted the council to define the Church prior to considering the world and to suggest that there is a first moment in which the Church constitutes itself as the Church before it turns to consider its mission in and to the world. Clearly, the Church is not defined or constituted without reference to the problem of human existence, but the world does not enter into the definition or constitution of that problem. The council did ask, "What, in the light of the Word, is the meaning of the Church?" Its answer to that question included in part the asking of the other question: "What, in the light of the problem of human existence, is the meaning of the Word (including the Word about the Church)?" It did *not* ask, "What, in the light of human existence as a political problem, is the meaning of the Word (including the Word about the Church)?"[34]

If, however, existence is a political problem and project, then the world cannot be considered to be external or subsequent to the real business of human living. The world (or at least the world as intended in discussions of the Church-world relationship) is not simply "the theatre of human history," as the council called it; the world *is* human history, it is what human beings not only have made together but *are* together. Individuals are individuals within that world; it makes them what they are and they make it what it is. Individual self-realization occurs within the general political, social and cultural self-realization of the world; the world realizes itself through the individual self-realizations. To paraphrase Peter Berger and Thomas Luckmann, the world is a human project, and the individual is a worldly product.[35]

As, from an earlier anthropocentric standpoint, the religious question is not separable from the problem of individual self-realization, so, from the standpoint of political theology, the Church's self-realization is not separable from the problem of the world's self-realization. As an individual's faith is a particular instance of the project of human existence, so the self-constitution of the Church is an instance of the self-realization of the world. The Church does not come to be except in the world, in reference to the world, and even in part because of the world. The Church is a moment in the world's self-realization.

These conclusions suppose, of course, that what Christian revelation interprets is not only the drama that defines an individual's existence but the tragi-comedy of political existence as well. This is something of what Gutierrez, for example, means when he tries to make concrete Karl Rahner's abstract statement that the Church is the sacrament of what God's grace is doing also outside the Church.[36] For Gutierrez this formal statement means that the Church "must be the visible sign of the presence of the Lord within the aspiration for liberation and the struggle for a more human and just society."[37] This too helps to explain what he means when he speaks of the Church's self-consciousness being mediated by the consciousness of the world in which it lives.[38]

Something like this view of the Church-world relationship seems implied in the perspectives of *Octagesima adveniens* when Pope Paul VI says that "at the heart of the world there dwells the mystery of man discovering himself to be God's child in the course of a historical and psychological process in which constraint and freedom as well as the weight of sin and the breath of the Spirit alternate and struggle to prevail."[39] At the heart of the *world* the mystery of sin and grace, constraint and freedom, constitutes the great issue of human history. History, the world, is constituted by that constitutes the Church; if the world is unintelligible at its heart without the Church, the Church is by that fact unintelligible without the world. Church and world define one another.

It remains, however, that there is nothing to relate if Church and world are not distinct. The distinction lies in the fact that the Church is that community of men and women who constitute themselves around the person of Jesus Christ, because of him, in his name, and for his sake. The problem of human existence, individual and social, is for them interpreted and resolved in Christ. This is not a private moment nor an act of withdrawal from "the world." It occurs in the world, and it is a moment in the world's self-realization. For the world is not what lies outside the Church; the world includes the Church, and without the Church, the world would not be what it is. Christian believing, hoping, loving are political acts, moments in the realization of the world. If this is the case, then there is not some first moment in which the Church becomes the Church and a second moment in which the Church considers its relation to the world. The Church's self-constitution is itself an act within and with reference to the world.

A recognition of this may be impeded by the fact that historic, especially Catholic, Christianity includes certain objective representations and bearers of its constitutive meaning and value: the Scriptures, the living memory of its tradition, patterns of worship, creeds, etc. Without these, Catholic Christianity would not recognize its own distinctive self-realization: these are constitutive of the Church's coming-to-be in the world.

But the objectivity of these bearers of the Church's self-constitutive meanings and values is misunderstood if it is thought that they bear those meanings and values prior to or independently of the questions about human existence that mediate the Church's self-interpretation and self-realization. Meanings and values are borne only when they are received by persons and communities. Such reception is always a concrete act, in concrete circumstances, with concrete personal and social significance. Only the assumption that the reception of the constitutive Christian meanings and values is exhausted by the problem of individual existence allows one to think that the objective bearers carry meanings and values constitutive of the Church prior to its engagement in the world. The reception of those meanings and values, even when they are restricted in reference to questions of individual existence, *is* the Church's engagement in the world. But when the questions are given their full reference to questions of existence, both individual and political, that engagement can become self-conscious and self-critical.

CLERGY AND LAITY RECONSIDERED

Vatican II's typologies of clergy, religious, and laity describe their respective relationships to the world. The clergy and religious typically do not involve themselves in the world, but minister to the Church's self-constitution and testify to its transcendent destiny. The laity typically realize their Christianity in the world by their worldly activities, although they also have roles in the Church's self-constitution.

It was suggested above that this role-differentiation implies a priority to a distinct moment of ecclesial self-constitution. Schillebeeckx, for example, in an early essay, refers to evangelization as the "primary, religious" mission of the Church.[40] This causes no problem if the word "primary" refers to the distinctive centering of its constitutive meanings and values around Jesus Christ. But there would be some problems if this were to be taken to mean something prior to a second and secondary mission of the Church to the world. To identify the primary mission of the Church as "religious" is also unfortunate if it suggests that the secondary mission is not religious. This is possible only on the assumption that the meaning of the religious is exhausted by the private and individual realms.

If, however, the relationship between Church and world is reconsidered along the lines suggested above, then the council's typologies also need to be reconsidered. The central and constitutive meanings and values, to which the clergy minister, are themselves politically significant. The religious "state" is in itself a political statement; and the life for which the vows free a person may be a life in the world.[41] It is not only, and not even typically, the laity who mediate the political significance of the Church's faith; this is an inescapable part of its meaning for and in the lives of all Christians. As Schillebeeckx puts it:

> The relationship between the Church and the world was clearly not fully thought out in all its consequences at the council and the "definition" of the layman and, although less obviously, that of the office-bearer is consequently not entirely satisfactory. Every form of being a Christian, in whatever kind of service or function in the Church (either lay or clerical), is a manner of being a Christian in the world. Even religious life cannot be interpreted in any other way than as a specific manner of being in the world. The Church is the "universal sacrament of salvation", . . . the sign of salvation in and for the world. All Christians are implicated in this sign, each according to his own service or function in the Church.[42]

The immediate political significance of Christian existence is most clearly visible in grass roots communities, particularly but not only in the Third World, in which the gospel is preached and received through the mediation of an interpretation of the social and political context and the group gathers in conscious opposition to the structures and styles of life of the larger society.[43] That there is a danger, as the Latin American bishops at Puebla and Popes Paul VI and John Paul II have pointed out, that these communities may reduce the principles on which they gather to particular political interpretations and programs is undeniable; but it would be a mistake to think that the great Church does not run a similar danger in the secularized societies of the West. For their privatized understanding of the constitutive meanings and values of Christianity is itself of immense political significance. These Churches show a tendency to locate the *specificum Christianum* primarily in a cultural opposition to a vaguely described "materialism" and a specifically described sexual morality. The political and economic structures and practices of the society tend to be taken for granted.[44] A sign of this is that direct political action is typically assigned to the laity who remain in a world from which the Church, in the persons of the clergy and religious, has effectively and even on principle emigrated.

But that attempted or recommended emigration is itself, at least on the analysis given above, a political option based on a particular, although often unconscious and uncritical, interpretation of the relation between the Church and the world, an interpretation which, somewhat ironically, has been taken over from the liberal political theory of the Enlightenment. The clergy and religious are not typically to be involved in the world because the world is now regarded as "autonomous," and its autonomy is the condition as well for the freedom conceded at the council to the laity in their typical sphere of activity in the world.

But if the autonomy of the world—at least in the form in which it was asserted both in the council documents and in the "theology of secularization"—must be called into question, then so must the allocation of typical responsibilities to clergy, religious, and laity. The growing sense that there is not only a distinction but also, in certain senses of the words, an opposition between Church and world makes it difficult to represent that opposition practically by the council's opposition of the typical activities of clergy, religious, and laity. What is really needed is a return to the original opposition which did not counterpose clergy and laity, but the whole Church, clergy, religious, *and laity*, to the world.[45] Becoming a Christian would itself then be seen as a political act within and over and against the world, and the differentiations within the Church would be so many different ways in which the directly political significance of belonging to the church is articulated.

There is, then, a valid point to the concerns expressed in recent years about the blurring of clerical and lay roles. But it consists less in the growing activity of priests and religious in the world than in the danger that the greater involvement of the laity in Church-internal activities may itself reflect or result in an ecclesiastical narcissism and privatization of the laity themselves. But this restricting of the gospel's implications ought also to be stressed with regard to the clergy and religious as well. Some fear, perhaps not without reason, a new clericalism; but the danger will not be overcome by having clergy and religious stick to their own "religious" and supposedly "pre-political" tasks. The clericalism really to be feared is that of those clergy, religious, and even laity whose efforts to make explicit and critically effective the political character of the gospel are undertaken without competence or critical inquiry. What constitutes such competence and inquiry is, of course, a nice question, on which, it seems, some lay persons would differ from at least some of the clergy and religious who have become involved in secular and political issues. For many concerned Christians the issue is a question of how accepting one should be of the differentiation of the Church and the world typical of modern liberal and secularized societies in the West.

There will, of course, remain different gifts in the Church, some of which will be more useful and suitable than others for articulating in theory and practice the political character of the gospel. But these differences will not be based on some mythical pre-political religious meaning, nor are they likely to be distributed neatly within the lines of the canonical and theological distinctions among clergy, religious and laity. None of these groups is, except by custom and, of course, training, less likely to be the recipient of the needed gifts and competence. In any one of them may appear the critical intelligence, the willingness, and the courage that constitute a call to the special ministry of articulating the political implications of the gospel and of provoking and challenging the whole Church to assume, consciously and critically, its inescapable political responsibility.

NOTES

1. Pope John Paul II, "Opening Address at the Puebla Conference," III, 7, cited from J. Eagleson and P. Scharper, eds., *Puebla and Beyond: Documentation and Commentary*, (Maryknoll: Orbis, 1979), p. 69.

2. Pope John Paul II, "Address to Priests in Mexico City," *Origins* 8 (1979): 548–549.

3. See *Origins* l0 (1980-81): 10-12, 15-16, 136.

4. The distinction between the "hierarchical structure" and the "life and holiness" of the Church recalls Yves Congar's attempt to construct a theology of the laity in terms of a distinction between "structure" and "life"; see *Lay People in the Church: A Study for the Theology of Laity* (Westminster: Newman, 1954). Congar's theology had a visible influence on Vatican II's teaching on the laity.

5. See E. Schillebeeckx, "The Typological Definition of the Christian Layman according to Vatican II," in *The Mission of the Church* (New York: Seabury, 1973), pp. 90–116.

6. See E. Schillebeeckx, "A New Type of Layman," in *The Mission of the Church*, pp. 117–131.

7. See P. Guilmot, *Fin d'une Eglise cléricale? Le debat en France de 1945 a nos jours* (Paris: du Cerf, 1969).

8. Schillebeeckx, "Typological Definition," p. 115.

9. As Guilmot and Schillebeeckx both show, the council's positions clearly reflect the state of the theology of the laity reached at the end of the 1950's.

10. *Acta Synodalia Sacrosancti Concilii Oecumenici Vaticani II*, III/III (Typis Polyglottis Vaticanis, 1974), p. 62.

11. Ibid., III/I, p. 282.

12. Ibid.

13. See LG 33, 35; AA 24.

14. See LG 31; PO 8; GS 43. See the *Relatio* for LG 36: "Although clergy and religious may sometimes exercise some 'lay' activity, especially to supply for certain deficiencies, in other words, in supplementary fashion, still, generally speaking, they cannot take the laity's place for this sort of activity" (*Acta Synodalia*, III/I, p. 288).

15. *Acta Synodalia*, III/I, p. 218.

16. See F. Klostermann, "The Laity," in H. Vorgrimler, ed., *Commentary on the Documents of Vatican II* (New York: Herder and Herder, 1967), I, p. 235.

17. For perceptive comments on the effect of such an approach on contemporary discussions of ministry, see C. Duquoc, "Concepts of Ministry," *The Tablet* 350 (1979): 101–113. For the historical development, see E. Schillebeeckx, *Ministry: Leadership in the Community of Jesus Christ* (New York: Crossroad, 1981), esp. pp. 52–65.

18. See LG 36; AA 7; GS 21, 36, 41. The council did not make use of the term "secularization."

19. See F. Klostermann, "Decree on the Apostolate of the Laity," in *Commentary on the Documents of Vatican II*, II, pp. 323–334.

20. See *Les deux visages de la théologie de la sécularisation: Analyse critique de la théologie de la sécularisation* (Tournai: Casterman, 1970), pp. 24–25.

21. See G. Gutierrez, *A Theology of Liberation; History, Politics and Salvation* (Maryknoll: Orbis, 1973), pp. 168–172.

22. See Schillebeeckx, "A New Type of Layman", p. 129.

23. See *Les deux visages de la théologie de la sécularisation*, pp. 26–27.

24. See *Les deux visages de la théologie de la sécularisation*, pp. 173-200, and, in the same volume, F. van den Oudenrijn, "La théologie de la sécularisation: une idéologie religieuse de la société unidimensionnelle," pp. 155–172.

25. Y. Congar, "Apports, richesses et limites du Décret," in *L'Apostolat des laics*, Unam Sanctam 75 (Paris: du Cerf, 1970), p. 179.

26. Congar, "Apports, richesses et limites," p. 180.

27. Congar defends his distinction in *Un peuple messianique: L'É-glise, sacrement du salut; Salut et liberation* (Paris: du Cerf, 1975), pp. 171–177.

28. See, for example, C. Davis, *Theology and Political Society* (Cambridge University Press, 1980), pp. 2–3.

29. Gutierrez, *A Theology of Liberation*, p. 149.

30. Gutierrez, *A Theology of Liberation*, p. 135.

31. This, of course, does not mean that the commitment itself goes unquestioned. Gutierrez asks *both* types of questions. And both types are needed if there is to be a genuine and critical correlation between contemporary practice and Christian faith.

32. See J.B. Metz, "The Church and the World in the Light of a 'Political Theology,' " in *Theology of the World* (New York : Herder and Herder, 1969), pp. 108-110.

33. D. Sölle, *Political Theology* (Philadelphia: Fortress, 1974), p. 45.

34. See, for example, the extremely limited significance assigned to the world in the self-constitution of the Church in *Gaudium et Spes* 44.

35. P. Berger and T. Luckmann, *The Social Construction of Reality: A Treatise in the Sociology of Knowledge* (Garden City: Anchor, 1967), p. 61. Their statement is that "Society is a human product" and that "Man is a social product."

36. "The Catholic must think of and experience the Church as the 'vanguard,' the sacramental sign, the manifestation in history of a grace of salvation which takes effect far beyond the confines of the 'visible' Church as sociologically definable"—K. Rahner, "The New Image of the Church," *Theological Investigations* X (New York: Herder and Herder, 1973), p. 16.

37. Gutierrez, *A Theology of Liberation*, p. 262.

38. Gutierrez, *A Theology of Liberation*, p. 260.

39. Pope Paul VI, *Octagesima adveniens*, 37.

40. Schillebeeckx, "Typological Definition," pp. 114-115.

41. This is well recognized in a recent document of the Congregation for Religious and for Secular Institutes, which quite transcends the limited perspective of *Lumen Gentium* and other conciliar documents; see "Religious Life and Human Promotion," *Origins* 10 (1980-81): 530-541. This document is included in the Appendices of this volume.

42. Schillebeeckx, "A New Type of Layman," pp. 129–130.

43. See *Les groupes informels dans l'Eglise* (Strasbourg: CERDIC, 1971) and the sociological study of K. Dobbelaire and J. Billiet, "Community formation and the Church: A Sociological Study of an Ideology and the Empirical reality," in M. Caudron, ed., *Faith and Society*, (Gembloux: Duculot, 1978), pp. 211–259.

44. It is this form of Christianity, which he calls "bourgeois religion," that is the object under criticism in J. B. Metz' two recent books, *Faith in History and Society: Toward a Practical Fundamental Theology* (New York: Seabury, 1980), and *The Emergent Church: The Future of Christianity in a Postbourgeois World* (New York: Crossroad, 1981); for a summary statement, see the latter, pp. 1–16.

45. See Schillebeeckx, "A New Type of Layman," pp. 117–121.

Agnes Cunningham, SSCM

RELIGIOUS PROFESSIONALS IN "POLITICAL MINISTRY": THEOLOGICAL CONSIDERATIONS

At the 1983 convention of the Catholic Theological Society of America, attending members engaged in a heated, difficult and unusual discussion. The conversation, if it can be called that, was unusual because, for perhaps the first time in its history, the Society was addressing a question that impinges on a theology of religious life. It was difficult and heated because of conflicting perceptions and loyalties, pre-existing biases and incomplete information regarding an individual person and a complex event: the Agnes Mary Mansour case. "L'affaire Mansour," as it might be called, has indeed become a *cause célèbre* in the history of the Catholic Church in the United States, although, I am convinced, its entire and true account has never been told in a public forum. From one point of view, the incident has been invested with more significance than is warranted. Like the religious habit, the name, Agnes Mary Mansour, has become synonymous with a number of issues which lie beneath the surface of the words, generating tension and division while giving rise to false questions and suggesting inadequate measures toward understanding and reconciliation.

I refer to this situation because, at the 1983 convention, I was one of the opponents of the proposal to issue, in the name of the Society, a statement of protest against the ecclesiastical authorities whose actions led to the unhappy outcome of the "case." More importantly, it seems to me, I asked at that time for the establishment of a research committee to study the question of the religious or priest—the "religious professional"—in political or public office. Only in this way, I maintained, might we, as theologians, be able to speak responsibly and effectively to a phenomenon that gives every indication of being increasingly present and problematic in the United States in this moment of history.

The Catholic Theological Society of America did endorse a statement of protest, and to date the research committee has not been established, but the question of priests and religious in political office in the United States is more critical now than ever before. The Woodstock Center has recognized this reality and the papers in this volume attest to courageous steps taken to explore the issue at the levels of both *theoria* and *praxis*. My own contribution to this discussion is, necessarily, a limited one. Neither the topic under consideration nor the complex issues that derive from it have reached a point of maturity in my own thought. Furthermore, the question is far from developed in the thought of the theological community in the United States or even in the universal Church. Consequently, anything I have to say on the subject must necessarily be articulated in a general and tentative manner. With this *caveat*, I propose, in the following pages, to assess the concept of "political ministry" in the light of a number of theological perspectives; to examine a series of tensions that arise from underlying and frequently non-articulated ecclesiologies; finally, to suggest several questions for further study, given the context within which the topic under consideration is experienced and must, therefore, be evaluated.

A PHENOMENON—A DILEMMA

The articles in Part II of this volume bear witness to the fact that priests and religious do indeed hold political office at several levels of government in the United States. On the whole, their experiences are positive. Difficulties encountered because of a conflict of ideologies seem to have been minor and few. The women and men who share their stories manifest high motivation and a strong sense of commitment. Because of their dedication, the poor have been served, needed reforms have been initiated, improvements in living conditions have been realized. Church-state conflicts or "cases of conscience" do not seem to have figured significantly in the experiences related here. Still, "concern over the clergy in political office has been coextensive with the history of the nation," according to Robert L. Spaeth (cf. Part IV). He argues further that the world in which priests and sisters might engage in formal public service has "never existed" and "never will exist." The Code of Canon Law (278, 3; 285, 2; 287, 2; 289,2) and the repeated admonitions of Pope John Paul II have moved the debate into a critical arena. What has been a phenomenon is becoming a dilemma. The concept of "political ministry" for "religious professionals" needs to be assessed in the light of a number of selected theological perspectives on ministry as it has been developed historically in the Church.

POLITICAL MINISTRY

Joseph Simon, S.V.D. (cf. Part II) identifies the characteristics of political ministry, as he perceives them: 1) full-time participation in political office; 2) appropriate qualifications; 3) permission from the competent ecclesiastical superior; 4) integration of one's clerical or religious character; 5) commitment to one's chosen state of life; 6) personal authenticity. Apart from the specific focus deriving from political life, these points could apply to any area of ministry. However, a number of theological perspectives need to be invoked as criteria for assessing political involvement as "ministry." These perspectives focus on ministry as charism, *koinonia*, worship, proclamation and mission.

Ministry perceived as *charism* is, essentially, a biblical concept. Several basic texts are particularly helpful in exploring this understanding of ministry: Romans 12, I Corinthians 12, Ephesians 4:7-11. Reflection on these texts leads us to arrive at a foundational understanding of ministry as a charism in the Church. Ministry exists because the Spirit of Jesus is present and active in the faith-community, pouring out the spiritual gifts to be expressed in a diversity of services. These gifts are given to individuals, not for their own sake, but for the good of others—that is, for the "common good": the building up of the body of the Lord. Each ministry is as unique as the charism from which it flows and all exist together in complementarity, contributing to the growth of all the members to the measure of the fullness of Christ's stature. The Spirit of God, as Paraclete and Comforter, knows the needs of the Church in every age. Thus, a charism and its corresponding ministry may be temporary or permanent, local or universal. The charism is given to be used for the good of the entire Church. Therefore, the presumption is that a charism is to be used; indeed we might say it must be used in response to the needs of the Church in a given age, place and culture. The first charism given to the Church in every age is exercised in a ministry of love. That is the gift that must impel and direct every other service.

From the perspective of *koinonia* (*communio*, communion), ministry is rooted in the tradition of the early Church. For the patristic writers, the community of believers was the true Body (*corpus verum*) of Christ. In the communion shared by those who were baptized into Christ, there was no longer "Jew or Greek, slave or free, male or female. All are one in Christ Jesus." With this understanding of ministry came the recognition on the part of early Christians of the necessity of the *sharing* of ministries, so as to allow for the fullest possible participation of all members of the community in the life of the *ekklesia*. No one was to be excluded arbitrarily from a role of service to the community, although there were distinctions and limits, such as the reservation of certain offices (*episkopos, presbyteros*) to male Christians. With this concept of ministry, we find the development of liturgical, contemplative and caritative services—all directed to the care of the entire community. Ministry perceived as *koinonia* was coordinated by the local *episkopos*, whose responsibility it was to identify the needs of the local Church, to call forth men and women to respond to those needs and to assure the unity of all services in faith and love.

A third perspective on ministry is to perceive it in terms of *worship*. This concept of ministry is laden with ecclesiastical developments that occurred with Constantine's recognition of Christianity in the Empire. With the emperor's friendship there came changes in organization and the exercise of authority; new understandings of theological formulation; changing intuitions regarding ecclesiology. For a variety of reasons to which history attests, diversities in ministry began to diminish from the fourth century on. Increasingly, the sacramentality of the Church was carried out in multiple "sacramental" actions. At the same time, administration of these actions was gradually reserved to ordained ministers: bishops, priests and deacons. All were male. All were clerical. The form of liturgical worship was "institutionalized" while external signs and norms of unity assumed greater significance than in the preceding centuries. Ministry as charism and *koinonia* became associated with monastic life, as it flourished. Ministry as worship, in the sense explained above, became the characteristic of the "institutional"—as distinct from the "charismatic" (monastic) Church. This situation was to perdure for several centuries.

While ministry as worship prevailed in the Church, another perspective was also developing. This was ministry perceived as *proclamation*. In the earliest centuries of the Christian era, the Church was served in a unique manner by the confession of faith expressed in the witness of the martyrs. Only if we seek to understand the theology and spirituality of martyrdom which developed in the early Church can we acknowledge the martyrs' witness as true ministry. For the early Christians, baptism into the death and resurrection of Jesus Christ meant incorporation into the Body of the Lord in a revolutionary manner.

To be allowed to suffer and die as Christ, the Martyr, had suffered and died meant to re-live the passion of the Lord. The final victory—death—was the signal that another Christian had, at last, *become* "totally" *Christ*. Martyrdom, however, was to give way in time to other phenomena in the Christian's desire to seek a lifestyle that was marked by a "more radical witness." Monasticism and religious life became, at the heart of the Church, that charismatic, prophetic "*ecclesiola*", witnessing to the universal call to holiness. As the Church emerged from the Age of the Martyrs, it was to face a new challenge: That of articulating in unambiguous and faithful language the teachings that had been preserved and transmitted "from the beginning." Theological debate and doctrinal definition, in turn, became a ministry of proclamation by which the Church was enabled to announce in ever more simple yet detailed expressions her faith in Jesus as Lord.

The final perspective which helps to clarify our understanding of ministry is *mission*. This focus is primarily the fruit of the Second Council of the Vatican. We have known the Church as *communio*; we know the Church as *missio*. *Gaudium et spes* has enlarged the horizons of that arena to which the Church is to bring Christ, the light of the nations. To the extent that each of us is aware of being Church, to that degree have we sought to make our own "the joy and the hope, the grief and the anguish of the men (and women) of our time, especially of those who are poor or afflicted in any way" (*Gaudium et spes*, l). The underlying inspiration in ministry perceived as mission is the concept of the Church as the People of God, on pilgrimage to the Kingdom. The vision before the eyes of this people is the unity of the entire human family, when all men and women everywhere will be brought to the Father through Christ, in the unity of the Spirit. The perspective of mission as a focus on ministry is a gift of the Spirit to the Church in an age when global consciousness and access to the concerns of men and women everywhere have reached a new intensity.

How can these theological perspectives on ministry be invoked as criteria for assessing the validity of "political ministry"? Like Dulles's five models of church, each one is incomplete in itself. Ministry, in fact, is all of the realities we have just considered: charism, *koinonia*, worship, proclamation and mission. Indeed, it is all of these and more. However, it is possible to distill a certain number of constants that seem to characterize a theology of mission as it has developed through the centuries. In the first place, ministry is always the exercise of a charism given by the Spirit to the Church, through individual members—all of whom are gifted. Second, ministry is given for the sake of the Church, in response to her needs in every age. Third, because the Church is the Body of Christ, ministries are as diverse as the members of the Body, through whom Christ acts and ministers. Fourth, just as a human body is able to act because of its organic "institution" and supportive skeletal system, the Church organizes and oversees the exercise of her ministries, in order to assure unity in fidelity to her Lord. Finally, the Church, as a *communio*, shares in the mission of Christ, bringing the Good News to all nations, announcing the coming of God's Kingdom. In other words, ministry, rooted in the charisms given to individuals, flourishes in a believing, worshiping community so as to find full expression through proclamation of the Good News in a mission that envisions all of humanity.

At first glance, it may not seem clear that the criteria suggested above provide an appropriate assessment of political ministry on the part of priests and sisters. The perspectives on ministry and the constants derived from them may seem too concerned with the Church *ad intra*. Are there not other considerations which might be taken into account in an attempt to address the phenomenon of priests and sisters in political office and to resolve the dilemma which seems to characterize that experience? The examination of a series of tensions that result from the presence of the Church in the world may be helpful, at this point.

THE CHURCH IN THE WORLD: THE CHURCH FOR THE WORLD

By reason of its rootedness in the community of believers which is *ekklesia Christou*—the Church of Christ—ministry of any kind is vulnerable to the tensions that mark the telling of the Good News and the breaking into human history of God's Kingdom. The Church is both divine and human: sent in mission to the world and, thus, "not of the world"; at the same time, inextricably "in the world." The Church is in the world because it is involved in human history, human experience, human life and destiny. It is also in the world, as St. Augustine tells us, to the extent that we are citizens of the world because the false love of the world reigns in us.

This paradoxical situation has resulted in relationships between the Church and the "world," marked by any one of a number of tensions. For our purposes, these can be identified as: 1) the sacred and the secular; 2) church and state; 3) authority and leadership; 4) clergy and laity; 5) incarnation and eschatology.

The Sacred and the Secular. This tension is not peculiar to the Roman Catholic Church, nor is it reserved for Christianity alone. The earliest recorded religious history of humankind bears witness to the dialogic movement between attraction to the "sacred" and awed repulsion from it on the part of men and women who hungered for an experience of the "divine," yet found themselves rooted within the limits of earthly time and space.

Christianity carries forward this tension resulting from our experience of the transcendent and the here-and-now. For many, Christianity is, essentially, a flight from this world. Jesus called all to his kingdom, a kingdom "not of this world." The followers of Jesus are hated by the world, which had hated him, first. The world has rejected the light and has not known either the Father or the Spirit of Truth. Preoccupation with the cares of the world stifle the Word of Life. Those who are faithful to the end are promised the rewards of another life and a treasure stored "in heaven." This sketch of Johannine and Matthean themes seems to verify the reality of the chasm that exists between the transcendent point of view which Christianity brings to life and preoccupation with the daily concerns of human existence.

This picture, however, is clearly one-sided and incomplete. Jesus came that we might "have life" and have it "more abundantly." The parables of healing in the gospel accounts reveal his desire that the wounded, the ill, the dispossessed, the marginalized possess the fullness of humanity. The Hebrew concept of a redemption measured in terms of health, family and possessions was not rejected by Jesus, but rather, transformed into a symbolic representation of the redemption and reconciliation he had been sent to accomplish. The Christian, it would seem, is challenged to face the paradox of tension between the sacred and the secular. Contemporary developments in theology, reflected to some extent in the documents of Vatican II, affirm this challenge. Creation is good; we are called to grapple with the "sin of the world" so that, in Christ and through Christ, all things may be restored and brought to the Father.

Church and State. Within the seemingly all-encompassing horizons of the sacred-secular tension, one particular experience emerges as a more focused arena of conflict. This is the area that has been identified historically by the term, "Church-state relations." Tension arising from these relations has been with the Church from the beginning. In part, the ambivalent attitude discernible in early Christian attitudes toward the state resulted from two factors. In the world into which Christianity moved—the ancient Near East and the Mediterranean world—religious and civil functions were understood to be inseparable. This was true both in the Roman Empire, where emperors were gods, and in the Jewish concept of the state.

Throughout the centuries, the drama inaugurated in the conflict between the Christian Church and the Roman state has been re-enacted in many other theaters. The difficult question of church-state relations has had to be faced in every age and in every nation. The struggle ultimately can be expressed as one of avoiding extremes. In the past these were identified as Caesaropapism and Papal Theocracy. Today we speak of paying the price for state patronage or of adhering to a new species of "Ultramontanism." The challenge and the tension are critically germane to the subject of this study, if we review the history of the Roman Catholic Church in the United States and assess the impact on Catholic life of our experience of the separation of Church and state.

Authority and Leadership. The tensions between sacred-secular and church-state relations imply a dynamic exchange in which at least one of the two parties is "other" than the Church. When we address the question of authority and leadership, however, we are concerned with a tension that arises within the community of believers itself. The contrast between Johannine and Pauline churches in matters of structures of office and administration is frequently suggested as a concrete example of the difference between authority and leadership within the Church.

According to some writers, leadership positions in some of the New Testament communities flowed from the charisms or spiritual gifts bestowed on given members and exercised by them in the *ekklesia*. In other words, office flowed from charism. In other communities, the exercise of authority belonged rightfully to one who had been mandated to office. The "charism" of leading or presiding in the community was a result of the office to which one of the members had acceded. Of course, the ideal situation existed when office and charism were united in one and the same person. The charism of leadership then became a powerful factor in the efficacious exercise of authority.

Here again, the history of the Church advises us that authority and leadership, at times, were felicitously found united in the same administrator. At other times, leadership resided in one who held no mandated office, while the official exercise of legitimate authority lacked the charismatic dimension of true leadership in the Church. Attached to this question, obviously, is the meaning of obedience, of "creative revolution," of "conscientious objection" in matters of Church doctrine or, more frequently, ecclesiastical discipline. Among the "retrievals" of Vatican II were the rediscovery of authority understood as service in the Church and the concept of collegiality, particularly through consultation in view of decisions to be made. Interpretations of these conciliar principles quickly penetrated areas of Catholic thought and action not directly envisioned by the Council Fathers. Out of the attempt to apply these principles to expectations regarding the exercise of authority and authentic leadership in the Church, particularly in the United States, have come a conflict and a tension that seem to portend serious consequences. This situation is directly related to the involvement of priests and sisters in political office.

Clergy and Laity. The tension between authority and leadership in the Church has been closely linked, historically, to the tension between clergy and laity. This is true both in regard to the universal Church and to the Catholic Church in the United States. "Investiture," "Trusteeism," "Catholic Action" are only three terms out of many which highlight critical developments in the difficulties that have marked clergy-laity relationships, particularly since the Middle Ages. Since Vatican II, the mode and intensity of the tension have changed. However, the problem remains far from resolved. The restoration of the permanent diaconate and the emergence of "lay" ministries are two factors which have given rise to new forms of the clergy-laity tension. Another significant influence has been the women's movement, with the unique impact it has brought to relations between women and men regarding decision making and roles of power in the Church.

The ecclesiology of Vatican II certainly calls for a Church that is the whole People of God on collaborative pilgrimage in this world toward the Kingdom—already here, yet still to come in its fullness. Uncertainty of role and function, for both laity and clergy, in an age when the understanding of "ministry" and "ministries" is in transition, undoubtedly contributes to the clergy-laity tension. Another critical point can be recognized in the preparation of the laity for service in the Church through theological and religious education programs now widely available to them. This has tended to highlight the widespread lack of continued education programs for priests following ordination. The fact that women—often women religious—have been in the forefront in pursuing theological and ministerial preparation has, again, added to the already-present tension. This becomes evident as women religious increasingly enter new areas of service in the Church formerly not open to them. The results can be described, negatively, in terms of "threat" and "confrontation." Positively, a contribution of creativity and challenge ought rather to emerge from such experiences.

Incarnation and Eschatology. Each of the areas of tension considered above has led us to an increasingly focused and intense field of ecclesial relationships. With "incarnation and eschatology," it would seem that we have entered a completely distinct sphere of concern. In fact, at this point the tension results from concepts that underlie every other area of tension we have seen. This tension speaks more directly to the political involvement of priests and sisters, since it has to do with the nature of the witness-value attached to a state in the Christian life perceived as "professional," because its members are, in an ecclesial sense, "public persons."

Here, we are once again invited to consider the challenge of bringing the sacred and the secular together, as humankind has sought to do from the dawn of religious history. Again, we experience the paradox of being members of the Lord's Body— Church "in the world, but not of it"; a Church "sojourning as a stranger" here on earth, as the Apostolic Fathers would say, but sent in mission to every nation. The tension that emerges from the apparent dichotomy between incarnational love and eschatological witness reaches into the heart of the vocation to priesthood or religious life in the Church. Its implications are readily obvious for priests and religious who question the restrictions placed on their involvement in what they perceive as a call to a ministry that enables them to further the works of the Kingdom of God in an arena where Christians encounter, not gladiators or wild beasts, but the devastating evils of injustice, oppression of the poor and systemic structures whose dehumanization of men and women "cries to heaven for vengeance."

RELIGIOUS PROFESSIONALS IN POLITICAL MINISTRY

At this point, it is appropriate to return to the initial idea with which this paper began. The *theologoumena* underlying the concept of "political ministry" as well as the areas of tension attached to it reveal the ecclesiological principles which impinge on the topic. Indeed, the question of priests and sisters in political office is, fundamentally, an ecclesiological question. It is in the context of ecclesiology that the general, tentative reflections developed above can be brought to bear in a specific manner on the phenomenon that has become a dilemma and the paradox which is, finally, a challenge in the lives of those persons who can rightfully be called, "religious professionals."

Priest and sisters involved in public service through political office seem to identify their engagement as *"political ministry."* If "political ministry" is, indeed, going to qualify as ministry, in an ecclesiological sense, it must be in harmony with those theological intuitions which validate any Christian service. I do not want to introduce here the debate over "restricted" and "extended" concepts of ministry. Efforts to establish a more exclusive understanding of ecclesial ministry, reserving that term to the functions of the ordained, continue to meet some resistance in the Church. At the same time, however, opposition to an inclusive concept of ministry has not ceased to come from active members of the laity, who choose to serve the Church in roles that respect the autonomy of Catholics who are neither priests nor religious. The present ambivalence attached to the term, "ministry," does not facilitate the task of identifying specific "ministries." This, however, is an endeavor in which both "lived experience" and theological research have a contribution to make.

The designation of political involvement as "ministry" may or may not be appropriate. Further, it may or may not be advisable. What is evident is that the criteria suggested in this paper seem not to have been invoked or applied, ordinarily, in the case of priests and sisters in political office. One valuable consequence of the present study may be to highlight the importance of "testing" the experiences of religious professionals in public service. This could be achieved by a process of spiritual discernment that uncovers the presence—or absence—of those elements considered essential for any activity to be recognized as ministry in the Church. Such a process might also lead to the discovery of guarantees to be assured when priests or sisters, in accordance with minimal ecclesiastical requirements, seek political office.

Basic to the process of spiritual discernment just suggested is the acknowledgment of priesthood and religious life as states of life or vocations that, in a very real sense, "belong" to the Church. This affirmation can be maintained, even though a distinction must be made between priests and sisters in the Church.

The statement that "priesthood belongs to the Church" is an ecclesiological statement. Priesthood is rooted in the sacramentality of the Church. Through Baptism, we share in the priesthood of Christ. We become a "priestly people." Some members of this people are "ordered" to ministerial priesthood. In this capacity, they manifest the sacramental, hierarchical character of the Church in which they exercise priestly ministry. They assume positions as "public persons" in the community of believers.

There seems to be an unspoken expectation in the *ekklesia* that the "public service" given by the priest will take place within the Church. The entrance of the priest into public service through political office is frequently perceived as an anomaly, even when the reasons for this perception cannot be expressed clearly and convincingly by an individual or a community.

This inability to translate a deep-seated "Catholic intuition" regarding the role of the priest is not surprising, particularly today, when questions arise from many quarters in the Church regarding the need for a "new theology" of priesthood and when the emergence of multiple ministries, among other factors, points to the necessity of a new understanding of ministerial priesthood and spiritual leadership in the Church. We seem to have come to a place where awareness of a priest's "belonging to the Church" as a "public person" is more clearly affirmed and more directly challenged than ever before. To what extent does the presence of the priest in political office promote or hinder the efforts by which priests and people together seek to assess and meet the needs of a Church-in-mission? To what degree does a priest's exercise of "political ministry" assure and enhance the role of the believing community as a ministerial people? At what point is there an essential conflict between the exercise of priestly ministry and participation in political office? These are questions which need to be asked at many levels of ecclesial life. It is too early to anticipate the answers that might be offered in response to them, once experience, reflection and dialogue have explored the issue.

If "priesthood belongs to the Church," religious life can be said to be "born of the heart of the Church." It is not outrageous to claim that the Church could not be Church without religious life. The corollary to this is immediately evident: religious life cannot truly exist or flourish without the Church. These statements represent another way of expressing what we read in Pope Paul VI's Apostolic Exhortation, *Evangelica testificatio*: "Without this concrete sign there would be a danger that the charity which animates the entire Church would grow cold, that the salvific paradox of the Gospel would be blunted, and that the 'salt' of faith would lose its savor in a world undergoing secularization" (3). In the same document, we find an expression of what is understood as the specific witness to be given by religious in the world: it is the "splendid and striking testimony that the world cannot be transfigured and offered to God without the spirit of the beatitudes" (50).

There is an emphasis in conciliar and post-conciliar documents as well as in statements from ecclesiastical authorities that seems to highlight the "sacred" and the *ekklesia* as the appropriate arenas for the participation of religious in the mission of the Church. In one instance, this sharing is identified as "collaboration in 'her enterprises and objectives in such fields as the scriptural, liturgical, doctrinal, pastoral, ecumenical, missionary and social.' " Without much hesitation, women religious in the United States have interpreted such texts widely in practical, concrete action. Involvement in political office seems to be one door through which sisters have walked to address what seem to be the roots of many of the evils in society: faulty or inadequate legislation, lack of integrity on the part of many political officials, disregard for the worth and dignity of the human person, especially the poor.

This is not the place to do more than recall the problems which touch on religious life in the United States today, because of conflicting understandings regarding the nature of that life and the appropriate role of women religious in the Church. There can be no doubt, however, that the scenario actually being played out in that regard cannot disregard, from either side, the interpretation and evaluation of the involvement of sisters in political office. Where women religious are actively engaged in public service without opposition or conflict with ecclesiastical superiors, there is still no evidence that the question is on the way to right resolution.

It would seem that, in the case of women religious more than of priests, "political ministry" is likely to be perceived as a misdirected activity or an inappropriate "ministry," both by members of the laity and by persons holding ecclesiastical authority. This perception is based on one understanding of the role of religious in the Church. That understanding and that role still have meaning today. However, the renewal of religious life which followed the Second Council of the Vatican has brought about new roles and, in consequence, new understandings of who religious are and what they are to be about in ecclesial service. Religious, themselves, in returning to their roots, as the Council mandated, have had new insights into the way in which their original, "founding" charism is to be exercised in a new time and place. In either understanding or perception of religious life, fundamental theological principles are at stake. Furthermore, there is a perception of religious either as "clerical" or as "lay."

It is just this point that women religious, especially, would argue, on canonical grounds. Indeed, a good part of the renewal undertaken by women religious in the United States since Vatican II has been motivated by the intention to "get down from the pedestal" and to stand with their lay sisters in forthright, positive Christian service in the

Church and in the world. The misunderstandings and conflict resulting from the past decade and a half of renewal in American religious congregations are a matter of concern in the entire Church in the United States. Efforts toward reconciliation are certainly being pursued with good will and hope. It is possible that "political ministry" is one of several issues that will have to be taken into serious consideration, as that pursuit continues.

As the phenomenon of priests and sisters in political ministry continues to be a dilemma in the United States, it will become increasingly imperative to reflect theologically on the culture in which the Church "sojourns" and to which she is in mission. As James Hug has shown in an article on ministry, "Social Sin, Cultural Healing" (*Chicago Studies*, Fall, 1984), the past twenty-five years in the United States have been years of overwhelming change, disappointment, disillusion and too much of the "reality" that T.S. Eliot found human nature cannot bear. Aside from the national dis-ease of this past quarter of a century, we have been sharers in the changing moods and moments of the civil rights movement, the women's liberation movement, and the growing conviction, especially among "religious professionals" in the Church, that the inherent values of a nation dedicated to the pursuit of "liberty and justice for all" are consonant with gospel imperatives and that the democratic process can be an effective vehicle for the transmission of those imperatives into our culture.

What is to be the future of priests and sisters in "political ministry"? I am not able to venture even a tentative response to that query. In this paper, I have suggested selected criteria by which such ministry might be evaluated. I have sought to identify ecclesiological principles underlying areas of tension and conflict. I have attempted to probe and reflect without prejudice to either side of the question. I would like to hope that the phenomenon which I have called a dilemma *can* become a paradox and a challenge in our midst. It will take all our faith and love to make that journey.

Part 2
VIEWS OF THE PRACTITIONERS

The heart of the matter, the genesis of the "sensus fidelium" regarding the relationship between church people and politics must be the experience of the practitioners themselves. This section records the experience of some of those men and women. Several who have actually served in political offices offer their reflections, a kind of "wisdom literature" of this unique religious-cultural phenomenon. Thomas Gannon's essay on how and why Robert Drinan came to Congress provides a kind of paradigm for the period of the 1970's. Carol Coston's posthumous reflections on the career of Clare Dunn, the first sister elected to a state legislature, and Larry O'Rourke's on Geno Baroni, who held the highest federal post ever occupied by a priest, are fascinating and edifying illuminations of stars whose light has been dimmed prematurely. Carolyn Farrell and Roland St. Pierre record their rise to election as city mayors. Joseph Simon, Ardeth Platte, and Jacqueline Slater tell their stories of serving in city councils and struggling with local politics, their experience being perhaps the most representative of the involvement of many priests and religious engaged in political ministry today in rural as well as urban areas. Elizabeth Morancy, now in her fourth term in the Rhode Island state legislature, and Theodore Hesburgh, who has served in 14 government posts, reflect on their unique experiences. Mary Sean O'Reilly, a judge and court master for the state of Texas, describes her experience in a ministry that attracts increasing numbers of religious men and women: legal advocacy, the criminal justice system and the judiciary. Finally, the section closes with the eloquent statements of Robert Drinan, on the occasion of his forced resignation from the Congressional race in 1980, and of Agnes Mary Mansour, on the occasion of her forced resignation from the Sisters of Mercy in 1983.

189

Thomas M. Gannon

REVEREND FATHER CONGRESSMAN*

The grass-roots movement in the Third Congressional District of Massachusetts that, on Nov. 3, 1970, sent the Reverend Robert F. Drinan, S.J., to Washington as the first Roman Catholic priest elected to Congress in the twentieth century really began on a primary election day in 1968.

In the Third District contest that year for the Democratic nomination for U.S. Congress, three peace candidates divided 52 per cent of the vote, but the incumbent, Philip Philbin, took the rest and the nomination, and later returned to Congress to begin his fourteenth term. The supporters of the defeated candidates, realizing their mistake, vowed that in 1970 they would unite behind a single candidate and take Mr. Philbin's seat away from him.

In the summer of 1969, Fr. Drinan, dean of the Boston College Law School, travelled to Vietnam as part of an ecumenical fact-finding mission. He returned to the United States more of a dove on the war than ever. A few months later, in October, 1969, participation in the Vietnam Moratorium identified hundreds of people as potential recruits for the effort to unseat Mr. Philbin. Throughout December, 1969, and January, 1970, an ad hoc executive committee of what came to be known as the Third District Citizens' Caucus met to discuss prospective candidates and their qualifications. Arthur Obermayer, an industrialist from Newton whose electronics firm specializes in defense contracts, suggested Fr. Drinan. The latter, when contacted by Mr. Obermayer, showed interest in the nomination. Meanwhile, other po-

---

*Several priests and religious, currently or formerly holders of political offices, were invited to contribute their reflections to this volume. Among those who declined, for reasons of their own, were former Congressmen Robert Drinan, SJ, and Robert Cornell, O. Praem.

tential candidates were screened and interviewed by the executive committee, and the caucus itself was more extensively organized.

Finally, on Feb. 21, 1970, over a thousand people met in Concord to hear the candidates speak, then choose a nominee. Originally, there were 12 candidates, but 9 dropped out, leaving Harry Stevens, one of the men who had lost to Mr. Philbin in 1968, John Kerry, a decorated veteran of the Vietnam War and a recent convert to the peace movement, and Fr. Robert Drinan. All day long, delegates to the caucus met by town or city to discuss how their community's votes should be cast. Mr. Stevens withdrew, leaving only Mr. Kerry and Fr. Drinan. On the fourth ballot, Fr. Drinan received the required two-thirds majority. The Third District Citizens' Caucus had a candidate for Congress.

The campaign began slowly. John Marttila, who had worked for the Republican National Committee trying to bring young blacks into the Republican party, signed on as campaign manager in mid-March. Older members of the caucus set out to raise the funds needed to mount a successful challenge to a long-term incumbent like Mr. Philbin. Student volunteers from the colleges and universities in the Boston area started showing up for work at Drinan headquarters.

Then came the invasion of Cambodia and the shooting of four students by National Guardsmen at Kent State University. The stream of student volunteers swelled to a flood. John Marttila put them to work canvassing 40,000 households in the Third District. The canvass, whose results were tabulated by computer, then transferred to voter registration lists for use on September 15, primary election day, identified not only potential Drinan voters, but potential Drinan volunteers. These latter helped to complete the canvass and to inundate the district, in massive door-to-door leaflettings, with Drinan literature.

The candidate himself, on leave from Boston College, campaigned vigorously—on college campuses, at factory gates, in supermarkets, on radio talk shows. At the start of the campaign, only 16 per cent of the voters in the district knew who he was. As the campaign progressed, the figure soared to over 75 per cent. In the meantime, the Democratic incumbent, Mr. Philbin, confident that he would turn aside Fr. Drinan's challenge easily, campaigned hardly at all.

On September 15, the Drinan organization was ready. Despite bad weather, the voter turnout was heavy, and the Drinan staff made sure it was their people who turned out. Citizens who, when canvassed, had indicated a preference for Fr. Drinan were telephoned repeatedly and urged to go to the polls. Transportation was provided if they needed it. And go to the polls they did. Fr. Drinan polled 28,000 votes to Mr. Philbin's 22,000, and the nominee of the Third District Citizens' Caucus had become the nominee of the Democratic party as well.

Throughout the primary campaign, a major topic of conversation was Fr. Drinan's status as a Roman Catholic priest. Before he made himself available for the nomination of the Citizens' Caucus, he had sought and won from his immediate religious and ecclesiastical superiors, not an endorsement of his candidacy, but assurance that his quest for public office was indeed compatible with his status as a priest and a Jesuit. Still, the question of Fr. Drinan's priesthood remained in people's minds, and was raised on radio talk shows, in letters to newspapers, and in conversations with the candidate and his supporters.

Though his staff had armed his canvassers with an answer to the objection that "a priest should not be in politics," though he had toyed with the idea of arranging a public confrontation to air the priesthood issue fully (as John F. Kennedy did with the Catholic issue at Houston in 1960), and though he had gathered (but did not use) a series of endorsements of the legitimacy of his candidacy by religious leaders of all faiths, Fr. Drinan's general approach was to dismiss it as a non-issue, and pass on to more important things.

In retrospect, he felt he had acted correctly, and his staff regretted that he and they had "wasted" so much time agonizing over the question during the summer. Fr. Drinan's primary victory made his candidacy credible and virtually ended public discussion of the propriety of a priest in politics.

Private reservations about that propriety are another thing, however. Public opinion polls taken at the end of the general election campaign revealed that over 30 per cent of Third District voters still objected to priests in politics. Opposition to Fr. Drinan's candidacy on the grounds of his priesthood was, surprisingly, strongest among Catholics. The candidate himself attributed that opposition to the profound alienation of the ordinary citizen from politics. It was, they believed, a dirty business and their priests ought to stay out of it.

Other Drinan staff members thought that their candidate was a lightning rod for change in the Church. Men and women who did not like English in the liturgy or guitars in the sanctuary could express their resentment at those reforms by voting against a priest in politics. Still others thought that professional politicians in Massachusetts (most of them Irish or Italian Catholics) were jealous over the instant publicity given to Fr. Drinan. After years of handshaking at dreary party affairs, after years of handing out pocket calendars and matchbooks in an effort to get their names before the public, they resented the relative ease with which Fr. Drinan, because of his priesthood, became not only well-known locally, but a national figure as well.

One Drinan volunteer, herself an agnostic, credited the Catholic resistance to Fr. Drinan's candidacy to an overly spiritualized notion of the priesthood: "I don't know why they can't see that he's a man. They think that because he's a priest he isn't a man."

Another Drinan volunteer spoke of talking to a Catholic with eight children, a public school principal who was struggling to make ends meet. At the beginning of their conversation, he advanced extremely rational arguments about separation of Church and state (most non-Catholic opposition to a priest in politics, incidentally, focused on this issue, with special emphasis on the centralized structure of the Church of Rome). As they continued to talk, however, it became clear that he blamed the Church's teachings on birth control for his economic difficulties. Fr. Drinan and all priests, he felt, lived in ivory towers and did not know what life was about.

A final element in the Catholic opposition to Fr. Drinan's candidacy was, paradoxically, anti-Semitism. Several prominent members of the Citizens' Caucus were Jewish, several leading contributors to the candidate's campaign were Jewish and many of his student volunteers were Jewish. The combination resuscitated a centuries-old prejudice in some Catholics. Fr. Drinan, they believed, was but a front man for Jewish interests.

A few people in the Drinan camp felt that, given the time, money, energy and technology poured into the campaign, the candidate would have walked away with the primary election if he had not been a Roman Catholic priest. In the light of the polls and the number of times the issue was discussed during the primary campaign, the feeling is understandable. It is not necessarily accurate, however, for the impact of Fr. Drinan's priesthood on his candidacy was positive as well as negative.

It surely helped to make him easily recognizable by the electorate. By November 3, 90 per cent of the people in the Third District could identify him. Children in the Burger King in Waltham came up to him and said: "We know you. You're Fr. Drinan." His priesthood won him votes as well. Some Catholics with a traditional, somewhat embattled mentality undoubtedly cast their ballots for him because "he's one of our own and we've got to stick by him." One voter told a Drinan volunteer that on primary election day he had gone into the polling booth still undecided about whom to vote for and finally settled on Fr. Drinan simply because he was a priest. The volunteer's interpretation of the incident was that "people associate a priest with a real concern about humanity."

An intensive socio-psychological study of the attitudes of Third District voters would be required to assess with complete accuracy the impact of Fr. Drinan's priesthood on his candidacy. For the present, however, there seems to be considerable truth in the assertion of one Drinan worker that "if Fr. Drinan hadn't been a priest, his candidacy would never have gotten off the ground."

Victory in the Democratic primary did not assure Fr. Drinan of election to Congress. State Representative John McGlennon was already running hard as the Republican nominee, and Philip Philbin, understandably reluctant to relinquish a House seat he had held for so long, refused to accept the primary results. Instead, he mounted an independent campaign as a "sticker" candidate, urging voters to ignore the Republican and Democratic nominees and instead to paste his own stickers on their ballots.

In the general election campaign, as in the primary, the Drinan effort was fueled by the energies of 3500 volunteers, more than half of them over 30. The motives of these volunteers were undoubtedly as varied as the volunteers themselves, but perhaps the motives of two of them will serve to illustrate those of so many others. Anne Marie Goggin, 21, had been 1969–1970 student body president at Regis College near Boston. "I got into it slowly," she said. "I had heard of Fr. Drinan, and I wanted a graduation speaker who would say the kind of things Drinan said. So I wrote to him and he agreed to come. We talked then about his potential campaign. Later, after he was nominated, he sent me a letter asking for volunteers, and I started working. I don't know that I was radicalized by Kent State and Cambodia, but I did get more involved after those two things happened."

The campaign had a distinct personal meaning for her. "It's helped me to find myself," she said, "to find out what I want to do with my life. I always wanted to go to law school. Now I know why. Now I can see the law as a tool for the service of the people. So the campaign is both goal and discovery for me. The goal is Fr. Drinan's election, of course, and the discovery is the process whereby I've learned what things are most important to me. This is the kind of thing I want to be involved in, in the particular sense of Fr. Drinan's election and in the general sense of what things in life are worth doing. This is a place where I can contribute, because I have a lot of time and some energy."

The Drinan campaign was a personal affair for Tom Vallely, too. On August 13, 1969, while he was serving with India Company, 3rd

Battalion, 5th Marine Regiment, in a region of South Vietnam called the "Arizona Territory," 20-odd miles south of DaNang, his unit walked into a North Vietnamese ambush. Tom Vallely won a Silver Star by collecting hand grenades from wounded comrades and using them to knock out two enemy machine gun emplacements. "When I was in Vietnam, still in the field," he said, "I read about this Citizens' Caucus. My first thought was that it was some phony, white liberal caucus. But when I came home, I thought I'd check this guy Drinan out. I did, and I started to work as a regular canvasser. Then in July, I quit my job and came on fulltime."

Why did he decide to oppose the war he had fought in? "You just start thinking about these things. You look at the over-all situation. Like last week, 43 men were killed in Vietnam. I remember when 43 men were killed a day. You ask yourself: 'Why do I have to kill these people? Why do my friends have to die? Why are we here?' Well, our two governments sent us. When you capture one of these people, you don't even want to hit him, he's so scared, so nervous. Then I read the statistics—about the political prisoners, the government, the deaths. So I thought I'd do something about it, I suppose. Maybe I owe something to the friends I left there, the friends in my company."

The speedy liquidation of the war in Vietnam through a device like the McGovern-Hatfield amendment was only one of the issues Fr. Drinan campaigned on in the period between the primary and general elections. Congress, he said, should reassert its responsibility in the formation of foreign policy instead of servilely yielding it to the President. He criticised the increasing militarization of America, and called for a reordering of domestic priorities that would provide more funds for housing, education and health care. He scored the President for increasing unemployment (a serious problem in the Third District) without stopping inflation. And, toward the end, as the campaign became increasingly vicious, he repeatedly preached the "politics of reconciliation," based on mutual trust, respect and love.

Mr. Philbin based his bid for reelection partially on the literally thousands of favors he had done for his constituents during his 28 years in Congress. Another, more important issue was the depressed state of the economy in the Third District. As defense contracts were cut back, unemployment rose in the electronics industries concentrated in the area. Mr. Philbin, citing his seniority in the House (12th out of 435) and his status as vice-chairman of the House Armed Services Committee, campaigned on the slogan "Philbin means jobs." Much of his support came from organized labor, especially the International Brotherhood of Electrical Workers, whose members were frankly afraid of losing their jobs and openly hostile to Fr. Drinan with his call for reductions in defense spending.

Mr. McGlennon, the Republican candidate, associated himself with the Nixon Administration. He supported the President's time-table for withdrawal from Vietnam and disagreed with Fr. Drinan over the foreign policy role of Congress. The House and Senate, Mr. McGlennon believed, should follow the President's lead rather than strike out on their own. He was cautiously optimistic about the state of the economy, saying that "the President was getting a handle on it," and that "we are almost out of the woods." In any event, he argued, as a Republican he could work better with the President and thus bring more jobs to the Third District.

An anti-Drinan issue that both Mr. McGlennon and Mr. Philbin shared was that of law and order. Mr. Philbin associated Fr. Drinan with radicalism, extremism, Marxism and totalitarianism. He charged that the latter's campaign was staffed by "minions of the New Left" (in the last few days before the election, Fr. Drinan took a cue from Mr. Philbin and addressed his workers as "dear minions"), and was fi-nanced by "golden streams" of money flowing into the state from out-side (the Drinan campaign was indeed expensive, costing $120,000 in the primary alone, but 88 per cent of the contributions came from Massachusetts).

In his speeches, Mr. McGlennon accused Fr. Drinan of emotional instability and called him a "left-winger" and an "extremist." He also used radio spots—effectively, if not necessarily ethically. One spot be-gan with youthful voices shouting "off [kill] the pigs," then took a state-ment by Fr. Drinan about civil disobedience out of its original context (the Nuremburg war criminal trials) and implied that the priest en-couraged disrespect for law. Another featured more young voices shouting "Hell, no. We won't go." It tried to link Fr. Drinan with stu-dent unrest wherever it occurred.

Editorial writers and columnists in the Boston *Globe,* the Water-town *Press* and Leominster *Enterprise* came to Fr. Drinan's defense, condemning his opponents' tactics. Lawrence O'Brien, Democratic National Chairman, denounced the introduction of "Agnewism" into the campaign. On Oct. 29, 1,200 Drinan supporters jammed Boston's Faneuil Hall to hear Sen. Eugene McCarthy of Minnesota warn that "the devices of the demagogue . . . are again abroad in the land," and to hear the candidate himself renounce the "verbal violence" of his op-ponents. Indeed, during the last few days of the campaign, Fr. Drinan pleaded repeatedly with his youthful workers, asking that they not be embittered by the tactics used against him.

Yet there was deep resentment in the Drinan camp. "Philbin is sort of a tragic figure," one worker said. "He's an old man whose seat is being taken away from him. What he's said is not half as insidious as McGlennon, because McGlennon knows what he's doing. He knows he's quoting Fr. Drinan out of context, he knows he's distorting, he knows he's being unfair. It's really incredible that the campaign has become so ugly and base."

The Drinan staff at first ignored the charges about their candidate. Later, they admitted they had been wrong. "We should have put out a clarification right away," said campaign manager John Marttila. "It was a tactical and an ethical mistake on our part. That's the problem with the liberal movement in this country. They endure this kind of thing. They ought to tell these other people that they're not going to take it. You have to fight back."

As the campaign neared an end, Fr. Drinan's strengths and weaknesses as a politician came into sharper focus. To some extent, his failures were those all politicians experience. Some speeches fell flat on their faces but, as an aide explained, "in this business you can't stay high all the time."

Other liabilities were more peculiar to Fr. Drinan's own candidacy. His outspoken ways were a problem. They alienated some people, and made him especially vulnerable to quotation out of context. "I wish we'd read his books carefully beforehand," said Dan Payne, his press secretary. "Then we'd have known what we might have to defend." For a time, the candidate, himself an amateur, fretted about giving responsibility to his largely amateur staff. Fr. Drinan's capacity for seeing the several sides to a single question sometimes hurt him too, because it kept him from making the narrowly political statements that many people apparently expected to hear. He once hedged on an endorsement of Sen. Edward Kennedy because he thought his questioner was leading him into a discussion of the incident at Chappaquiddick. On other occasion, when asked if he supported the Black Panthers, he singled out three innocuous Panther proposals and said he was in favor of them. His opponents naturally interpreted his statement as an endorsement of the entire Panther program.

On balance, however, his staff agreed that his strong points outweighed these deficiencies. "He has never weakened on the issues," said Jerry Grossman, an organizer of the Citizens' Caucus and the campaign's finance director. It was, after all, Fr. Drinan's stand on the issues that won him the nomination of the caucus and attracted so many volunteers.

"The exciting thing about Fr. Drinan," said Joan Snitzer, 17, "is that he's willing to give young people responsibility." For John Marttila, the candidate's vitality was a factor. "His great strength is that he's got spark," he said. "Drinan's alive, and when you're with him, you know it, and that's what makes a man." The candidate's idealism worked in his favor, too. Housewives in supermarkets told him: "We need more men like you." Volunteers saw in him a chance to "initiate a new, more moral politics." Finally, as the months passed, Fr. Drinan's skill as a campaigner noticeably increased. "At the beginning," said one aide, "he was just a priest in politics. Now he's put it all together."

Even before the Drinan campaign was over, people were already probing for its meaning. One of the most perceptive comments was offered by Stephen Jigger, a Drinan volunteer who graduated from Harvard in 1969. "Some people think that this election is a test of the system," he said, "but it's too much to say that. This is a special district. It's been reapportioned to include highly educated, suburban communities like Newton, Watertown and Waltham, and the redistricting hurt Philbin. Sure, a large effort with a lot of money can produce a victory, but if Philbin had done anything, he would have won.

"This election shows the impediments the system works under," he continued. "In Newton, Concord and Lincoln, you had people with money who were politically interested. You have universities around, so there's student manpower available. Yet with all that money—we were spending $5 or $6 a vote in the primary—and with 40 or 50 full-time people, with hundreds of volunteers, it took all this to defeat an incumbent Congressman who has done nothing in 28 years except a few favors for his constituents."

On October 22, a Boston *Globe* poll showed Drinan with 35 per cent of the vote, Philbin with 26, McGlennon with 22, and 17 per cent undecided. A second poll a week later showed Drinan had lost three per cent, McGlennon had gained two, and 18 per cent of the voters remained undecided. Supreme confidence still characterized the public posture of the Drinan operation, but Frank Maloney, a Drinan volunteer employed at the Raytheon electronics installation in Waltham, was less sure of the election's outcome. "The silent majority didn't vote in the primary," he said. "A lot of bitter, hostile people couldn't care less about a primary. It's going to be tight."

The last weekend of the campaign, the Drinan organization mounted a maximum effort. The candidate appeared at rallies, dances, cocktail parties, lox and bagel breakfasts, and ham and beans dinners. His television commercials were shown during the Tonight Show, the David Frost Show and the Boston Bruins' hockey games. His volunteers fanned out through the district for one last leafletting.

On November 3, election day, the Drinan staff held a "Breakfast of Champions" at 5:30 A.M., then set out to employ the same techniques that had worked so well on primary day. Once again, voter turnout was heavy. There were reports of irregularities—Philbin workers electioneering and distributing stickers in illegal proximity to the polls—and John Marttila complained about them in a statement issued at noon. At 8 P.M., the polls closed. The voters had rendered their verdict.

Given the inherent difficulties of a "sticker" campaign, Philip Philbin had run amazingly well, polling 46,755 votes. John McGlennon had confounded the pollsters by winning 60,785 votes and finishing second. Robert Drinan had won only five of the Third District's 31 towns and cities, but his pluralities in Newton, Watertown and Waltham put him over the top with 63,863 votes. It had been a very close race indeed, but Fr. Drinan, who had weathered a storm about his priesthood during the primary campaign and fought off a series of smears during the general election campaign, was going to Congress.

Carol Coston, OP

THE LEGACY OF
SISTER CLARE DUNN, CSJ

On January 12, 1982, in the Arizona legislature, the following tributes were given to Sister Clare Dunn, CSJ, the first Catholic sister elected to a state legislature in the United States. She and Sister Judith Lovchik, CSJ, her longtime friend, campaign manager and co-worker in politics, had been killed July 31, 1981 in a head-on collision with another vehicle. At the time Clare was the elected Assistant Minority Leader in the House.

> I would like to speak on behalf of the Republicans who did not always agree with Sister Dunn. . . . I think that all of us have great respect for her abilities as a speaker, great respect for her abilities as a debater, great respect for her as a hard-working legislator and certainly I add to those in that respect. But, I think what we are going to mainly miss here is the fact that, in my opinion, we have lost the conscience of the House, we have lost a champion of the poor, we have lost someone who could speak and remind us that there are unemployed in the State of Arizona, that there are women who do not have equal rights, that there are minority groups who do not have every opportunity that is supposed to be granted to all of us as citizens of this great nation. My concern is who will step forward to remind us of these facts. Who will be our new champion? We have our lobbyists from industry, the farmers, the cattlemen and every other group you can conceive of here at the legislature, but Sister Dunn represented those people who did not have a lobbyist or the lawyers, those people who did not have a voice, except for legislators like Clare Dunn. (Rep. Donald Kenney, R-Phoenix)

Sister Clare was the first person that exposed me to the legislative process. She brought me to Phoenix in her car and she shared some of her thoughts. . . ."Chuy, remember that it is not what people feel about other people that counts, it is what you are going to sacrifice for the poor, the elderly, the disadvantaged that God will recognize you for." If more humans would be like Sister Clare, the world as we know it, would be a better place to live. Therefore, I would like to commit, in public, my political career to the memory of Sister Clare. (Rep. Jesus Higuera, D-Tucson)

The other thing I want to share with you is that among the Navajo people, there is always the saying that when you go through life you will recognize that the good people never last long, that is somebody that is pure in the heart, pure in the spirit, and pure in thought will not be among you, the living, for long. . . .You will just see a glimpse of them. They will come into your life, you will see them, you will hear them, you will feel them and they will be gone. (Rep. Daniel Peaches, R-Window Rock)

Who was this woman so remembered? Why was this nun in politics? Could a socially conscious, feminist Democrat accomplish anything in a Republican controlled legislature noted for its support of vested and wealthy interests, its chauvinism and its disdain for the poor? Were there accomplishments commensurate with Clare Dunn's seven years' struggle as a legislator?

Sister Clare Dunn, CSJ, was born Fern Lois Dunn on November 13, 1934, in Arlington, California. She grew up on a farm where she loved to work in the fields with her father. After high school Clare worked as a secretary and later entered the Sisters of St. Joseph of Carondelet in 1956 where she became a government and history teacher. In 1965 she was assigned to teach at Villa Carondelet. At both the Villa and Salpointe High she encouraged her students to become politically involved, and in so doing she herself became an elected McGovern delegate to the 1972 Democratic convention.

I first met Clare in 1972 when she was appointed a McGovern delegate to the credentials committee. This contentious committee met in Washington and Clare told stories about her first immersion in national politics. One irate delegate inquired angrily, "How can you, a nun, vote against Mayor Daley? Don't you know he is a Catholic?" Other lobbying efforts typically began with the person claiming credentials such as, "my uncle is a monsignor" or " Sister so and so, my aunt . . ."

Later that summer Clare participated in the NETWORK Legislative Seminar. This first event of the Catholic social justice lobby attracted about 150 nuns to Washington to learn the political process integrated with a faith perspective. Clare helped organize an added event during which Mrs. George McGovern and McGovern staffers presented his views on issues and encouraged participation in the campaign. Clare returned to Arizona and ran the state campaign for McGovern.

Subsequent political experiences and a growing reflection on societal and individual suffering led Clare to a personal conviction that "injustice in society is not the will of God," and it became clear to her that "the place where injustice is most often redressed or multiplied, usually the latter, is the arena of government." She compared this insight to her original decision to become a nun:

> My decision to run for the House in 1974 was the natural result of my commitment to serve people, a new expression of what I had pledged to do so many years before. By working for laws that are just, by trying to introduce into the political debate the moral considerations attendant on issues of health care, tax laws, energy output, employment practices, interest rates, to name just a few, I hoped to witness to God's care 'for the least of our brothers and sisters,' God's concern for the marginal and the powerless, God's personal attention to the orphan and the widow, described so eloquently and so often in the Old Testament. ("Politics is My Ministry," Saturday Magazine, Scottsdale *Daily Progress*, Fall 1979)

This decision, first made in December 1973, was controversial within her congregation and elicited painful discussions and personal disappointments. The Provincial Council initially refused her permission. Clare had been asked to meet with the Most Rev. Francis Green, bishop of the Diocese of Tucson. He discussed the difficulties of political life with her; and although he neither endorsed nor supported her, he did not raise objections to her candidacy. The council then received a negative reaction from a spokesman for Bishop Edward McCarthy of Phoenix. This negative response was affirmed later in a private meeting between the bishop and the Provincial, Assistant Provincial and Clare's regional superior. After the Provincial Council met subsequent to the bishop's meeting, Clare was informed by the Provincial that the bishop's objections were significant and she could not run for office as a Sister of St. Joseph.

On 24 April 1974, Clare wrote a lengthy letter to the Provincial Council in which she outlined her convictions and the evolution of the decision to seek office. In May, Clare and about a dozen CSJ supporters met with the council. During this discussion Clare spoke of her decision as a matter of conscience and the Provincial, Sister Mary Brigid, asked to meet with her another time privately. As a result of this discussion on May 20, Clare received permission to become a candidate.

Like many other women religious in the 1970's Clare took the Vatican Council's call to renewal seriously. These women were persuaded, not only by their own experiences of change within religious communities, but also by the clear challenges to promote structural changes in documents such as Pope Paul VI's *Call to Action* and the Synod statement on *Justice in the World*. Clare's own introduction to the Church's social teaching began in a Catholic high school in Los Angeles, 1960 when another sister on the faculty suggested, during a heated political discussion in which Clare was extolling Richard Nixon who was then running for President, that she read *Rerum Novarum*.

> I almost asked "What's that?" but was vaguely aware that an ancient papal encyclical bore that name. I got hold of a copy and found myself studying it with eagerness and astonishment . . . From there I went on to statements of succeeding popes and conferences of bishops which strongly underlined the rights and dignity of the individual human person and the need to make this broad spectrum of rights and responsibilities effective in every social, political and economic system. The discovery of this whole body of social morality, unknown to many members of the Church because it has not been promulgated with the same enthusiasm as other moral principles, not only had a profound effect on my teaching, but also prepared me for my later decision to enter politics. (from "Politics is My Ministry")

Given this long gestation period of internalizing Church justice teachings and acting on the challenges they contained, it was most irritating for Clare to find official church resistance to her being in politics—an irritation increasingly shared by many other women religious.

Clare's efforts to arrange a dialog with Bishop McCarthy of Phoenix were unsuccessful. Eventually she received a letter from him in which he admitted that it was not within his power to "forbid" her candidacy. However, he opposed it because he felt it would "affect adversely the efforts of the Church in Arizona pastorally and in its efforts to be an influence for social reform and improvement."

Clare did not agree with the bishop's judgment and in a homily several years later summarized her own views on the subject:

> I see the Church's presence in politics as an important force against the familiar evils of discouragement, cynicism, and despair. Christians should have a great capacity to absorb discouragement. They can give to each other, and to their co-workers in the struggle to build a more just society, the patience and hope that come from being able to take the long view—an amazing grace, grace that may elude us at times, but never for long. Because we know so well the unfinished character of Jesus' saving act, we should be able to reach out to the future without anxiety, trusting that we are, however painfully and mysteriously, participating in the work of salvation. The German theologian, Dorothee Soelle, calls it a "revolutionary patience" which refuses to abandon messianic hope even in the darkness of the present political climate—and it is dark indeed. (St. Cyril's Church, Tucson, 12 October 1980)

Clare was no stranger to the need for "revolutionary patience" and referred to being in politics as both "a burden and a joy." In a speech entitled "Ministering to the Body Politic" (Denver, Feb. 1981), she described the decision to move from teaching into politics as a "decision which I never regretted but which has often prompted me to grumble like the beleaguered Job: 'I was in peace, but he dislodged me.' "

However, Clare did not feel that her political ministry dislodged her from her congregation's traditions. On the contrary, she described in the same speech how their priest founder, John Medaille, in the 17th century "directed our first sisters to divide up the city, which happened to be LePuy, France, in order to 'learn what disorders prevail in each quarter and so they may remedy them.' " She felt then in 1974 that the legislature "metaphorically speaking, happened to be in my quarter." And that this institution was "meting out injustice with regularity and impunity, routinely impervious to human needs." She used even stronger language in a speech to the Sisters of St. Joseph: "And the stench of evil that arose from that place was so great, the need so profound that I had to act. It was not an easy decision. . . and my superiors, understandably, had many concerns. But courage, or perhaps I should say, rashness, triumphed and we moved together, into a new and untested response to human needs."

Clare was not alone in criticizing the state legislature. She agreed with the publication *The Sometimes Government* (1971) in which the Arizona legislature received an infamous rank of 43rd among the fifty state legislatures. The rating was based on minimum standards of democracy and efficiency: functionality, accountability, informedness, independence and representativeness.

And so in January, 1975, when Representative Clare Dunn first entered the State House, she was painfully aware of its inadequacies. By June, 1975, she wrote: "I knew that the Arizona House was anachronistic and regressive in its procedures and this has been more than confirmed in this session."

She decried the access of the powerful and wealthy to the system and described how the attorneys for banks, insurance companies and big business wrote legislation dealing with their industries to the detriment of consumers and taxpayers' interests. She bemoaned the compressed time schedule which mitigated against thorough study and debate.

As that first disappointing and unproductive session drew to a close, Clare was told "don't give up, hang in there." Her response was "I have never entertained the idea of giving up or giving in. To the contrary, the more I learn, the more I plot change. While it is not very satisfying to fight a rearguard action of trying to keep worse things from happening to the citizenry rather than promoting and enacting constructive legislation, we at least gain some experience and position ourselves to do more in the future." And in this same speech—typical of her positive attitude toward a difficult task—she already had her eight goals outlined for the next session. ("Resume of the First Session of the 32nd Legislature" June 4, 1975)

During her seven years as a legislator Clare received high praise for doing her homework and, as evidenced in her memorials, she was a formidable debater—never to be taken on lightly. In her first term she was put on the Banking and Insurance Committee (in the Republican controlled House Democrats did not have choices). She later described this as a "blessing in disguise" because as she took university classes in insurance and economics and studied assiduously, she began to see the enormous economic implications—especially for the poor and women.

She was equally diligent in approaching her work on the Ways and Means Committee. Steve Emerine, a reporter for the *Arizona Daily Star*, noted that "she quickly became one of the more knowledgeable members." Arizona has incredibly complex tax laws, but Clare studied hard and Mr. Emerine observed that "it was a joy to discuss the problems of property valuation and taxation with Sister Claire because—unlike the majority of legislators—she understood Arizona's laws and knew the inequities they contained."

A letter from a constituent at the time of her fourth campaign in 1980 illustrated her continuing study: "You far surpassed the men in the Forum on taxation May 22. You were the one who had a grasp of the subject and could express your thoughts clearly to the audience. Press on!"

Since the early 1970's Clare supported Common Cause's agenda of opening up the system, and she lobbied publicly for legislation dealing with open meetings, campaign financing, elections and ethics. She supported reform measures for written records of debate, roll call votes and the state's use of tax dollars. In her first term Clare joined other progressive Democrats in a lawsuit which asked for proportional representation on committees. The suit failed, but by 1978 the committee membership was proportional in all but two committees, and the Speaker of the House gave even Democrats a choice in committee assignments.

As a member of the minority party Clare did not introduce numerous bills "since the majority does not allow minority bills of a major consequence to move through the legislature." She proposed some alternatives through a few bills and amendments but saw her major responsibility in calling the majority party to "accountability to the average citizen." (from " Tucson nun seeks religious goal of peace, justice in state legislature," by Marguerite Bantlin, *Tucson View*, June 2, 1978)

In a speech to the Arizona Nurses Association, Nov. 9, 1979, Clare admitted that "legislative victories are sometimes measured by what was prevented—by an injustice that was derailed." An example of preventive action was the setting up of the House Special Interim Committee on Nuclear Power. Clare insisted on its creation, much to the dismay of the Arizona Public Service officials. In the aftermath of the Three Mile Island nuclear accident she thought it important for Arizona to hold hearings on the Palo Verde Nuclear Plant and review everything "that could affect the public health and safety before the plant becomes operational—not after." (speech to American Association of University Women, October 13, 1979)

In 1980 Clare was still trying to prevent problems. This occurred in a contemporary rendition of the biblical injunction against usury as Clare tried repeatedly to warn the Banking and Insurance Committee that their emergency act removing usury limits contained a loophole which opened the door to loan sharks. In an interview with the *Phoenix Gazette*, June 7, 1980, Clare described her efforts: "I explained it over and over on the House floor and pleaded with them not to pass the bill that way. I became like a broken record, making speeches on the floor trying to get anyone to listen." After the bill passed the chairman belatedly recognized the problem and had to set up a subcommittee to repair the damage and possibly request a special session of the legislature. Clare was not appointed to the subcommittee.

Clare had set the agenda on which she would be judged as early as 1974. In a letter to the Provincial Council, April 24, 1974, she pointed out: "If a Sister of St. Joseph were elected to a legislature, she would cast a vote on issues of human need and human rights. She would speak in a public forum in defense of the powerless and the weak. She would seek justice and decency for the poor and the working people through legislation." The closing line of the speech announcing her candidacy June 7, 1974, was "I want to go to Phoenix to struggle for social justice."

There is no question that Clare had unlimited opportunities to "struggle for social justice." An examination of her voting patterns, floor speeches, presentations to an overwhelming number of groups, conferences, forums and annual meetings, reveals that there were numerous opportunities and occasions for Clare to intervene in interests of social justice.

But how was she evaluated by others—constituents, colleagues, reporters and friends? One immediate assessment is the fact that she was re-elected for four terms, despite a resurgence of right wing politics which dislodged many of her progressive allies. Letters from constituents spoke of their enthusiasm for her values and issues, the hope she gave them, the pride they felt in her. Her campaigns were always able to attract numerous hard working and intelligent volunteers. Richard Deuriarte, the Phoenix *Gazette* Legislative Reporter, wrote on Sept. 6, 1980 that "Sister Clare is credited, even by House Majority Leader Burton Barr, a Phoenix Republican, as being one of the central figures in the reorganization of the old state Atomic Energy Commission, now structured as a much more powerful Radiation Regulatory

Agency." In another article on Feb. 16, 1981, Mr. Deuriarte reported on the "outnumbered cadre of Democratic lawmakers" which seemed to be "winning more battles than its very minority status (17 to 43 GOP members) would dictate." He explained that the group had been a minority since 1966 and in the past was incompatible, antagonistic and disparate. But now they are sticking together on the issues, and part of the credit went to Clare, "the feisty, intense House Assistant Minority Leader. . . (who) serves as the point for the liberal wing of the caucus. She is the one who will point out, as she did to the House Banking and Commerce Committee recently, which special-interest groups are receiving legislative tax relief and other favors—and who is being ignored."

Writing about the 1978 elections the *Tucson Citizen* described Sister Clare and then noted: "Though we cannot support her philosophy, we still note she is a leader of the House liberal bloc who has earned the grudging respect of the House GOP leaders. They fear her ability to pick apart some of their less well thought-out proposals and arguments."

And the *Arizona Daily Star*, editorializing about "Sister Clare's successor" on August 4, 1981, began with the statement: "Sister Clare Dunn was buried yesterday, and now the Pima County Board of Supervisors faces the impossible task of replacing the irreplaceable legislator."

Richard Bird, in a Ford Foundation funded "Program for Legislative Improvement in Seven States," commented that in his seven years working with legislatures Clare was "the outstanding legislator . . . I have never met anyone so sensitive to people's needs, willing to listen, capable of tackling problems which she has never confronted before as Clare Dunn." One is reminded of the earlier reference to "revolutionary patience" when Mr. Bird noted that "she has done this despite an institutional atmosphere in the Arizona Legislature which is designed to frustrate people like her."

Sister Barbara Sullivan, CSJ, lived with both Clare and Judy for seven years and was the treasurer in all four campaigns. She felt Clare's greatest sense of accomplishment was in gaining the respect of all the legislators by doing her homework, knowing the issues, learning the complexities of Arizona law and especially for being consistent in positioning herself with the poorest and least represented citizens. A second accomplishment, in Barbara's view, was the satisfaction Clare felt in continuing her role of teacher. She taught hundreds how to impact the system, how to understand the hearing process, when to lobby, which amendments would be strongest for needs, etc. She shared her political experiences and gave hope to other social activists. In writing for the NETWORK Quarterly, she encouraged involvement among religious women: "I see sisters not only as lobbyists and legislative observers at the state capitols but staff members as well. Religious generally possess the intelligence and the skills to fill many legislative positions, and once inside the system, would have a significant opportunity to influence legislation . . . I get really excited about the difference that sister-power can make in a political campaign." (NETWORK Quarterly, Vol. III, No. 2, Summer 1975)

For their friends and supporters at NETWORK, Clare and Judy were examples of "sisterpower," models of political ministry and of an integrated spirituality which provided sustenance for this demanding work. Clare and Judy's partnership in ministry was an important aspect of Clare's effectiveness. Judy's gifts in research, speech writing and organizational skills were complemented by Clare's public speaking and debate skills. Judy was referred to as the "61st Legislator" in an acknowledgement of her efficient presence at hearings Clare was unable to attend and her prodigious research to back up Clare's committee responsibilities. The representatives knew that to take on Clare was to take on Judy also and the two together were formidable!

Since Clare was the first nun to be elected to a state legislature it should be asked: What special legacy did she leave for women religious or others who share similar values and lifestyle? I would suggest two legacies in particular—her spirituality and her feminist perspective.

Clare's spirituality was integrated, that is to say there was harmony not dissonance between and among her work choices, prayer, lifestyle, congregational commitments, personal relationships and party affiliation. Clare was a nun whose prayer, congregational history and lived experience led her to work as an elected representative from the Democratic party. But for her, party loyalty was strictly on the basis of issues; party affiliation was a "useful vehicle by which I was able to enter the political environment and serve in the manner in which I felt I could best express my concerns as well as my gifts. I can assure you from my experience that there is no comparison between loyalty to the party and loyalty to my conscience." ("Perspectives on Political Ministry." NETWORK Election '76 Workshop, Los Angeles, March 27, 1976)

Clare continued to live in community and was sustained by the sisters both in Phoenix and Tucson. They shared at all levels—salary, office, car and all the "burdens and joys" of public office. And they could find time and money to share with others. I received a letter from Clare, Jan. 13, 1980: "When we get our Christmas money counted—we plan to send small contribution to NETWORK—still pushing NETWORK out here and still appreciating every jot and dot of what you write and think you are doing an ever better job—just real proud of your longevity and commitment and accomplishments." Many CSJ's helped out in her campaigns and in the process both gave an example of Clare's "family" support, and also experienced an extended sense of community as women and men—all ages, different races, various degrees of sophistication—worked together on a common project. Everyone shared a belief in what Clare stood for and a sense of contributing to something important. The campaign illustrated her values of participation and shared decision making: Each major campaign staff position was a partnership—one nun and one layperson; all decisions were made at the weekly campaign meetings open to all volunteers. On the Thursday before Clare's first election 10 sisters arrived from Los Angeles to assist in the final effort. They walked from house to house, phoned registered voters, met fellow-campaign workers and celebrated the whole experience in shared Eucharistic prayer.

As the news about Clare's effective campaign spread throughout Arizona another candidate called George Miller, a key advisor and supporter, and asked "How can I put together a similarly effective campaign?" George answered: "Tell me how many nuns you can get."

In addition to her community support, Clare was also sustained by her own prayer and reflection. Her love for the Psalms was well known and she often began her day by meditating on them outdoors within sight of the Arizona mountains. She also drew inspiration from the Old Testament prophets who thirsted so intensely for justice. In many ways she was the uncomfortable embodiment of Isaiah who cried out: "Woe to those who enact unjust statutes and write oppressive decrees." But as she reminded her colleagues that certain issues do have moral considerations many of them were no more receptive than Isaiah's listeners. As Clare spoke murmurs and rumblings echoed throughout the chamber—"here comes anguish and tears" or "it's that goddamned nun again."

The former farm girl also loved gardening and said she prayed best while working in the earth. She laughed when she was appointed to the Agriculture Committee: "Won't they be surprised when they discover that I know how many bushels to an acre, the right time to plant potatoes, and how many cuttings of alfalfa to expect per year."

Clare's experience inevitably led her to a feminist perspective: "the decision-making of women will be shaped by different values. I believe women have learned something from having been excluded from power so long. They have suffered. Suffering teaches you something about the use of both power and money." ("Sister Clare Dunn: Representative for the Powerless," by Sister Martha Mary McGaw, CSJ, *St. Anthony Messenger*, April 1975) And when she spoke to women's groups, which she often did, one could see that Clare was already doing what she advocated for others:

> What I want to say to women is that they cannot wait around until they have every answer and all kinds of expertise. It is more important to get started. . . As with everything, it is only experience that will beget sophistication. Pain and defeat will be our most treasured teachers. Maturity and seasoning will breed self-confidence. Discipline, endurance and just plain hard work will establish our credibility. ("Woman—Shaper of Society," Theresian Conference, November 19, 1977)

Clare herself wrote what may be the most realistic description of the significance of her political ministry. A letter to me in 1980 concluded with this comment: "The whole thing—our political work—is still a good front operation for getting a lot of things done in the state and in the Tucson community—I am not at all unhappy with the way things have worked out—feel good about it in fact—appearances to the contrary notwithstanding, feel like we have accomplished something."

And if Clare's photograph, which now hangs in the Minority Caucus room, reminds her colleagues there of the values she stood for, and if her spirit provides them the courage to grow bold and stand for the poor and for justice—to share her "anguish and tears"—then one could hope to hear more often in legislative chambers across the land the exasperated sighs of "it's that goddamned nun again."

Lawrence M. O'Rourke

GENO C. BARONI, PRIEST AND PUBLIC ACTIVIST

A few weeks before his death on August 27, 1984, in Washington's Providence Hospital from mesothelioma, a rare abdominal cancer, Monsignor Geno C. Baroni talked about how he would like to use the enormous power of the Roman Catholic Church in the United States to build homes for the poor and elderly, to restore neighborhoods, to provide medical care for the uninsured, to force a nation too heavily committed to military might to negotiate reductions in nuclear arms.

Baroni spoke of coalitions of believers in which men and women of conscience, no matter their preference of religion, would confront the White House, Congress, governors' mansions, and city halls across America with demands for justice and peace. As Geno Baroni faced death, he found consolation in the role he had played to bring the Catholic Church into the forefront of social activism. He spoke also of his unfinished agenda. But he spoke in disappointment too of his inability to convince religious communities to invest their pension funds in community development programs. "They don't understand all they can do if they would only try," Baroni said in June.

In his final year, Baroni worked with religious communities in a vain effort to have them "leverage"—one of his favorite words—their pension funds to force banks to make loans to families to rehabilitate homes, to businessmen to start new enterprises and expand right in the old neighborhood.

Baroni, though a liberal Democrat, had come to accept that liberals expected too much from government and relied on it too heavily. He wanted government, the business community and a third sector made up of churches, associations and neighborhood groups to collaborate in improving the capacity of self-help, community-based institutions, including local parishes, to work from the bottom up for a better life.

Baroni often said that the Catholic Church had to be more than a critic and cheerleader. It had to use its pulpits and its financial resources in the political arena to turn preaching into practice. He was aware of the limitations on the Church's power and the potential for abuse. At the end of his days, Baroni felt the Church had done much, but not enough, to feed the hungry, shelter the homeless, and minister to the ill.

A few days before Baroni's death, President Ronald Reagan said in a speech at a prayer breakfast in the Reunion Arena in Dallas that religion and politics are "inseparable." The president provoked a controversy when he said religious activists had a right and obligation to work for government policies reflecting their moral beliefs. Geno Baroni, who practiced that approach all of his adult life, could hardly have disagreed with a narrow interpretation of the president's statement. "What's he really mean by that?," Baroni would probably have asked, shrugging his shoulders, shaking his head, and looking every inch a wily ward leader in a black suit.

One thing Geno Baroni would not have tolerated was government turning its back on the poor. He spoke with disdain of "trickle down economics." He said the Democrats had to learn how to manage better. They had lost the public confidence, he said, because they had become too paternalistic and in the process had forgotten how ordinary people must be involved in arranging their own neighborhoods and living conditions.

Baroni rejected the idea of big government being called on to solve all of humankind's social ills. Baroni loved to explain his theory of a combination of government, private enterprise, and non-governmental voluntary private sector, including the Church, with an elaborate and frequently incomprehensible series of circles, triangles and connecting lines. Before his hospitalization, he would, on the slightest excuse, fill a blackboard or tablecover with his roadmap for a greater involvement of the Church and its neighboring institutions "where people live."

The point of Baroni's artwork, as indeed the point of most of his public service, wasn't the specific design, but the notion that the Church he served and loved had a moral obligation—and probably the best opportunity in the land—to guide the concerns of the country toward the solution of social problems. Baroni spoke with great sadness of his brother priests who were absent when Dr. Martin Luther King, Jr. led the March on Washington along Pennsylvania Avenue in 1963 and who shielded their eyes from injustice and inhumanity. He spoke with disdain of pastors in the suburbs who collected used underwear for inner-city residents, but who would not join in some way in convincing the power structure in City Hall that the poor needed jobs and better homes.

Baroni acknowledged that only a few priests—he considered himself "unique"—had the personality and inclination to testify before Congress and City Council, to work their way along the corridors of political power, to stick their neck out further than the cardinal or bishop was willing to stick out his. "I put my neck on the block so that when it was cut off, that would be my head, not Cardinal O'Boyle's on the floor," said Baroni.

As he reviewed a career as a priest in public service, Baroni said, "You cannot separate the Church from society. You cannot separate the Church from people's lives. I don't think a priest should be in politics, but that doesn't mean the priest shouldn't do anything about the issues that concern people's lives. I believe that as a priest I am part of the community and that I have to make a contribution not only around the altar, but that I have to share in responsibility as a citizen. The notion that we are all on the way to heaven as we gather around the altar is difficult to sustain if the neighborhood around the church is going to hell," Baroni said.

"We live in an organized society," Baroni said. "Therefore we need to have an informed and organized way for the non-governmental sector, including the Church, to be involved in changing public policy. It is in the public arena that decisions are made that affect people's lives. We of the Church community cannot be absent from that. The Church has a special respect for human dignity and the value of every individual. For that reason, the Church must be involved and concerned."

In Baroni's scheme of things, the non-governmental voluntary private sector made up of parishes and other neighborhood groups was equal to government in addressing the problems of big cities. Baroni was a sergeant in government. But as the founder and first president of the National Center for Urban Ethnic Affairs, he was the commanding general of an army of people all across the nation. Many in that army felt an alienation toward government.

Baroni loved to tell a story about his brothers-in-law, men of European immigrant stock, who felt that government was doing everything for blacks, nothing for them. (The story, like many of Geno's stories, was more a parable than an accurate account of dinner table conversations. But it worked.)

Baroni saw it as his mission to tell government that while the blacks had the broken back from mistreatment, the urban ethnics had a broken arm from neglect, and both had to be treated, or neither would get well. For Baroni, this was part of his ministry as a priest.

Despite a deeply-held belief that priests, on the frontline of community and parish life, have an obligation to be involved in public service, Baroni accepted and publicly endorsed, the instruction by Pope John Paul II to priests to get out of political office, a directive that forced the retirement from Congress of Robert Drinan, S.J., and would have, if in effect, blocked Baroni's own service within the Federal government. But Baroni was quick to add that a ban on service in elected public office, or even appointed office, did not create much of a problem for somebody like himself who knew the craft of politics. Baroni had more influence on public policy outside the Federal government than he had while serving within. In some respects, his going inside the Carter Administration was a mistake. That analysis of Baroni's public service was held by many, though not all, of his co-workers through the years in and out of the government. Baroni readily conceded that he lost some of his effectiveness as a critic when he joined the Carter Administration. But he insisted adamantly that he made the right choice in 1977 when he joined Carter.

Baroni also saw a distinction between public service and what he called the "profession of politics." He noted, for example, that there is a long history of the institutional Church being involved in matters of state. He pointed to Pope John Paul II's own statements about his native Poland, including his threat to return to Poland if the Soviet Union invaded that country.

Geno Baroni saw his function as a priest to be the shaping of a political agenda. Though seriously ill in 1984, he seized every chance he could to applaud the bishops' 1983 nuclear statement, and from his bed maneuvered to influence the bishops' statement on economic policy and development. He offered advice and consolation to his wide circle of friends in Congress. He encouraged Archbishop James L. Hickey of Washington to testify on Capitol Hill against U.S. military intervention in Central America.

From his earliest years of adulthood, he was a man intensely occupied with current events and their consequences for people. He strove to connect people who shared his perception that the country had abandoned its principles in a thoughtless rush to self-destruction. Those who knew Baroni in his seminary days, as a young priest in Altoona and Johnstown, Pennsylvania, and Washington, D.C., as a civil rights activist and as a fighter for the rights of urban ethnics, as a political adviser and government official, remember the pile of eight or ten newspapers he would consume a day, the mound of books being read in progress, his knowledge of what was taking place on Capitol Hill and the White House. And people remembered his ability to simplify all this, to encourage people to enter the system to make sense of it.

In doing this, said the Rev. J. Bryan Hehir of the U.S. Catholic Conference, Baroni served the Church by keeping in the forefront of concerns of the hierarchy the pressing social issues of the day. In his days as an unofficial lobbyist for social issues on Capitol Hill, Baroni did more than preach the Gospel to the heathen members of Congress. As Gerald McMurray, staff director of the House Subcommittee on Housing and Community Development, recalled, Baroni somehow managed to convince politicians that what he was asking them to do was not only the right thing to do, but also in the best interests of their own constituencies and reelection chances. While doing this, said McMurray, who watched Baroni closely for years, Baroni never exploited the fact that he wore a Roman collar. "But the collar gave him entré into offices where others pleading causes were unable to go," said McMurray.

Only on the most difficult days of his illness did Geno Baroni lay aside the *New York Times* and *Washington Post* without having devoured them from front page to back. Telephone callers and visitors during the evening television news hours had to compete with Tom Brokaw and McNeill-Lehrer. From his hospital bed he worked his network, gathering intelligence for Hickey, gently reminding members of Congress and Capitol Hill aides what would be the right thing to do for the poor and the cities. His ability to spot opportunities for progressive policies remained without equal.

Geno Baroni remained perhaps the "most plugged-in" man in Washington. But that wasn't surprising. He has always been a political professional, one of those rare human beings who can see the multiple dimensions of political issues, who can weigh interests, and understand the necessity of wheeling and dealing, and who can bring to politics a transcending purpose, the promotion of decency, justice and peace.

But for all his experience, wisdom and success as a politician, Baroni had a curious, somewhat contradictory, attitude toward the role of the Church and its ordained and professed ministers in politics. He said they should plunge into public life, but not into politics. Nor should they run for election nor accept appointment to partisan political office, Baroni insisted.

He was sensitive to the irony in urging upon others a practice he did not follow for himself. As U.S. assistant secretary of Housing and

Urban Development during Jimmy Carter's administration, Baroni held the highest office ever attained by a U.S. Catholic priest in the Federal government. He was nominated to that position by Carter in March, 1977, and confirmed the following month. It was a policy position with considerable political sensitivity. Baroni, after many years as an outsider confronting and advising government, was suddenly on the inside, with the responsibility to manage an office and programs, to safeguard a budget, and, as a team player to defend Carter politically.

In that job, Baroni achieved several successes. He helped persuade the Carter Administration to reverse itself and support creation of the National Consumer Cooperative Bank. He helped sell Congress on the Neighborhood Self Help Act. He served as the spokesman for neighborhoods inside Federal government. He shepherded through an amendment to the Urban Development Action Grant program that permitted Federal urban redevelopment dollars to flow to nonprofit groups, like neighborhood organizations built around parishes.

Baroni loved to tell the story about how he went to Capitol Hill and testified in favor of the Consumer Cooperative Bank plan when Carter, the Treasury Department, and the Office of Management and Budget opposed it. Baroni arranged through friends on Capitol Hill to be summoned as a witness on the bank bill. He followed to the witness stand a Treasury Department official who denounced the bank plan. Baroni, by prearrangement, was asked in a casual way what he, as an urban activist, thought about the bill. He said he thought it was fine.

The phone in his office rang shortly thereafter. It was an aide to Secretary of Housing and Urban Development, Patricia Roberts Harris, calling to say that she had just been admonished by the White House because one of her assistant secretaries—Baroni—had defied the administration position on the bill. Baroni suspected that Secretary Harris was privately delighted with his independence because she too supported the Consumer Bank.

"I always believed it was better to ask forgiveness than to seek permission," Baroni said.

That sort of independence caused trouble for Baroni inside the Administration. And with no experience at running a large bureaucracy, he was an atrocious administrator. He drove some of the dry bureaucrats and officials in HUD crazy with his verbal style. "Baroni was used to thinking out loud, fishing around for ideas and testing them against his audience until he was sure he had found common agreement. He couldn't do that in government. They wanted 'yes' and 'no' answers on paper and in conferences, and he wouldn't give them, or maybe he couldn't," said an official who worked with—sometimes, against—Baroni at HUD.

On most days Baroni wore a Roman collar to HUD. He was formally addressed as Monsignor or Father, but it didn't seem to confer any special status when it came to bureaucratic infighting. His priesthood and record as an activist outside government may have hampered his effectiveness with some officials who thought he would let his Christian beliefs, his compassion for the poor, sick and homeless, overcome his loyalty to Administration policy.

But Baroni's greatest problem in HUD was philosophical, and perhaps that means moral. He was confronted by experienced urban planners who thought in broad sweeping terms. Baroni talked about people in neighborhoods. Where planners saw bricks and mortar, Baroni saw people in pews, bars and ethnic groceries.

A lawyer who represents cities in Washington said the Carter people had grand designs for cities and a great deal of money to put them into effect. But the Carter people didn't understand that city was place, but it also was people. Baroni understood the human force. He knew what made people cry and laugh, risk and fear, make peace and share love. He knew because he remembered the lessons of his own childhood in a strong, though desperately poor, neighborhood. He remembered those to whom he had ministered in the parish parlors, the alleys, and the streetcorners of one of Washington's worst slums as an assistant pastor. He knew neighborhood people all across the nation. They wanted to preserve their neighborhoods, to retain traditions, to build on strengths of Church and ethnicity.

"I came to Washington determined to save the world. When I realized I couldn't do that, I decided to just save this country. When I found out I couldn't do that, I thought it would be enough to save the city. When I couldn't do that, I thought it would be okay just to save one neighborhood," said Baroni. "When neighborhoods go," he said, "cities go."

Baroni in HUD was the champion of the revitalization of black, Italian, Hispanic, Polish, Irish and other ethnic neighborhoods. "Unless you understand the ethnic and racial factor," he said, "you can't understand the cities."

Baroni felt he had a special understanding of ethnicity and race acquired through his service as a Catholic priest. He never argued that his priesthood gave him any superior understanding, but rather that his experience—gathered as a priest, but not because he was a priest—equipped him to offer advice on national urban policy.

"My time in Federal government was a logical extension of my work as a parish priest at SS. Paul and Augustine," said Baroni.

Geno Baroni's sensitivity to peace and justice began to take form during his childhood in a small mining town, Acosta, in Pennsylvania. Born in 1930 to Italian immigrants, Baroni grew up in a community where labor unions were still viewed by some bosses as communist intrusions on the American way of life.

Guido Baroni, Geno's father, was a fighter for the union. Geno's mother, Josephine, was always the first to cross the street with a pot of soup or a few extra vegetables for a neighboring family without a job or struck by illness.

Growing up in that family and community, Baroni came to young adulthood as a confirmed New Dealer, a partisan Democrat, a strong unionist, and a believer in a supportive community. The Church should play a role in guiding that community, Baroni came later to realize. But the churches and churchmen of Baroni's early days were often more willing to side with the mineowners and operators who supported them than with the soot-covered miners, their wives and children, who filled the pews on Sunday mornings.

As a seminarian in the 1950s, Baroni began to read about some of the great figures of the social justice movement in the United States. He was particularly impressed by the teachings of Monsignor John A. Ryan, the pioneer social philosopher. Baroni several times read the 1919 bishops' program of social reconstruction, which Ryan drafted. Many of the ideas advanced by the bishops were considered radical at the time. They have since become law. The right of workers to organize, minimum wage legislation, health, unemployment and old-age insurance, a federal housing program—these proposals flowed from the mind and conscience of one of America's great social justice activists.

Baroni, reviewing his own life, listed Ryan, Dorothy Day, and Monsignor George Higgins in the forefront of his list of heroes. Baroni read *The Catholic Worker* during the long days in the strict, traditional seminary in Emmitsburg, Maryland. That and other liberal journals were available in the seminary library, and they caught Baroni's attention. The faculty members neither encouraged nor discouraged such reading, Baroni recalled.

He was trained to be a parish priest, to become pastor someday, as he put it, "of East Snowshoe." When he was ordained in 1956, Baroni said, he saw ahead a life of administering the sacraments, tending the rectory, preaching on traditional Church teaching. He had no great dreams at his ordination of power or glory. "I felt my education in grammar school and high school had left me unprepared for very much," Baroni said.

His first assignment was to Sacred Heart Parish in Altoona, a working-class parish. "I was scared silly," said Baroni. "I was really surprised to find myself a priest." He was there only two months when he had an idea, and he advanced it to the pastor. How about a mass on Labor Day honoring workers? The pastor liked the idea and the word got around that Baroni was responsible.

So when the police in Altoona were unable to negotiate a contract with City Council and turned to arbitration, they picked as their representative on the panel the new 26-year-old priest, Geno Baroni. "I was never much of an orator," he said, remembering his first appearances in the pulpit. "The pastor would stand in the back of the Church and time me and critique me." But the working class people in the pews sensed they had a champion in Baroni.

One day in the fall after his ordination, the pastor called him in for a little talk, Baroni recalled. "He told me that it was okay to do what I was doing, to have a Labor Day mass and to side with the police and to support coalminers and railroaders against their bosses. Then he told me something that has stuck with me and irritated me the rest of my life. He told me that I was never going to make bishop doing that kind of thing."

Baroni said that looking back over his career, he's afraid the pastor was right. Not that Baroni wanted to become a bishop. But he listed several priests who in his judgment should have become bishop, and were prevented, Baroni said, because those responsible for promoting such appointments in the United States were suspicious of their records as social justice activists.

He saw in this the contradiction within the Catholic Church hierarchy. "The bishops and the clergy profess, and I think, do believe, that we should take seriously the command of Jesus to comfort the afflicted, shelter the homeless, feed the hungry and serve as peacemakers," Baroni said. "But they too often fail to realize that merely preaching this Gospel is not achieving it. The political reality is that somebody has to give voice to these principles, and to work to put them into effect. As a priest, I say that you can't celebrate at the altar without celebrating the pain and problems of the community. Minimum wage, housing, jobs are moral issues. You cannot separate action on those issues from religious belief. They are questions of right and wrong, questions of justice.

"It is the responsibility of the Church, through its members, to address questions of justice, and to struggle to achieve justice. The Church, if it fails to engage itself fully in the pursuit of justice, fails to meet its responsibility. I think that the Church has abdicated its responsibilities too often and left too many questions of justice to government."

Poverty and injustice greeted Baroni on his first assignment as priest. As assistant pastor in Altoona, one of Baroni's biggest jobs was to meet the people when they came to the rectory for a few dollars to help tide them over rough days. It was in that process that he discovered how little money the parish had to help and how many parishioners were up to their necks in debt to local finance companies.

"One of the young people in the parish worked at HFC, and I asked her one day how many of our parishioners were on the books at HFC. 'You'd be surprised at how many, father,' she said." In the seminary Baroni had read about the Antigonish Movement, a cooperative in Nova Scotia. He liked the connection between the parish and the working people that Antigonish encouraged. With that in mind, Baroni said, he decided to start a cooperative at Sacred Heart.

He raised the subject at meetings of the Holy Name Society and the Sodality. "I told the people, why should they pay 20 percent or more to HFC when we could raise the money in our own parish, have our people pay six percent interest, and give most of that back to our own people who had deposited the money." The pastor agreed, but with a condition.

"He said yes if he could pick the treasurer," said Baroni. "He picked a treasurer who was a daily communicant and an accountant at a local hospital. That didn't work out so well. The man's wife died and he went off with a nurse and took all the credit union's money. Fortunately the credit union was bonded."

Baroni said the first reaction of parishioners was, "Great idea, father. You organize it and set it up and run it and we'll put in a few dollars." The people in the pews were too used to having their priests run everything, Baroni said. But involvement of the Church and its clergy in public life does not heighten that risk, Baroni said. "First of all, there are very few priests or nuns who are interested in public positions. In the nearly four years I served in the Carter Administration, not a single priest or nun ever came up to me and said, 'That looks like important interesting work you're doing. You got any suggestions on how I might get into it?' "

Baroni refused to run the credit union. He forced parishioners to become its founders and officers. This was the first of many such experiences for Baroni. He would conceive an idea, spin it off, then step back while others made it work.

The credit union that Baroni started in Altoona with $150 and 25 sponsors now has 7,000 members and assets in excess of $9 million.

Central Pennsylvania was too confining a field for Baroni. He came to Washington in 1960 and was assigned to Sts. Paul and Augustine Parish at 14th and V Streets, one of the most rundown and tough neighborhoods in the city. It was an area identified with narcotics, prostitution, rats running through hallways of overcrowded and untended tenements, holdups and murder.

"At first impression, that neighborhood was hell on earth," Baroni said. "Then I began to walk around and talk with people, and it wasn't long before I saw the suffering of human beings on those streets. And I realized that it wasn't enough just to celebrate Mass and to be there with the sacraments. We had to go out to the people and deal with their concerns. The old people couldn't afford medicine. Heads of families couldn't get jobs. The police were hassling the kids. We wouldn't be moral if we just left these people to take care of themselves or to welfare. Welfare was a moral issue. That destroyed families. A woman couldn't have a man in her house or she'd lose her welfare. The government spent a fortune checking out people's private lives and couldn't find any money for jobs. They were moral issues, and the solutions had to be political. I could preach all I wanted, but the people with power didn't hear me until I started to organize a community and the politicians began to realize its political power.

"Political decisions are often moral decisions. As such, I felt a need to get involved to help shape those decisions."

When the Archdiocese of Washington assigned him to Sts. Paul and Augustine parish in Northwest Washington, Baroni recalled, "They told me it was the 'colored' parish, but the priests were okay." Fortunately for Baroni, the pastor was Monsignor George Gingras who was Cardinal Patrick O'Boyle's principal contact with the black community. Baroni took advantage of every opportunity Gingras gave him to test in practice some of the social justice ministry projects Baroni had been reading about.

Soon, with Baroni doing the organizing, Sts. Paul and Augustine had a tutorial program. H. Rap Brown and Stokely Carmichael were early volunteers. Baroni started a preschool program that was to serve as a success story for President Lyndon B. Johnson's formation of the Federal Head Start program. R. Sargent Shriver, Johnson's first war on poverty director, said he watched Baroni's programs develop at Sts.

Paul and Augustine because they were something he thought the Church should have been involved in for many years, but had failed to try.

Baroni opened summer camps and school lunch programs. He converted an abandoned convent into a center where community people could gather. He brought together young street toughs who said the police were hassling them and area police officials.

Baroni's reputation spread, and the invitations followed. He was drawn quickly into working with area Protestant and Jewish church leaders. They formed a "Tuesday breakfast club," said the Rev. William Wendt, then rector at St. Stephen's and the Incarnation Episcopal Church. Christian clergymen of several denominations would sit for hours drawing up schemes to involve their bishops and institutions in social action on Washington's streets.

Baroni met considerable resistance from his own hierarchy, although not from O'Boyle. The cardinal, a native of the harsh Pennsylvania coalfields, was ready to let Baroni test the water. "Geno's job was to stick his neck on the block for O'Boyle to see how far out it could go before the head was cut off," said Floyd Agostinelli, an urban affairs aide to O'Boyle and Geno's friend.

Through his involvement with the Protestant and Jewish clergy, Baroni was drawn into civil rights marches, appearances on Capitol Hill and before Washington's City Council. One morning his picture appeared on the front page of *The Washington Post*. There was Baroni, in his black suit, Roman collar, and hat in the second row of marchers past the White House on Pennsylvania Avenue demonstrating for stronger Federal legislation to guarantee blacks in the South the right to vote. One of the bishops spotted Baroni's face and complained to O'Boyle that priests of the diocese were not supposed to join Protestants in civil rights demonstrations.

O'Boyle summoned Baroni to his office. "What were you doing yesterday, father?" the cardinal inquired.

Baroni humbly explained to his eminence. O'Boyle listened, and then said, "I was pleased to see you wearing your hat, father. I like my priests to wear their hats in public." That was the end of the affair, and Baroni seeing daylight, ran toward it.

When Dr. King called for the March on Washington in August, 1963, O'Boyle named Baroni to coordinate the archdiocesan response. One of Baroni's greatest disappointments, he recalled, was his inability to get other priests of the archdiocese to march. O'Boyle offered a prayer on the steps of the Lincoln Memorial and stood there while

King delivered his "I have a dream" speech. But Baroni and fewer than a half dozen other priests joined the line of march.

After Dr. King and his marchers for civil rights were attacked on the Edmund Pettus Bridge in Selma, Alabama in 1965, Baroni and Agostinelli convinced O'Boyle that Catholic priests from Washington should be permitted to join clergy of other denominations in Selma for a renewed effort to march to Montgomery. O'Boyle agreed to let Gingras, Baroni and two other priests of the Archdiocese of Washington go. Matthew Ahmann, directing an inter-racial effort in Chicago, said the participation of the Washington priests—for which he gave substantial credit to Baroni—opened the way for priests across the nation to tell their bishops: "Cardinal O'Boyle is letting his priests go. You should follow his example."

O'Boyle began to trust Baroni more and, increasingly, to listen to his advice about social justice issues, particularly as they developed in Washington.

Tentatively at first, then with growing enthusiasm, O'Boyle began to attend meetings and to reach agreements with non-Catholic clergy. Baroni was instrumental not only in bringing the archdiocese into the civil rights action, but in starting to crack the barriers of creed which had kept the Catholic Church from a full engagement in social justice ministry.

"The Cardinal had an excellent record on civil rights within the Church," Baroni recalled. "He had moved early to desegregate the schools and hospitals. But he was reluctant to get into civil rights activities outside the Church. He did not have much experience working with Protestant bishops. He had the traditional Catholic tendency to shy away from such coalitions."

While serving as an assistant to O'Boyle for urban affairs, Baroni performed the traditional functions of a priest as an assistant at Sts. Paul and Augustine. Those included meeting in the rectory front parlor with parishoners who had fallen months behind in their rent payments and faced eviction. At first, Baroni called landlords and pleaded, as a priest and often as a fellow Catholic, for a few more months' grace for the tenant. "It wasn't long before I realized that while I was wearing myself out dealing with individuals, the larger answers were in legislation." So he began to appear on Capitol Hill more and more for changes in welfare laws and employment practices.

Once Baroni made an impassioned appeal for Federal law changes to promote jobs for the unskilled inner-city young people. Rep. Mendel H. Rivers, D-So. Car., listened. The next day Baroni was startled to find a truckload of watermelons delivered to the rectory, a gift of Rivers.

As tensions built in the 1960s throughout the country, including Washington's black ghetto, Baroni began to be identified as a civil rights street priest. Chuck Stone, a black journalist, described him as "the most relevant white man in Washington." When Dr. King was assassinated in Memphis in April, 1968, Baroni and his Protestant and Jewish colleagues were ready. They had long anticipated that it would take only a spark to turn the city's streets into a firestorm. The big supermarkets were burned out. The streets were not safe for most whites, but Baroni was able to walk along 14th Street during the riot. The clergy coalition, through prearrangement, worked with a supermarket chain to bring basic foodstuffs into church buildings to feed those left without access to stores.

Baroni's reputation was also growing within the institutional Church. In 1969, he was asked by the bishops to co-chair a National Task Force on Urban Problems. In November, he laid out an agenda for the 1970s.

The U.S. Catholic Church, he argued, represented "a crucial force that might well be decisive in determining the future life-style of our rapidly urbanized society." In developing its urban mission policy, the Church, said Baroni, should explore these assumptions:

—The Catholic Church has traditionally been an urban church, indeed an inner-city church, with a body of knowledge and techniques useful to achieving the assimilation of poor people into the mainstream.

—The people who live closest to black ghettoes are Catholic, and they view the Catholic parish as "the major, if not the only, cohesive force in their neighborhoods."

—Dioceses and parishes lack the urban policies, personnel and organization needed to deal with this major confrontation between blacks and ethnic whites.

Baroni proposed, for the first time, the creation of a "national fund for human development" in the United States. This was to become the Campaign for Human Development, one of the U.S. Church's most profound achievements.

As Baroni developed this concept, he did not want it to be a fund for charity, although he recognized that the church had a traditional charitable instinct and responsibility. He saw the Campaign as a source of money for neighborhood revitalization. He saw it using its money as "leverage"—a favorite Baroni word—to encourage banks to put up money to allow families to renovate their homes, young families to buy in the old neighborhood, and business people to start new enterprises and to expand.

The riots in Washington, Detroit, Newark, Philadelphia, Los Angeles, Gary and elsewhere had a deep effect on Baroni. He sensed, he said, the growing hostility between the blacks and those who live next door in the cities, the ethnic Catholics to whom Baroni felt a special kinship. He began to realize, through his contacts with his own family and friends, that American society was being torn apart and that those being blamed for lack of progress on the civil and human rights fronts were often Roman Catholics, those who had close identification with their Church and ethnic heritage in the big cities.

He saw this as being in large measure a failure of the Church, in its teachings and through its parishes, to prepare Roman Catholics for changes in American society and to form coalitions for common purposes that transcended racial differences. Baroni said he understood the hostility of working-class whites to blacks who were aggressively demanding jobs, equal housing and educational opportunities, and, then, affirmative action to redress the wrongs of two centuries in America. To understand that hostility, said Baroni, was not to condone the violence or injustice that resulted from it. He felt that the Catholic Church, commanding the allegiance of the majority of ethnic Americans, was in a position to bring people together. Baroni saw that an essential element of this moral process was a political agenda.

Baroni broached to his friends, including members of the Catholic Committee for Urban Ministry, a national support group of activist priests, sisters and lay people, the idea that he might accomplish more by working with ethnics rather than with blacks. Some of his friends felt that by going in that direction, Baroni betrayed the civil rights movement, that he turned away from the victims toward the oppressor racists. Baroni was hurt by this attack on his integrity and commitment to civil rights. He put a political coloration on his new path. "I saw the people who had voted for Bobby Kennedy in 1968 switching to George Wallace," he said. "I knew that the Democratic Party and the social principles for which it stood were going to be badly hurt until somebody was able to deal with the legitimate concerns of the white ethnics. I decided to make that my mission," Baroni said.

This question of vocal public support for the Democratic Party was always a troublesome one for Baroni. Privately, with friends, he spoke enthusiastically in favor of the Democrats. He identified with the Kennedy wing of the party and for a time was a confidant of several members of the Kennedy family. Baroni said he felt awkward in that role, and he withdrew from it, although, as he lay ill, he cherished notes from Sen. Edward M. Kennedy and Ethel Kennedy. Baroni said he did not want to be cast as a chaplain to the Democrats. Later, while in the Carter Administration, he declined on several occasions to offer prayers at meals and meetings. He saw his role as assistant secretary of Housing and Urban Development, not as Jimmy Carter's captive Catholic priest.

Baroni said tokenism would be a serious problem for any man or woman from the ordained or religious ranks who entered public service. He said anyone offered a public position should consider carefully whether the tender was made because of the person's qualifications, or if it were an effort to enlist a representative of the Church into a partisan cause. Baroni struggled to explain effectively the distinction between public service and partisanship, both to others and to himself. In his analysis, Baroni seemed to be ruled more by instinct than intellect. His explanation of how to tell the difference between public service and partisanship was akin to the observation of a Supreme Court justice that defining pornography may have been intellectually impossible, but "you'll know it when you see it."

In 1970, Baroni, with start-up money from the Ford Foundation, opened the National Center for Urban Ethnic Affairs, an organization dedicated to working with city people, the majority of whom were working class. Through that work over the next six years, Baroni was drawn ever more deeply into national politics.

Baroni advised President Gerald R. Ford and members of his administration on how to respect the rights and meet the desires of ethnic Americans. Baroni said this never involved reverse discrimination and was not, as some critics charged, "pandering to the racists."

Baroni saw his service to the ethnic Americans as a continuation of his Roman Catholic priesthood. He said that he was partly motivated by the reality that the crack-up of inner city neighborhoods meant the destruction of Catholic parishes. Baroni's Center funneled money from Ford and other sources to groups often associated with local parishes. Several priests in inner-city neighborhoods received foundation money through Baroni's Center.

Along the way, Baroni used his Center's money, his prestige and contacts, to encourage others to engage in public policy formulation. He gave active support to the creation of *Network*, the Catholic social justice lobby organized by women religious. Baroni often said he had more success with the sisters than he did with fellow priests in getting them to become concerned about the pressing issues of the day. Baroni said one of his proudest moments was the support he gave to *Network*. He said the joining together of religious women for the purpose of influencing U.S. domestic and international policy was an appropriate and necessary step in the awakening of the Church to its responsibilities in the search for justice and peace on earth.

He was especially proud of his early sponsorship and support for two women later elected to the U.S. House of Representatives, Barbara Mikulski of Maryland and Marcy Kaptur of Ohio.

Baroni's blurred distinction between public service and partisan politics figured in 1974 in a dispute between Baroni and George Bush, then chairman of the Republican National Committee and later vice president under Ronald Reagan.

Baroni in 1974 was co-chairman of a meeting on the role of ethnic Americans in the 1976 bicentennial observance. The invitation to Baroni came from John W. Warner, President Ford's choice as administrator of the American Revolution Bicentennial Commission. Bush heard complaints about Baroni's performance at the meeting and he sent off a biting letter to Warner.

"In selecting Gino (sic) Baroni to chair the meeting," Bush said, "the Commission seems to have cast its lot with the more radical ethnic people—and people with very liberal views who would not represent the matrix of our great ethnic communities."

According to Bush, under Baroni's "direction and insistent leadership," these themes developed:

—"This group would have an ongoing purpose which would not end with the Bicentennial."

—"A lasting racial/ethnic coalition—militant in nature and 'activist' in orientation would emerge. The creation of a new urban 'power bloc' was envisaged."

—"Little mention was made of the traditional values which unite the ethnic groups in this country. Rather, a special film was shown that left the impression that the Commission's goal should be putting together racial coalitions for social action."

Warner responded that Bush's complaint put a "shadow" on the "good will and integrity" of the Commission, the participants, Baroni and his co-chairman. Warner said Baroni and co-chairman James Gibson "both discharged their duties responsibly."

But in his analysis, Bush was not all that far off the mark as far as Baroni's intentions were concerned. He did, in fact, want urban ethnics to form a political power bloc, one influenced by the teachings of the Catholic Church. It was Baroni's lifelong thesis that the work of God on earth could most effectively be accomplished through political action and that in the U.S. system, power blocs, votes and success were inextricably linked.

Baroni's own step into federal service in the Carter Administration may have seemed then, and still today, as a giant leap from the ordained priesthood to politics. But for Baroni, it was only a logical step.

Baroni's first move toward service in the Carter Administration came while he was sharing coffee and bagels in the Chevy Chase, Maryland, home of Mark Talisman, a representative in Washington for the Federation of Jewish Agencies. Baroni had watched with dismay as several bishops, including Joseph Bernardin, had mishandled a visit to President Ford in the White House briefing room, when they left reporters there with the distinct impression that they favored Ford over Carter, the Democratic nominee. The press reports upset the bishops who felt they had been misunderstood. But astute political types like Baroni began a rescue operation.

Carter was also running into trouble with Catholics largely on the issue of abortion. His support for the U.S. Supreme Court decision in *Roe v. Wade* had led to several confrontations with Catholics and threatened to dominate his campaign to win votes from Catholics. Carter was cast onto the defensive before people who had for years been considered dedicated to the Democratic Party, particularly working class whites, including the ethnics with whom Baroni had considerable credibility.

From Plains, Georgia, where Carter was nursing some early battle wounds, came a call to Baroni in Talisman's kitchen. Could he help Carter get out of this mess?

Carter already knew that Baroni was at work trying to work out a graceful way for the bishops to edge away from their apparent statement of support for Ford. Baroni agreed to offer guidance to Carter on how to appeal for the votes of the Catholic ethnics. Baroni advised Carter to take seriously the concerns of Roman Catholics over abortion and not to dismiss the issue, as he indicated he might, as one of interest more to the bishops than to lay Catholics. "I told Carter he would also make a mistake in trying to find and exploit any differences among bishops on this issue," Baroni said. "I told him he might be able to do this on other issues, but on abortion, the bishops were going to stay together, and any effort to divide them could hurt Carter badly."

Baroni also advised Carter and his campaign strategists to look for specific issues that would appeal to inner-city Catholic voters. Baroni talked about his own experience with urban ethnics, the lack of responsiveness of urban programs, the insensitivity to ethnic culture.

Baroni insisted later that if he had been asked by Ford for the same campaign advice, he would have given it gladly, and that, in fact, what he told Carter was essentially the same as he had previously advised Ford. But suddenly Baroni was a campaign strategist for the Democratic presidential candidate he wanted to see elected.

Baroni did more than advise. He suggested, arranged and advanced a visit by Carter to the Polish Hill District in Pittsburgh, a neighborhood that is almost entirely Catholic and where the local church and its priests play a major role in shaping political attitudes. Baroni arranged for Carter to walk through the neighborhood, to greet the bartenders, butchers and grocers, shoppers and retired railroaders and steelmen. Then he had Carter stand on the front steps of the church, wearing a Polish Power T-shirt, and speak to an audience that included Catholic school children in their uniforms. It was a great story and produced photographs that helped to turn around the Carter campaign. The divisions between Carter and the ethnic Catholics were for the moment forgotten in the appreciation of the economic issues which unified them.

Even as he entered Carter's campaign and thus engaged in partisan politics, Baroni held back a bit of himself, an indication, he conceded, that he was troubled by the role of priest in politics. On Polish Hill and later in the campaign, Baroni worked behind the scenes. He said he was reluctant to have Carter and his strategists exploit the fact that they had a Catholic priest on their team.

But Baroni nourished his contacts with the Carter campaign team through the campaign. He telephoned senior campaign aides with advice and he suggested to his old friends in the urban ethnic movement that Carter would make a better president than Ford. Discreetly, Baroni campaigned for Carter. On election night, Baroni was in Carter's suite in an Atlanta hotel. Baroni said he went to Atlanta to experience the excitement of election night at Carter's headquarters, and he was invited to Carter's suite by an aide who happened to spot him in the crowd. Baroni began to take advantage of his earned access to the Carter staff. It was part of the inevitable process that Baroni began to urge Carter to appoint to office some of the people who had worked over the years with Baroni. Baroni felt he was entitled as a contributor to Carter's campaign to get something in return.

He worked the telephones and his contacts to get White House staff jobs for his associates Marcy Kaptur and Vicky Monjiardo, and Baroni wanted a job for himself. He said he had his eye on the chairmanship of a commission on neighborhoods. But that went to another political adviser. Baroni said he was surprised when he got a call from Patricia Roberts Harris in March 1977, asking him to become assistant secretary of Housing and Urban Development. Baroni was to be responsible for neighborhoods, voluntary associations and consumer protection. In a way, he served as an ombudsman for the department. It was through Baroni that ordinary people were able to get their opinions voiced inside the rooms where decisions about their neighborhoods were being made.

Baroni was pleased by the invitation to join the Carter Administration as a sub-cabinet officer. He checked out the offer with a few of his friends. Several urged him to turn it down. They said he could be much more effective for the causes he believed in outside the Administration than from within. No one seriously raised with him any potential conflict of interest between his role with Carter and his priesthood, Baroni said. He raised the issue with a few friends and let them know he didn't have any problem with the idea of a priest in government.

Baroni decided to take the job. He was at the time assigned as a priest to the archdiocese of Washington. He told Archbishop William Baum that he had been offered a government position and wanted to take it, but would not if Baum objected. Baum did not object.

Baroni saw his work within HUD as a continuation and fulfillment of his priestly ministry. He believed that he was bringing to government all the accumulated experience and wisdom he had acquired as a priest serving the poor and alienated.

As with all jobs at that high a level, there was for Baroni a steady pulling in toward the political consensus. "He did make himself a pain in the neck on neighborhoods. When he'd come into a meeting, some people would say, 'Here's Baroni. Here comes the neighborhood,' " a HUD associate recalled. But politics, the art of compromise and the possible, inevitably requires concessions. Baroni, in order to retain his influence, was forced to submerge his conflicts with the Administration, to defend it publicly, and to limit his contacts with his former colleagues, including priests with whom he had worked in CCUM and through the Center.

Baroni said he did not compromise his principles at HUD, and the evidence and testimony from former associates supports that. But in the process, Baroni sacrificed effectiveness within the bureaucracy. As he spoke about moral commitments, he lost his acceptance as a politician and simultaneously began to be typecast as a priest who was out of his element in the Federal government. Baroni said he never felt he was being used as a priest by Carter and his senior staff. But Baroni sensed the possibility of that trap of tokenism.

In this way, Baroni's roles as priest and politician inherently collided. The more he, identified as a priest, advocated a position as moral, the more it alienated some listeners as the special pleading of a churchman. Baroni did not masquerade as an expert on Catholic theology, nor did he cite Catholic teaching to his colleagues at HUD. Rather he relied on his own experience, his own feelings for what was right, and he brought a practical politician's instinct for what could be attained in the political process. But some of his HUD co-workers persisted in dismissing Baroni's arguments as tainted by his priesthood. Baroni was never confronted directly with this attack, but he and his friends sensed it and were frustrated by their inability to deal with it. "The reality is that he was a priest, and that was a factor even though Geno didn't want it to be," one aide said.

On most days, Baroni would wear his black collar to the office, and he was known to many HUD employees as Father Baroni. He occasionally was called on to listen to the personal problems of employees and to administer the sacrament of reconciliation to those employees. Conversely, HUD workers who needed help or special favors from Catholic institutions—like admission of a parent to a Catholic nursing home or admission of a child to a Catholic college—would enlist Baroni's help.

Baroni saw no conflict between his role as a priest and his role as a public figure. His bridge between the two callings was his determination to use his office to press for the protection of the poor and disadvantaged, especially the Catholic urban ethnics he had championed from 1970 to 1976.

As an outsider, he had been lecturing government officials on the need to change the system for the involvement and delivery of social services. No longer could Federal government alone subsidize housing, food, education, welfare assistance, jobs and other social services that the underclass and working-class needed for decent survival, Baroni said. As a private citizen, he had lobbied for more involvement by the private sector and greater participation by the non-government, private voluntary sector, made up of neighborhood associations and churches for the most part. Baroni saw himself, as did others, as an enabler, a facilitator, to bring the sectors together. It is difficult to imagine anyone in modern American society who had more impressive credentials to do that pulling together than Baroni.

Baroni saw no conflict between his obligations as an ordained priest and the sworn promise he delivered to Vice President Walter F. Mondale to "preserve, protect and defend" the Constitution of the

United States. No conflict between the two obligations ever developed during his four years in office, Baroni said. If it had, he said, he would have submitted his resignation to HUD.

Baroni was sensitive to the fact that as a priest he could be forced to be more public than he would care to be on the center stage of politics in Carter's election bid. Baroni said about a year before the first term ended that he would be leaving the Federal government, no matter what happened, at the end of Carter's first term.

During the second campaign, Baroni, in his role as a HUD official, did facilitate several trips that Carter tried to use to his political advantage. Baroni saw that as a function of his position within HUD, and not as a partisan political act. This is not to say that Baroni stood aloof from the campaign. Directly and through his surrogates at the White House, Baroni sought to alter campaign strategy. He wanted Carter to campaign in cities as the champion of policies that promised better housing and schools, and more jobs—issues Baroni felt would have outweighed Carter's weaknesses in the minds of urban ethnic voters.

Early in 1980, before Reagan won the nomination, Baroni began to believe that Carter was finished. He said as much to friends. Baroni loved the mechanics of politics. He delighted in predicting how states would go in the election. In 1980, he confirmed what was well known among his friends—Baroni had an uncanny sense of the political mood.

Baroni's advice to Carter to campaign against Reagan on issues that would attract support from blue-collar urban ethnics went unheeded. Baroni suggested several events that Baroni believed would renew the 1976 coalition that got Carter elected the first time. But those events, somewhat to Baroni's distress, were rare and inconsequential. Carter was preoccupied with the U.S. hostages in Teheran. Baroni wished he could have convinced the president to see more of America's neighborhoods.

Looking back at his career in Federal government, Baroni said he had no regrets that he accepted Patricia Roberts Harris' bid to join HUD, but would not advise it for any other priest, and, in fact, does not believe any priest should do it. Baroni said he did it because he was "unique," that his career as a priest equipped him to carry into government the same interests he had held as a priest. Repeatedly, Baroni stressed that his service in government was an extension of his ministry as a priest.

Asked if he saw a difference between the role of the lay Catholic and the role of the Catholic priest in public service, Baroni said, "Yes. I think it is 99 percent the job of the lay people. I think priests should create the climate, be encouraging and supportive. I got involved in what I did by accident."

His participation in federal government, Baroni said, was "unique because I lived in Washington, so I got involved in national legislation on redlining. I found out you had to go to Congress if you wanted to change minimum wage. This was affecting thousands of people in the neighborhood, city, and parish. It didn't make any difference to me whether they were parishioners or not. They were people who needed help and it is the job of the Church and its people to extend that help."

Baroni said he suspects that most U.S. Catholic priests and religious men and women who enter public service do so because of the circumstances of their ministries. "They see it as a natural continuation of their work as Christians," Baroni said.

It would be a disservice to Baroni if his career, however, is examined primarily in terms of his Federal government service. His contribution to the Church and to the country far supersedes the limited contribution he made in the Carter Administration.

Baroni was a principal figure in moving the institutional Church into the world to assume a major role in restructuring policies that influence and impact on people's personal lives, dignity and human rights. Baroni helped convince Catholic Church leaders and many religious women and men in this country that they had a moral obligation, a gospel commitment, to go beyond the St. Vincent de Paul approach of charity to seek involvement in the political process.

Baroni embodied a human rights, civil rights, social justice, political-economic fairness ministry. Baroni and those who worked with him made legitimate within the Church the idea that the Church's job is not simply to pick up the pieces of defective social arrangements, but to reshape, restructure and redesign those arrangements according to moral standards.

Baroni made the social justice ministry a religiously significant calling for the Church.

Carolyn Farrell, BVM

LET THE VOTERS DECIDE

In the fall of 1977, I had no idea that women religious in politics would be a major topic of interest in 1984. For me, when I decided to seek election to the Dubuque City Council, being a woman was the most important consideration in my decision. No woman had ever served on the City Council. The fact that I happened to be a BVM, a Sister of Charity of the Blessed Virgin Mary, rated about equal in importance with the fact of being Irish or a Farrell. It helped to tell who I was.

It is important to remember that my story begins before Pope John Paul II or the Drinan case of 1980. I was very much a woman of the 70's. In 1968, renewal began to take place within our religious community. We were able to return to our own baptismal names, wear contemporary dress, live in apartments, minister in the place and way we discerned God's call. We were free to become involved in the civil rights struggles, protest against war in Vietnam and enter into the Woman's Rights movement. No one told us how to act. Indeed, it was a fast-paced period of growth for me.

Considering my personal gifts, and trying to decide how I could best serve the Church at that time, I accepted a position as principal at St. Patrick School, Dubuque, Iowa. This was my first major decision and risk, following renewal. I now think of myself as young—I was in my early thirties!

The age factor does seem important to me as I look back to that time. At that age, I entered into the arena of administration and into all the committee work such a position either required or suggested. I found that I enjoyed the work at St. Pat's and the committee work was both stimulating and exciting. I didn't realize at the time how much of an extrovert I was and how much I thrived on interchange with people. I soon found myself the first chairperson of the Dubuque Catholic School Principals' Organization. This position put me in touch with the public school sector as well as the colleges in the area. These connections proved to be important for name identification and support when I ran for the City Council.

Given the freedom to move into society at large, my personal characteristics—high energy, great capacity for enjoying people and challenges—thrust me into a variety of civic committees and groups within the local area. At the same time, these same personality traits drew me into deeper involvement with the government of the BVM congregation. I was elected a senator to represent our part of the country in the BVM Senate, our major decision-making body. Later I was elected to serve on our Administrative Board as a ministry delegate. I thrived on the activity.

In describing this intense activity, it is important for me to emphasize my deep belief, then and now, regarding the need for systemic change. My conviction that some systems were oppressive or restrictive was just beginning to grow as I became more aware of the world of the 70's. It seemed to me, my conviction was a call and a ministry to work for change within structures to achieve positive renewal and growth. I felt called to work within systems using unrelenting effort and a loud voice on certain days.

As I participated in these various groups, my awareness of being a woman increased. In the educational circles, I often found myself the only woman in the group. I soon noticed that most positions of authority were held by men. Within both school systems, men held the decision-making roles at the superintendent and secondary school levels. All principals at the elementary level in the public school system were men, while the Catholic schools had sisters. Each Catholic school was connected to the parish and pastor through its school board. My experience was one of tension and struggle between the pastor and schoolboard. As the principal caught in this situation, I perceived it as a male/female struggle for power.

The more experience I gained, the more I realized the struggle a woman has in achieving a leadership role within the structures of our society whether Church, education, business, or government. I continued to believe good leadership could effect change and, in time, renew worn-out structures. My stance remained the same: such activity is ministry in the best sense of our understanding of Church.

In 1974, I left St. Patrick School and became Director of Special Programs at Clarke College in Dubuque; in 1975, I also assumed responsibility for the Clarke Summer Session. My entrance into higher education brought with it the same type of committee involvement and the awareness that it was also a man's world at the decision-making level of college administration. During this period of time, many special programs for women were developed and offered at Clarke. From the base of "Special Programs," we were able to develop a Division of Continuing Education. My involvement in this area of education did two things for me: it raised my awareness of the difficulties women face returning to school and work; it also expanded my contacts in the city.

During this same period of time, two major events took place in my life which eventually led me to run for the City Council. I was asked by Alan Thoms, Mayor of Dubuque, to serve on the Dubuque Civil Service Commission. No woman had ever served on this committee, and he suggested that with my background in education I would be a valuable asset to the Commission. The chief task of this particular Commission is the administration of entrance and promotional tests to police and firefighters. Other related personnel matters also fall within the Commission's review.

I pondered the appointment to the Civil Service Commission. In those days, there were no open meeting laws so I felt free to discuss the position with Alan. I had met him through an ecumenical discussion group and we had become friends. He was part of the "male power group" in the city and provided my introduction to city government. I decided I could do the work, and said I would be willing to serve on the Commission.

It never occurred to me that my religious vocation was an impediment to such civic service. I believed the same talents used in committee work regarding education and religious life could be helpful in city government. I also felt that it was an important breakthrough for a woman to serve on the Commission.

I never asked anyone in authority in my religious community if I could or should serve in such a role. It never occurred to me to ask. Looking back, I think I felt called to use my own reason and conscience in a mature way, to decide if I could and should handle the task. The BVM congregation supported adult, life giving behavior, and I felt I was responding as a responsible BVM. I continued to operate with this principle in mind as months and years later, I accepted the invitation to serve on the Governor's Advisory Council on Volunteerism, to co-chair IOWA SHARES in Dubuque, and to take a position on the Iowa Campaign Finance Disclosure Commission. In fact, as I became better known I was asked to serve on state *ad hoc* committees and attend various statewide conferences. I used to laugh and say that I was recruited in order to represent Northeastern Iowa, Democrats, Catholics and Women all in one. The truth was, I attended so that a woman would be present.

My civil service involvement brought me in contact with City Hall-elected officials and staff. I enjoyed both the work and the people I met. I discovered I was accepted as a woman and a religious. These affirming relationships were a critical influence in my decision to run for the City Council.

A second major influence was an invitation by Governor Ray to serve on the IOWA 2000 task force committee. This was my introduction to statewide committee work. The experience was stimulating, enriching and affirming. Working at this level, I found that I was accepted as a woman and a religious. The project put me in touch with a network of active people in the State of Iowa. I discovered my involvement unleashed a desire to become more active in the political process.

With this background, 1977 became the year I decided to run for the City Council. The decision had been in process for many months. My successful involvement in civic work, educational circles and BVM government reinforced my inner conviction that I could be effective on the council. Oftentimes, teasing took place. "There's no woman on the City Council—why don't you run?" This type of affirmation urged me onward to consider the challenge of elected office. It was time to act.

Permission? I visited with Joan Keleher Doyle, BVM, then president of the Sisters of Charity, BVM, and also the president of the Leadership Conference of Women Religious at that time. I shared with Joan my interest in running for the City Council. She encouraged me to run for the office. Later, I went to Alan Thoms, who had been encouraging me to seek the position, and told him it was now or never. We began to campaign.

Meanwhile, before the public statement announcing my candidacy, I went to the Chancery to visit with Reverend Jack Dalton, chancellor of the Dubuque diocese and secretary to Archbishop Byrne. I told Jack of my plans and indicated I would like the Archbishop to hear of my candidacy before the public announcement. He was supportive and he assured me he would share my plans with the Archbishop at lunch that day. I left feeling good; I felt that I had done the polite thing. I never knew or thought I needed his approval to run for the City Council. I never heard a word from the chancery office.

The following day I announced my candidacy and the campaign began in earnest. In time, the campaign raised the following question: Is there a violation of the principle of separation of church and state when a woman religious seeks and is elected to public office? I think not. However, it was a great topic to discuss at the time of such an election.

I can remember answering this question more than once for an inquiring reporter at a Candidate's Night. Each time I responded with a somewhat simplistic remark that I supported the First Amendment. I certainly didn't want the Church telling the state what to do, nor did I want the state telling the Church what to do. I continued by saying that I had the support of my religious community and the local Church authority had said nothing—as was proper. The Church was neither endorsing me nor speaking against me; the decision belonged to the voters.

No one ever challenged my response. The fact that I was a "nun," as the townspeople so often said, did not violate the United States Constitution. The Congressional roster reveals a number of men who are ordained ministers. It has been said on occasion that they are not "practicing" their ministry while serving in Congress. Their "church status" does not seem to impede their work for the country nor does it challenge the First Amendment. In 1984, Rev. Jesse Jackson is a candidate for president. His role as a minister has not disqualified him as a viable candidate for public office.

Beyond the legal question of constitutionality came the real question: Should a woman religious seek public office? This question kept discussion moving across the bridge table, at the Chamber of Commerce office, in the union hall, around the shopping center, and on the radio talk shows. Everyone had an opinion.

Comments from the daily call-in talk show, SOUNDOFF, gave a flavor of Catholic Dubuque as it pondered the possibility of a "nun" on the City Council.

"Nuns should stay in the schools where they belong."

"Praying doesn't mix with politics."

"She looks like an ordinary housewife." (Return call) "What is wrong with looking like an ordinary housewife?"

"Will she have enough time for her prayers if she is on the City Council?"

"How can a woman with a vow of celibacy wear earrings?"

This was the bottom line in the fall of 1977: the appropriateness of a vowed woman serving in an elected position. With a quiet official Church, the citizens were left to exchange their own thoughts with their neighbors. Consciousness raising did take place. The advice I received from my campaign committee was to stay out of the discussion, state and restate my experience and capability to serve at the council table. It is also important to remember that throughout this whole discussion, there was an undercurrent of concern: Could a woman serve well at the Council table?

The women's issue was not central to the campaign. The out-front statement declared the city needed qualified council members to serve the citizens of Dubuque. The campaign stressed downtown development, highway 561, and the Iowa/Wisconsin bridge. These were the key issues in that election. As a woman, nun, candidate, these were the major issues I was called upon to discuss and debate. And indeed debate did take place on the issues, but visibly I was a woman and even without the title "Sister" everyone knew my religious commitment. Only once was I challenged in pubic by a local citizen who shouted at me that I was "out of place" running for the City Council. I kept cool and assured him he had a right to his opinion. The audience was embarrassed and the candidates' panel continued without further disruption.

The most challenging criticism I received as a religious seeking public office, from some Dubuquers, was the fact that I did not pay taxes. I have not heard the same concern stated regarding other religious or clerics serving in public office. Some citizens believed that as a non-tax-paying person, I should not have a say in the use of the tax dollar. This was a critical issue since the major role of the council is to approve the city budget and allocate taxes to support city services.

I defended my position by stating that I did pay all sales taxes; our apartment rent helped our landlord to pay his property tax; my personal income was nonexistent due to my contributed services to a religious institution, and such an arrangement is approved by U.S. law. The counter response contended that I was outside the system, and therefore I should not hold a decision-making role in the system. This position is reinforced by tax-free status of land and buildings owned by religious congregations.

As with the question of whether a nun should serve in public office, the local taxpayers discussed this question in the city forum of free speech and exchange. Not many folks took this criticism seriously, but those who held it never changed their minds.

The abortion issue was never part of the campaign rhetoric. It was not a city issue. During my four years on the council, it never surfaced as a cause for consideration under any agenda item. It seems fair to say it is the issue that causes the most grief for religious and clerics who serve in public office. I did not have to deal with it while I served on the council. However, in 1980, I did work for Senator John Culver in his attempt for re-election as senator from Iowa. At the same time, I actively worked for the passage of the Iowa Equal Rights Amendment.The pro-choice issue was key in both of these elections. Both Culver and the Iowa Equal Rights Amendment lost, and I received hate mail calling me a "baby killer" among other epithets.

In my story, I have deliberately focused my reflection on my personal involvement and background before moving into public office. It is very difficult to be elected to a city, state, or federal position. It takes name identification, a broad base of support, money, and a platform built on strong issues. I could not have been elected if I had not had my background and previous experience. The fact that I was a nun was only one part of the story.

Today, with the intervention of the Vatican in the United States political process, it strikes me that we may lose sight of the crucial challenge built into our democratic system of election. Voters do think and support the candidates of their choice. Issues and personalities, as well as money, are paramount in the process. Women religious running for office are in the same category as all other candidates. Voters, emotionally or logically, select candidates of their choice. To survive in such a process means a candidate has been accepted by the electorate after a long and strenuous campaign with issues out front and personalities bared to public scrutiny.

The voters had to decide if I was qualified to represent them at the council table. I believe that is the way the process should work here in the United States. There was no prohibitive or questioning stance from the official Catholic Church to hinder the discussion. The citizens were able to decide, in a democratic way, if a church commitment was an impediment to a candidate for public office.

Dubuquers recalled Gaylord M. Couchman, a Presbyterian minister who served on the City Council in 1968. Businessmen wondered if a woman could understand the city budgeting process. Local tax payers pondered the advisability of one "out of the taxing system" serving on the council. Supporters declared my experience and background spoke for itself.

The voters did decide: I was elected to the Dubuque City Council.

The votes cast at the polls during November 1977, ultimately led to my selection as Mayor of Dubuque in 1980. Dubuque had a strong city manager type of government at that time. This system requires the election of mayor from the members of the City Council by the Council itself. The mayor is an extra time position for the person selected to serve in that role.

During my four-year term on the City Council, one member was passed over as Mayor. In late December 1979, and January 1980, the great story in the city of Dubuque was the Council's decision to elect me mayor instead of Jim Brady who was often called "the maverick."

Being a nun/woman religious never emerged as a handicap for me in the selection process. I had served two years on the Council, as well as Mayor pro tem during my second year. My activity within the city and at the council table earned me the respect of the city and the members of the Council.

I was so involved in the city discussion regarding my selection as mayor over Jim Brady that I was amazed that my election as Mayor of Dubuque was national news. The two years on the Council caused me to think of my political activity to be within the normal range of city government. Dubuquers had taken me for granted but the idea of a "Nun/Mayor" became a novelty to the press and media folks. The national attention forced me to analyze carefully my relations with the press and media.

I believe strongly in the freedom of the press and I am aware of the responsibility that accompanies this right. I attempted to deal honestly with all press and media people. I returned phone calls and gave both TV and radio interviews when possible. I quickly became aware of the power of press and decided to use it to promote women—and women religious. Such a decision is a risk and a challenge.

Such activity is subject to editing. The end product is never known until it is aired or printed. Live interviews require quick thinking and honest responses. As with television, my image came across to the public to ponder and evaluate. To my advantage, I enjoyed the exchange with interviewers and found it an exciting challenge.

A memorable interview took place with the "Des Moines Register" and its radio station during the Spring of 1980. I was Mayor at the time and Fr. Drinan had just received his directive to withdraw from Congress. The same day the story broke, I was called by the "Des Moines Register" and asked if this request applied to me. The statement, including the phrase, "clergy could not serve in public office" was read over the phone to me. I immediately responded that women religious had never been considered clergy and it did not apply to me. That response became national news. Within a week, "Good Morning America" had a live interview with me while I was in Washington, D.C. Again I was asked the question of the relationship of the directive to Fr. Drinan to me. I replied in the same manner as before. David Hartman then asked about some of my responsibilities as mayor and I can remember telling him that the real work was in zoning issues.

Beyond publicity, as the choice of the voters, I chaired all council meetings, work sessions, and public hearings. My name appeared on all official documents as Carolyn Farrell, BVM. I was invited to represent the City of Dubuque at the various functions in Dubuque and other parts of the state. Lobbying for highway 561 found me leading groups of men to the Department of Transportation in Ames, Iowa and Washington, D.C.

It was a full year of intense activity for the city. There was no conflict between my religious commitment and my position as mayor. A fun thing was to be asked to give both the welcome and the invocation before a formal dinner. Most of the time, it was one or the other.

I am not impressed with titles or positions, but I am aware of how such status enables you to be a public figure and therefore able to present a personal message or image. I used my role as mayor to present women as capable and involved citizens. Without saying it, this was also true for women religious.

The voters risked in deciding that I should represent them at the Council table and as mayor. It was their decision. My public service in their behalf was my response within the democratic process that is the United States.

Roland H. St. Pierre, OMI

THREE TERM PRIEST-MAYOR

My unexpected venture into the nebulous world of politics began quite by accident at a 1969 political gathering in Plattsburgh, NY. That year, I had accepted to serve as master of ceremonies at the annual dinner of the local Republican Party. Two weeks later, the local Democrats demanded equal time and similar service at their election-year event. Since I was a lifelong Democrat, I complied.

While introducing the incumbent Democratic Mayor in the course of that evening, I noted that, during his first four years in office, this individual had not really administered City Hall. Certain influential parties were making the decisions behind the scenes—usually for their own gain. Adding that he would automatically be re-elected to a third two-year term, I concluded: "This means that you have just two years to shape up or ship out, even if I have to run against you myself in 1971. And you had better beware for I do have a strong platform already: PLATTSBURGH, ALBANY, WASHINGTON and ROME—in that order!"

Many citizens of Plattsburgh never let me forget those words throughout the two ensuing years. Their reminders became legion in 1971 when no viable candidate came forward to oppose the incumbent whose policies and procedures had not changed one iota despite my 1969 warning. I, therefore, sought permission from my Major Superior to seek political office, specifically that of Mayor of Plattsburgh, N.Y. The avenue was cleared and I was on my way.

If my Order, the Oblates of Mary Immaculate, had insisted that I take a leave of absence while competing in the political arena, I would not have entered the field. I do not believe in leaves of absence. Nor do I believe that a religious or a priest is a second class citizen relegated to the sole task of praying for a certain congregation and caring for its spiritual needs, that he or she has no right to work towards bettering the condition of all fellow citizens by means of a political office if no other qualified candidate is available. Be that as it may, I am not an across-the-board advocate of clergy in political office. Such should never be our normal course of action. However, when a fully qualified religious person is a citizen in a municipality or region where a political office is not being administered properly and no capable layman seeks the post, then he or she should obtain the necessary clearance to run for the position and remain in it for whatever time is necessary to clear the air and render unto the electorate the services that they justly deserve.

THE INITIAL CAMPAIGN

On 28 June 1971, the annual caucus of the City of Plattsburgh Republican Party chose me as its candidate for Mayor. I accepted on one condition and I spelled it out clearly to all in attendance: "If you find a better candidate before the filing date, I will bow out of the race." The campaign was on!

From that moment on I did not preach at St. Peter's Church where I was serving as pastor. My Provincial proposed another Oblate Father's name to the Bishop as interim administrator. I bade farewell to my people in the parish bulletin on Sunday, 25 July 1971, writing: "Normally, I would deliver a final message from the pulpit. However, the venture that I wish to undertake prevents me from doing so. I also wish all to know that the priesthood means more to me than anything else and that I shall remain a priest, doing priestly work in everything that I undertake." On 29 July, I officially became the Republican candidate for Mayor of Plattsburgh.

I handled the campaign personally and ran it extremely low key, preferring to meet and talk with as many people as possible, stressing positive points and letting my opponent's record speak for itself. The theme of the campaign was *"Positive Programming for Progress"* and the platform proposed four distinct elements:

1) Less talk, more action in City Hall,
2) A dollar's worth for every dollar spent,
3) Personal involvement of all citizens,
4) Sane and sound development of Plattsburgh's potential.

In a city where two-thirds of the population is Catholic the priesthood was thought to be a political liability. It was felt that the majority of the Catholics would want to keep their priests in Church and away from elected office. I did not go along with that theory. I maintained that the Catholic majority would want the best for its City's administration. The primary advantage of being a cleric is that people expect justice from you right down the line, even when it hurts. They expect you to be honest and to exercise charity in difficult cases. I am sure that my fellow citizens would have been visibly upset if I had removed my collar in the course of the campaign. And I never did!

Only one writer proved negative during the campaign in the Letters to the Editor that appeared in the local newspaper on a daily basis. She proposed the separation of Church and State as an issue to be considered in the light of my candidacy. All other contributors backed my move wholeheartedly. When I appeared on the panel show "You Can Quote Me" over WCAX-TV in Burlington, Vermont (directly across Lake Champlain from Plattsburgh), the moderator, Charles Lewis, asked me, "Father St. Pierre, if you are elected Mayor of Plattsburgh, what is the first thing that you will do? Place a Chapel in City Hall?"

My answer was spontaneous: "No. I shall place a Confessional in City Hall. That is what it needs!"

There were three debates between the mayoral adversaries in the initial campaign. The incumbent underscored one of the abiding issues prevalent in the Plattsburgh area when he reminded everyone that he had lived in the City all his life and knew what the people wanted in City Government. My response was a bit simplistic when I answered that, although I had been in the area for a mere five years, I had already fallen in love with the City and desired to provide its citizens with what they wanted and deserved.

I planned a simple strategy in this initial campaign: let the incumbent hang himself. Several controversial issues worsened day by day and it all turned to my advantage.

First, there was the constant bickering between the six City Aldermen (five were Democrats) and the Mayor during the weekly Thursday evening Common Council Meetings. These happenings were aired live over a local radio station and were fast becoming the most entertaining comedy of the week. Then there was extreme division over the proposed site of a new Civic Center. Factions of citizens were intent on constructing it in a crowded area of the City, a preposterous locale for such a project. Nonetheless, there was lack of leadership by the administration in setting things right. City streets were in pitiful condition with no relief in sight. The Police Force openly condemned the Democratic City Judge for unequal distribution of justice and vowed to defeat his party. The Police Headquarters itself was relegated to a depressing basement section of City Hall and could not operate properly.

When I spoke of disarray at City Hall, the voters knew exactly what I meant. After all, they had been listening to the Common Council broadcasts filled with intra-Democratic squabblings.

Then came November 2, 1971 and the election . . .

Ninety-five percent of all eligible voters in Plattsburgh cast ballots that day. In the mayoral race I garnered sixty-nine percent of the vote, beating the incumbent by better than two-to-one. The six man Common Council was split down the middle: three Democrats and three Republicans with only two incumbents re-elected.

The battle was ended and the task of bringing efficient government to the City of Plattsburgh was about to begin.

AN AMATEUR REGIME

The front page of the local Press-Republican which had endorsed the incumbent carried this banner headline on November 3, 1971:

AMATEURS TAKE CITY HALL: G.O.P. REGIME STARTS JAN. 1

The same day, a front page Editorial stated: "None can argue that this is a clear mandate from the people of Plattsburgh; that they want a new government ever so badly; that they want the entire thrust of city government to change, to reflect, in essence, those platform points espoused by Father St. Pierre and his Republican slate."

The election was over but the fight to establish an honest, efficient and caring City Administration was still two months away. True, my victory had disbanded the long-reigning Democratic political machine and promised a change of character to City Hall. However, a great deal of groundwork had to be accomplished to lay the foundation for the task ahead.

My first move was to fly to Washington, D.C. I spent ten days there to establish personal contact with those officials of Federal Agencies who could provide sorely-needed help to small cities such as Plattsburgh. Here, my priesthood stood me in good stead. Everyone wanted to view this new breed of political animal, the first Catholic priest elected Mayor of a city in the United States.

I set up appointments with officials at various Federal Departments: Transportation, Commerce, Housing and Urban Development, Environmental Protection, Parks and Recreation and Civil Defense. I even made a stop at the Pentagon because of the Strategic Air Command Base at Plattsburgh. Throughout this tour I collected data on legislation affecting small cities, on grants available to same, and I listed the names of the proper officials to contact for these offerings. This laid the foundation for the many moves needing Federal backing that I would make during my tenure as Mayor.

While in Washington I received an invitation to visit with the President of the United States who was interested in meeting Plattsburgh's first Republican Mayor in a generation. I declined since it would have cut into an already overcrowded schedule and would have prevented my making all the contacts that I had programmed.

Once back in Plattsburgh, I listed all the priorities facing the new administration and began the research necessary for the implementation of the many reforms that would be required of it. There was an evident waste of municipal funds in useless projects. Patronage and nepotism reigned supreme in the local hiring practices. Planning and programming were lacking in most areas.

The incoming regime had its job cut out for it!

THE NEW ADMINISTRATION

January 1, 1972 dawned and the inauguration of the country's first priest-mayor took place at the Clinton County Courthouse with Supreme Court Justice Norman Harvey presiding. The time had come to roll up one's sleeves and get the show on the road.

The summary of the platform that I had written for the Republican contenders formed the basis of the approach that I intended to use in governing Plattsburgh. It stated: "We aim to provide sound business administration, leadership and government in the City of Plattsburgh, bringing growth and progress to an area that cries for development. Government costs money: we will give the people the facts. Our objective is to make Plattsburgh solvent, to keep our young people with us, to handle every problem without delay so that City Hall will truly reflect the will of the people."

The Charter of the City of Plattsburgh calls for a strong-mayor form of government. The Chief Executive presides over the Common Council, the Legislative Body of six Aldermen, and breaks all ties. He is also empowered to summarily assume the responsibility of personally heading any city department should a problem arise.

During my first two weeks in office I personally audited every city department. I concentrated on the work load required of each, on the number of employees actually involved as compared to the amount truly needed, on the finances allotted, the expenditures made and the procedures used in spending. It quickly became evident to me that the city was the victim of excessive waste both financially and in terms of manpower.

I immediately tightened up the finances. Any expenditure of fifty dollars or more had to be authorized by the Mayor. State purchasing contracts were to be utilized whenever and wherever possible. Overtime, outside of acute emergencies, was banned. These somewhat drastic maneuvers did not occasion the uproar that I had expected. Both the citizens and the city workers realized the excesses that had prevailed in the past and welcomed the opportunity to co-operate in rectifying the situation.

I then turned my attention to the excessive size of the city work force. This was a more difficult undertaking since family security was at stake. I had come into office with nothing to lose, nothing to gain and no interest in higher office or currying favor. I was, therefore, able to espouse a hard line on some very difficult decisions. Once I ascertained that the people affected would be covered by unemployment benefits, I trimmed the city payroll with a sizable layoff of surplus personnel—all deadwood.

Over the years the Plattsburgh work contingent had become the illegitimate child of patronage and nepotism not merely in the unskilled labor market, but also in the professional fields. Persons without needed qualifications were heading important departments. This practice had to be eradicated. Wherever possible, I established a new formula for the jobs offered by the City of Plattsburgh. Every position gained Civil Service stature. Thus, the Mayor, as appointing officer, could present to the Common Council for confirmation the best qualified candidate from the top three finishers in the competitive examination or from all applications in the non-competitive fields.

The by-laws of the Plattsburgh Housing Authority prevented my effecting this procedure in that area. The Mayor alone had the authority to appoint anyone that he chose. As long as I held the post, there would be no problem. The appointees had definite six-year terms, but, once a term was complete, the Mayor was free to appoint anyone that he desired. That, in my opinion at the time, was the only area that I had left unguarded simply because there was nothing else that I could do.

Upgrading the city streets, modernizing utilities and renovating the parks were sorely needed in Plattsburgh. Programs in these areas were practically non-existent. Instead of paving the streets previous administrations had made a career out of caring for people's driveways.

The contacts made in Washington were tapped. The Federal grants obtained allowed the complete repair of major roads. They also permitted us to replace some seventy percent of the underground sewer system, separating the sanitary sewers from the surface drains. We renovated an existing park and built two new ones so that each section of the city had a suitable recreation area, one that was pleasant and safe for young and old alike.

The inadequacy of Police Headquarters also concerned me. With rising construction costs and my preference for using a pay-as-you-go system even for capital improvements, I decided to combine a new police facility with a Civil Defense Readiness Center, thereby obtaining eligibility for a Federal Grant that would absorb a goodly portion of the cost. To avail myself of a proper site without removing any property from the tax rolls, I transferred the Public Works operation into part of the voluminous space occupied by the Water and Sewer Department. This change proved beneficial to both departments.

Shortly after the new headquarters was dedicated, the Chief of Police retired. Two factions arose within the Department, each promoting a favorite candidate for a temporary appointment to the open post. I invoked the City Charter and personally assumed command of the Police Force until the pending Civil Service Test was administered. Once the results were in, I appointed the man that I found most competent among the top three finishers. The Common Council backed me unanimously in these moves.

Many problems came to the fore during the six years that I headed Plattsburgh's government. None ever dealt with the realm of religion. City government is big business and must be handled as such. The basic difficulties lay in differences of opinion with one or the other of the Aldermen who felt that, as legislators, they should be part and parcel of the executive branch of the city. The Thursday evening Common Council meeting became known as my "weekly kindergarten class" because what could not be ironed out during the session was cleared the following day with an executive order.

CONCLUSION

Throughout the six years that I spent in Plattsburgh's City Hall I encountered no church-state confrontations. The closest thing to such a happening came from a retired military man who asked me why I was not wearing a business suit as Mayor. Pointing to my collar, I retorted, "This IS my business suit."

What surprised people the most was that, although a lifelong Democrat, I had run twice as a Republican and in my final campaign as an out-and-out Independent taking on both parties and had won each time.

In June of 1977, as I moved into the final quarter of my third term as Mayor, I decided that there was little more that I could contribute to the betterment of this North Country Community. A local businessman had apprised me of his interest in seeking office should I decide to leave. He had excellent qualifications and I figured that my presence was no longer required at City Hall. I soon announced that my political career would come to an abrupt end on December 31, 1977.

As I reviewed my political career, I took great pride in the appointment of fully qualified professionals to head key city departments. I was especially grateful that all were now officially civil servants and enjoyed full tenure before I left. I had combed the countryside for them, hiring an electrical engineer from Illinois to direct the Municipal Lighting Department, a former chemical company executive from Massachusetts as Manager of the city's pollution control system and a professional engineer from New York as City Engineer. These persons had come aboard to serve the city at large. They would outlast any Mayor.

Another achievement that I considered noteworthy was the lowering of taxes. In two of my six years as Chief Executive the citizens of Plattsburgh had no city tax whatsoever.

I have watched City Hall from a distance since leaving its precincts. Patronage has returned to the housing authority area. These posts that provided their occupants sixty dollars per meeting in my day now produce well over one hundred dollars per session for each appointee. New positions have been created outside the civil service structure to reward a few political backers. All in all, however, our basic reforms remain intact.

On January 12, 1978, at the request of my Provincial and the Bishop of Ogdensburg, I accepted the post of Catholic chaplain at the dubiously famous Clinton Correctional Facility, Dannemora, N.Y., part of the State Prison System. Just recently, I transferred to the new State Prison in Altona, N.Y.

The questions most often thrown at me these days by friends gleaned since my 1966 arrival in Northern New York are: "How can you stand it in prison? Don't you miss the limelight of politics? When are you coming back to City Hall?"

My answer is simple and straightforward: "Inmates are my kind of people. They are easier to deal with than politicians will ever be. And, God willing, this will be my FINAL PRIESTLY TASK!"

Amen.

Elizabeth Morancy, RSM

POLITICS AS A
MISSION OF MERCY

The Elmwood neighborhood of Providence that I represent in the Rhode Island House of Representatives has been called the international district. The population is about 45% white, 30% black, over 20% Spanish speaking, and now has an emerging Indo-Chinese Hmong population. Some call it a microcosm of the world, but as I campaign on the streets, attend local meetings, greet the children, and listen to the struggles, pain, and also joys of the people, I know that above all else, my constituents in Elmwood have become for me the Many Faces of God. And as I define my position of State Representative as ministry I also feel the six year experience has, in so many ways, been their simple, profound ministry with and to me.

My academic background provided a natural preparation for involvement in politics. With a B.A. in history and an M.A. in political science, I taught government in high school and college. But it was three other influences that motivated me more directly to seek political office.

When American women's congregations started to struggle with the Vatican II mandate for renewal, nuns began to search for the roots of their orders. We Sisters of Mercy again claimed a heritage which recalled that Catherine McAuley and her co-workers in nineteenth century Ireland sought to address unmet needs and in so doing challenged both Church and government on behalf of working women and the homeless women in Dublin. The desire to return to the original commitment of the Congregation once again energized some of us to respond to the Gospel call for ministry with the economically disadvantaged. This renewed priority was further strengthened by interaction among religious communities throughout the country.

The social teachings of Pope Paul VI also provided us with common direction as we sought to discover how best to live out our orders' charisms in contemporary society. It was specifically the Pope's *Call to Action, the Eightieth Year Letter*, that brought forty-seven of us to Washington, DC in December, 1971. We founding mothers of NETWORK decided that the encyclical's statement, "Politics is a demanding manner to live out the Christian meaning of service to others," must be concretized. Our new Social Justice Lobby would do just that.

Moving into the Elmwood neighborhood of Providence in September, 1972 provided the experiential component that finally drew me to politics as a ministry. Elmwood was a typical core city neighborhood; racially mixed, large pockets of substandard housing, federal target area for revitalization funds in the early seventies, local community organization. As I participated in neighborhood efforts to clean up lots, fight crime, improve housing, it became clear that the people who had power to change some of these conditions were the elected officials. I began to say, "It's important who is making the decisions." Then I began to think, "Why shouldn't I become a part of that process?"

Given the complexities of our time and the power centered in our social structures, it seemed so natural to seek to influence the governmental processes that often determine the quality of peoples' lives. And I do not think it is coincidental that some of us chose to do it during the time when Pope Paul VI encouraged Christians to penetrate the economic and political centers where decisions made were having enormous impact on the way people could live.

I have served three terms in the Rhode Island General Assembly. During the past six years I have tried to minister in the Gospel spirit that is so wonderfully expressed in Mary's *Magnificat*. "For the God who is mighty can do good things through me. Yahweh . . . has exalted the lowly. She/He has filled the hungry with good things . . . ." As Mary perceived her role to be God's instrument for freedom and empowerment, I have always labored to make my presence in this policy-making body a sign to the powerless that some within the system seek to be instruments of justice and liberation. In a very special way the sensitivity that Mary's song reflects is a unique expression of her womanhood. And I have to bring that same compassion and care that is uniquely feminist to a patriarchal structure that so often exalts the mighty and favors the rich.

As a State Representative from a struggling urban neighborhood I have worked for social change through the legislation I have sponsored and the issues I have raised.

The major proposals for which I have developed legislation include fair housing, emergency shelter appropriations, handicapped rights, sexual assault, and criminal justice. Each has become a priority because my constituents have expressed a need or the social justice and women's groups with which I work have surfaced the concerns.

An amendment to the R.I. Fair Housing Practices Act which would prevent discrimination in rental and leasing solely on the basis of families having children has been a proposal for which I have worked the longest and hardest. In 1979, just after my first session in the House of Representatives two different people approached me concerning the problem. One of the persons was a single parent whose three children were not wanted by the landlords who owned decent apartments that were affordable. The second person was a young black attorney who had just moved to Rhode Island and wanted to rent an apartment with his wife and son as quickly as possible so he could concentrate on his study for the State's Bar Examination. My investigation of the issue led to a five year effort to end this discrimination in Rhode Island. The best part of this effort for me has been the realization that I have participated in a human rights struggle that particularly involves the economically disadvantaged, women, minorities—the very people whom I intended to serve through legislative office.

As Coordinator of the local Social Action Conference of the Sisters of Mercy in the early 1970s, I was one of several founders of McAuley House, a soup kitchen-hospitality place. I have since become a volunteer at the shelter which developed because of a need expressed by the guests of McAuley House. The experience motivated me to secure appropriations from the legislature to aid the work of sheltering the homeless. The stories from the people themselves directed my energies and set my agenda.

Several women's groups have also influenced my priorities. Of principal importance has been my participation as board member of the Rhode Island Rape Crisis Center. I have received an eye-opening education about the extent of sexual assault and the traumatic effect on the victims. My contribution has been to bring the issue into a forum where laws can assist the victims and educate the public. In addition to other efforts, I have sponsored marital rape legislation, the Rape Crisis Center Confidentiality bill, and State medical coverage of rape exams for victims with no health insurance.

My ministries prior to that of legislator never brought me into contact with the developmentally disabled, so people have wondered how I happened to be the author of two laws that expanded the parent subsidy program for handicapped children and their families. Another Sister of Mercy, Arlene Violet, was an attorney for a protection and advocacy agency. They wanted the existing law expanded to help parents whose children were treated out of state by including them in the subsidy statute that covered children within state institutions. I successfully sponsored the two laws that now financially assist parents to keep their children home instead of sending them out of the state for the necessary medical help. It was a meaningful process for me to sponsor the legislation that had been created by the experience of another Sister of Mercy in her political ministry.

When the State Advisory Commission on Women decided to address the growing problems of the women's prison, I was asked to represent the Legislature on the Committee for Incarcerated Women, since they thought I was probably the politician that would be most interested. From its inception our group has had significant influence in securing new programs for the women and our constant pressure has been a significant factor in the Correction Department's decision to develop a more humane facility for the women. As one of the negotiators for the whole Committee, I am especially delighted by the fact that sometimes a few determined committed women can successfully confront the male power structure on behalf of other women.

In order to raise justice issues within the legislative arena, most Americans choose to get elected through a process that includes running as a member of a political party. (This in itself is now a significant controversy.)

The issue of partisan politics seems to have surfaced because of the implied prohibitions in Canon Law. Since I run as a Democrat I have had to justify my party affiliation. It seems to me that the Vatican has formed its opinion on the basis of the impression of the European political parties which are far more ideological and doctrinaire than American political parties. As an example of this difference, one can point to Democrats in Congress, Senators Kennedy and Pell and Congresswoman Shroeder, who have consistently fought the Reagan policies while some of their colleagues in the Party from the South have supported the President. Republicans like my Congresswoman Claudine Schneider have been equally critical of the present administration's militarism and social cuts, while many Republican senators such as Helms, Thurmond, and Hatch have supported Reagan faithfully. It would not be correct, however, if I claimed that "partisan politics" cause no difficulties for religious candidates.

In Rhode Island the Democratic Party has been dominant during the last forty-five years. The House of Representatives itself consists of one hundred members, only fifteen of whom are Republicans. When any group exerts such control, accountability is weak. In politics, patronage swells, self-serving legislation increases, and powerful in-terest groups make headway when one party has a comfortable he-gemony. The year 1981 was characteristic in Rhode Island politics. That year we had a key bill that would give Rhode Islanders attending in-state private colleges a $500 tuition credit (among major recipients were the Catholic institutions), several patronage job bills, a proposal to raise the salaries of state office holders at a time when we could not afford it, and a few anti-abortion bills that were unconstitutional. Each of these bills was supported by the Democratic leadership. I voted against all of them. Later in the year it was reported to me that my district was to be one of the two Providence districts that would be elim-inated in the re-apportionment plan because I was not loyal to the Party. When the initial maps were unveiled, sure enough, my district was split and drawn into the two surrounding ones. I simply argued against the proposal, offered an alternative based on the population realities, and stated I would run for re-election under any condition. When the plan was finalized, my district was intact and the changes reflected the true population shifts of the city. I still do not know the dynamics that altered the actions within the Party.

Causing far greater tensions than party politics, for me, has been the Church politics of abortion. Rhode Island is the most Catholic state in the nation—two thirds of the population identify themselves as Catholics. The hierarchy is active concerning the issue. There is a vocal Right-to-Life movement. The Legislature has passed most of the anti-abortion bills irrespective of their constitutionality. In my first session in the House I was faced with an Informed Consent bill that was de-bated in the Judiciary Committee on which I serve. After extensive tes-timony was received, the majority of us felt the legislation was medically incorrect, legally unconstitutional, as well as harrassing to women. When we would not vote the Bill out of committee, the Right-to-Life groups vented their anger through personal attack. They were particularly harsh on me, implying in one of their newsletters that I was not in good standing with the Church or the Sisters of Mercy. This first attack since being elected really hurt. Since that time I have pe-riodically been singled out by them, but I have learned to place the unpleasantness in perspective.

My position on abortion has been clear. I am personally opposed to it. It is a tragic commentary on our society. But I also feel that we must distinguish how one views the issue and how one deals with it in a pluralistic society. It is my opinion that we cannot legislate the pro-hibition. Rather we must decide the greatest causes of increased abor-tions and address those issues more effectively. This position, however, is not acceptable to most of the hierarchical Church; consequently, the conflict continues. In reality it is a no-win issue.

A question that must be asked about any politician is: How is she/ he perceived by others? A recent comment by one of my colleagues reflects one view of me. Referring to my unwillingness to amend my bill that would give absolute confidentiality to the records of rape victims, allowing for judges-only inspection, my peer observed "Representative Liz is a very nice person but she's too inflexible. In politics you always have to accept compromise."

There is another view of me, too. One colleague in the Legislature delighted me when he told a group that I was the strongest supporter of women in the House. He stated that I was more than an E.R.A. advocate, that the "feminization of poverty" became more understandable because I consistently related the experiences I encountered in my daily ministry that demonstrated the effects of Reaganomics on women. Because my goal has been to do just this, I was happy to hear the comment and hoped that my presence in the General Assembly made the plight of the economically disadvantaged more visible and more difficult to ignore.

Every member of the General Assembly knows that I choose to work as well as live among low income people. Last year there was a proposal in the House of Representatives from the Governor that would further limit the number of people who would be eligible for medical assistance from the State. The measure, part of the Executive's plan to address the State's deficit, was slated for passage. In the floor debate I related my experience of being with Hmong refugees at the welfare office and told of their fear of having no medical coverage. I urged rejection of the proposed cut. The bill was postponed that day. After the debate the Speaker of the House and the Majority Leader told me that I had the experience and they would certainly respect my opinion. When the bill was brought to the House floor again, the section to which I objected was deleted. I felt it was an important victory because it represented the very reasons for which I sought political office.

The six years that I have spent in the Rhode Island House of Representatives has been a time of profound impact. One month after my first election I heard a speaker define ministry as, "making private pain a public issue." This immediately concretized the essence of politics from my perspective: this would be my goal in the Rhode Island Legislature. As I have worked to bring the needs of economically disadvantaged people to public awareness, my own life has been affected. I am part of the process of integration that faith and politics ignite.

Individual concerns that are truly the Gospel issues of human dignity have become public issues for legislative reform. What is viewed as holy and what is seen as secular are fused into a reality that seeks justice and equality. The call to live from a spirituality that is creation-centered is so much more real to me now. I am part, in a very personal way, of a process that can demonstrate that all efforts to improve the quality of people's lives are a reflection of the Gospel mandate to "bring good news to the poor, to proclaim liberty to captives, to set the downtrodden free, to proclaim God's year of favor." (Luke 4)

Truly Pope Paul VI envisioned a crucial Gospel response for our contemporary world when he proclaimed that, "Politics is a demanding manner to live out the Christian meaning of service to others." (*Call to Action*)

Joseph Simon, SVD

PRIESTS IN POLITICS: WHERE WERE THEY WHEN WE NEEDED THEM?

The decision to run for an elected government position need not always come about because one is interested in politics, even though the interest is there. My decision to run for office was like that. The reason I did choose to run was the fact that, for the five positions open on the City Council ballot, only one name had been submitted. This is not an uncommon situation in small towns. At the same time, the city was preparing to request federal funding to make needed repairs in its water and sewer system. What was needed was not only council members, but members who were willing to help the city deal with the complexities of state and federal bureaucracy that inevitably accompany the granting of such funds. I was asked to run as a write-in. I did so and was elected.

With a background in history and a deep respect for James Cardinal Gibbons (my favorite figure in the history of the American Catholic Church), the realization that politics means involvement has always been my ideal. I have always been fascinated with, not only the workings of government, but how against all odds the first Americans were able to carve out a great country because they made its problems their own. And Cardinal Gibbons throughout his life, though eminently a churchman, was just as eminently an American, and proud of it. He was not afraid to speak out. He was not hesitant in acclaiming his devotion to his country and, in whatever way he could, taking a position on the events of the day. He was influential, not because he told his people how to vote, but because he clearly showed by word and deed what should be the Christian approach to political issues.

Another reason drove me to the conviction that to be effective one must be involved. While studying Church History in Rome, I remember unnerving a professor after class one day, by openly questioning the wisdom of the "Non Expedit" and "Non Licet" decisions of the Vatican that forbade Italians from taking part in elections after the Papal States had been confiscated by the Italian government. I was frustrated by his inability (from my point of view) to understand how much the Church had lost during those crucial years by not having well-meaning Catholics, with the backing of the Church, speaking out and holding office, or even voting. Who knows how much misery for the Church and for Italy could have been avoided had those two prohibitions not stood in the way. The image of his annoyance and my frustration will never leave me. I hope by now, Father Droulers has forgiven my American impertinence.

My Roman days go back to the early 1960's. My adventure into the real world of holding political office dates to the 1970's. My interest in politics and the Church's role in political action goes back to the 1950's and 1960's. I was a young black seminarian then, studying in the South. At that time I was one of many, black and white, who watched the civil rights movement get under way in earnest. We heard some politicians speak of the moral issue involved in the civil rights movement. We heard many ministers echo those same thoughts. We listened to the overwhelming silence that came from our own Church, as few, if any, from the hierarchy and the clergy raised their voices. And as the civil rights movement increased and was successful, we saw the moral leadership that emerged from that movement as so many ministers of various religious persuasions got involved. The greatest disappointment we black seminarians felt was the absence of the Catholic Church in this movement. Wherever civil rights marches went, wherever political action and involvement was needed, we saw ministers of various faiths there in the forefront. By their presence, these ministers showed that they were not only interested in the values of the civil rights movement, but that they were also concerned about the people that made up that movement, and about the change that needed to be made. And so, they could not be content with preaching support and giving instructions from their pulpits. They felt they had to be involved personally.

The consequence of such personal commitment was lasting. Their action showed that, indeed, the civil rights movement was not only a moral issue, but that the supporters of civil rights had justice and righteousness on their side. Moreover, these ministers demonstrated that they and their churches were involved in the movement and with the people of the movement. What happened? As the political influence of non-Catholic church leaders expanded, their moral leadership triumphed. They became the heroes of those struggling for civil rights. Their names were not only connected with the civil rights movement, but with political leadership as well. The Catholic Church had offered no such leadership and involvement. By its absence, it was left behind as far as black America is concerned. It has never caught up.

In truth, that phenomenon characterizes better than anything else what makes the American political situation different from much of the world. In general, on the American scene, political power and political influence cannot be exercised for very long from the safety of the sidelines. The so-called "Moral Majority" is the latest victim of this American phenomenon. Their emphasis was to focus on one or other "moral issues" as the criterion for supporting or rejecting a candidate. Their plea was "We have weighed this candidate in the moral scale that we have established, and found this candidate wanting. Unless you want to feel our moral indignation (and God's, too, since He speaks to us and we speak for Him!), you will follow our lead." It worked for a time. But then two things happened. First, people began to realize that they were not being convinced, they were being told what to think, how to think, and what to do. And, secondly, it soon became evident that the only quality some of the candidates supported by the Moral Majority had was the fact that they were supported by the Moral Majority. More and more Americans realized that they were being short-changed by following the dictates of this group that preached from the sidelines, seeking to place their people in office. Without getting their hands dirty they sought to pull the strings. It is just not the American way. And so, their influence is fading.

The American Catholic Church had discovered this wisdom a long time ago, although it seems to have forgotten it in recent times. Today we can appreciate the feeling of dread that must have gripped the American hierarchy in the last century when the Vatican suggested that it would be a good idea to start an American Catholic Party. The thinking of the Vatican was that, with a Catholic Party, the Church could, as it did in many places in Europe, exert political influence more effectively. Respectfully, but firmly, the answer of the American hierarchy was that this would not work in the United States. They argued that this would create more problems than it would solve. More importantly, the American bishops know Americans would not allow themselves to be led, politically, from the sidelines.

As Americans, we can understand the trepidation of the American bishops. The Vatican position is also understandable. The Vatican and most of the world at that time did not understand Americans and their politics and, in many ways, most of the world, and the Vatican, still do not. In other forms of government and political party systems, a party must have at least one cardinal point that separates it from all the others. In the American political system, it is more or less political issues and approaches that separate one *candidate* from another, rather than one party from another. As Americans we know that the mythical or mystical reason why a person belongs to one political party rather than the other defies the scope of human wisdom. And here lies the problem. For Americans, politics is a question of issues rather than a question of party programs and platforms. It is mind-boggling for non-Americans when, even after a hard fought and bitter election fight, the various parties cooperate to make the government work-rather than to do all in their power to bring down the government. For most of the world, and that includes the Vatican, political parties and party politics have to be in some way divisive. We Americans believe, on the other hand, that political parties are an element in our system that promotes a government that is responsive to the needs of the whole society. For me, the American system best exemplifies the meaning of the term "loyal opposition": opposition to the party in power, but loyalty to the country. Viewed in this manner, politics loses its quality of divisiveness and contention.

In working on the boards of the Eastcentral Intergovernmental Association (regional planning) and the East Iowa Regional Housing Authority, both of which cover five counties and are made up of people of differing political persuasions, I have found that issues are much more important than party affiliation in determining policy. When we consider the needs of the region, funding, programs, housing for the needy and the elderly, the question that never comes up is what party controls this or that area. The only question of consequence that is debated is whether or not this is the best way to serve the people. Perhaps that is not always true of all areas of the United States. I would venture to say that where politics are practiced most successfully it is characteristic.

It would be naive to think that every American who enters politics does so purely for what can be given and not at all for what can be gotten out of it for personal gain. But, I do have enough faith in the American system and in those who serve it to say the vast majority of elected and appointed officials are in politics to render service, service to their constituents and service to their country. Furthermore, the points and policies they choose to support and fight for, come not from party platforms, but from their own commitment to a particular policy or approach to social problems and their solutions. And if the party platform supports their position, all well and good. However, if that is not the case and they must go contrary to the party platform, that will not ordinarily change their position or cause them to change political parties. How best to serve their constituents is the bottom line.

In every community, no matter how small, the concerns are the same: how can the lives of the citizens be improved? When a city budget is considered and taxes are assessed, and when the scope of government services is determined, the poor, the sick, the jobless, and the elderly are the specters that haunt every city council chamber. And at times that awareness can take a strange twist. With the turning over of most block grants to the states to be administered, Iowa has come up with a point system for applicants, in which the first three hundred points are determined by the state before any application is submitted. Some of those points are based on what the state classifies as "local effort." In reality what it means is how much in taxes is being asked of the people. For the last four years I have argued that the only way we could score higher, and thereby be eligible for grants, would be to raise our very low tax rate. After being turned down a number of times because we received only one hundred and twenty of the possible three hundred points, the rest of the council finally agreed with me. Hopefully, our next application will meet with greater success. Certainly we will have more than one hundred twenty points to start with.

Here again, for the American, participation is the issue. Since the religious and religious institutions don't pay taxes, my effort to effect an increase in taxes would have been futile if attempted from the sidelines. But, because I am a member of the city council and had to defend my position and show why I believed it was the best thing for the citizens, the rest of the council was willing to support a stand which they could see would prove financially beneficial to the city in the long run. My concern was no longer theoretical. It was not theoretical some years ago when I supported the city's effort to obtain housing rehabilitation funds. That program was always filled with headaches for local governments. The council did not realize how many headaches we were inviting until we actually began the program. And yet, in the end we were glad to accept the problems because of the better and warmer housing it provided for many elderly and needy citizens. It was good government.

Good government is achieved because people are willing to use their time and talents, to get involved, to help influence and inform the process. Legislatures on the national and state levels, seem, in their wisdom, to have done all in their power to make the government process almost unintelligible. Time, patience, and some familiarity with the perversity of legislatures in this respect are needed to help the local level of governments plod through the maze created to confuse them. When people who have the time and the talent do not place these qualities at the service of local governments, then these local governments are forced to hire outside consultants and experts to help them obtain and administer funds from state and federal agencies. I think a good case can be made for the position that a person with such talents and time owes it to his local government to offer that time and talent so that the city will not have to pay an expensive consultant to provide such services.

We must, however, make a distinction between active participation in politics and political ministry. Here it is not a question of intensity, but also the amount of time committed to the political scene. Participation in politics can take many forms. It includes everything from voting or working for a particular candidate, to holding an office. In many cases, holding what is commonly designated as a political office may have nothing to do with party politics in the strict sense. Frequently in small communities, election is by default because no one else chooses to run for that office. In such cases, a person is elected or appointed to a particular position, not because he/she belongs to a particular party, but because he/she is willing to serve. I know of one small community near my own (and the situations are probably legion across the country) where, for the last three elections, the mayor has refused to run or to place his name on the ballot. He has been elected overwhelmingly each time. Why? Because his community trusts him and knows that, if elected, he will do his best.

To me, all of the above should be characterized as participation in politics, rather than political ministry. For, while an individual is participating in political action and his/her dedication to what is being done is complete and whole-hearted, the allocation of time in some situations is not. Participation can be a part-time job. These part-time jobs are carried out while the cleric and/or religious is engaged in clerical or religious ministry as their primary role in life. The time and energy one gives to this kind of "participation" does not subtract from the main focus of one's activities: religious service to the people of God. For myself, time spent functioning as a member of the local city council, the regional planning organization and on the regional housing authority, is small, in comparison with the energy and time given to my main ministry, being academic dean and teaching in a college seminary. That I see as participation in politics. Political ministry, on the other hand, would reverse the order, and clerical and religious work would become part-time. While it is much easier to justify *participation* in politics for clerics and/or religous, I think that, in certain instances, a full-time political ministry is justifiable as well.

In the American Church today, the shortage of priests and religious is a fact. Because of this fact, bishops and/or religious superiors must look long and hard in considering whether or not some can be spared to devote themselves totally to political ministry. Certainly, for the most part, priority must be given to a ministry of a religious nature. There are other considerations that must be borne in mind. Bishops and religious superiors make judgments on the training, character, and other personal qualifications of an appointee to a parish or another type of religious ministry. The same type of considerations should be made, I think, when granting permission to engage in political ministry. We cannot escape the fact that anyone who takes up political ministry still continues to be a cleric and/or religious. And while the political acumen or political zeal of such a person might be praised or condemned, no one ever forgets when a position is taken on a particularly sensitive issue. And when that happens, it does no good for that person to say: "I am speaking of my own position and not that of the Church." It will be difficult for ordinary people to understand that distinction. Personally, I don't think ordinary people should have to make that type of distinction. For political ministry ceases to be a ministry and becomes only politics when the character of one's clerical or religious state ceases to be an influence in one's behavior or priorities in the political arena. Perhaps a layman can make the distinction between the position of the Church and his/her own moral view. I don't think a cleric or religious can or should.

What any candidate is expected to bring to an office is not only particular qualifications, but the whole character of his/her life. For a cleric or religious entering the political ministry that should certainly be a reason why political ministry is chosen. It is true that candidates are elected by their constituents because of trust. But that trust is not placed because of one or the other quality, but rather in the whole person, in the complete individual. Willy-nilly, the commitment of a cleric or religious to his/her chosen state must be a characteristic on which the election turns. It would be demanding too much of people to solicit their trust politically, when they can see that one places little value in the commitments made to the Church and its teaching. Authenticity in the candidate is an absolute requirement. I would hope that bishops and religious superiors would be just as diligent in assessing these personal qualifications before granting permission to engage in political ministry, as they are in determining clerical and religious assignments.

If clerics and religious can be found with those characteristics and, at the same time, if they are interested in political ministry and can be spared from other ministries, I think, on the American scene at least, political ministry is a viable and at times a necessary ministry for the Church to be engaged in. First of all, we have the question of perception. We find ministers of other faiths in offices, elected and appointed, at all levels of government. Are they any less ministers of the Word and shepherds of God's people than Catholic clerics and religious? One cannot believe that the vast majority of Americans feel that way. What Americans see is church ministers adding their spiritual leadership and ideals to the governmental process in an effort to solve or at least relieve the daily problems that people face. These ministers don't seem to believe that their participation in American politics and political action demeans or compromises their commitment to the Gospel. The only question that Protestant America (and Catholic America, for that matter) can ask is: Why? Why is it necessary for the Catholic clergy and religious to be so aloof? Why are they such a special brand of religious leaders? Too often, Americans have to come to the conclusion that politics per se is dirty business (what does that say about the non-Catholic minister?), or that the Catholic leadership has clothed itself in a mantle of spiritual superiority.

Leo XIII, in "Longinqua Oceani", viewing the American relationship of church and state, added a caveat. American Catholics, he stated, should not look upon the system in this country as "the most desirable status of the Church." Perhaps it isn't for many places and countries, but it is for us. Furthermore, it is the only status that we have, can have, or would want to have. James Cardinal Gibbons made that point clear as he took possession of his titular church. He stated that if sometime in the future American Catholics found themselves in the majority in this country, they would not want to change the relationship of Church and state, for, he concluded, it offers freedom and protection without interference. Be that as it may, it is also the system that we have to live in and live with.

From our earliest times, it has been a truism that for ministers and the clergy to exert continual political force, they have to engage in political action directly. At the same time, there has never been a revolution without political pulpits and active ministers. This is certainly true on the American scene. I return to my original premise that the loss of the influence of the Church among Black Americans can be traced, at least in part, to the absence of political action and involvement on the part of the Catholic Church during the civil rights days. It was also a mistake that the Church should not have made had it been cognizant of the history of the black man in this country. Among Black Americans, the church has always been the center of life, social and political. In the days of slavery and after emancipation, the church leaders were the ones to whom Black Americans looked for guidance and support. Even such economic elements as insurance companies and banks have their origin in the church and church organizations. Somehow we forgot all of that during the civil rights days and we let others stand without us. Too often the question is asked, and justly so: Where was the Catholic Church then? Also, with justice, I think, many Blacks can legitimately ask: "If you were not willing to aid us actively in those dark days, why should we accept your leadership now?" I would deeply regret that, at some future time in regard to another matter of national importance, the same question would have to be asked again.

What can Catholic clerics and religious bring to the political process of this country? First of all, they can bring the feeling that the Church is interested, interested enough to allow them the time and opportunity to engage directly and actively in the issues of today. They can bring the character of their whole lives, which will mean much as legislation is prepared and presented. I have felt that very often my ideas are listened to with interest, not only because I have done my homework, but because others realize I have no political axe to grind. The office or the commission that I might serve is not looked upon by me as a stepping-stone to some higher position or office. In other words, people perceive that I am not just putting in time at this particular position so that I will be able to get something better and more important in the future. They also perceive that while there are questions of direct moral issues, I am interested as well in all of the problems and political issues that face governments. Being a member of the Regional Housing Authority has been particularly gratifying to me in this way. The question of public housing, for the elderly and the needy, is always a sensitive issue, especially in the more rural areas of America. Resistance to the introduction of such housing into a community is at times fierce; partly it is a fear of what public housing can become, partly it is a resistance to the very idea that such and such an area should even need public housing. It became very difficult to keep up the resistance when a priest member of the housing authority supported the report which showed the need for such housing and also stood behind the promise of the housing authority that dire images of what public housing could become would never be allowed to materialize in this area. The position of the housing authority was accepted along with the housing. And we have kept our promise to the communities. The result has been communities that at one time opposed such housing are now firm supporters, even at times requesting more such housing for the elderly.

Are there exceptions? Should a cleric and/or religious, with the right personal qualifications, be allowed to accept *any* political office or appointment? I think not. While I strongly believe the Church, through its clerics and religious has an active place in political ministry, I firmly believe there are some areas in which such a ministry should not be exercised. Two important areas I would see political ministry by priests and religious excluded, are in law enforcement and the administration of justice on the judicial level. These are not policy making areas or positions in which laws are enacted and, therefore, influenced. While I think it is self-evident why law enforcement should be excluded, the same is true in the administration of justice, either in the role of prosecuting attorney or judge. In both cases policies are already set. And, in most cases, prior judicial decisions have already determined the action and the direction a judge must go. One is therefore forced to act according to those principles and prior decisions, whether or not they correspond to one's own beliefs or moral judgment. Take, for instance, the Supreme Court decision on abortion.

But in the halls of Congress, or on other levels of government, where policies are set and laws enacted, the chance to exert effective influence is still present and there political ministry can be most effective. Voices can be raised and action taken to remove or prevent discriminatory policies and legislation from ever becoming the law of the land. There the forces of the Church's teaching can be marshalled in the most effective manner.

I firmly believe that the Church can and must play an active part on the political scene in this country. But I also believe that it has to be done in a manner that is consistent with the American system. And that means the role of the Church must be exercised through the moral and spiritual principles with which it has evangelized its people. Further, I believe, somehow the leadership of the Church as well as its clerics and religious must be seen to take an active part in the important issues of the day. People need to know that many issues—civil rights, care for the needy and elderly, and many others—are indeed moral as well as political issues, as evidenced by the willingness of clerics and religious to be part of the political process and not merely spectators and sermon-givers from the sidelines. There is no substitute for positive, active participation in the political process.

What I have found time and time again is that political activity offers numerous opportunities to exercise one's primary ministry. It is amazing how often fellow "politicians" find it easier to approach someone engaged in their type of work and disclose their particular problems, feeling they have found someone who can understand them. That in itself makes the cleric or religious a powerful force for good. In helping the personal healing process, one is enabled not only to influence the political process, but also to influence those who influence the political process. By enlisting the aid of many others in this way, we will make amends and pay back-dues for those times we have been so conspicuously absent when we should have been so openly present. The American system, once again, is the only system we have. It offers great opportunities. We are the only ones that can restrict our ability to make use of those opportunities. We can preach from the sidelines and fade away as time passes. Or, we can be ever active and reap the fruits of gratitude from those who saw us present when we were needed the most.

Ardeth Platte, OP

PUBLIC OFFICE: AN OPTION FOR ONE, A MANDATE FOR ANOTHER

Elected public office for me is a mandate. It provides me an opportunity to live my commitment to social justice. As a woman I am able to identify with the excluded and bring to my ministry the dimensions of empowerment, mutuality and cooperation. As a religious rooted in Gospel values I am able to affect public policies by applying the vision of an economic, social and political order that includes the participation of the poor and disadvantaged of the local community. While public office is a conscience mandate for me, I believe it should be open to all religious persons as an option.

FACTORS INFLUENCING MY VALUES

My journey to public office as City Councilwoman evolved over many years. Events, individuals and groups of persons have deeply influenced my study, planning, decisions and actions.

In the 1950s I was a student. During the next decade as an educator and administrator, my experience, reflection and prayer led me to support the Civil Rights Movement, Poor People's March on Washington, the renewal of religious life, the Vietnam and draft protest, and the Black and Chicano power movements. My convictions were strengthened by working closely with expellees, ex-offenders, and persons in poverty in the 1970s. My search for moral teaching on justice led me to the documents of the Church, and my search for skills, strategies and hope led me to the Network legislative seminar in Washington, D.C.

My father has had an enormous influence on my life over the years. It was no real surprise in the early 1960s when Dad traveled to live and work in Mexico and Guatemala among the Indian people.

From the midst of a simple life style, he shared his stories about the people in these Third World countries. His letters home were like the epistles of the early Church in which the Gospel message and the essence of religious living were linked.

My Grand Rapids Dominican family, like many other religious communities of women throughout the United States, assumed more responsibility for renewal in the post Vatican II era. We discerned as women, and as religious, new applications of church values and teaching in society. We developed a new consciousness of justice and a solidarity with the poor. One of our chapter recommendations in 1969 asked us "individually and corporately to effect social change by making our own convictions known to national and local leaders, so that social injustices in the areas of housing, employment, health, education and law enforcement may be corrected."

During the past fifteen years we have recorded support for sisters actively assuming leadership in diocesan, civic, regional, and national organizations and movements to promote justice and oppose oppression. Women religious enthusiastically pursued these new ministries. We were impacted and re-energized by the influence of our own generous families and friends, the experiences of religious renewal and the benefits of educational development. We were moved by our potential for future contributions to the Church and society. Women inside and outside of religious congregations began to choose more active public roles.

SAGINAW EXPERIENCE: TOWARD POLITICAL MINISTRY

After a number of years as an educator in various locations in the State of Michigan, in 1966 I became principal of inner city St. Joseph High School in northeast Saginaw. The city is a fairly typical midwest industrial city. More than 90,000 people—comprised predominately of white, black and Spanish-speaking people—lived within its eighteen square miles. More than two-and-one-half times the number of people living in the city lived within the metropolitan area. Since this was a new community to me, I tried to associate closely with the people and learn from them their needs and hopes.

The facts I learned were staggering. Unemployment among black and Hispanic youth was unduly high. Many persons were ill-fed, poorly sheltered and lacking health care and education. Our neighborhood surveys substantiated the desperate human need and the poverty area deterioration.

There were daily opportunities to supply material necessities. Feeding the hungry, clothing needy people, attending court hearings for the imprisoned and providing housing and counseling for battered women and their families were familiar services provided day by day. I felt little prepared for those experiences in the inner city. During the first year I even questioned at times my own capacity and vision to respond to these human needs.

It was heart-rending to tell Mary that her missing son had been found in a ditch, dead, hands tied behind his back and a shot through the head. I had been called to identify him in the emergency room. The frequent, violent deaths and injuries, the extensive incarceration and school expulsions, the desperate food and health care needs were beyond anything my previous experience had prepared me for.

Peter called me one day to his jail cell and requested that I deliver his poetry to a woman friend. When I entered Beth's house I found her lying on the couch, a trail of injections evident on her arm. Her two small children were playing on the floor seated in the middle of rubbish. Mice scattered as I walked into the room.

I observed young people gathering on street corners, women searching for food for their families and persons constantly looking for work, frequently turning to illegal trades.

All of the human destruction that I witnessed touched me deeply. I was convinced that everyone, every household had a right to certain basic requirements for education and employment, but I came to realize that the violent effects of poverty cannot be remedied on an individual basis. Like many others, I discovered how naive it is to believe that caring people can pass out Thanksgiving and Christmas baskets to meet the needs of hungry families while public policies make it impossible for them to feed themselves the rest of the year. Powerlessness, dependency and poverty are indigenous in the economic and political fabric of present society. Persons do not choose these conditions. Nor do I believe that dignity and rights, love and justice are separable.

Alternative Education Center

In my second year as principal of St. Joseph High School we added a night school to the high school program to respond to adult literacy needs. Two years later community college classes were begun. In the next years expellees, dropouts, adults, persons referred from prisons, agencies and the streets entered a variety of alternative educational programs. St. Joseph Educational Center was born. Persons who had been eliminated from the mainstream previously because of circumstances or policies in traditional settings returned for educational development at the Center. The direction, designs and decisions of the Center were determined by the same people. Significant, successful cornerstones were alternative teacher and curricular models, scheduling diversification, inclusive decision-making, respect for uniqueness, self-determination concepts and ideas from disadvantaged and minorities for the development of self, neighborhoods and the community.

To best accomplish our goals and incorporate these values we reconceptualized education and made it an integral part of the real issues in the daily lives of the people who attended the Center. Volunteers from all walks of life shared their specific skills within the Center. Probation officers, police, lawyers and prosecutors facilitated lively discussions regarding people's rights and criminal justice. Nutritionists and health care personnel provided new ideas regarding child development and physical well-being. Business, trades and industry personnel enriched students with a range of possibilities for job application and in skill-building needed for various work-sites. Re-integrated ex-offenders motivated youth in new directions for life-giving ventures. Feminists presented information regarding self-destructive patterns in women and steps to be taken to begin a life of independence and self-fulfillment. Media experts developed useful public media resources and skills as tools for community improvement. Neighborhood organizers enhanced student skills in examining neighborhood problems, social analysis, goal-setting and directions for solutions.

Students of the Center organized themselves around neighborhood issues such as properly located traffic signals that would result in saving lives. They were successful in negotiating a resolution of a problem related to a railroad underpass. They sought and gained neighborhood improvements and housing rehabilitation, and worked to stop redlining. This involvement strengthened the demand for reinvestment in poverty areas rather than continued disinvestment.

In each action, we learned together about structural ills. Our approach was exemplified in a 20th century translation of the scriptural command to feed and clothe the needy in Matthew 25:

> When you changed those structures that generate hunger, thirst, and loneliness, when you created or operated structures through which (men) could finally feed themselves in a community of justice and love, it was to me that you did

it. And when you abstained it was to me that you did not do
it. (Laurentin p. 123, Sourcebook on Poverty, Development
and Justice, CHD, 1973. p. 45)

In 1977 I resigned in order to work full-time with exoffenders in
developing a plan to provide services and system changes for incarcerated persons returning to the city. Ex-Offenders Unite for Equal
Opportunity, funded by the Campaign for Human Development,
planned and originated numerous ways to reduce recidivism. Many of
the plans that they formulated have influenced projects now being implemented in the city.

As I was transformed in the process of designing alternative
models for decision-making and new structures, my own growth in
awareness, empowerment, and strategies for change enabled me to
identify public practices and policies that keep people oppressed. I began to see and understand the racism, sexism and classism in Saginaw,
and came to realize that I was being called to do something about it in
the public policy arena. I had the confidence that the church agreed
with me:

This view of the church's ministry and mission requires it
to relate positively to the political order, since social injustice and denial of human rights can often be remedied only
through governmental action. In today's world, concern for
social justice and human development necessarily requires
persons and organizations to participate in the political process in accordance with their own responsibilities and rules.
(Quest for Justice, J. Brian Benestad and Francis J. Butler,
USCC 1981)

POLITICAL MINISTRY

My formal political ministry began in 1973 when I decided to run
for City Council. In an active door-to-door campaign, I stressed my
bias toward the poor, my priorities rooted in Gospel values. I spoke to
the need for changes in public policy to bring about a more just and
unified Saginaw.

Under the charter of Saginaw elections are non-partisan and are
at-large rather than by geographic or ward representation. The nine
male city council members were selected and their campaigns financed

for the most part by a small committee of Saginaw citizens from industry, lending institutions and business leadership. For each election this United Saginaw Citizen group ran a slate of persons selected and endorsed by them to fill each vacant seat. All other candidates seemed to have little opportunity to win. The disadvantaged of all races, women, minorities, and justice-minded persons encouraged my candidacy and pursued my election. The effect of an involved community believing and participating in the electoral process did impact on the election and became more of a consideration in future decision-making. My own political ministry gave encouragement and support to other people seeking control over their own local affairs. Again, I was confirmed by the church's pastoral wisdom:

> Unless combatted and overcome by social and political action, the influence of the new industrial and technological order favors the concentration of wealth, power and decision-making in the hands of a small public or private controlling group . . . participation constitutes a right which is to be applied both in the economic and in the social and political field. (Justice in the World I, USCC 1972, pp. 35-38)

ELECTED PUBLIC OFFICE

In November, 1973 I took the oath of office as City Councilwoman in Saginaw. There were four vacancies to be filled in the at-large election. The other three persons elected were members of the United Saginaw Citizen slate.

Broad citizen participation, accessible and open meetings and the dissemination of information pertaining to local government have been priorities for me. With others of like mind I persistently designed as many ways as possible to include persons who had been excluded from influence and control over matters that affect their lives. My concept of citizen participation provided an alternative to forms of cooptation, consultation or social therapy so frequently used on poverty people. Improvements and services must be owned by persons who work to gain them.

During the first meeting I received unanimous support from all Council members to remove all sexist terminology in future titles, documents and proposals. During the first few months I plotted the geographical residency of all members of boards, commissions, and task forces on a city map to highlight the narrow representation of people in any advisory or decision-making capacity. This has been changed. The participation requirement to include women and minorities is now formalized in an affirmative action plan.

In the selection of the commission that makes decisions regarding public housing, we insisted on the legal right of tenants to be represented on the commission. Persons who are tenants of public housing and are directly affected have been selected by appointment since that time.

We removed the prohibitive rules of order of Council sessions which discouraged participation previously. The meetings are now more accessible to the public, and structured to encourage identification of citizen and neighborhood problems. The process for seeking solutions has been brought into an open forum. Neighborhood organizations have gained new strength. Saginaw Neighborhoods, Inc., has a third party contractual arrangement with the City. It provides organizers for neighborhoods concerned about the cycle of disinvestment and human needs. This formalized process of marshalling resources of an area by community organizers is annually supported, improved and strengthened. Our policy of empowerment enhanced the public policy to improve housing, land use, human services and public improvements. We were able together with neighborhood organizations to gain disclosure from lending institutions and a Mortgage Appeals Board. Fair Housing, Urban Homesteading and the cooperation of developers, lenders, government and citizens slowed the cycle of deterioration. Through a Woman's Conference we drew consensus for the establishment of a Rape Crisis Center and Home for Battered Women. We developed a policy to allow city properties to be used for vegetable gardens and to facilitate vacant land to be sold to adjacent neighbors.

With community participation assured, elected officials take more seriously the problems of housing abandonment and recycling, unemployment and comprehensive inclusion of affected groups in affirmative action and contract compliance policies. The city budget is debated and becomes more visible and open to the public. Citizens have gained more control over income and expenses with this knowledge. This motivates greater effectiveness and efficiency in rendering government services.

The mass transit system was improved when handicappers participated in the planning sessions. Emotionally disturbed and drug abusers defended their rights to live in housing within the community. Lower income people used their expertise to design community self-sufficiency programs, and ex-offenders shared knowledge of the best alternatives to prisons in a community setting and have assisted in their development. Local concerns also extend to our stewardship of the land, of water, air and natural resources. Together we were able to remove the PCB that was stored in an industrial plant in our area. At other times we have challenged toxic and hazardous waste burial policies and keep a watchful vigilance on industrial pollutants.

During my third four-year term as city councilwoman, the dissolution of slate politics and the eradication of handpicked representation has resulted in a more diverse group of elected officials. The transition reflects a city improved by the representation of minorities and women.

Neighborhood participation and empowerment has had a "ripple effect" in other ways. Empowerment at a local level teaches people to bring those same skills and vision to working on national and global issues. It is difficult for people who are not involved in saving their own neighborhoods to fathom the strategies needed for saving the world from destruction. People empowered in strategies and tactics to improve their local community have gained skills in public policy for other levels of political action.

ADVOCACY FOR JUSTICE

After a second term for City Council and a strong showing at the polls, I joined a small group of persons, motivated by the Diocesan Call to Action in 1978, in forming an organized effort to work for peace and justice in Saginaw. We believed that movement for effective action had to show the linkages from a global perspective. Our advocacy group sponsored a Home for Peace and Justice to unite people of all faiths and to focus on particular issues. The home provides human and material resources, educational workshops and facilitators for direct legal and political action. Typical issues include registration and the draft, disarmament, criminal justice, poverty, women's problems, employment, etc. Organizing efforts have made us more aware of the local and national connections and the linkage of local issues with global concerns.

There is an even more direct connection between my work with this grass roots organization and my role in public office. My life and ministry is integrated in a unique way. My participation with persons seeking peace through public vigils, demonstrations and civil disobedience is confirmed, concretized by a vote at City Council for a Nuclear

Weapons Freeze. My participation in lobbying with people for full employment is consistent with my vote for diversification of economic development, jobs for youth and community self-sufficiency programming in the city. My joining with the concerned people petitioning to stop the nuclear power plant under construction in a neighboring city is strengthened by a vote at Council to reject the plant because of safety deficiencies and the mounting rate cost which is injurious to residents. This natural linkage is also evident in stands regarding toxic pollutants in the river streams that run through our cities and state.

POLITICAL MINISTRY: A MANDATE

Political ministry is a mandate for all Christians. In today's more complex society, the Christian mission of charity and service requires an understanding of and action upon the broader dimensions and root causes of poverty, hunger and injustice. The human condition and earth condition are mirrored in social, economic, and political institutions, structures and systems. Our concern for social justice, human development and transforming the earth requires participation in the political process. It is a ministry that dismantles power in the hands of the few and enables the participation of all.

Those of us who have chosen religious life have in the nature of our commitment to religious life itself, a greater necessity to show or live the way, not simply to tell the way. The option and actual choice by women religious to seek elective and appointed public offices, to work for candidates and to lobby, reflects their involvement in justice and peace as constitutive of holiness.

The history of religious congregations is rich with dedicated work in the poorest areas of the world and in service to the global family. The apostolates include schools, orphanages, hospitals, parishes and prisons where the basic human needs of God's people must be met. These are the same issues and needs that ministry addresses today through creating public policies that support direct needs and services.

It is the experience of women religious in service and charitable ministries that has awakened them to the public policies and practices that cause hunger in the world of plenty, malnutrition and desperation in the midst of technological genius, and direction by decision-makers that leads to destruction rather than the renewal of the earth and the human condition.

It is essential for lay and religious to be involved in the shaping of public policy so that the commitment to renew the earth will not be frustrated. This gift of the Spirit should not be thwarted by human law.

Political ministry includes women and men, lay and religious in the invitation to transform the earth. At the same time the Code seems to deny religious who dedicate themselves as witnesses and participants in the totality of Christian life to share in the actual transformation. Religious life signifies love of God and love of God's people. It encompasses the 'yes' response to shaping the future for humankind on earth.

Political ministry is so integrated into the life and heartbeat of the human endeavor that I believe it cannot be selectively separated or compartmentalized.

The experiences of political ministry have been life-enhancing for me. My perception of the dignity of persons is deeper. My understanding of social sin and unjust systems is keener. My convictions regarding community, empowerment, collaboration, protection of resources and global connections are firmer. These perceptions and convictions are not theoretical principles or tenets held separate from the events of history. It is impossible to claim to love people in the community and yet to allow oppressive and exploitative policies and systems to exist unchallenged. Political action flows from incarnated values of the Gospel.

It is the open option that is important. Holding public office may be an option for one, and a mandate for another. Church and society can only gain by keeping this choice open for persons who hunger and thirst for justice and peace in every part of our world.

Theodore M. Hesburgh, CSC

THE PRIEST AS MEDIATOR
AND AMBASSADOR

May I confess at the outset of this personal account that it is difficult, if not impossible, to write of oneself or one's activity without straining objectivity and, at times, credulity. However, I cannot make the point that needs to be made without at first giving this personal account, as requested by the editors of this book. Please bear with me.

I can hardly remember a time during the last thirty years when I was not doing one or two or even three different tasks for the federal government and, one would hope, for the common public and private good as well. In fact, I added up the years of service, admittedly part time, and they came to forty-five.

It began during President Eisenhower's administration. Sherman Adams called from the White House one Sunday afternoon in 1954 and asked if I would, if appointed, accept an appointment to the National Science Board, a group of twenty-four persons, mostly scientists of national reputation, who govern the National Science Foundation which had been established by the Congress in 1950 to promote fundamental scientific research and education. I responded that my education had centered on philosophy and theology, not science. Surprisingly, he said that President Eisenhower wanted a philosophical and theological dimension represented on the National Science Board. "Well," I said, "if they can stand some philosophical and theological observations, I can certainly learn a great deal about science."

Twelve years later, after serving the maximum two statutory terms of six years each, I could honestly say it really happened that way. I had learned much from the experience, having passed through the atomic revolution, the space revolution, and the beginnings of the electronic and biological revolutions in science. Before, it had largely been a *terra incognita*. From all of the personal friendships with many of the world's greatest scientists, my life was enriched and still is, as we now join arms again against the nuclear threat to humanity. Obviously, the experience and learning enhanced my capabilities as president of a major research university (one of the few Catholic universities world-wide in this category) and prepared me to represent the Holy See for fifteen years as its Permanent Representative to the International Atomic Energy Agency (Atoms for Peace) whose headquarters are in Vienna.

As Chairman of the National Science Board's International Science Committee, I found myself on occasion exercising my priestly ministry, hearing confessions, preaching and offering Mass at remote Antarctic posts, including the South Pole, while carrying out other official duties. Some might argue that Church and State were confused here, but there was a warm welcome and no complaints everywhere I appeared.

As Chairman of the Board's Committee on Social Science, I was able, against the strong opposition of many Board members, mostly natural and physical scientists, to institute a program and eventually a well-supported Office for Social Science Research and Education. It is still well and healthy today, although often under fire.

Three years after this National Science Board appointment, I had another call from the White House in the fall of 1957, asking if I would accept appointment to the newly-created U.S. Commission on Civil Rights. There were to be six members, three from either political party. After consulting my Provincial Superior and obtaining his permission, I agreed. Later they called back to ask my political affiliation; they had already appointed three Republicans. I told them I was politically an Independent, so I was put into a Democratic slot. The opposite happened later when the Democrats were in power. They substituted me for a Republican slot, although, in fact, I was neither.

We commissioners were sworn in at the White House for what was then considered to be a two-year term. Fifteen years later, as President Nixon was re-elected for a second term, I was abruptly terminated. He had named me Chairman of the Commission when he assumed the Presidency in 1969. He had also asked me to become Director of the War on Poverty Program, but it had become so politicized in the large cities that it seemed inappropriate for me to do that as a priest, so I declined. He appointed Donald Rumsfeld who subsequently became Secretary of Defense.

I should say for the record that I had, as Chairman of the Civil Rights Commission, disagreed strongly with the administration regarding both the substance and the tactics relating to the achievement of equal opportunity for all Americans. I was, therefore, ripe for dismissal. A few days later, I also submitted to the President my resignation as a commissioner. It seemed proper not to be looking over the shoulder of the new Chairman.

I cannot think of any moral task of greater importance to America during those years than the task that faced the Commission: to create new laws and new legal structures, a new equal opportunity for those then denied it in the area of voting, education, employment, public accommodations, and in the administration of justice.

We held public hearings throughout the United States, but especially in trouble spots. We published over a hundred volumes of studies in all areas of concern. Over seventy per cent of our recommendations (almost all highly controversial) were enacted into federal law during the decade of the sixties. The federal civil rights legislation of 1964, 1965 and 1968 changed the face of the nation. To our original mandate to enlarge equal opportunity for those denied it by reason of color, race, religion, or national origin, I was able during my time as chairman, to add sex to the list. Subsequently, age was added as well by my successor as chairman, Arthur Flemming.

I found the years of service on the Civil Rights Commission enormously rewarding as a priest and as an American citizen. We were able to really change America by totally eliminating peacefully (most of the time) and by law, a system of apartheid every bit as bad as South Africa's, despite the fact that we have more blacks in America than any African state, except Nigeria.

I really believe that the struggle for racial justice and the creation of legal structures to counter centuries-old prejudice was a priestly work. I found that just by being a priest, I was, through no merit of my own, endowed with great moral authority in the eyes of my colleagues. I must say that I encountered very few Catholics on our staff or state committees, but they were all very happy to work with me because I could speak as no other commissioner could, from a moral and spiritual base that was unique—and very necessary. They gladly printed my minority statements in our annual reports, and were forever urging me to elaborate the religious and moral dimensions to whatever problem we were discussing in public hearings. When the situation really became tense during some of our hearings, the staff would pass me a note on yellow legal paper saying, "Give them the theological reason why Christians should practice racial justice. That will settle things down because they are fundamentally good people." After one of these tense hearings, a Southern governor said to me: "You really bother me because I'm a Christian, son of a minister, and

I know you're right and I'm wrong, but it is so hard to change my ways."

I know that subsequently there were many priests and religious men and women involved in the civil rights movement, but in the late fifties and early sixties, it was a lonely spot for a priest to be, especially in the South. Even so, looking back over my forty years as a priest, those fifteen years of service on the Commission were among my most priestly and apostolic—I do not regret one single day of this service.

During the Kennedy years, I was given an additional task to those two already mentioned: membership on a State Department Commission on International Educational and Cultural Exchange, chaired by John Gardner. This lasted about three years. We produced a slim volume, *Beacon of Hope*, which is still relevant in this area. Again, my main task at the University was enhanced, and I was able to be a better board member of the private Institute for International Education and the Rockefeller Foundation Board. These were intertwining circles, each one reinforcing the others.

During the Johnson years, I served briefly on the Commission to study International Economic Development in the Third World (the Perkins Commission) and on the Policy Planning Board of the State Department, as well as continuing on the Civil Rights Commission. At least my mother was happy when Lyndon Johnson gave me the Medal of Freedom at the White House in her presence.

During the Nixon years, in addition to the Chairmanship of the Civil Rights Commission, I was appointed to the (Gates) Commission on an All-Volunteer Armed Forces, which was legislated by Congress following our report. It also alleviated the Vietnam tension aggravated by the military draft. This volunteer situation is still in force and working reasonably well for the military. I had an easier time in the University once the draft was dropped.

During the Ford years, I was appointed to a nine-person Amnesty Board to deal with those civilians and military personnel who ran afoul of civilian or military law during the Vietnam War. This was one of my most difficult government assignments. The Board was philosophically divided on amnesty, with me at one end of the spectrum and a Marine General at the other. We had court-martial transcripts of literally more than a million pages to review. The Board had only a year in which to work. The work load was so heavy that the Board was doubled by President Ford and at my suggestion, another priest, Monsignor Frank Lally, was added. The staff, at the end of our year of service, ran a computer check on the decisions we rendered as judges in individual cases. I was happy that the two priests led the eighteen-member Board as the most forgiving.

With Ford Foundation support, the University of Notre Dame's Center for Civil Rights published four studies on the work of the Amnesty Board. The first, which outlined a whole program of Presidential amnesty, was accepted by the newly-elected President Carter. He enacted civilian amnesty the day after his inauguration and military amnesty a short time later.

President Carter also appointed me U.S. Ambassador in October 1977 to head an eighty-person Congressional and civilian delegation to the United Nations Conference on Science and Technology for Development, to take place in Vienna during September of 1979. We had a largely State Department staff with another Ambassador, Jean Wilkowski, as Staff Director. Two years of intense preparation, with many studies and reports, were required. Jean and I individually circled the globe several times to attend preparatory conferences and help many developing countries prepare for the Conference.

Jean and I led a small delegation to China where we met most of the ministers of the Beijing Government as the guest of Feng-Yi, their highest Minister for Science and Technology. We also met many university leaders and Science Ministers in the provinces. At first, the Chinese officials called me the Chinese equivalent of Ambassador Hesburgh. When I visited the only Catholic Church and priests then operating in China, and when they learned that I was offering Mass every day in my hotel, wherever we were, they began to call me Hesburgh Shen-fu, Hesburgh the Priest. They still use this greeting when I occasionally meet them in Vienna or Washington or Notre Dame.

I was able to write President Carter's opening statement to the U.N.C.S.T.D. Conference in Vienna, and the new lengthy U.S. Policy Statement. Both of these statements were among the most liberal of U.S. official policy statements regarding our obligation to help the developing countries through financial and technical assistance. The fact that I was primarily a private citizen with no career at stake, and working without government pay (although I was entitled to an Ambassador's salary) enabled me to obtain support for these two statements. Also, my past government involvement had gained for me many allies and very helpful colleagues, a great network. It was also reasonably important that at the same time, I was Chairman of both the private Overseas Development Council and the Rockefeller Foundation (replacing Cy Vance who was then Secretary of State). Also, I was able to assemble a delegation with some of the best known international scientists as members, so that their support was enormously helpful.

Again, it was ultimately a work of intertwining circles reinforcing one another.

When sworn in at the State Department after Senate approval, it was remarked that never before had a priest been a United States Ambassador. In response, I made the point that priests were essentially mediators, and an Ambassador's task was not unlike that, although between humans, not between God and humans. Mediation is a frame of mind, as well as a professional task.

During the last two years of the Carter administration, I was appointed Chairman of the U.S. Select Commission to study Immigration and Refugee Policy. This was a two-year task for sixteen commissioners, four Cabinet members (Secretary of State, Attorney General, Secretaries of Labor and HEW), eight members of Congress of both parties, all from the Senate and House Judiciary Committees, including the Chairmen, Senator Kennedy and Congressman Rodino, and four public service members.

Again, there were lengthy studies, meetings, consultations, and public hearings from coast to coast at ports of entry. We published a dozen volumes and managed to agree on a new policy that was more humane and effective than the current patch-work of prejudice and inefficiency that allows millions of illegals to be abused while living in the shadows. Our recommendation for appropriate amnesty for illegal aliens was unanimous. Unfortunately, after three years of follow-up work by a National Committee of fifty distinguished citizens for immigration reform we still do not have a new law, but it is coming I trust, in 1985. It must come.

During the Reagan administration, I have had only one assignment: to spend a few days in El Salvador as one of the official international observers during the last election of a new constitutional Assembly. If other tasks were longer, this was certainly the most threatening, as we spent election day in a helicopter, dropping in and getting out of the voting places in the eastern zone where the guerrilla forces were trying to prevent campesinos from voting or us from seeing them vote in large numbers. Gunfire all day, mostly in our direction; but even then, I was able to bury, in San Miguel, a mutilated soldier who had been killed a few hours before while protecting a voting place. For his mourning mother's sake, I was glad to be there as they carried his body to the cemetery without a priest or even a last blessing. I offered a Requiem Mass for him the next day.

As we were taking off that morning, I told our helicopter crew and fellow observers that at least they would get absolution if we were shot down, but that after seeing all the violence on both sides, if we were caught in a fire fight on the ground, I was not going to use the M-16 provided. So much for the first Salvadoran elections.

There have been other governmental tasks that I have omitted, such as Chairman of the Board of Visitors at the Naval Academy in Annapolis (where we completely revised the curriculum), a post on the Board of Visitors at the U.S. War College in Washington (where I unsuccessfully tried to have it renamed the Peace Academy).

Now that I have detailed the various public service tasks performed during the past thirty years, may I, for the remainder of this account, address myself to the personal instincts, principles and general attitudes that guided me in saying yes or no to various invitations to serve, as well as the modality of service in those cases where I did say yes.

First of all, I decided early in my priesthood that I would never run for any elected office or ever endorse a political candidate or join a political party. My reasons are perhaps somewhat convoluted, but at least sincere. I believe that partisan politics tend to divide people who naturally take sides. I felt that as a priest, it was my task to unite and to mediate, not to divide. Also, while I know many upright and honest political persons, it is difficult to raise money for a campaign without the danger of compromising oneself, and if elected, one does have some obligation to one's supporters, although one may not agree with them in principle. I made these decisions, I might add, without knowing the precise Canon law on the subject and have not thought otherwise because of the new Canon Law. These were personal, not legalistic, convictions. Perhaps having said this, it might strengthen the case somewhat if I add that I have been invited to run for several political offices: for Senator from New York and for the Vice Presidency, to mention two. Also, I have never sought to impose my views on others who may well have had their own good reasons for running for office. Father Bob Drinan's case is particularly relevant here. He provided much needed leadership in the House Judiciary Committee for the total revision of the Federal Code. This most important project has not moved forward since he left the House.

On the other hand, I have always been open to appointment to government service under certain conditions.

First, I have only accepted commissions that had some moral dimension to which I felt I had something special to contribute as a priest involved in the apostolate of higher education.

Second, it was important to maintain personal integrity and independence by working as a volunteer without pay.

Third, as a religious under vows, I would not engage in governmental activity that did not have the approval and support of my religious superior, the Provincial. I should add parenthetically that I am grateful beyond measure for a long succession of understanding and supportive religious superiors.

Fourth, I always operated as what I am, a priest, wearing clerical garb, not disguising myself as a layman. I never had to compromise myself as a priest or as a religious. I offered Mass and prayed my Breviary each day, and it was no secret, although I never flaunted these integral parts of my life.

Last, I always tried to perform to the best of my ability, did my homework, and asked for no special privileges. I should add that I was almost always the first priest and the only Catholic in these various tasks. The friendships that grew out of these activities were almost always with non-Catholics who are still today among the very best and most caring friends I have ever known. There were very few conversions, but I hope some enduring understanding and certainly growing respect on my side and theirs. All of this was fallout, perhaps little to be expected from government service. In a way, I was trying to practice what Cardinal Suhard of Paris called "The Apostolate of Presence"—most of the work was mediatorial, therefore priestly in a deep sense.

Because of these conditions, there were appointments offered that I could not honestly accept. Perhaps the most significant of these was the Administrator of NASA, just as the Apollo Program to the moon was being launched under President Johnson. It did not seem appropriate that a priest have the ultimate decision on six billion dollars of commercial contracts annually granted for the Apollo Program, with all of the political and commercial infighting that would be involved. I do confess to being fascinated with the space program and would welcome a chance to see spaceship earth from afar on the space shuttle, provided that I could offer Mass up there each day. Silly? I don't think so. At least it is consistent with past practice and I am sure that the Mass was offered on another explorer craft, the Santa Maria.

One more observation. All of these governmental activities have provided wonderfully rich university archives for future university research and several centers for present research on continuing problems, such as human rights (nationally and internationally), immigration and refugee problems, and others, particularly international development in the Third World, now carried on in our Kellogg Institute for International Studies.

In recent years, and with the advent of the new Canon Law, there have been new and serious discussions about the involvement of priests, brothers, and religous women in public or governmental service.

As one who has little input into whatever decisions that will be made in this area, may I only offer this record of governmental service and ask what may be the relevant questions regarding this record.

1. Has it compromised my priesthood in any way, or has it augmented and enriched my priestly apostolate?

2. Has it compromised the Church, or has it put the Church (or at least one of its representatives) on the cutting edge of some immensely pressing moral problems in our times?

3. Has it involved the Church politically, or has it enabled the Church to give moral leadership (again indirectly through a priestly representative) in seeking a humane, just, and compassionate solution to these difficult moral problems?

4. Would the Church or the priesthood have been better served if the activity outlined in this record had been forbidden or proscribed, or is what was done precisely what one might expect of the Church or priests in times of great moral crises?

After this lengthy and personal account, may I at least give my answer to the above questions: No, to the opening part of each of the four questions and a sincere yes to the latter or alternative part of each question. In my judgment, without the government service described, both my priesthood and my Church and my educational apostolate, and the Good News of Christ and the common good of my fellow citizens and the world would have been less well served.

I cannot speak for other countries or other governments, but in the cultural setting of the United States, where so much public good is provided by the volunteer efforts of its citizens, both in and out of government, it would seem that priests and religious can fulfill an important role and should—if they are able and willing—exercise moral and spiritual leadership, as well as fruitful mediation, where they are often desperately needed.

Jacqueline Slater, CSJ

"IT WAS I WHO CHOSE YOU"

Until the fall of 1976, running for public office was the farthest thing from my mind. The fact is that as of January 3, 1984 I completed six years (3 terms) as alderman on the Minneapolis City Council. Today, as I write my reflections on that period of my life, I explore anew what led to my decision, what conflicts and controversies made my choice the challenge that it was, what people expected of me and what I learned from my experiences.

Complex factors led me into the political arena: my personal background, the changes in the Church and religious life, and the opportunities that arose.

I grew up in St. Paul, Minnesota where I received my education in Catholic schools within walking distance of my home. I never thought of myself as a leader or a follower, but just one of "the gang." Peer pressure prompted me to attend daily Mass during Lent and Friday night stations. Two of my friends wanted to be nuns. I did not. But after a bout with rheumatic fever as a senior in high school I softened to the idea and told God if he wanted me, he'd have to arrange it. After graduating with a degree in chemistry from the College of St. Catherine, I became a quality control chemist for a local brewery.

My family was not very political. We seldom discussed politics. My Dad was a union man and a Democrat, and my Mother followed his political thinking. I voted in my first presidential election in 1956, the year I entered the convent to become a Sister of St. Joseph of Carondelet. By 1961, I was teaching science in Waverly, Minnesota, the home of then U.S. Senator Hubert H. Humphrey. The following year was the beginning of Vatican Council II which initiated the changes for the Church as a whole and our religious congregation as well. We were alerted to be aware of the signs of the times and to help interpret them. A new type of leadership was emerging—collegiality. Obedience was described as listening to the Spirit and to each other. We began to discover who we were as individuals and how we could promote the building of community. The way was open to experiment with all aspects of our religious life to determine what permanent changes we would make. We experimented with our religious garb, our housing arrangements, our prayer life, our schedule, and our type of ministry.

During this time of transition I left my secondary school teaching position to complete my Master in Science teaching degree. In 1972, St. Stephen's, an inner city parish school serving a large American Indian population, was in danger of closing its doors unless one or two teachers would work without remuneration. Two of our sisters who were teaching there made a plea to our congregation for help. Although I was a ten-year veteran science teacher in secondary schools, I was between jobs. I volunteered to teach 6th, 7th and 8th grade science and math that fall in the heart of the Sixth Ward.

In June, 1973, two of us moved into the first stage of a proposed ten-stage New Communities development in Cedar-Riverside, located in the West Bank neighborhood of the University of Minnesota. Thirteen hundred units in six high-rise buildings replaced the rundown houses in a four-square block area. We were attracted to the project because it was a new venture building a community from the ground up. We described it as a multi-racial, multi-economic, multi-life-style community for students, professional people, families and the elderly. The project hoped to capture the diversity of cultures of the world community associated with the university and to attract the urban pioneers of all descriptions who were willing to forsake the "faint heartbeat of the suburbs" for the vital and vibrant community called Cedar Square West.

Most of the "new community people" were unaware of the controversy which surrounded this Urban Renewal Project at the edge of the Sixth Ward. Long-term residents had fought bitterly along with University anti-war activists to prevent the development from taking place. With the influx of more than 2000 people to the area the ranks of potential voters swelled, enabling a young Democrat to oust an 8 1/2-year Republican incumbent from his City Council seat in November, 1973.

Meanwhile, there were forces operating that would draw me closer to that contest. In the Spring of 1974, the federally-mandated citizen advisory group was expanded to include representatives from "the new neighborhood". I was elected to the Project Area Committee (PAC) and subsequently to be its Vice Chairman. I plunged right into all the activities, attending meetings several nights a week. Battle lines were being drawn between the new neighborhood and the old, and like the overpass which connected them, I hoped to be a reconciler by espousing the causes of the old neighborhood while living in the new. By now I was immersed in neighborhood politics.

Having completed my third year at St. Stephen's I decided not to return. I would now donate full time to my new neighborhood. I was elected PAC chairperson and received a better Urban Studies course than any university could offer.

By the fall of 1975, it became more apparent that our new alderman was voting against our neighborhood's interests. A friend and PAC delegate from our complex told me I ought to run against him. Instead, several of us joined the volunteer committee of an American Indian woman who challenged him. This was my first political campaign. Most of us were inexperienced and no match for the incumbent. He was re-elected for his second term.

The 1976 precinct caucuses were scheduled for February. Back in 1974, my first precinct caucus, I stayed until after 1 a.m. without being elected. I had stated my opposition to the 1973 Supreme Court decision on abortion. Although by 1976 I was well-known in my neighborhood, and had been politically active, I did not want to be turned down again.

Strangely, the abortion issue was never brought up that year. I was elected 1st Vice Chair of our precinct and a delegate to the Senate District Convention. Since I headed our delegation at the convention I could choose the committee on which I wished to serve. A friend advised me to choose Nominations Committee, to help me understand the structure of the Democratic Farmer Labor (DFL) party.

I was chosen chairperson of the committee and I believe that was what helped me get elected as a state delegate that year, and therefore a delegate to the 5th Congressional District Convention. I continued my education in party politics by getting into the Nominations Committee for both the 5th District and the State. Because of my PAC involvement I was most interested in city government, and the 5th District encompassed most of Minneapolis. Several of us from the District Nominations Committee were later elected or appointed to City government positions. I caught on quickly to the political process and found that I had become a seasoned veteran in a little more than three months, an achievement that often does not happen in a lifetime of political activity.

Having ventured deeply into partisan politics I decreased my activities on the PAC but remained a delegate representing my area of the neighborhood. I was also appointed or elected to other boards: Christian Sharing Fund, Catholic Charities, and the Minneapolis

Community Action Agency, an organization which could receive and allocate federal funds for poor people.

Meanwhile, I was appointed by our Province Director and her council to be on a three-Sister team heading our Social Justice Secretariat. We formed a network with our other three U.S. provinces in working on local, national and international social justice issues. All my areas of interest seemed to coalesce in my Secretariat activities. I became a member of the Joint Religious Legislative Coalition (JRLC) which unites the efforts of various religious denominations in our metropolitan area who lobby for state legislation on which we all agree. Lobbying at the legislature brought me in contact with my political friends of a few months back.

The Hennepin County Women's Political Caucus sponsored a meeting in December, 1976, for women who had in the past or might consider in the future a run for public office. I was introduced to a Republican woman who had come razor-close to defeating an incumbent Democrat for the city's 10th Ward Council seat in the last election. She told me that if ever I decided to run, she would tell me everything she knew about getting started. I had received several telephone calls from 6th Ward constituents who asked me to consider a challenge to the incumbent, but I was unsure if this was something I wanted to do. When I continued to receive calls, I discussed my dilemma with several of our sisters including our assistant province director. One sister suggested that I list the pros and cons, but everyone I spoke with gave me encouragement to forge ahead. Sister Clare Dunn of our Los Angeles province had been elected to the Arizona House of Representatives. I would not have to plow new ground defending a political ministry. Still I was struggling with my decision.

Two days before a January meeting of 6th Ward women, I decided definitely to run. When I awakened that morning three thoughts popped into my head: "I should run. I can win. I will win."

The night of the meeting some women were cautious about giving me their backing. Was I willing to work hard enough to win? Did I understand how hard it would be to unseat an incumbent? What other support did I have? How could I raise enough money? What about volunteers? Could I devote the time to contact the delegates and alternates? Would there be any difficulty with the Church because I was a nun? I satisfied the group on this last question by saying my religious community had a State Representative in the Arizona House.

I had no practical knowledge of the personal demand, but I committed myself to give whatever it took to win. The assembled group decided to back me; some were ecstatically enthusiastic, others mildly skeptical.

Shortly after, some of us drafted a letter of announcement to delegates and alternates. I received a couple of campaign contributions for postage and launched out into the deep. However, I had not yet discussed my political involvement with our Province Director. When we met she seemed generally pleased that I was running for office until I mentioned my changed position on the abortion issue. Before the Senate District Convention I had done more serious reflecting and praying concerning the issue. I believed that from a governing standpoint, we should preserve the opportunity to choose (essentially a recognition of free will) even if some people would make wrong choices. For me to be able to make my choice (pro-life) I would have to allow others to choose according to their consciences. My life decisions are based on my value system which differs from others. I concluded that in the political realm, the difference between a democratic, pluralistic society and a totalitarian state was being able to choose according to differing value systems or being forced to comply with one. I believed we would only be acting humanly if we lived by the law in our hearts rather than by one which was imposed from outside. Therefore, a pro-choice position seemed closer to my thinking on the matter.

When our General Superior was in town I met with her. We also discussed my pro-choice position. She wanted to know if I had "the permission of the Ordinary" to run for public office. I had talked with the Archbishop in a light, informal, social conversation where he teased that it was too bad he did not live in Minneapolis so he could vote for me. Sister told me I should write to the Archbishop and ask his permission. And further, that she thought any campaign literature of mine should state clearly that I was a *Sister*. When I wrote to the Archbishop I related that I had been requested to ask his permission to run for public office. In his letter back to me he said he thought I had already discussed the question with my superiors when he talked with me, but he thought I should abide by their wishes in these matters, and that he personally preferred to see the laity assume these positions.

However, since no one had given me a direct "No" and because I felt this mission was as much a part of my personal call from God as was my original religious vocation, I did not turn back. In deciding whether to include "Sister" on my campaign brochures, I was convinced that I should not. I was not trying to hide the fact that I was a nun, but I was not advertising it either.

The ritual of the endorsing convention took place on March 19, the Feast of St. Joseph. As a Sister of St. Joseph, I claimed I had special help with St. Joseph "on my side." After nominating speeches, seconding speeches, a question-answer period and the first ballot, I was ahead by two votes. The opposition was horrified, but they recovered to begin the strategy of "working the floor." My opponent's campaign workers tried to convince my delegates to vote for him. Fear tactics were used. "If she is endorsed, she will lose to the former incumbent who just happens to be here watching the proceedings." "She's a nun. Do you want a nun to represent you on the City Council?"

The votes shifted on the third ballot as the greater experience of the incumbent's forces prevailed. He was now ahead by two votes and some people had left the convention, expecting a marathon session. In the ensuing ballots my opponent led by eight votes, but his lead slipped to four votes by the sixth ballot. We finally agreed to a "no endorsement convention" on the seventh and last ballot.

The blocked endorsement of the incumbent was a political victory for me. I started campaigning the old-fashioned way, knocking on every door that I could, trying to meet every potential voter while doing my own needs assessment of my ward. The Sixth Ward was a high density, inner city, racially and culturally diverse ward which encompassed five neighborhoods and the Central Business District, contained most of the liquor licenses in the city, fifteen senior citizen public housing high rises, and most of the city's many group homes, half-way houses and board and care facilities.

One of my helpers, a black man from Chicago, lived in a "cracky-old" building that had been carved up into sleeping rooms and shared baths. His neighborhood was rough, and the police came often to break up gang fights between the blacks and the Indians. Smitty was an ex-prizefighter. He wanted me to see the degradation in his area but he said I "shouldn't go alone" and that he would "be my bodyguard." Several times as we made our way through the multi-unit buildings, he grabbed my elbow, steered me down the hall saying loudly, "We're all finished in this building." Some chemically-dependent residents dissolved in tears at our visit, while others were more belligerent. He introduced me to his friends as "the alderman." He loved to go with me to the affluent buildings in my ward. He would wear a brightly-colored shirt and tie on such occasions to "wow the ladies." Sometimes in the senior citizen high-rises he would encounter someone who would slam the door in his face. On a couple of occasions that happened to me, too. But we met many lonely people who were grateful for a sympathetic or understanding ear (that listening which is at the heart of ministry). I heard of many problems, many stories.

Even as a candidate I put people in need in touch with people who could help them. The deteriorated housing, the chemical dependency, the unemployment, the lack of safety and security for residents and business people were problems that seemed to call out to me to be addressed. My platform was shaping up to be: to make inroads in the areas of housing, economic development for jobs, and increased security and safety.

As the election drew closer, candidate forums increased in number, and questionnaires multiplied from any group who wanted to know where I stood on issues of concern to them. The political "pros" were predicting that I would come in third in our three-way race. I was predicting an upset. I worked harder than ever to deliver that "handful of votes" which would determine the winner. On election day eve we put a door-hanger on every knob in the sixth ward. One side read, "We didn't want to disturb you, but please vote in the DFL primary tomorrow for Jackie Slater." On the other side was a bit of hyperbole, "Unlike others, her integrity can never be questioned." It was a not so subtle reference to the fact that the incumbent had been indicted but cleared of perjury charges just three weeks earlier, and the former incumbent had been convicted of breach of the peace when he hassled a neighborhood newspaper photographer who attempted to take his picture against his wishes. I won the primary election by 267 votes, but the "door hanger" piece became a campaign issue in the general election. Besides if all the votes which had been cast for my primary opponents were transferred to one of my general election opponents, I would need a lot more votes to win in November.

I was not elected yet, and my principal opponent was willing to do or say almost anything to prevent my becoming the next 6th Ward alderman. He attempted to use the fact that my campaign manager during the endorsement process was a lesbian, to generate an anti-gay vote for himself. He charged that I did not respond to the Minnesota Citizens Concerned for Life questionnaire because I was "pro-abortion," and of course, he questioned *my* integrity. I had become a convenient focus for the continuing struggle over these issues. Despite all his charges I won the general election by 900 votes.

There were six of us newly elected to our thirteen-member Council in November, 1977. Four were women, bringing the total number of women to six. Three of us were Democrats, giving the DFLers a majority.

As a member of the majority caucus, I took part in the negotiations for council leadership positions and committee chairmanships and membership. I was satisfied with my committee assignments which were: Government Operations Chair, Community Development, Intergovernmental Relations, and Licenses and Consumer Services. I was ready to begin my new ministry.

On the morning of January 3, 1978, I was inaugurated for my first term on the Minneapolis City Council. One of the first hurdles was managing my time between committee meetings, appointments, phone calls, and dictation. I had to prepare for committee meetings by reading and studying reports in order to ask the right questions and judge if I had received enough information to vote intelligently. Constituents who came to testify at a public hearing expected their alderman to be present to hear every word, while the person who called the office expected to speak to the alderman. Still others wanted the alderman out in the ward, rather than trying to solve their problems from the "Ivory Tower" of City Hall. Of course, people expected their representative to be on hand for neighborhood meetings, dedications, open houses, ground-breakings, annual meetings, breakfast, luncheon and dinner meetings to represent the City. An alderman had to be familiar with all issues connected with the city in order to explain them or defend them. When the media got on to something they thought was controversial or that they could make controversial, there could be a storm of letters, phone calls, requests for interviews from TV stations, newspapers, even journalism students to follow up on the story. An alderman was on call 24 hours a day.

My first challenge on the Council was a so-called abortion issue. The decision concerned allocation of City Health Department funds for education programs. One was for young women who were pregnant and planned to keep their babies and another was for young women and their sexual partners on prevention of pregnancy. Both programs were educational in nature since no funds could be used to fund abortions. The previous council had voted the money for the program for young women who would keep their babies (the perceived pro-life program). Parliamentary procedure allowed for a reconsideration motion by the new Council to make a different allocation of the funds if it chose. (A change was likely because there were more women on the Council and this was perceived to be a "women's issue.") The lobbying began about ten days before the first regular Council meeting of the year.

The "funded program" was organized by Sister Mary Meyer, one of our nuns, who was also a friend of mine. The second program was operated by two individuals who ran a clinic which performed abortions and had access to clients who had chosen abortion as a solution to their "unwanted pregnancy." (Their program was the perceived pro-abortion one.) Both programs were worthwhile, but the political issue was over who would win the battle of perceptions. I met with Sister Mary and asked her if she would be willing to split the grant money between the two proposals which would mean both groups would then seek a matching grant from other sources. Although it would be more difficult for her organization, she agreed.

I then talked with the administrator of the other program who also agreed to a split, not 50-50, but 3/4-1/4 with her group getting the larger share. I was the deciding vote on this issue because six aldermen would not vote for any split and the other six would only support the 3/4-1/4 option. The night before the council meeting I figured out the parliamentary procedure to accomplish what I set out to do.

The vote to reconsider the previous Council's action passed 7-6. The next motion was the 3/4-1/4 option. Then a substitute motion was made to give Sister Mary's program all the money. That failed 7-6. I made another motion to amend the 3/4-1/4 to 50-50. That died for lack of a second. Having voted on the prevailing side of the failed motion for total funding for Sister Mary's program, I moved reconsideration. One of the alderman supporting the 3/4-1/4 option recognized that I was about to vote to give all the money back to Sister Mary's program and said that if I would withdraw my motion to reconsider, he would move my previous 50-50 motion. It passed 7-6. I lobbied the Mayor to sign the council action, but he vetoed it and his veto was sustained. Sister Mary's program got all the money, I got "flak" from all sides. I had successfully engineered a no-win situation for myself, having alienated those on both sides.

Another battle was fought over the granting of a liquor license to a black man in one of the more conservative wards. Constituents were pressuring their alderman to deny it because they did not want a black man to have a "bar" in their neighorhood. It was traditional to honor "aldermanic courtesy" by voting the way the ward alderman asked. Since I voted in committee to grant the license, my campaign manager, who was working for another alderman, came to instruct me about being a "team player" and finally to put pressure on me to vote against the license on the council floor. I explained to her the reasons for my vote and reminded her of my campaign slogan, "It doesn't have to be politics as usual." It really shocked me to hear her ask, "You mean you actually *believed* all your campaign rhetoric?"

When she was unable to get me to change my mind she said that

I might as well get "the Catholic Church" to pay off my campaign debt, because there would be no help from the DFL. My campaign committee's debt approached four thousand dollars. I did not change my vote, but the ward alderman changed his mind. The license was approved. The next several months I made donations to my campaign committee from my salary until the debt was paid in full. I did not ask for help, and none was offered.

Several of my colleagues were unhappy that I beat my predecessor. Also, they did not know me. They believed they could tell me how to vote and that I would "obey orders." But I asked for reasons, and if they had none or they were not very good, I would vote according to the knowledge I had.

When I first began having conflicts with my DFL colleagues, the Republicans, particularly the women, came to my rescue. There were partisan reasons, of course, in capturing another potential vote for the minority caucus, but beyond politics, we were becoming friends. I had heard how Council leadership would isolate someone who did not follow the caucus agenda. It was the majority leader's job to "maintain caucus discipline" in getting the necessary votes to pass or block Council actions. My first term on the Council we had one of the newcomers as majority leader. She negotiated for the leadership postition as part of the power struggle in our organizing process between the North and Southside DFLers. We were evenly split in number with the Northsiders being traditionalists and mostly incumbents, the Southsiders liberals and mostly newcomers. As majority leader she had power in name only. An actual power vacuum was created as we each "did our own thing." Knowledge is power, but often she did not transfer information, and in some cases she never received it in the first place.

By contrast, the Minority leader was a veteran Council member and well-organized. The Republicans were happy to furnish me with information because I would be more likely to vote with them on a particular issue if background information rather than political persuasion was the basis for decision. The President of the Council often crossed caucus lines to get his votes for an issue, but if I did, I was charged with lacking loyalty to the caucus. I paid little attention to the charges, and they submerged until another issue would revive the old contentions.

By the end of my first year in office, I began organizing for the February endorsing convention for my second term. There was evidence that some of my colleagues joined efforts of political foes in my ward to try to force me out of office. But I was much stronger politically than any of them realized. My main opponent in my second term election was the former Republican incumbent who ran against me in the first election. Essentially his campaign was a re-run of the previous general election. Someone circulated a smear piece about me concerning the abortion and gay rights issues, but it backfired. The second time I beat him 2 to 1, and even my detractors preferred to see me re-elected rather than him.

However, one of my biggest conflicts was about to begin. I had prepared the ground for many projects during my first term and during my second term they were coming to fruition. Still there were some political old-timers who wanted to give me my "come-uppance." As a conscientious, hard-working alderman I had become one of the stronger members on the previous Council. I should reasonably have moved into a stronger position in the Council committee structure. Instead, one of my colleagues in negotiating for his own rise in power and that of a newly-elected friend of his, acquiesced in the "caucus package" for organization which gave me a somewhat lower status than I had my first term. Since our eight-member Caucus did not need my vote to pass their package, I let them know they would not have it. I voted no on both the president and vice-president choices as well as some of the committee assignments.

From my perspective, my caucus had settled for personal gain at the expense of the strongest position for our caucus, our council and our city. Even with a stronger majority leader the caucus seemed to self-destruct. Decisions appeared to me to be based on pettiness and that carried over into the neighborhood organizations who "took political sides" in endorsing their favorite or "most powerful" alderman. I continued to work closely with two of the five neighborhoods in my ward, but I was often at odds with the others. Still, most of the proposals I worked on were funded and the projects completed, from Urban Development Action Grants for housing renovation to Economic Development Agency support of an American Indian shopping center. I negotiated for changes or alternatives for "bad projects" and voted and worked against them if their originators refused to compromise. I was a formidable foe to those who simply wanted to win the battle to do things their way or to get something funded that was not worth doing.

I believe that I was a controversial figure on the Council, not because I was a nun, but because I challenged the system. To some extent I was successful in changing it, but bureaucracies retain a good deal of inertia and oftentimes what looks like an upheaval settles back after the disturbance has passed. I did not set out to be a reformer, but I did attempt to refine the processes as I worked to accomplish my goals.

I tried to be as fair as possible with all the people. For most, that is all they expected. But some thought they would get whatever they asked because of who they were. That might include the representatives of a powerful corporation or a powerful neighborhood organization. I felt there was no sense in my being alderman if I allowed myself to be controlled by whatever special interest group currently wielded the most clout. I understood how the political games were played and for what reasons. There were times when I got caught up in them too. A couple of times I helped to develop our Caucus' package for allocation of block grant monies and made trade-offs to insure projects in my ward were funded, while others less involved had their project funds trimmed. In the political sphere I could receive high marks for my endeavors, but personally I felt uneasy. I wrestled with the idea that I might be becoming just another politician. I wondered if I wanted to continue. The personal demands and sacrifice associated with being an alderman were immense. Therefore it was with mixed feelings that I sent my delegate/alternate letter before Christmas announcing that I planned to run for a third term.

The ward boundaries were changed to equalize population distribution after the 1980 census. Some of my political adversaries had been appointed to redraw the boundaries. They cut from the areas where they thought I was strongest and added as much new territory as possible. They tried to have two sets of endorsing conventions, one within the old boundaries to determine where my support was and a second after redistricting. They counted on taking the endorsement for their candidate or at the very least blocking mine. Outwardly I was dealing with these political threats, but inwardly I had decided I would not seek a third term after all. I felt great relief and release with my decision. I really did not want to go through the rigors of another campaign year. I had accomplished more than many aldermen do in such a short time. I was ready for the Lord to dismiss me from my task.

My secretary intended to retire at the end of my second term so I did not have to tell her immediately, but I did want to tell my aide so that she could begin job-hunting. I told her not to tell anyone else because I wanted to wait for the appropriate time to make my announcement. I was awaiting the DFL's decision about whether there would be one or two endorsing conventions. If there were only one, it would have to be after redistricting which could push it as late as June. The DFL decided on one convention with the new boundaries. The 6th

Ward convention was scheduled last after filings for office had opened. The right time never came for me to make my announcement. I was in the race for a third term.

This race was different. I was up against the sophisticated elite of political circles. The intended heir to my chair quit his job early so he would have time to campaign. The "new ward" was designed to give him the best advantage. He had friends on the Council who would brief him on the issues and friends in "high places" who would help him raise money.

It is a truism in politics that the longer you stay in office the more enemies you make. In the many conflicts and controversies that I encountered over the years, some internally with other Caucus or Council members, others with groups which operated within my ward, I witnessed the struggle to seize power and control people and events. Campaign '81 was a classic example.

The new Sixth Ward included an even larger gay population than before. Several gay activists organized for a block party along the street where the gay bars were. They planned a celebration modeled after the Castro Street events in San Francisco. There had been considerable anti-gay activities occurring in the city, and I was opposed to any confrontation that I thought the block party would invite. I refused to sign the permit. The full City Council agreed with me. The courts did not. The judge ruled that we had abridged the gays' First Amendment rights. The gay block party became a campaign issue, and a substantial number of the delegates and alternates to the endorsing convention were gays or lesbians.

I was the deciding vote on de-funding the Minnesota Tenants Union. They had earned the reputation of getting after "slum landlords" through their activities of organizing tenants. I came to believe that their reputation was better than they were. After a couple of years of working with them I discovered a pattern to their strategy. They played one group off against another: landlords, tenants, aldermen, inspectors, judges, and lawyers. They also knew how to manipulate the media. Their defenders seemed to believe that for the MTU "the end did justify the means." Those who knew how they operated and how I had given them my unquestioning support in the past were amazed at the courage I exhibited in casting my vote against them in spite of incredible pressure from all sides. With close to 90% renters in the Sixth Ward, defunding or defending the Tenants Union became a major campaign issue.

The stage was set for a difficult campaign. At least a third of my new constituents were moved by redistricting. Some were so angry about the change that they threatened to boycott the election in protest. Six of my sixteen senior citizen high rises were transferred to other wards and they were part of my stable base of support in a very transient ward. The overwhelming majority of my constituents were renters, and the new boundaries encompassed a larger gay constituency. Against this backdrop there were four gay men, a Tenants Union staff person, and an Hispanic activist who were challenging me for the endorsement. The preceding week was an agony of anticipation for me. Anxiety causes me to lose my appetite. I had to force myself to eat. But by the morning of the convention I was calm. Suffice it to say that everything was stacked against me. I came in second, but there was no endorsement. And the man for whom the ward had been "designed" came in third. Some of my delegates voted for him to keep him in the contest to preserve a "no endorsement." If he dropped below a certain number of votes, he would have been excluded. Not very many people knew he was gay, and the disclosure of the fact in the local gay newspaper may have given him some hesitancy about continuing the race. Within a week he had dropped out, and some of his supporters came to volunteer for me.

Primary election day started out as a beautiful, sunshiny day. Most of my supporters made it to the polls early. My opponent expected the young people living in apartments to vote for him on their way home from work or school. About 4 o'clock a terrible thunderstorm hit the city. It rained with lightning and thunder for several hours. I am not sure if the weather put a damper on the election results, but it lent a psychological effect to the outcome. I won the primary election, and by the general election I received the largest vote total I ever got. Since that occurred with the new ward boundaries it would be more difficult than ever for someone to unseat me.

Now I was a seasoned City Council member and the opportunity I had to exert leadership was becoming more apparent. One TV newsman said that we had "the potential of being the best Council this City has ever seen." But it did not work out that way. Four of us southside DFLers proposed to drop the position of majority leader and to transfer the powers to the Vice-President. By suggesting the move we incurred the wrath of a northside DFLer who fought to keep his position. Once again there was a power struggle for leadership and committee assignments. The alderman who first suggested the plan was also the first one to back away from it. He sought a compromise that would have given him membership on the two most powerful committees. But I offered an alternative to his plan which the rest of our caucus accepted so he lost out, and he and I were often at odds with each other after that. In addition, the deposed majority leader appeared to seek ways to cause dissension or division in our caucus.

I did not have a "leadership position" *per se*, but my knowledge, experience and involvement in shaping the direction that the Council and the city were taking increased immeasurably. I chaired the Intergovernmental Relations Committee which gave me an important tie to all the other governmental units. At the same time, angry supporters of my primary opponent who felt cheated that they were unable to defeat me in the last election continued to snipe at me whenever possible and to search for the bigger issues they might use against me in the next campaign.

However, by December 1983 I determined there would be no next campaign for me. I had never planned to run for more than four two-year terms. A whole year of tough campaigning would force me to postpone work on a city housing policy and other priorities I had set for myself. The physical stress of the job was beginning to leave its mark. Slowly I began to realize it was time for me to move on. I made my announcement public six years to the day that I first decided to run.

Now that I have finished the course, the proposals, projects, letters, phone calls, controversies, conflicts, motions, resolutions are all part of my "aye" for final roll call. For the most part I avoided the pitfalls of allowing myself to be pressured or "sweet-talked" into unworthy schemes. I did not fear to challenge others when I thought they were wrong, or to admit when I was wrong. Most people expected me to do my job and to get results. Some put me on a pedestal, a convenient target for others. Many forgot I was a nun or never knew. Their expectations were based on who I was as a person, or on what I had already been able to accomplish.

As for me, I have learned political skills, I know more about myself and more about the other people who have touched my life—the loving, supportive friends who were there when I needed them, those who challenged me when I thought I was giving my whole self, those I fought in one battle or other who later became friends, and those who are more distant from me than before.

I am grateful for the time I had in public office. Still I wonder why the Lord called me when he did, and why today there are those in the Church who oppose political ministry so vigorously for priests and religious when the Pope himself is so involved in it. If we really are a people struggling to bring about the Kingdom of justice, love and peace, then political solutions rather than military ones are the best course for us to pursue. It may not be clear what forms this new ministry will take in the future, but we must not fear it. For our work becomes a ministry when empowered by the Spirit. To those who are called the Lord's message is clear, "It was not you who chose me, it was I who chose you to go forth and bear fruit. Your fruit must endure, so that all you ask the Father in my name He will give you." (Jn.15:16)

Mary Sean O'Reilly

TRIAL ADVOCACY AND PUBLIC OFFICE: AN AMERICAN RELIGIOUS WOMAN'S EXPERIENCE

Being born and raised in the Southwest, I came by a pioneer spirit in an honest way. And having grown up during the Second Vatican Council, I developed my sense of church during a time of great openness in the Catholic Church. The Council's spirit of search and the adventure of the Gospel paralleled my desire to spend my life working with people in a caring and creative way.

My experience of being an advocate began at an early age. Although I was the second child in a family of nine girls and two boys, I was always the trouble-shooter and spokeswoman. Actually, I perceived myself as a third parent and assumed a lot of authority with the other children. Fortunately for them, and with gentle suggestions from my parents, I learned that authority carries a lot of responsibility. That sense of responsibility was centered in my conviction about being fair even if firm. I believe this sense of fairness has permeated my experiences as a trial attorney and remains a central value to me now as a member of the judicial system.

I was about sixteen when I began to develop an interest in the legal system and to distinguish it from legislative politics. This interest was intuitive and it became increasingly important to me during the next four years. I was also developing an interest in the church and a curiosity about religious life. I was studying the documents of the Vatican Council in my high school religion classes as they were being published. I was very attracted to the principles of social justice found in *Gaudium Et Spes*. I was struck with its stance on the dignity and value of each person and its conviction about the need for global justice. Thus, the values and challenges of the Council documents became the catalyst through which I explored the possibility of becoming a woman religious. *Gaudium Et Spes* and *Lumen Gentium* remain crucial points of reference for me today as I search and grow in my understanding of Gospel demands.

Sixteen years ago I joined the Sisters of Mary of Namur in Fort Worth, Texas. They are a small international Congregation whose ministry priority is working among the poor. When I joined the Congregation in 1966 I asked to study law because I thought that practicing law would give me access to the political system in a constructive way. I thought that helping families as a civil trial lawyer would be a concrete way of living out a serious commitment to those who are disadvantaged. It also seemed to me to be a valid expression of the church's concern for social justice in American society. I was aware of the emerging Legal Services Corporation and was attracted to the notion of practicing poverty law.

My interest in becoming an attorney was respected by the women in leadership in the Texas Province. Those women encouraged the development of my gifts, insights and skills as well as the talents of other sisters. This openness resulted in a variety of new ministries for many of us and in my obtaining a law degree.

In January, 1978 I began my 3 1/2 year experience as a Legal Services attorney. I worked in the Family Law Unit and spent most of my week in the Family Law Courts with low income women. During that time, I worked with over 600 women and children, using my professional skills to make the legal system work for them. Because of this access to the courts, these families had options and alternatives to desperate and inhuman situations. I obtained protective orders and child support in many of these cases. At least a third of these cases involved child or spousal abuse.

Because much of my work with victims of family violence was among the very poor, I sometimes saw the desperate side of life that includes death. For those who live in abject poverty, the struggle for basic housing and jobs can make life seem hopeless. Pressures build from the effects of drugs, lack of communication and ignorance. Too often, the result of such pressures is violence. In less than three years I experienced the violent deaths of four clients: one child and three client-relatives in domestic violence incidents. Two other clients took their own lives in similar situations. The child who died was born prematurely after his mother went into labor in the courtroom with me. She was seven months pregnant and had been badly beaten. Three weeks after the baby died, the beatings resumed and my client shot and killed her husband during a five hour beating episode. She was arrested and charged with murder. I obtained a good criminal attorney for her and the grand jury later dismissed the case, finding the death to be a matter of self-defense.

The saddest of all my cases involved the deaths of two young women, one black and one white, who were senselessly murdered by their husbands. Both were killed in front of their children, both were killed with handguns, and both had been turned away by the police and district attorney's offices after begging for protection against the men who were threatening to kill them. One woman was shot in the head as her 21 month old daughter sat in her lap.

After over 600 hours of legal research I filed a civil rights action in state court on behalf of the surviving children of these two women, ages 23 and 25. The seven surviving children were all under ten years of age. The lawsuit, seeking money damages, was filed against the police department and district attorney for excluding a class—battered women—from protection against criminal assaults when the men inflicting the injury were spouses. Although the lawsuit was not successful in recovering money or in distinguishing the legal doctrine of immunity, it did effect practical changes in our county. Both law enforcement agencies have become more responsive to the plight of family violence victims. The issue of the prosecutor's immunity was carried to the Supreme Court of the United States over a period of two years. The media kept alive the issue of assistance to such victims and educated the public to family violence dynamics.

The state court, in denying my petition for relief, wrote that there was "no decision from any court which conclusively establishes that a prosecutor may exclude a particular class from protection," i.e. battered women. That judge went on to say, although public policy requires that prosecutors be given absolute immunity in determining what criminal actions should be brought, that is not to say that plaintiffs (here, the surviving children) may not vigorously and legitimately contest that position.

My varied legal responsibilities during those years of research and writing were very special in that they helped me realize the power and injustice of the criminal justice system. As I worked month after month on careful and tedious research I also continued my daily routine in the family courts. Those very different activities were a striking contrast of the diversity in advocacy expressions and the urgent need for the legal system to work effectively for those whose very lives may depend on it.

It took a lot of faith for me to deal with the horrible reality of those situations involving death and so much pain. I learned that one must have a deep sense of hope to share in these kinds of experiences and encourage families to go on. The courts could not and did not solve all the problems faced by these and many other families, but the legal system did offer them concrete alternatives that were an improvement over their previous situations. I considered it an important part of my call to Christian commitment to be involved in these experiences in a caring and hope-filled way.

Being part of the legal system has also afforded me the opportunity to stretch the growth lines of that structure in legitimate ways. My years of work with victims of family violence gave me the experience, reputation and drafting skills to work on state legislation for domestic violence protections. The result was improved laws that expanded options and protections for victims of family violence. It was also a sobering experience for me to learn that law and politics are fiercely loyal allies. It requires strong and committed leadership in each of these areas to effect change.

When I left Legal Services in 1981 I opened my own law office. I continued my work with low-income women and children for the next 2 1/2 years. Throughout that period of time I took as many cases as I could manage, spent about 25 hours a week in court, and had to turn away 40 to 50 requests for assistance every month.

During this time I was still an active member of my religious community. Based on many experiences and comments of others, I think that being a woman religious helped establish my credibility with clients and with other professionals. When I started practicing law I was held to the same scrutiny as other young attorneys, but oftentimes both lawyers and judges had positive presumptions about my work for the legally-marginalized women and children I served. Most of my clients and their families also trusted and cooperated with me because they knew, as one older black woman said, that I was a "Church lady." Many clients were non-Catholic but they frequently asked me to pray with them and I did.

The Pastoral Constitution (*Gaudium et Spes*) of the Vatican Council states that we Christians must collaborate wholeheartedly in establishing an order in our world that respects all human freedoms. That document also reflects on the prophetic role of church in which we all participate. This is the search for justice and peace that Jesus showed us by His life. It is the new command of love that holds the secret of our world's transformation.

Several years ago, at a meeting on apostolic concerns, one of the sisters said that her ministry experiences had "radicalized" her understanding of mission or vocation. The same realization is true for me.

An important result of my trial attorney experiences for six years was the development of my own spiritual life. Being so close to human pain and suffering has deepened my sense of prayer, humility and commitment to working toward caring for one another. I am repeatedly impressed with the verses of Isaiah (58:6-8) that reveal it is *our* wounds and not those of the poor that will be quickly healed if we break the unjust fetters, shelter the homeless poor and do not turn away from the needs of our kin.

I believe that a part of my stewardship is to develop the talents and aptitudes that I have received. Those gifts include a sense of self-worth and self-confidence that I remember always possessing even as a child. My sense of vocation has always included a desire to be the best person I can be and to use my gifts in accordance with gospel imperatives. For me, this is an essential and primary aspect of my who-ness and my who-ness in relationship to the church. I have never experienced a sense of compromise or ambivalence in living out my Christian commitment and religious vocation as a practicing attorney or recently as an associate judge in the Family Law Courts.

I also believe that my work with poor and abused women gave birth to my conscious feminism and the commitment I have to work for economic justice for and with women in our society. In case after case I have seen, from both sides of the Bench, how economics can and does define the quality of life, or lack of human quality, for poor families often headed by women. My perception of the women's movement is that it is an effort to integrate the values of mutuality and participation for all in the day-to-day dynamics of our society. I perceive this as a positive way of looking at the abilities and contributions of each person as person, rather than limiting our expectations of each other to traditional roles. An essential aspect of this integration requires close analysis of the economic as well as social barriers that some people experience because of their gender.

These last three years have been years of intense reflection and search concerning my relationship with the Sisters of Saint Mary. The heart of those reflections centers on the very traditional expression of religious life now being promoted by Vatican authorities. Our Congregation has moved more and more toward this expression as being the exclusive direction for our sisters. Our new Constitution excludes more contemporary expressions of living out the vowed life, especially in the areas of authority, community life, and diversity in ministry. For me, this is much more than a matter of life style and includes the questions of self-definition and the participatory role of women religious at the threshold of the twenty-first century church. It is also a matter of great importance for me because of the integrity with which I try to live and the way I make life choices. I have come to believe and accept that there are legitimate conflicts about the role of church authority. I also believe that many of the women now leaving traditional religious life are searching out new ways for women to be involved in the life of the church. New expressions of community already exist in various liturgical, peace and justice groups. It is exciting to think of new directions growing out of the valuable tradition I came to know and love during my sixteen years as a Sister of Saint Mary.

Because I had made the decision to seek a dispensation from my Congregation before I had any knowledge of my court appointment there was no struggle in the decision to accept this position. I did ask and receive the permission of my Bishop to continue my legal ministry as a Court Master while I was still a member of my Congregation. I also know that this was not the situation for other churchwomen in recent months who have had to seek a dispensation from their vows in order to pursue their commitment to the people of God through political ministries.

I know that the judicial and legal systems are different than legislative politics. I know the importance of legislative advocacy and the need for political decisions to be made by persons who take seriously the challenge to live according to the Gospel. Being involved in the judicial system or in the legal system *is* political in the classical sense. It is action on behalf of the body politic; it is preserving order in society for the good of all society.

My appointment as a Family Court Master for the Texas District Courts is a new expression of advocacy that gives me the opportunity to preside over the kinds of hearings that I was involved with as a trial attorney. I think my unanimous appointment by the family law judges was based, in part, on my work with poor women and children for the last six years. This is a non-partisan appointment that gives me a courtroom and bailiff and the opportunity to hear five to six cases a day.

As a Court Master I listen to problems involving paternity, child support, visitation rights and protective orders to prevent property destruction and physical harm. Many of the people who appear before my court cannot afford legal counsel. My position gives me a lot of discretion about giving instructions, re-setting hearings, awarding interim attorney fees, granting probation rather than jail time, ordering counseling and arbitration, and closing the courtroom when the hearing involves such difficult issues as sexual abuse or custody matters. I have found parents more conciliatory and responsive to the court or social workers when they are treated with respect and given the needed time and privacy to deal with the litigation. I have the option of using the court system wisely and efficiently. I am sure that this position will hold many new insights for me as my experience broadens.

I have always thought of my roles as a citizen and as a church person as being part of the same reality. I perceive the expectations of the various publics I serve as a Court Master to be basically the same as those I met in practicing law, i.e. to be fair, honest, professional and committed in my advocacy. Over the years I have tried to articulate the insights I have gained from experiences with poor women and to work for structural changes that will benefit those in our society who have been disadvantaged by the legal system.

It seems to me that important human decisions and issues should be addressed by those of us who know that life is a precious gift to be guarded and respected for all. *Gaudium Et Spes* observes that "We can justly consider that the future of humanity lies in the hands of those who are strong enough to provide coming generations with reasons for living and hoping." The document also makes the joys, hopes and griefs of our world one with the concerns of the followers of Jesus. Thus, the journey to God's Kingdom is inextricably bound up with this earthly journey in which we all participate. What better way to advocate the Gospel message than by living out Gospel values in every place and space the Lord has graced us to be.

Robert F. Drinan, SJ

MAY 5, 1980

It is with regret and pain that I accept the decision of the Holy See.

I went to Congress, chosen by a citizens' caucus, to work for justice in America and for peace throughout the world. These are the clear objectives ardently recommended by the Second Vatican Council and by all modern popes.

I have spent 10 of the 27 years of my priesthood as a member of Congress. I am certain that I was more influential as a priest in those 10 years than in my previous 14 years as dean of Boston College Law School.

For a decade I have had a voice and a vote in the resolution of the difficult problems confronting this country and the world. I worked for the termination of the war in Vietnam. I helped to eliminate the military draft. I was a leader in the abolition of mandatory retirement based on age.

Human Rights Missions

As an attorney I was intimately involved in developing substantial improvements in the law relating to copyright, bankruptcy, civil liberties, crime, privacy and other areas.

I had a central role in the impeachment proceedings in 1974.

As a member of Congress I participated in important human rights missions to Argentina, Central America, the Soviet Union and elsewhere. I was one of the first to see the tragedies of the "boat people" in Indonesia and Southeast Asia.

This Sunday I will fly to Amsterdam to participate in a two-day international conference to liberate Anatoly B. Shcharansky, the Russian human rights activist sentenced to 13 years in prison for alleged spying.

Grateful for Opportunities

I am grateful to have had these opportunities as a moral architect. I can think of no other activities more worthy of the involvement of a priest and a Jesuit.

I am proud and honored to be a priest and a Jesuit. As a person of faith, I must believe that there is work for me to do which somehow will be more important than the work I am required to leave.

I undertake this new pilgrimage with pain and prayers.

Global hunger and the arms race have been the two interwoven agonies of mankind which have disturbed me more profoundly than any other problems confronting the human race. I hope that in God's providence I may be given an opportunity to work to alleviate world hunger and to stop the arms race.

Agnes Mary Mansour

MAY 11, 1983

On the evening of May 9th, I requested with deep regret, sorrow and limited freedom, a dispensation from my perpetual vows as a Sister of Mercy.

My request was directed to the Holy Father, Pope John Paul II, through his representative, Bishop Anthony Bevilacqua of the Brooklyn Diocese. Bishop Bevilacqua had been asked to meet with me as an *ad hoc* delegate of the Holy See and to mandate that I immediately resign my position as Director of the Michigan Department of Social Services or be subject to a canonical process leading to imposed dismissal from the Sisters of Mercy.

In order not to act in defiance of the mandate of the Holy Father, and at the same time to honor my freedom of conscience and my continuing commitment to the people of Michigan, especially the poor who are served by the Department of Social Services, I requested and was granted what, for me, was the least of three undesirable alternatives.

Because my situation was continuing to cause strain within the Catholic community, in early April I requested a leave of absence from the Sisters of Mercy for the duration of my appointment as Director of the Department of Social Services. My hope was that the leave would eliminate what some saw as an obstacle to having a religious sister administer a public office.

Although my religious superiors granted the leave on April 11th, the Apostolic Delegate asked that the news of this leave not be made public at that time.

It was not until my meeting with Bishop Bevilacqua on May 9th that I learned the Vatican had overridden the religious community and that a leave of absence was not an option open to me.

The reasons that led me to request a dispensation from my vows are many and complex and include what I consider to be faithfulness to the Church, to the people of Michigan and to my religious community.

Faithfulness to Church

From the beginning of my considering and finally accepting the appointment as Director of the Michigan Department of Social Services, I have acted in good faith seeking the necessary approvals and communicating in every instance honestly and openly. It was my understanding that the needed approvals were granted knowing my opposition to abortion and my position on Medicaid funding for abortion; and knowing, likewise, the Vatican's concern relative to a religious holding public office.

The approvals were granted precisely because the mission of the Department of Social Services is very much in keeping with the mission of the Church and very much in keeping with the special emphasis by the Sisters of Mercy on service to the poor.

Of my four vows, the vow of service to the poor, sick, uneducated and oppressed has always been the primary one for me and the one that has given meaning to the other three vows including obedience.

Throughout my conflict with Church authorities, I have attempted to be faithful to my vow of obedience by discerning honestly with my religious community and others what should be done. I believe in a tradition of obedience more fully developed in the Church since Vatican II. This for me is an obedience born out of mutual dialogue and openness to seek the truth.

Throughout these difficult days, my religious order has supported me and has made several unsuccessful attempts to dialogue with Church authorities with the hope of reconciling differences.

The directive I received on Monday, was not the result of a dialogic, objective process, but of a unilateral one where neither I nor my religious superiors were ever given the opportunity to appropriately present our case.

I do not feel that I should or could witness to an obedience which, for me, would be irrational and blind. To the contrary, the mandate presented was not of obedience but of compliance that did not include an objective review of the issues at stake even though the disciplinary consequences were great.

Faithfulness to the People of Michigan

Having in good faith sought and received the necessary approvals to serve as the Director of the Department of Social Services, I made in equally good faith a commitment to the people of Michigan. If I had not received approvals initially, I would never have accepted the position.

Although I am well aware that I am dispensable and that there are others available who are highly qualified to direct the Department of Social Services, I do not consider it responsible or just to cause another transition disruption to occur. This concern becomes even more acute given the harsh economic realities of our state, the current human emergency with approximately 15% or 1 out of 7 Michigan citizens on public financial assistance, the present controversial budget debates and the new directions already taking shape within the Department of Social Services.

But more importantly, if I agreed to Vatican demands, I would have allowed, in no uncertain terms, Church intrusion into state affairs and Catholics would once again be suspect and possibly denied the privilege of public service.

Faithfulness to Religious Community

To be faithful to the Sisters of Mercy, my vows, my Church, and even God, I must first of all be faithful to myself, and further, I must be free to be faithful.

My positions on the issues associated with my current circumstances are a matter of conscience. My decision to request dispensation from my vows is also a matter of conscience. This is a decision my religious community has accepted and respects because they know it is a decision that only I can make.

For the support of the Sisters of Mercy and the manner in which they have handled my situation I am both proud and grateful. Although I have become canonically separated from the Sisters of Mercy, it is a formality that cannot easily break the habits and bonds of 30 years. Additionally, I will continue through my work in the Department of Social Services to be connected to the very heart of what the Sisters of Mercy are all about. This, when all is said and done, is what really matters and what I hope I can now begin to give my full attention and energy to.

Part 3
VIEWS FROM THE AISLE

In this section we have invited reflections from several persons who bring a special perspective to our subject as concerned bystanders or as actors involved in the ecclesial or political context. Kenneth Untener of Saginaw, Michigan, offers a bishop's view. Emily George provides the double perspective of a religious superior and that of an official witness to the events surrounding the cases of three sisters whose involvement in politics was challenged by church authorities. Alan Geyer of the Center for Theology and Public Policy discusses the subject from the point of view of "vocational democracy" and his long experience with church activists. John Danforth, a Republican Senator from Missouri, is an ordained Episcopal priest who sees no contradiction in his double role and has often waded straightforwardly into the dilemmas of religion and politics on Capitol Hill. Richard Celeste, Democratic Governor of Ohio, has appointed religious professionals to state offices and defends his policy on several grounds. Finally, Peter Steinfels, editor of *Commonweal*, raises the issues of complicity with coercive systems and the danger of neo-clericalism in registering his objection to the involvement of religious men and women directly in the functions of government.

Kenneth Untener,
Bishop of Saginaw, Michigan

CHURCH PEOPLE AND POLITICS:
A BISHOP'S VIEW

I am happy to be invited to share some of my reflections on the question of the involvement of priests and religious in political or civil offices. In doing so I write from the practical perspective of a Bishop who might be asked to allow this in his diocese. What are some of the basic questions that would surface? How might these considerations apply differently to a priest or a religious?

I will approach the subject from this point of view. Before doing so I would like to limit the topic a bit and clarify some terms. My focus will be the United States. Political systems vary greatly from country to country and one should be cautious about generalizing. Also, I will not attempt to distinguish clearly between various elected offices among themselves (e.g. city council, U.S. Congress) or between elected offices and appointed offices. Some distinctions would have to be made on this basis but there are some factors common to all, and my comments will be in the latter vein. Finally, when speaking of priests I generally include both diocesan and religious priests, and when speaking of religious I usually have non-ordained religious in mind.

What are some of the basic questions that might arise if a priest or a religious were considering political office and asked the Catholic community for input? It would certainly be a challenging discussion. People who agree on the conclusion may do so for very different reasons. I suspect that the following concerns would surface in one form or another:

1. *Political and civil offices are inappropriate because priests and religious are supposed to be sacred persons set apart from the world.*
This view of priesthood and/or religious life has been consider-

ably modified by the Vatican II Constitution on the Church and developments since then. Through baptism and confirmation, all Christians are set apart, not just priests and religious. All are called to holiness. All constitute the priestly people of God. While there are distinctions within the commuity, these are not based on the belief that some members are more sacred than others. If one accepted the premise that political involvement is inappropriate for people who are sacred, then one would have to say that it is inappropriate for everyone who is baptized and confirmed.

The truth of the matter is, however, that this has not yet been fully communicated to the Catholic community. Most Catholics still see baptism as primarily the washing away of sin, rather than a journey through the water to a new, holy way of life. The fact that chrism is used to consecrate every Christian in baptism and in confirmation is not nearly as prominent in the consciousness of our people as the use of chrism in the ordination of a priest.

2. *Politics is a dirty business and priests and religious should stay out.*

This is much like the first concern, and is actually the other side of the same coin. Once again, if the political arena is unholy, then it is so for all members of the Church. The underlying assumption, however, that politics is a dirty business, would have to be challenged. It may be that "dirty tricks" or unfair tactics are used from time to time, but that is true of any field of human activity. There is nothing in itself unholy about politics.

The Pastoral Constitution on the Church in the Modern World has provided the basis for a much more positive attitude toward the secular task. The process of building a better world is now seen to be related closely to the task of preparing the way for the kingdom of God. Some fundamentalists (among others) would see it very differently. For them, the world is inherently sinful, destined to be annihilated at the end of time. The world is a sinking ship, ruined by sin, unsalvageable. We are doomed to sail on it during this life, but not sink with it, for the Lord will rescue the just and place them on an entirely new ship on which they will sail blissfully for all eternity. In this perspective, enterprises that are not specifically religious are seen only as a necessary means to an end, never worthwhile in themselves. Any effort to build a better world through political or civil involvement is a dead end street. Thus, priests and religious should devote themselves to the radically different enterprise of building the kingdom of God.

If, on the other hand, one sees the building of a better world as part of the process of preparing for the kingdom of God, then involvement of any Christian in politics takes on a different perspective.

3. *Priests and religious are not competent in the political sphere.*

This may or may not be true in individual cases, but it certainly cannot be accepted as a general statement. It would be more correct to say that because a person has authority in the religious sphere, which touches all of human life, he or she cannot necessarily claim authority in all human spheres. There may have been a time in our immigrant Church when pastors were accorded all-encompassing competence by the people, but that is not the case today. Such competence would have to be established in each individual case.

Nor can we accept the assumption that priests and religious by their very lives are one step removed from the real world and therefore incompetent. Again, there may have been a day when that was true—many priests and religious lived a sheltered life. It is certainly not true today. Priests and religious have full access to the flow of information available to everyone else, and they are part of the mainstream of life "out there" in the world.

4. *In politics one sometimes has to compromise certain values for the sake of others, and this would place a priest or a religious in a position incompatible with his or her state of life.*

Once again I find it difficult to say that it is morally acceptable for a Catholic lay person to do this, but not a priest or religious. There is no question of conflict of values often present in political or civil life. Every Catholic citizen faces the same conflict when voting. What do you do when faced with a choice between two candidates, one of whom is anti-abortion but in conflict with the Church's position in other areas of human life, and another who is the reverse? Any vote would be something of a compromise. The person in political office faces similar choices. It certainly could happen that such a person would have to resign rather than compromise in a specific instance, but that would be true for a lay person as well as a priest or religious.

5. *Priests and religious shouldn't get into areas that belong more properly to the laity.*

I see this as a valid objection. It is not so much a matter of questioning the competence of priests and religious in this area, but of recognizing distinctive roles. Generally speaking, political and civil responsibility should be exercised by lay people. Priests and religious cannot claim to be the sole agents of goodness in the world. Political or civil responsibilities should be assumed only by way of exception. There would have to be some special reasons. I am not suggesting that justifying reasons would be next to impossible to establish. A religious, for example, might have extraordinary abilities that respond to a special need in the community. I am saying, however, that such cases constitute an exception.

6. *The Church should stay out of politics.*

Since this statement is made in a variety of contexts (e.g. the Bishops' Peace Pastoral) I would like to make some general comments. The Church, as a corporate entity, should stay out of politics in the sense that it should not tell people how to vote, form its own political party, and so forth. Nor should a priest or religious, on behalf of the Church, do any of these things. On the other hand, the Church has the responsibility to preach the gospel in all areas of human life. When we tell business people to be honest, people do not accuse us of meddling in business. When we tell doctors to respect human life, we are not thereby "getting into medicine." When we tell laborers to do a fair day's work we are not perceived as getting into labor management. I find it strange that when we tell our government to do any of the above, we are suddenly getting into politics. It is one thing to preach to people in all areas of human endeavor. It is quite another thing to "get into" these areas.

Having said that, we can now examine the question of whether or not a priest or religious in politics represents the corporate reality of the Church any more than a lay person does. In other words, does a priest or religious officially represent the Church in such a capacity? Obviously, he or she need not. It may be, however, that they would be perceived by some people as officially representing the Church, and this has to be taken into account. My guess is that this perception would apply more to a priest than a non-ordained religious, but it could happen in both cases. We are dealing here with the perception of the public, and it would vary from case to case. In my own experience, we have had a Sister on the City Council of Saginaw for some years, and she has not been perceived as being an official representative of the Diocese or of the universal Church. The public seems quite capable of making the necessary distinctions.

7. *Political involvement interferes with the priest's role as gatherer of the Eucharistic community.*

This presents a serious concern. I do think that we have to distinguish between the role of a priest as "gatherer" (along with some others in pastoral leadership) and the role of religious. There is a tendency to lump priests and religious together in regard to this question of political involvement, and I do not find this helpful. In the popular mind, priesthood and religious life seem to be different sides of the same coin. Women religious are sometimes seen as something of a female counterpart to priesthood. This is probably because they have in common such things as celibacy, life-long ecclesial commitment, Church titles, and so forth. In reality, the two are quite distinct and each ought to be treated in its own right. Statements that begin, "Priests and nuns should not . . . " are questionable from the start.

Generally speaking, I do not think it is appropriate for a priest to be in a political or civil office. On the other hand, I think that such a role could be very appropriate for a religious. Let me explain.

In many ways, the role of the priest is summed up and expressed in his function of presiding at the Eucharist. A priest is a gatherer, a shepherd. Everything the people do is brought to the Eucharist and flows from it. Their identity as the community of disciples is based upon bonds that transcend ethnic, social, political differences. It is the role of the priest (and other pastoral ministers) to gather the people as sisters and brothers in the Lord, and to remind them of the implications of this in their daily lives.

Such a role, it seems to me, is not helped by political involvement. Our political process is a dialectic. It is not built on a consensus model. Furthermore, the style that has become part of the process removes it even further from the consensus model. Opponents and opposing positions are characterized and caricatured in extremes, highlighting the most vulnerable aspects. Hard lines are drawn between factions, and issues are decided on a win/lose basis.

Digressing for a moment, I might point out that this adversarial style has come to be regarded as the normal way for members of almost any organization to interact. It is a style that is "in the air" everywhere—labor negotiations, school boards, law suits, etc. Catholics in this country have absorbed it into their bloodstream and find themselves acting this way on parish councils, parish commissions, even as ordinary parishioners. Lines are drawn, supporters are sought out, votes are taken, and that is that. Opposing positions are characterized in their weakest terms, opponents are villified, questionable motives are ascribed, faith is challenged, questions are raised in the style of cross examination. While this way of doing things may be an acceptable way of life for various organizations, and may not be a process evil in itself, it is not the style to which the Church is called in conducting its affairs. We should not forget that we are called to a different model.

To return to the question of the involvement of priests in political office: I am not generally in favor of such involvement, not because politics is evil or compromising, but because it can interfere with the role of a priest as gatherer. The concern is functional, not ontological.

On the other hand, strange as it may seem, such a role may be appropriate for religious. Theirs is essentially a prophetic way of life. Prophets sometimes do "outrageous" things. They are not necessarily gatherers of a defined community. They challenge us, console us, awaken us, and evoke reactions that range from great joy to great anger. They can represent and voice the cry of the people.

Furthermore, prophets tend to focus on specific aspects of the gospel message. This is quite different from being the chief teacher in a defined community, which is the role of the shepherd. They hold the same truths as the entire community, but they forcefully dramatize certain of these. In this sense they have more freedom than the person who preaches day in and day out to one specific community.

If we view religious as prophets rather than as quasi-"priests," then it seems that there could be circumstances in which political office could be an appropriate channel for them to exercise their prophetic role. The questions raised earlier would have to be taken into account, of course; but if these can be dealt with, then religious need not consider political office as always and everywhere in conflict with their way of life. Such a role would be by way of exception, but exceptions could be appropriate.

The whole question is a very complex one, and one should be careful about absolutes. Much of what I have said has been "on the one hand . . . on the other hand." That is the nature of the issue. I certainly do not mean to offer a rigid prescription. My intent is simply to contribute to the dialogue as we search for answers. These reflections can serve as background for the specific considerations that have to be taken into account in each case. There are priests who are not in the role of "gatherers" and this raises questions about the relationship of religious life and priesthood that have not been considered in this short piece. The most basic concern, I believe, has to do with this distinction and as I said, I do not think that it has adequately been taken into account. Current reflections in the Church on the nature of ordained priesthood and religious life could be very helpful in the future.

The issue will be with us for many years to come, perhaps for all of our time in history. After all, Jesus Himself posed the underlying tension when He said on the one hand, "they do not belong to the world any more than I belong to the world," and on the other hand, "I have sent them into the world." (John 17: 14,18)

Madonna Kolbenschlag, HM

INTERVIEW WITH
SENATOR JOHN DANFORTH

KOLBENSCHLAG: What are your personal convictions about religious professionals, whether ordained or not ordained, serving in public office? Does it compromise the American understanding of the separation of church and state in any way?

SEN. DANFORTH: Clearly not. In fact, the Constitution makes it clear that there cannot be a religious test for holding public office. Therefore, there is nothing in the Constitution which sets any limitation on the identity of who can hold public office, other than certain age restrictions, and the fact that the President has to be a naturally born citizen. There can be no religious test for holding public office. That is absolutely clear in the Constitution.

KOLBENSCHLAG: Does the candidacy of religious professionals compromise the political process in any way?

SEN. DANFORTH: I don't think it does. And I can't imagine ruling out people who are of any particular background or belief or affiliation. As far as elective politics goes, all of this is a matter for the public to consider. They can consider whomever they want. That is their right as citizens. They can vote for someone because that person is physically attractive, or because of a candidate's image or family life. The voters can vote on whatever basis they wish for the candidate of their choice. But as far as one's state of life somehow compromising one's ability to serve in public office, I don't see it.

KOLBENSCHLAG: I'm reminded of the time when Jack Kennedy ran and we hoped that his candidacy laid to rest all the fears about people who had affiliations with the Roman Catholic denomination. But do you think that some of the events that have happened recently such as the forcing of Sister Mansour in Michigan to choose between her office or her vows, and the recent forced resignation of the priest in Parliament in Canada—do you think these events have raised fears about Catholic candidates again? Is the situation of the Catholic different from someone in another denomination?

SEN. DANFORTH: Well, I think that the Catholic church is more hierarchical than many churches, and the clergy and laity seem to be more subject to rule and discipline. You know, when the news broke that Father Drinan had been told he couldn't run again by the Vatican—the presiding bishop of the Episcopal church was the chaplain for the day in the Senate. And I'm told that Moynihan was presiding. And he beckoned to Bishop Allen and asked him, "Have you come to get Danforth?!" But we are just not that disciplined I guess. I think that it's much more likely that the Catholic hierarchy would simply say to somebody, "You can't do that." Obedience is one of the conditions of the Roman Catholic ordination. That is much less likely with Protestants.

KOLBENSCHLAG: Looking at this question from another perspective, then, not of the state and of the people in a democratic society, but looking at it from the point of view of the church, do you believe that the candidacy of religious professionals can compromise the mission of the church in any way?

SEN. DANFORTH: No, I don't. That is, I think that the mission of the church is to proclaim the good news and to diffuse the Word, to extend the incarnation. Therefore, it would be very difficult to accept that and rule out whole areas of life, whole occupations, and say that this is an area that we're just not going to function in, or that we're not interested in. I believe to be ordained and to be in the world is simply to say that all of the world is an invitation to Christian activity and involvement.

KOLBENSCHLAG: How did you make your decision to become a candidate for public office?

SEN. DANFORTH: I have been interested in politics since I was a little boy. And all along I had the idea of maybe running for office. Although I was never a great life planner, when I went to college I still had that idea, the idea of going to law school and going into politics. That was more or less my meandering way, the way I was going. I took some religion courses in college. I majored in religion and believed at the time that I had a calling to change my vocational plans and to go into divinity school, and then go into the parish ministry or into the teaching of religion. So, I changed my plans. I did go to the Yale Divinity School. I did not like it. I increasingly had a hard time seeing myself, at least at that point in my life, my early twenties, as being either in the parish ministry or teaching religion. So I reverted to my original intention of being a lawyer. By that time I had two years of divinity school behind me, and I wanted to finish what I had started. And I asked the dean of the divinity school if I could do it. And he said yes, after about a week's thought, because it took a change of the rules to do that. He said it's like being a strip-tease saint. And there were about six other former seminarians at law school when I was there. Gary Hart and myself and Jerry Brown of California, being the three most destined for politics.

KOLBENSCHLAG: Why did you seek ordination then?

SEN. DANFORTH: Well, by that time I was on my way to getting two degrees, and I really didn't know about ordination. And I didn't want to have any role to play in deciding that. I wanted to be told. I didn't want it to be a question of here's some milepost, in other words, some achievement. I wanted to be called. And I had a bishop—now retired—an absolutely marvelous person, very pastoral, a very non-directive man. And I remember meeting with him one day. "What do you want to do?" he said. "I don't know. What do you think I should do?" Well it was Alphonse and Gaston, we went back and forth—but finally I made my decision. But I knew I didn't want parish ministry.

KOLBENSCHLAG: So you did feel a call to ordination?

SEN. DANFORTH: Yes, I did. But it was never as clear as I wanted it to be.

KOLBENSCHLAG: I wonder if you feel that in your service as a political professional you have maintained your identity as an ordained priest. Do you see them as different and separate roles in your life? Or have they, in a sense, merged?

SEN. DANFORTH: I think that I am a priest, and that is part of me. And there is no moment when that is not what I am. But that doesn't mean that I am acting all or even much of the time in a sacerdotal way. So I believe that when you're in a job like being the Senator, you bring to that job all that you are as a human being, all the experiences you ever had, all that's important to you. And my priesthood is very important to me. It is part of me. It's my background, it's my training, it's what I am, it's what I do, at least part of the time, and there's no doubt that it's a glass through which life appears to me. But that's not to say that I am operating as the Reverend Jack Danforth here at the Senate. I mean, when the vote bell rings and I troop on over to the floor and vote, I've tried to use my best judgment as a Senator from Missouri to do my best for my constitutents and for my country.

KOLBENSCHLAG: And all that you are bears on that.

SEN. DANFORTH: That's right. I'm other things too. I'm a husband and a father. And I think that being ordained is something which——it's not just an incidental or an overlay. It is something that is intrinsically part of what I am. And when I'm in the Senate that's what I am. I don't try to weigh my ordination on either my constituents or my colleagues. The closest I have come to mixing my roles was when I made a school prayer speech during the school prayer debate. It was a Bible-quoting speech. And I enjoyed doing the speech. But I apologized for it. I said, look, I didn't sign on to be the pastor of the people of Missouri. I'm their Senator. But I just wanted to make my case, and that was part of making my case.

KOLBENSCHLAG: You seem to be suggesting that you don't necessarily make a clear division between the roles. To be Senator is to represent the people, and you bring all of your roles to bear on that, even though you function in a very specialized way at the moment.

SEN. DANFORTH: Exactly.

KOLBENSCHLAG: So, do you think there are *any* roles that would be very inappropriate for an ecclesial person to assume, any offices, positions? There is definitely some controversy about offices like attorney general.

SEN. DANFORTH: Well, I was the Attorney General of Missouri for eight years. So, the answer to that question is no!

KOLBENSCHLAG: But what if your personal convictions were opposed to capital punishment, would that influence your view?

SEN. DANFORTH: I was in that position actually. Not for long, because when I was Attorney General the Supreme Court had, in effect, ruled out capital punishment. But while it was there—I was personally against capital punishment. It's easier to take a position in the Senate because I'm a legislator. There I took the position that it was a policy-making decision, and the Attorney General really is not a policy maker. My responsibility was to carry out the law.

KOLBENSCHLAG: Is there somewhat of a parallel between that situation and the Catholic person who has to enforce legislation for something he or she may regard as immoral, say for example, Medicaid funding for abortions?

SEN. DANFORTH: There is a kind of a conflict of interest in that. And I believe it's difficult to state exactly how you work it out. It isn't necessarily resolved because of ordination, unless your church has a position and it can impose that position on its clergy. If you have a church which is more collegial, then I suppose there could be more of a dilemma. It would be similar to the decision of a pacifist. A pacifist, whether or not it was an official position of his denomination would just decline to fight.

KOLBENSCHLAG: Could you conceive of any public policy situations or personal situations that might require you in conscience to resign your office?

SEN. DANFORTH: It hasn't happened yet. And, you know, I've been in public office now for over fifteen years.

KOLBENSCHLAG: Have you encountered any situations at all that presented a conflict of interest because of your convictions and your role?

SEN. DANFORTH: I don't think so. You know I am against the death penalty. I voted against the death penalty here in the Senate. I guess a public opinion poll would show that most of my constituents were *for* the death penalty. But I don't view that as a conflict of interest. My constituents know my views on the death penalty.

KOLBENSCHLAG: I think there might be some other governments where potential conflicts of interest might be more crucial. For example, you have more or less indicated that you do not see any problem with religious professionals in government. We have some people in the Catholic denomination who believe that they should serve only in times of emergency, in what has been referred to as "frontier cases." So, we have a situation like Nicaragua where the priests who are in government are claiming that they are serving because it's an emergency and they are needed. Now, without commenting on the present government of Nicaragua, what if, in fact, they should come into a situation where the policies and convictions or the stated aims of the government they are working for come into conflict with what they stand for as Christians? What would be the proper thing to do? To continue to serve the people and their need, or to resign?

SEN. DANFORTH: It's very hard to generalize on an answer to that. There are cases where you have a clear duty to protest. And thank God that really doesn't happen in this country, because you can protest any time you darn well please. I mean, we have in the Executive Branch, much less than in Congress, some faithful whistle-blowers. But there are cases where you clearly have an obligation to disobey. Nazi Germany was an obvious case. The fact that the government says we're going to exterminate six million Jews, well, you as clergy—as a human being—have to say, no, I'm not going to do that. So there are cases where there is a duty to disobey. But I think it's stretching it to say that therefore any time you disagree with anybody's policy you have a moral duty to throw a monkeywrench into your government. I think that maybe that was a notion of many in the 1960s—in other words—waging a guerrilla war for any precious little thought of your own. So, I think finding the point at which you take that position of disobedience is something that has to be decided prudently on a case-by-case basis.

KOLBENSCHLAG: You seem to see the American situation as being one that does not tend to provoke that kind of dilemma because there are so many other checks and balances on it. This suggests another question, I think, about the difference between our party system and the party system in some other countries. Do you think that our party system is less ideological and doctrinaire, and that this allows a religious person—or any person of definite convictions—a little more flexibility in participating in our system?

SEN. DANFORTH: Sure. Ours is not a parliamentary system. In the Congress we're really individuals. I don't know how Howard Baker does it. I mean, he's got a hundred prima donnas, each of whom is absolutely certain on every issue of having the perfect answer for everything.

KOLBENSCHLAG: So you're not selling your soul to a particular narrowly conceived agenda when you decide to be a Republican or a Democrat in this society, because those agendas often blur?

SEN. DANFORTH: I think that's true.

KOLBENSCHLAG: There have been questions raised about governors appointing priests and religious professionals to particular offices and others running as candidates. Do you think that religious persons could be easily exploited in our system? Do they run a greater risk of being mere "tokens" designed to promote the party's interest?

SEN. DANFORTH: No, I don't think so.

KOLBENSCHLAG: The First Amendment gives all of us the right to participate in politics, and that goes without saying. But do you think the state has rights too, like rights of recruitment, the right to draft individuals of exceptional capacity?

SEN. DANFORTH: Generally speaking, no. The state can't draft its public officials. There are an awful lot of good people I would want to see run for office or I would like to see in government. I would like to try to hire them, but they have other things that they want to do with their lives.

KOLBENSCHLAG: In the case of persons committed to the service of the church, if there is an obvious need, do you think those persons or the church itself has an obligation to consider the common good?

SEN. DANFORTH: To free the person up?

KOLBENSCHLAG: Yes, to free the person up for at least temporary service.

SEN. DANFORTH: I don't think it's an obligation. I wouldn't say that. Individuals and institutions should be free to reject—or accept—such an invitation.

KOLBENSCHLAG: Another question that is often raised is whether people who are tax exempt, at least in a limited sense, and who may or may not be exempt from military service, should be candidates for political office. That argument has sometimes been proposed as a reason for church persons not to stand for political office.

SEN. DANFORTH: Well, does that mean therefore that people who are taxed the most, namely people who have very high incomes, have more of a right or an obligation to be in public office than people who are poor and therefore not taxed? By the same reasoning, poor people who don't pay any taxes would never hold public office or shouldn't hold public office. And I think that that would be a very strange argument. As far as elective office is concerned, why can't the public make up its own mind? I mean, let them decide. If they decide that somebody who is the clergy shouldn't be elected, fine. That's their choice. The public might feel that a clergy person wouldn't play it straight, that this person would be grinding some axe. Their votes will reflect that. For example, I think that the intensity of the opposition to the school prayer amendment may have been a reaction to the political involvement of the religious right. I think that there are people in the country who, if they had a born-again Christian fundamentalist running for office, would vote against that person. If Jerry Falwell were to seek public office, he'd have a lot of people running for him. And he'd have a lot of people running against him because of his particular kind of ministry. And probably you'd have people who felt the same way about a Catholic priest running for public office. The public should decide. Whoever goes to the polling place and pulls the lever should decide.

KOLBENSCHLAG: There is an interesting article in a recent issue of *The New Republic* in which the author talks about the school prayer controversy and says that we have fallen into the trap of being bullied by the sectarians on one hand and the secularists on the other. And he talks about the revival of civil religion. Do you believe that's the fundamental religion of the United States, a sort of civil religion coming out of Jefferson, Washington, Lincoln? The fact that every inaugural address addresses God, but not Jesus, is cited by some as evidence of this civil religion.

SEN. DANFORTH: Yes, that makes sense. Americans generally have a very deep religious faith, a very historic religious faith. Some are committed to very specific creeds: they go to church, they read their Bible or whatever, they believe and practice their religion—it's got some substance to it. There are other people who think that religion simply means keeping the Golden Rule. There are all kinds of different beliefs. The language of "civil religion" makes room for everybody.

KOLBENSCHLAG: In terms of political candidacy, say you had been a pastor for many years and had built up a considerable reputation and were greatly loved by the people, and so forth. Do you think that the special credibility that sometimes goes with that clerical role would in any way create an unfair advantage over another candidate?

SEN. DANFORTH: No. Because I think that it would have, again, pluses and minuses. Say, if you were the pastor of First Presbyterian Church and you had ardent followers, some of them might vote for you because they thought you shouldn't be wasted in the parish and should be put in public office. Some might vote against you because they wanted to keep you in your church job. The people across the street at the First Methodist Church might vote for you because they want to get you out of the competitor's church, and they might vote against you because you're a Presbyterian.

KOLBENSCHLAG: You mentioned something about your own view, an incarnational view, and I thought maybe you could say a little bit more about that, the connection between the political and religious dimensions. Do you think the Kingdom of God will be accomplished through politics? Is that what you're about?

SEN. DANFORTH: No. I don't think it'll be accomplished through politics. But I think that we have a duty to try to further it and make things better, to try to be ambassadors of the reconciliation, extensions of the incarnation, and operate as God's people in God's world to the best of our ability. I think all of us have that calling. That's not just a clergy job. And, I think that it would be a mistake to say arbitrarily and artificially that one particular way of doing that should be ruled out, that certain occupations should be off limits. That, to me, would be not right.

KOLBENSCHLAG: Our society, for all practical purposes, works against any notion that there is a separation between the sacred and secular domain. Therefore, it would seem that if you believe in the incarnational view of life then there would be nothing that would be closed out. Is that your view?

SEN. DANFORTH: Depending on the specifics of denominational creed or an individual's own views, there are sometimes reasons for not being involved. Of course, a pacifist would not be a soldier. And I can see that a Catholic probably wouldn't want to have anything to do with abortion. But I don't think that that should be expanded into some view of compartmentalization or separation of "spheres."

KOLBENSCHLAG: We hear a lot about politics being dirty and corrupting. Do you think politics has really deepened your faith and developed your spirituality?

SEN. DANFORTH: When you're a candidate and you're under fire, you do an awful lot of praying! Seriously, we have to realize that the Kingdom of God will not be accomplished by human efforts alone—so the Christian officeholder finds it possible to work strenuously for goals which often fall short of perfection. The relationship between ordination and politics has to do with trying to extend the presence of God in the world. Politics is a calling. Not only does it *not* seem to be in conflict with my priesthood—it seems meaningful to me, fruitful. As an Episcopal priest, in my political role and political decisions, I'm doing my own thing. I mean, nobody gives me orders. And I think if anybody tried to, then the people of Missouri would feel that they'd been shortchanged. I just don't see that there is a conflict. To be able to celebrate communion and then come down to the Senate seems to me to be a wonderful thing to do. It seems to me to be closely related, of a piece. The people who show up at my communion service on Tuesdays have jobs and roles too. And I think that they feel that it has something to do with their lives, too, that their lives shouldn't be compartmentalized, that this is their way of being nourished for those tasks and roles. Christ, who was present once upon a time at a particular place, is present in them, and in their lives, and in what they're doing in the world. And I think that they believe that as much as I do.

Emily George, RSM

GOVERNANCE, DISCERNMENT AND MEDIATION: THE COMMUNITY AND RELIGIOUS IN POLITICS

I write about religious in politics from the perspecitive of someone en-gaged in the governance of her religious community. I am a member of the central administration of the Sisters of Mercy of the Union. I was also personally involved in what is now called the Mansour case. Agnes Mary Mansour and I entered the Sisters of Mercy of the Union together and have been close friends for over thirty years. I was with her the day she was released from her vows.

When Agnes Mary joined the Sisters of Mercy in 1953, she wanted to become a physician. She was a medical technologist, was certain to be considered for an advanced degree, and had been drawn to the Sisters of Mercy as a congregation heavily invested in health care. At that time, however, Sisters of Mercy were canonically barred from the med-ical profession, a situation that has changed dramatically.

Agnes Mary went on to become a biochemist. She subsequently taught as a college professor and then assumed the presidency of Mercy College of Detroit in 1971. As early as 1980 she began to discuss her leaning toward politics with her provincial, Helen Marie Burns. She sought additional counsel on this inclination from others, includ-ing the diocesan bishop. The effects of public policy on what she was attempting to achieve as an educator in a very depressed city intensi-fied her conviction that politics for a religious could be a legitimate choice of ministry. The ministerial directions of the congregation au-thenticated this point of view. Accordingly, Helen Marie and her ad-ministrative board encouraged Agnes Mary to continue her search.

In late spring 1981, Michigan's 17th Congressional district un-expectedly became vacant. Agnes Mary was ready. With the deadline

336

for filing imminent, and before she or Helen Marie could contact the new Archbishop of Detroit, Edmund Szoka, Agnes Mary's candidacy was in the press. The Archbishop did not make an issue of the oversight, however, and Agnes Mary went on to the primary election where she was defeated.

With the election of Governor James Blanchard three months later, Agnes Mary's name surfaced for Michigan director of social services. Supporting this possibility, both Agnes Mary and Helen Marie sought Archbishop Szoka's approval. Although he advised Agnes Mary to say little about abortion or else to adopt his statement as her own (she had worked out her own nuanced position with the help of other bishops and theologians), he approved her appointment as consistent with her gifts, with the works of mercy, and with the moral tradition of the church as it affected Medicaid funding. The remainder of the story has to be read against this backdrop.

As I recall what happened between December 1982 and May 1983, the five month period that spanned Agnes Mary's appointment as Michigan director of social services and her canonical dispensation, I have had to examine the role the provincial and central administrations were allowed to play in this serious congregational conflict with the hierarchy. In stating the matter this way I have already pointed to what I perceive to be the problem, namely, that the congregation was reduced to a passive role in the case; was, in effect, rendered impotent in mediating the difficulty between one of its members, Agnes Mary Mansour, and church authority. Essentially the hierarchy carried on no dialogue with the congregation nor thought it should. At crucial points in the controversy the hierarchy ignored the congregation altogether. Two examples immediately come to mind. Anticipating that there would be difficulty over senate confirmation of Agnes Mary because of the controversy generated by her stand on Medicaid funding, Helen Marie contacted Archbishop Szoka's office offering to meet with the prelate before the hearing. He never returned the call but rather informed Agnes Mary a few days later that he was withdrawing permission. The second example involves the failure of the Congregation of Religious and Secular Institutes (SCRIS) to reply to a six-point inquiry made by Mercy President Theresa Kane for clarification on the SCRIS mandate that Agnes Mary resign. When the answer was given it was two months after Agnes Mary's dispensation and it was authored not by SCRIS, but by the special delegate for the case who claimed to reflect Vatican thinking.

Bringing these facts forward, I believe, can help us discover the appropriate and necessary role persons in religious governance should play in dealing with the complex reality that politics has become for many of their members. While the focus of the Mansour case was on Medicaid funding, also at stake was the issue of religious persons with "ecclesial" identity in politics. Bishop Anthony Bevilacqua pointed this out to Agnes Mary in his formal precept demanding her resignation. Therein he quoted John Paul II's warning to religious at Puebla that they stay out of politics, a sentiment that the Bishop noted had also been addressed in the 1978 SCRIS document on Religious Life and Human Promotion (RLHP).

While the Medicaid issue, therefore, continued to carry the weight of ecclesiastical disapproval in the Mansour case, political office was not far behind and it became central a year later when Union Mercy Arlene Violet made her intention known that she would make a second bid for the office of Rhode Island attorney general. To avoid open confrontation with her diocesan bishop, Louis Gelineau, Arlene also announced that she was seeking dispensation from her vows. Shortly after, Bishop Gelineau released a press statement in which he said that the church did not consider public office appropriate for priests and religious. The reasons? Politics substituted for the real work of religious (RLHP) and the new Code forbade it. Furthermore, John Paul II had made his mind clear on the matter. To support an exemption in Arlene Violet's case would be to redirect the course the Vatican has set, according to Bishop Gelineau.

If Bishop Gelineau is correct then little more need be said about religious in politics. Best that persons in congregational governance get themselves and their members behind the Code as he has interpreted it. We know, however, that a few priests and religious continue in public office with church approval, a fact which suggests that the Code is not as ironclad as the Rhode Island bishop had made it out to be. Clergy and religious have been elected or appointed to political offices in a number of states, among them Arizona, Iowa, Michigan, Ohio, Minnesota, and New York.

The issue will not go away for religious themselves, particularly for women religious. Evidence of this is the action taken by the March 1984 general chapter of Sisters of Mercy of the Union regarding Arlene Violet and Elizabeth Morancy. (Elizabeth was seeking a fourth term as Rhode Island state representative). The chapter extended its love and concern to Arlene, now dispensed, and pledged continued effort to clarify the role of religious in public life. Wishing to address the distinctive character of Elizabeth Morancy's position in the legislature—a part-time service paying a token stipend along with a record of achievement on behalf of the poor—and not wishing to jeopardize the conclusions of a congregational study on the appropriateness of political ministry for Sisters of Mercy, the chapter instructed Theresa Kane to request an indult granting Elizabeth a dispensation from the canons prohibiting public office for priests and religious. [Subsequently the indult was refused and Elizabeth Morancy sought a dispensation from vows in order to continue her service in public office.—Editor's note] The spirit that moves women religious to persist in removing ministerial boundaries flows from the conviction that action in the public sphere is a contemporary manifestation of their historical works of service. Once sisters saw that the causes of human misery were embedded in social structures and institutions, they were no longer satisfied to serve only in therapeutic ministries. They experienced themselves called to influence and change systems. Movement in that direction has meant political involvement for many; and, for a few, public office.

What, then, is the role of religious governance as this movement gains momentum, even in the face of some episcopal opposition and the disapproval of the current pontiff? Can persons in leadership hope to mediate what has become controversial, if not conflictual? The answer is yes, because the issue of religious in politics is still too ambiguous to close experimentation and discussion. The initial place to engage the debate is within and among those religious congregations that believe their members have a place in the public sector. Ironically, for the Sisters of Mercy of the Union, this debate was begun not within the congregation, but prompted by an inquiry from the outside—from the Vatican.

In July 1982 Archbishop Augustin Mayer, SCRIS Secretary, wrote to Theresa Kane asking for her position on the candidacy of Arlene Violet, who was then making her first bid for attorney general of Rhode Island. The SCRIS request was phrased with special reference to canon 139 of the 1917 Code forbidding public office to clerics without episcopal permission, and canon 592 applying this prohibition to religious. Also cited was section "D" of RLHP which dealt with active political involvement as "an exception" for religious. Theresa Kane sought advice from the provincial administrators, from select outside consultants, and from the church-institute committee of the congregation, the research arm for the central administration on issues affecting the congregation's relationship with and in church.

The consultants described the historical conditioning of the two canons, noting the anti-modernist flavor that permeates the entire Code, as well as the particular hierarchical concern that diocesan curates be bound to their parishes. As a result, the consultants questioned the canons' relevance to contemporary times and situations and their suitableness vis-à-vis religious priests. More significantly, they were concerned about the application of clerical norms to religious as a merging of identities. This, they said, was of crucial importance. If non-ordained religious spoke and acted in the name of the church, how then did they differ from the clergy?

In treating of section "D" of RLHP, the consultants pointed out that while the SCRIS document was reserved about religious in politics it did not prohibit such activity absolutely. The critical question concerned ministry for non-clerical religious. Who ultimately decides?—the diocesan bishop or the religious congregation, especially if the latter is pontifical? Further, was political office the "exception" that RLHP indicated it was? Some consultants said yes. As reasons they cited such possibilities as: co-optation by the system; hardening ideologies; conflict of interest and identity in being both a religious and a politician. At base these consultants questioned whether or not the compromise inherent in the civil governing process and in legislating for a society of conflicting values contradicted the unambiguous radical witness to gospel imperatives which religious are required to give.

Other consultants took issue with what "exception" the RLHP document connoted, namely, that there were areas of human development fundamentally alien to, or at least secondary to, the religious calling. Most of these consultants were dismayed by one of the primary strains they detected in the entire RLHP document: the fostering of the old dualisms between the secular and the sacred, between the existential and the ideal—dualisms they saw as effecting the separation of religious from the world. These consultants further spoke about choices of ministry flowing from the baptismal commitment common to all members of the church. To this end they cited *Lumen Gentium, Justice in the World, Octogesima Adveniens,* and *Evangelii Nuntiandi.* To support their point of view they noted how insistent RLHP was that religious witness in defense of human rights, be just in every aspect of their lives, be open to the signs of the times, and be in solidarity with persons of good will in promoting a just social order. Given the condition of the world, these consultants believed that religious were among the best suited to dedicate themselves to the transformation of society and to be advocates for the voiceless. They saw political office as consistent with these goals.

How, then, to answer Archbishop Mayer's request to Theresa Kane? The consultants offered three diverse possibilities. The first was to spend little time on the subject, since Rome was not about to change, and to address the canons in general terms. The second was to wait until after the November elections (Arlene Violet was expected to make a good showing but not win) and in the interim to engage other groups and persons in the discussion, inculding the apostolic delegate and Archbishop Mayer. The third was not to debate the canons at all but to present Rome with the pastoral dimension of politics in the United States, supported by the impressive pastoral history of women religious in this country. This latter view would also have Theresa Kane dwell on the right of religious congregations to choose their ministries and would have the issue of public office subsumed under the evangelical imperative incumbent on the whole church to be involved in social justice concerns and in "human promotion."

By fall when Theresa Kane had gathered this information, the congregation was already planning for a spring 1983 session of the general chapter. Because of the timing, she wrote Archbishop Mayer that she would like to delay answering his request until the chapter could deal with the question of public office. This was faithful to RLHP which exhorts chapters to bring their members into thoughtful dialogue regarding politically oriented ministries appropriate to their own culture.

To prepare the chapter for this discussion, the central administration asked the church-institute committee to develop a statement premised on Archbishop Mayer's request. The committee was into the initial phase of its research when Agnes Mary Mansour was named Michigan director of social services. Within two months of her appointment, Detroit Archbishop Edmund Szoka withdrew his permission, thereby setting in motion the events that culminated in Agnes Mary's dispensation in May 1983.

A month earlier when the chapter delegates had gathered they were perplexed about what they were to do with the statement prepared by the church-institute committee. Without specifically raising the issue of what action the congregation might take should there be a conflict with the diocesan bishop, the committee argued that a case could be made, from RLHP itself, to allow public office for qualified religious. The committee indicated further that they could draw no definite conclusions about the subject in the absence of significant experience. They therefore urged continued experimentation and discernment. Only partially aware of what had transpired between Agnes Mary and Archbishop Szoka since February, the delegates could not comprehend the gravity or the immediacy of the situation. When Agnes Mary, herself a delegate, Arlene Violet and Elizabeth Morancy, a third term Rhode Island legislator, addressed the chapter concerning their real and anticipated conflict with the hierarchy, the delegates were outdistanced. Frustrated by the discussion and apprehensive about the central administration's increased difficulty with the Vatican over the tubal ligation issue, they voted to recess until fall.

By September the chapter was in a better position to deal with difficult issues; they were also minus one delegate: Sister Agnes Mary Mansour. Prior to the session a small group of delegates, concerned about what had happened and desiring to engage the chapter in a serious discussion, polled the delegates on aspects of the Mansour case they were ready and willing to consider at the forthcoming session. At the chapter participants also heard particulars of the story from members of the central and province administrations. As a result they decided on a two-pronged strategy. The first was a public statement decrying the injury that had been done to Agnes Mary, the church, and the congregation by the manner in which the case had been handled. The delegates called upon the hierarchy to establish and/or activate processes whereby justice could be served more adequately. As their second strategy the delegates mandated a study to test forms of political ministry appropriate to the charism of Mercy. The total membership of the Sisters of Mercy was to be involved. Specifically the study was to incorporate the experiences and the perspectives of Mercy sisters in the Latin American and Caribbean regions, as well as in the United States. The congregation is currently engaged in that effort.

So far I have described how the Sisters of Mercy of the Union were led to examine public office for their members and how this examination has been diffused throughout the congregation. Congregation leadership has played a role in this process, a mediating role in bringing diverse elements within and without the congregation to bear on the issue.

As the Mansour case and those involving the two Rhode Island Mercy sisters reveal, the leadership has been less successful in serving as a mediating agent vis-à-vis church hierarchy. If there has been anything fruitful resulting from the reaction of the hierarchy as it has affected Sisters of Mercy in politics it has at least defined and sharpened *the questions*:

> For the individual religious who considers public office (presuming she has her congregation's blessing) answers to two major questions regarding identity must be raised. First, does a religious in politics speak and act in the name of the church? Whose theology is operative in answering this question? Second, can one be a religious and wield civil

authority? Is there an inherent contradiction in mixing these roles?

Unanswered for the congregation is the question of fidelity to its mission and the naming of it ministries. If a congregation comes to a position, even provisionally, that a certain ministry (in this case, public office) is appropriate for some of its members, what should its stance be toward church authorities who unilaterally decide otherwise? Pushed to its ultimate, the question for a religious congregation might be: What price canonical status?

For the whole church—the persons served, the religious serving, the hierarchy guiding and preserving the charism—how will we ever test the evangelical legitimacy of public office for religious if we do not allow for the experience? Is it possible to cut off a gift of the Spirit too early? Finally, and perhaps the most important question in this category: Do the people served see religious in politics as persons zealous for the reign of God?

Questions like these will persist, even in an inhospitable ecclesiastical climate. They simply will not go away. As a result, the mediating role of persons administering religious congregations will continue to be tested. What will determine the long-term outcome is the degree of wisdom, charity, and courage both church and congregational authorities bring to the current struggle over religious in politics.

Alan Geyer

THE CHURCH AND VOCATIONAL DEMOCRACY: RELIGIOUS PROFESSIONS AND AMERICAN POLITICS

It is a very audacious thing for a mere Methodist to hold forth on the question as to whether Roman Catholic priests and nuns should hold public office. Some may judge it to be outrageous, remembering past Methodist antipathies to Catholic mixtures of religion and politics.

But I write out of seven years of happy experience in an ecumenical study center devoted to the mixture of religion and politics. At the Churches' Center for Theology and Public Policy in Washington, we have said from the beginning that our prime purpose is "to strengthen the vocations of Christian leadership in the political order." Roman Catholics, Methodists, Episcopalians, Baptists, Presbyterians, Disciples, Greek Orthodox, Lutherans, United Church of Christ folk, Quakers, Brethren, and Mennonites have joined in this purpose. The ethical and ideological differences among us cut across all denominational boundaries.

THE STRUGGLE FOR LEGITIMACY

Our Center has had a very positive experience in balancing the political nurture of clergy with the ministry of the laity in the public sector. What is common to all our participants is a double-edged vocational commitment to religious faith and political responsibility. That commitment means that most of our participants feel somewhat marginal in their own professions, whether clergy or lay, and are constantly caught up in a struggle for legitimacy. If clergy activists seem forever called upon to justify their political action, laity who serve as politicians or bureaucrats frequently lament the lack of vocational respect from their fellow Christians. Some public sector laity testify that

344

the Center for Theology and Public Policy is one place in the church where, at last, they feel they can stand on holy ground as the political creatures they are.

Clearly the vocational mixtures of religion and politics raise serious dilemmas for both the church and the political system. Those in fulltime religious vocations must cope with both the norms of the church and the norms of our democratic polity. It is possible to achieve legitimacy in one of those two realms and be denied legitimacy in the other. A clergyperson may be acceptable to government or party leaders as a candidate for public office but not to religious authorities—or vice-versa. Ecclesial values and the democratic political ethos are not identical.

NEGATIVE PRESUMPTIONS

It is the manifold presumptions against vocations in politics which make this a painfully contentious issue for clergy and other religious vocations. (My use of the term "vocations" in these pages frequently strays beyond the clerical and religious connotations of Catholic usage. That's an incurable habit of some irreverent Protestants.)

Historically, clericalism in Europe, Latin America, and the English colonies bequeathed a bad memory of special privilege, corruption, sectarian strife, and anti-democratic influence.

The American ethos, which has ritually insisted on the separation of church and state, has tended to extend that principle toward political inhibitions on religious leaders. Those inhibitions have been reinforced by the anti-political sentiments of the dominant Protestant culture. As early as 1832, Alexis de Tocqueville observed: "And when I came to inquire into the prevailing spirit of the clergy, I found that they made it the pride of their profession to abstain from politics." Catholics have tended to prove their Americanism by similar abstention. Whether it is pride or timidity which best explains clergy disaffection from politics in the 1980's is an open question.

The recent involvement of nuns in politics, most emphatically through what they unabashedly call *political ministry* through their Network lobby, is quite a departure from their abstention in earlier generations. That abstention was caricatured in Robert Penn Warren's prize political novel of the 1940s, *All the King's Men*, in which a veteran party boss declares to a rather innocent newcomer: "Politics is not like Easter week in a nunnery." Since the 1960s, nuns and nunneries have been caught in generational conflicts between their historic constraints and the activist imperatives of justice and peace.

Those priests and preachers who have become political activists in recent decades have typically confronted resistance from some of their laity, particularly from upper class business and professional persons, especially in predominantly white churches. Fears of a new clericalism and of unseemly controversy within the churches have strengthened the presumptions of many Christians against religious vocations in politics.

Current Vatican strictures against religious vocations in politics thus reinforce historic and widespread inhibitions in American society. At the same time all popes since Pius XII have given powerful impetus to political involvement by their uncompromising commitments to peace, economic justice, and human rights. It is this apparent contradiction between prophetic commands and vocational constraints that has so deeply troubled both Catholic and non-Catholic progressives on such issues.

PROFESSIONAL LIABILITIES

It would surely be folly to claim that all clergy and religious should present themselves as candidates to the electorate or to executive agencies. Many, if not most, should not. In a truly democratic polity, no profession is entitled to preferment for public office—of which we shall say more later.

It is also true that every profession brings its own peculiar liabilities to the give-and-take of political life. Of course, controversy is of the very essence of democratic politics. Churches have chronic troubles handling conflict. Many religious professionals have a trained incapacity to cope creatively with controversy and conflict. They may have an aversion to all dissensus—or, oppositely, they may give vent too readily to absolutism, moral indignation, and messianic pretensions which make the necessary political arts of compromise, conciliation, and consensus much harder to practice. They are likely to be naive about the struggle for power, thin-skinned in the face of attack, and humorless before their adversaries. For other clergy, politics can actually be an exhilarating escape from the full and demanding round of parish ministry.

None of these all-too-typical liabilities of religious vocations, however, warrants any principle of absolute exclusion from political leadership or public office. It is precisely because every vocation has characteristic limitations—and also unique gifts—that a truly free society needs a philosophy of *vocational democracy*. It is not only the church that may prescribe the dos and don'ts of public office: the secular polity rightly asserts its own claims on all its citizens.

PROFESSIONAL DEFENSES

Many, if not most, professions have armed themselves with defenses against sharing fully in the responsibilities of governing a free society. Church leaders need to become much more aware of the degree to which their own vocational defenses are matched by those of other fields of work. Clerical exemptions from politics lose some of their categorical imperative when viewed in cross-professional perspective.

As a political science professor, I once taught an evening class to working students ranging from the mid-20s to the mid-40s. One of their assignments was to write a term paper explaining why they were Democrats, Republicans, Socialists, or whatever. It was a very frustrating assignment for many of them—as I knew it would be.

A newspaper reporter said he couldn't be active in politics because it would be bad for his journalistic credibility.

Several public school teachers thought any political activity would debase the "objectivity" of their teaching.

A doctor and a businessman both asserted that they couldn't afford to mix politics with their professions.

And, to be sure, a minister expressed the fear that his congregation would oppose any partisanship on his part. "I have never expressed my political views in public," he declared.

PROFESSIONAL PROPORTIONALITY

It is these multiple professional excuses for a non-political lifestyle which have often permitted serious distortions of the policies, legislation, and service of governments at all levels in the United States. In particular, it is the gross disproportion of lawyers in public office which has made effective and humane governance hard to come by.

Thomas Jefferson was prophetic in warning of the troubles too many lawyers could impose on the prospects for free government in America. A lawyer himself, he worried greatly about the unprincipled young lawyers of his time who were much absorbed in the legalisms (he called them "wily sophistries") of the works of Hume and Black-stone. In a letter to H.G. Spafford in 1814, Jefferson wrote that the books of Blackstone and Hume "have done more towards the suppression of the liberties of man, than all the million of men in arms of Bo-naparte and the millions of human lives with the sacrifice of which he will stand loaded before the judgment seat of his Maker." Extravagant language perhaps, but Jefferson would rightly be distressed today by the litigiousness of public justice, the costliness of legal counsel, and the presumption that the legal profession has a virtual if not proper monopoly on access to public office.

At the very least, religious professionals offer some alternative experience and countervailing perspective to those offered by attorneys. Of course, there come occasionally those triple-threat personalities who combine multiple vocations in their political careers. Lawyer-priest-professor Robert Drinan, upon whom our Center in 1981 conferred the first Barbara Ward Award for Christian Leadership in the Political Order, was obliged to retire from a prophetic career in Congress precisely because of his pluralistic vocation. He stepped down with grace in the face of a Vatican directive—but Father Drinan, with a brave show of pride and wit, declared that his years of service in Congress were the most important "ministry" in his entire life. Many congressional colleagues and many church folk felt keenly that the forces for peace, civil rights, and economic justice were severely diminished by his forced retirement.

DOUBLE-STANDARD

There is an unexposed double-standard in all this. Priests may be employed by the government in a *military* capacity as chaplains but not in a *civilian* capacity as politicians or administrators. This is not said in disrespect for the military chaplain's public office. In fact, one of the most heartening developments in my recent experience has been the repeated invitation to address chaplains' conferences on the issues of peacemaking. In particular, the Roman Catholic priests who now head both the U.S. Air Force chaplains and the Air Force Reserve chaplains have been notably responsive to the teaching mandates of the U.S. Bishops' Pastoral Letter on War and Peace. They have provided open forums in which the chaplains of various faiths could hear and speak to divergent convictions on the ethics and politics of peace.

Why, then, should civilian public office, as a base for work for peace or social justice, be denied to clergy?

BLACK EXPECTATIONS

In our pluralistic religious culture, whatever the constraints on white clergy in political matters, the Black heritage fosters the expectation that pastors will become political activists. As a pastor in an interracial inner city church in Newark some years ago, I was struck by this pattern of conflicting role expectations: many white members were at least troubled at the thought of political action by their pastors, while Black members generally expected and even demanded it. Black clergy have been, and continue to be, the prime public champions of the Black political agenda. Adam Clayton Powell, Martin Luther King, Jr., Andrew Young, Jesse Jackson, and Walter Fauntroy all powerfully exemplify that tradition. (Apparently, Black Catholic priests have been less inclined toward political activism.)

What shall white church authorities say to this? Is it either un-Christian or undemocratic for Andy Young to be a mayor or congressman or United Nations ambassador? Is it illegitimate, on any grounds, for Jesse Jackson to run for president? Is it theologically or ethically wrong for Walter Fauntroy to represent the District of Columbia in Congress, even while he continues to pastor a Baptist church in Washington?

The fact that these preachers are all Protestants hardly relieves white Protestants from asking the same questions Catholics must now ask about such men. Is there any peculiarly Roman Catholic dogma, not shared by Protestants but central to Catholic faith and morals, which is violated by clergy politicians or bureaucrats?

THE POWERS OF MINISTRY

Perhaps the beginning of a healthy, humane perspective on this issue is to acknowledge that *all acts of Christian ministry have power implications*. Worship, Christian education, confession, counseling, visitation, administration, community leadership: none of these aspects of ministry takes place in a power vacuum. All of them are political, in some sense. A priest who maintains a constant silence in the face of grave public injustice becomes a partisan of the status quo: he is hardly non-political. A preacher whose moral convictions are dumped on her congregation only in monologues, without opportunity for talk-back or for alternative voices in her pulpit, has an unfair power advantage which may boomerang. A clergyman who lunches with the Rotary Club but never with labor union leaders or social workers is a biased political actor thereby. A pastor who visits the sick and prizes her special ties to physicians and hospital administrators, but never raises systemic questions about social and economic inequities in this nation's health care, sanctions the power and privileges of the medical-industrial complex.

Becoming conscious of these inescapably political dimensions of ministry does not necessarily argue for abandoning a congregation to seek a job on the public payroll or to be a candidate for Congress. Most clergy should continue in the work for which they were specifically trained: fulltime service to the church. But they should become much more self-aware of their identities as political animals, both in the generality of their human nature and the specificity of their profession.

POLITICAL ANIMALS

Over a period of some years, it has been my privilege to help conduct a number of clinics and conferences on the theme, "The Pastor as a Political Animal." The purpose of such encounters is not to recruit candidates for electoral politics: it is to help clergy become creatively self-conscious about the power dimensions of ministry in every role they perform. One of the inevitable outcomes is the discovery that pastors and politicians are engaged in many of the same tasks—not just hand-shaking and baby-kissing but the arts of public communication, promoting the common good, direct service to persons and families in special need, balancing the conflicting opinions and claims of their constituencies.

It is precisely these similarities between religious and political vocations which help equip some priests and pastors and nuns for public office. And it seems to me an injustice both to such persons and, more important, to the clamorous needs of society, to subject religious vocations to any absolute principle of categorical exclusion. Perhaps it could also be argued that the very principle of separation of church and state should be interpreted to mean that religious authority should not be permitted to impose any professional exclusions or excuses on a free society. (That is a line of argument which seriously tempts me but is beyond my present reflections on this issue. There is strong biblical warrant, however, for believing that the church itself has no monopoly on the understanding of justice. The record of government in civil rights over the past three decades, while it owes much to religious influence, has surpassed the performance of the churches themselves in some matters of racial justice.) After all, the norms of a democratic political order can, at times, have a redemptive influence on ecclesiastical institutions. That has been a large part of church history in the West.

PRINCIPLES OF VOCATIONAL DEMOCRACY

More positively, what principles of vocational democracy may help us think through this issue of public service for religious professionals?

1. *Vocational democracy requires vocational pluralism.*

No profession is entitled to a monopoly of political power. Having noted the perils of legalism and litigiousness which flow from an excess of lawyers, and also the baneful history of clericalism and inequities of medical entrepreneurialism, we may note the characteristic deficiencies of still another profession which has played a dominant political role at times: business. Shortly before joining the Nixon administration, loaded as it was with corporate executives, Professor Henry Kissinger wrote of the trained incapacities of such executives to cope with the political demands of foreign policy:

> The special skill of the executive is thought to consist in coordinating well-defined functions rather than in challenging them. The procedure is relatively effective in the business world, where the executive can often substitute decisiveness, long experience, and a wide range of personal acquaintance for reflectiveness. In international affairs, however—especially in a revolutionary situation—the strong will which is one of our business executives' notable traits may produce essentially arbitrary choices... The business elite is even less able or willing than the lawyer to recognize that the formulation of an issue, not the technical remedy, is usually the central problem. (*American Foreign Policy*, New York: W.W. Norton and Co., 1969, 32.)

Thus priests and nuns should not be cowed by the presumed expertise of lawyers or business executives in the work of government.

2. *Vocational democracy requires cross-professional leadership to cope with the complexity of modern government.*

Government has increasingly generated intellectual and practical needs which parallel the growing need for cross-disciplinary studies in higher education. One of our eye-opening experiences at the Center for Theology and Public Policy has been a pattern of serendipity: the unexpected discovery by professionals in one specialty of the insights they may gain from professionals in another specialty, often in the same general area of policy. Government itself doesn't always do a very good job of integrating the specialties required for its own best performance. Developing a holistic view of a complex, many-faceted problem is one of the prime requirements of public leadership today. One of our Center's most active policy panels has been in the field of urban policy. In one sense, urban policy is itself a specialty. But in another sense, it is the bewildering intersection of many specialties. It's only when you can gather together members of Congress and their staffs, bureaucrats, local officials, economists, social workers, urban health professionals, transportation experts, social ethicists, and inner city pastors—not to mention low-income workers, unemployed persons, and victims of systemic violence—that a rounded picture of urban policy and its challenges can begin to emerge.

3. *Vocational democracy lays burdens on every profession which serves serious human needs.*

Every profession must, in its own distinctive forms, nurture and celebrate politics as a vocation. No profession, on its own, is entitled to exemption from sharing in the burdens of governance. In an age when every area of human need has come into the purview of government, those whose work brings them into most intimate contact with those needs ought to be represented in the councils of government. This politicization of personal, family, and community problems can perhaps, with much difficulty, be made responsive to moral and spiritual values: it can hardly be wholly undone. Humane perspectives on the impacts of technology and social systems have become one of the highest requisites of public policy.

There is indeed a place for pastoral sensitivity and experience in both the legislative process and bureaucratic management. Pastors tend to be veterans of constituency service. If religious vocations are unique in any respect, they are servants of the sanctity of personhood in any and every institution. If they, too, can help to nurture and celebrate politics as a vocation, they may help mightily to overcome the anti-political prejudices which the churches themselves have so unfortunately fostered, to the detriment of the people.

4. *Vocational democracy requires a steadfast commitment to the common good.*

The fragmentation of American government by constitutional design—federalism, separation of powers, checks and balances—has been compounded in recent years by the surge of technical specializations, the proliferation of congressional subcommittees, the disarray of political parties, and the ascendancy of special interests and single-issue politics. Coherent government in the public interest has become a more and more daunting challenge.

While religious professionals sometimes take too narrow a view of their own ecclesiastical interests, or plunge into single-issue crusades with fractious fervor, many pastors do succeed in transcending such interests and issues: they achieve a more comprehensive perspective on society, its problems and its promises. Such an achievement is not necessarily a matter of personal virtue. It may simply reflect the fact that the institution which trained them and which they serve, the Church, is unique among private institutions in its commitment to the general welfare. At least, it is called to be a disinterested "Church for Others," even as Jesus Christ was and is the One for Others.

So there may be a special place, now and then, here and there, for a priest or a preacher or a nun in the vocation of politics.

Madonna Kolbenschlag, HM

INTERVIEW WITH
GOVERNOR RICHARD CELESTE

KOLBENSCHLAG: Do you believe that appointing priests or sisters to public office, or electing them, compromises the principle of separation of church and state in any way?

GOV. CELESTE: Not in my judgment. I've worked with religious people in Protestant denominations and in the Catholic religion, both in elected and appointed office, and I don't believe the fact that they served in government constituted a compromise in the traditional understanding of the separation of church and state. It raises a problem only if they were to purport to speak for the church in that role. If there is a dilemma of conscience, it stems from the fact that you take a Constitutional oath when you assume an elected or an appointed office, and each individual has to weigh the extent to which that oath is congruent with one's commitment to the church or religious order.

KOLBENSCHLAG: Is this compromised at all by the fact that sometimes although the appointing officer under whom this person serves has no problems and the clergyman or sister in government does not see himself or herself as a spokesperson for the church, but the general electorate or public might, even though that's an inaccurate perception? Does that complicate this question?

GOV. CELESTE: I think it may. In a way, it's less of a problem where the person is elected because when you're elected to office you go through a public clarification process. At least in the constituency you serve. I think the voters are pretty clear who it is they have elected in that office. The candidates have been tested and perceptions clarified by the electoral process, in a way that isn't necessarily the case when a person accepts an appointment to an office.

KOLBENSCHLAG: Could it complicate the political process in any way? Say, for example, if you were opposed in an election by another candidate who was a priest or a sister, would that present special problems for you as the competitor? Does the candidate who is a priest or a sister have an unfair advantage, or even a handicap?

GOV. CELESTE: Not in my judgment because I think a person who happens to be a priest or a sister would probably enjoy about the same opportunity of getting, for example, the Catholic vote as I could enjoy as a Methodist father of six Catholic children. You always have the question of particular appeals to the electorate. I'm an Italian-American. Does that give me an edge in a district where there are a substantial number of Italian-Americans, and my opponent is Irish? In my primary race for Lt. Governor in 1974, there was a Black candidate, there was a female candidate, each of whom were appealing to a constituency I wanted to win. I think it forces you to be clearer about what the choice is—why you're in the race, what it is that you believe and stand for—so that people will vote for you. I think very few people today would be inclined to vote for someone simply because that person happens to be a priest or a sister. My hunch is that the priest or sister may have to overcome more inhibitions on the part of the electorate, rather than gain by virtue of built-in advantages from, say, expectations of exceptional honesty or integrity.

KOLBENSCHLAG: There are fears right now about the mission of the church being compromised by the presence and involvement of priests and sisters in political offices. Do you think those fears are justified?

GOV. CELESTE: I think that if the expectation of the church hierarchy, in terms of mission, is a vocation in which all of one's time is spent in church-based ministry, then to be a candidate for public office, and hold public office, is clearly a distraction. It compromises the "mission" not in principle, but practically, in terms of time. If, however, one perceives the notion of ministry and service in a broader sense—which I think is the sense in which "mission" is now perceived by many religious—then it could be teaching, it could be administering a particular facility. Sisters run hospitals, for example. Well, I think you can minister as effectively as a member of a Governor's cabinet as you can as the administrator of a hospital. In that respect, the "mission" is not compromised. The trouble arises where, for example, I might ask a priest to become my director of rehabilitation and correction and we have a capital punishment law on the books. Part of his responsibility as the director would be to recommend, finally, whether I exercise clemency or permit an execution to go forward; that's tough.

KOLBENSCHLAG: One of the arguments often proposed is that clergy and religious should serve in government only in cases of absolute necessity, in countries, for example, where there is widespread illiteracy, or in situations where the body politic is not adequately organized to meet certain needs and people do not come forward. Or, it's so corrupt that there is a reason for clergy and religious to drop some of the other things they're doing and make themselves available for public service. Do you believe that that kind of restriction should apply to clergy and religious in the United States?

In other words, would you say that there is a need for their service in government here, or that there is no need?

GOV. CELESTE: I think the absolute necessity argument is absolutely elitist! It's a perfectly patriarchal idea. I mean *who* makes that judgment? Who makes the assumption that someone who happens to be virtually illiterate couldn't in fact turn out to be a strikingly capable leader in many respects?

KOLBENSCHLAG: There's a corollary question here, and that is, given the fact that there isn't a need for clergy and religious in any absolute sense, on the other hand, isn't there a necessity for everyone to participate if our system is to work? What Alan Geyer calls "vocational democracy"?

GOV. CELESTE: That's precisely what was implicit in my comment. There is a grave danger in assuming, "Well, America can get along without me." Sure it's quite possible that it can get along without any one of us at a particular point in time. But it seems to me that part of leadership in a democracy is weaving together different elements of background and temperament, and even different moral perspectives and experience, into the leadership team and the decision-making process. Democratic leadership isn't one person exercising his or her will, but it is a process of decision-making and consensus in which a number of people are involved and there is real give and take. My concern stems in some measure from the notion that one becomes contaminated by participating in this process within a political structure that is less than perfect and always will stand in need of God's grace and God's redemption. I hope that I can do God's work as a public official, but I don't imagine that what I'm doing is perfect. I must keep reminding myself that I'm going to do the best that I can with the knowledge and experience that I have and within the political context in which I operate.

KOLBENSCHLAG: You have appointed some people to government positions who belong to religious orders and have considered others, I'm sure. Knowing that it was a sensitive issue, what criteria did you use and were there any other factors that you took into consideration?

GOV. CELESTE: I chose the people for the jobs that I've asked them to do because of the *experience* and the *commitment* that they bring to their work. I'll let them be a judge of the controversial aspect of it. I hope there isn't any.

KOLBENSCHLAG: In other words, you treat that as if it were their business and not yours?

GOV. CELESTE: That's right. Anyone that I choose, either individually or as a member of some kind of group or constituency might be controversial. I've chosen six blacks for my cabinet. When you choose more than one or two members of a minority, some people begin to get upset. They—usually the white male political power structure—think it's too many. I've chosen six women for my cabinet. Some people are upset about that. I've chosen people who were not experts—for example, a tax commissioner, a woman who's a former County Commissioner. She's never been an accountant, or an auditor, or a tax expert. At first, people didn't believe that common sense was a sufficient qualification. Now they do, eighteen months later. But I'm a great believer that there are ways to make the whole more than the sum of its parts. We all have weaknesses, and we all have drawbacks in our experience.

KOLBENSCHLAG: Going back to what you said about the imperfection of the political system, are you suggesting that the synergy that's produced by having more varieties of experience and more commitment involved would help to make up for that imperfection?

GOV. CELESTE: That's right.

KOLBENSCHLAG: Would a priest or a sister serving as a public official, whether elected or appointed, be more vulnerable or less vulnerable to exploitation in any way? You mentioned experience and commitment. Are there factors which might make them less vulnerable?

GOV. CELESTE: I think that's a question that each individual constantly weighs. For example, I asked my Black cabinet members to take a particular interest in the Black constituency. Part of that is to tell me what I'm doing right, and part of that is to tell me what I'm doing wrong. I don't want to limit them to the Black constituency. So, I will have Black cabinet members work with groups that may not be used to working with a Black in a particular position, like the Commerce Director, who works with banks and savings and loans, and happens to be a Black. He goes out and meets with banks and savings and loan executives, most of whom have never met a person in this role who happens to be black. And sometimes he'll tell me when he feels uncomfortable in a particular role. If I say, "Would you represent me at the Hampton Alumni Association meeting?", he'll say, "Look, Dick, I didn't go to a black college or university. I think it would be inappropriate for me to be there." And he should say so. And similarly, if I were to say to Sister Pat, "Would you go to a Diocesan meeting of Senior Center Coordinators," she might say, "Look, that's one I'd rather pass up because I don't want to be there just to kind of dress up the occasion."

KOLBENSCHLAG: You're saying that, from your point of view, that it's up to the individual to resist tokenism.

GOV. CELESTE: Right.

KOLBENSCHLAG: You mentioned a situation where the issue of capital punishment could cause some serious questions for a person in public office who also had a religious commitment. Are there any other positions or issues that might cause that kind of conflict of interest?

GOV. CELESTE: The one that's been encountered most often is probably the issue of abortion. And I think it's a serious dilemma for anyone who's involved in the social service field. It's one that hospital administrators face, and that doctors face. It is confronted over and over again by parish priests in hearing confession. And I don't know how they resolve that dilemma. It is an issue that can come up in probably five or six different departments of state government. Right now, the Constitution of the United States can conflict not only with a person's individual conscience, but with what they believe would be their duty in any official capacity. And I think that's something that an individual needs to weigh very seriously. My view on that matter is to respect freedom of choice and to rely on an informed conscience. As much as I might disagree with the decision that the individual makes regarding abortion, I respect her conscience.

KOLBENSCHLAG: As Catholics we're living now with a situation where canon law forbids priests and religious to hold public office without special exemption. The fact of the situation is that the Vatican is resisting giving any exemptions. So we have an ambiguous situation in the United States, where sisters and priests in one state are allowed to function in state offices and be delegates to the Democratic convention; and in another state, they're forced to renounce their vows if they run for office, or they are suspended from priestly activity if they attend the convention as a delegate. This presents a special ambiguity for Catholic church people. How do you, as a governor, respond to this situation? Do you regard this as undue interference by the church?

GOV. CELESTE: Well, I feel about it a little bit the way I feel about having the president of Ford Motor Company telling me he doesn't want his plant manager to participate in my labor-management cooperation committee. I think he's wrong, but that's his business. In other words, I really regret the posture that, as I understand, really stems from very strong positions that the Holy Father has taken in a number of specific instances—particularly in this hemisphere—I might add, in contrast to the way he deals with Eastern Europe. The Vatican view has encouraged some bishops to believe that priests and religious should not participate in public service. But I think that view deprives us all of tremendous human talent and dedication, and potential strength of leadership. I know it's causing great ambivalence and frustration among many of the people I would consider to be among the best priests and sisters. And I think it's a shame that right now the hierarchy in the church is making it difficult for highly motivated, capable individuals—not all of whom agree with me politically, incidentally—to be candidates for political offices.

KOLBENSCHLAG: It might discourage them from political ministry in general?

GOV. CELESTE: Well, it may discourage people from becoming priests or sisters. I think if the boundaries of service are constrained in this way, particularly in a democracy, then there will be some people who may be turned away from ministry as a priest or sister.

KOLBENSCHLAG: Since the situation is ambiguous, and some get damned for doing it, and others feel damned for not doing it, should religious women and priests avoid getting involved in politics? Especially since, if the bishops do become involved, it does complicate the church-state issue?

For example, after Drinan was asked to leave his office, there were many reports that one Congressman in particular had quite a bit to do with it, and that he and other anti-abortion groups had lobbied the Vatican, saying that Drinan was compromising his position as a priest by supporting the Medicaid legislation. So, in effect, they bypassed the electoral process in order to get someone out of office. The question I'm asking is, if that's the kind of thing that's going to go on, might it be better for church people to stay out of politics?

GOV. CELESTE: Well, that's like saying that the four religious women who were killed in El Salvador should not have been there because of the risk that they might become involved in political controversy. I think that one of the lessons of feminism that we would all do well to learn is that politics is personal, and that the personal is political; and certainly thinking in global terms and not so much personal terms, it is very clear. There is no way we as Christians are above politics. We may not be in it officially in the sense that we hold an office, but if we are concerned about people eating, if we are conerned about equal justice, if we are concerned about survival of the human family, then there's a sense in which we are—and must be—thinking politically. My hunch is that the rest of human history is going to include an ongoing dimension of debate about what is appropriate political involvement for religious institutions and what isn't.

Calling for religious men or women and priests to withdraw from a particular office in order to avoid being implicated doesn't remove the implication. No concerned citizen can be apolitical.

KOLBENSCHLAG: You seem to suggest that you would agree with a statement that came out of the teachings of the Vatican Council, and much of Catholic social teaching, that a constitutive aspect of faith is working for justice. In other words, you can't omit it. Would you agree with that?

GOV. CELESTE: Absolutely. The problem of the appearance of being implicated seems to be what is involved in the issue of holding elective or appointed office. But if you're concerned about the appearance of being implicated, then the parish priest in New Jersey should not permit a campaigning candidate for the Presidency to come in and turn a church dinner into the appearance of endorsement. Again, it's manipulating the appearance.

KOLBENSCHLAG: So for Catholics, it seems to be a question of *who* is going to be allowed to be political. We have an interesting phenomenon taking place in the Catholic Church, where the Pope and bishops are saying, if you are an ordinary priest or sister, you shouldn't be involved in politics; and yet the Pope himself and the American bishops are becoming increasingly more involved in debate on political issues, and speaking out, and influencing people in political ways.

And, of course, the Pope's own activity suggests he's been the most political Pope we've had in this century.

GOV. CELESTE: That's why I made the comment about Eastern Europe, because there it seems clear that he is not disengaging from involvement but engaging, whereas in Latin America he seems to be counseling the Church to try to disengage.

KOLBENSCHLAG: Is this another form of elitism, in that politics is a game that should only be played by the hierarchy?

GOV. CELESTE: Of course it is. And I think it's a dilemma which is going to be a particularly acute for the American bishops, because they are operating in a clearly democratic milieu which is very different from the situation of the Pope and the Vatican looking at Eastern Europe.

And to try to distinguish between the pastoral dimension of the bishops' role in their Peace Pastoral or in the statement they're apparently contemplating on the economy, and the political dimension or impact, would be to try to draw an arbitrary line between thought and action or between faith and morality. Such a line is contrary to the imperatives of my Christian faith as I understand it.

KOLBENSCHLAG: We've certainly seen the controversy about the relationship of religion and politics heat up in the 1984 election. We've always had people in Congress, in state legislatures, and in local legislatures that are ministers, priests and sisters to a lesser extent; but do you think that this controversy will make it more difficult for church people to be involved in politics in a visible way? Or do you think it will, in the long run, create more involvement across the board?

GOV. CELESTE: I think that it may open the door for more involvement in the long run. In the short run, there are some issues that will make it extremely difficult. The opportunities for holding public office for priests or religious women are likely to be overshadowed by what I sense is going to come up very quickly; namely, a debate about reaffirming the constitutional separation of church and state because of Reagan's campaign methods. It's the first time I've seen a President systematically try to manipulate the symbols of religious faith, and to take advantage of people's genuine religious fervor, in a way that breaches the traditional protections that all religions have been assured of. In our pluralistic society, this can be extremely dangerous. My view is that he is an extraordinary hypocrite. When someone like this wants the state to insure that people can pray in school, I wonder. You know, my parents taught me how and when and where to pray, and encouraged me to believe I could pray anywhere. As I told somebody, those prayers may have been the only thing that got me through fifth and sixth grade math. But I don't ever want the government to write the prayers for my children.

KOLBENSCHLAG: The Church seems to have a deep concern about Church people being involved in "partisan politics." Is it possible to make a distinction between "partisan politics" and politics for the common good?

GOV. CELESTE: I always distrust people who try to make that distinction! I just think that it does a disservice to partisan politics. Being partisan doesn't mean not caring about the public good; rather it can express a commitment to the public good through the party you choose to work for. Sometimes people will use a distinction like that to be down on politics generally and act like there's something better. My view is that we operate in a political milieu if we get into elective office or appointive office, and it is not necessarily bad.

KOLBENSCHLAG: When you compare the party politics of the U.S. to that of other countries, say Canada, or Great Britain where they have parliamentary systems, my impression has always been that party agenda and the whole concept of party politics here is far less doctrinaire and ideological than it is in other systems.

GOV. CELESTE: That's right, and the fact is that an awful lot of what we end up accomplishing in the political arena isn't defined by a party line. For many issues, it takes votes from both parties to adopt a new piece of legislation. And if the position is to last, if it's to have any durability, it must be supported by people in more than one party. That's why I'm concerned about folks who sort of look down their noses at partisan politics.

KOLBENSCHLAG: So the goal of partisan politics in our society is far more the building of a consensus, ultimately, than it is taking rigid, ideological positions. Did we see that demonstrated in the process by which the Democratic platform was composed?

GOV. CELESTE: Yes—and it was a real contrast to the Republican platform in Dallas. I think it's ironic—I don't know whether you saw some of the surveys of people coming home from the Republican convention, which indicated that over half of the people at the convention didn't support some party planks—like the failure to support the ERA!

KOLBENSCHLAG: One last question. There are some who question whether people who enjoy tax exemption and, in some cases, exemption from military service, should be allowed to be candidates for political office. Do you think that's a valid argument?

GOV. CELESTE: My view is that if people are willing to elect them, let them serve. That's what our democracy is all about.

Peter Steinfels

SOME SKEPTICAL REFLECTIONS

Should priests and nuns hold political office? My first reaction is that the whole question should not be blown out of proportion.

Of course the question is urgent to those priests and nuns who feel they have political vocations, and to their friends as well, and to the communities which may look to these individuals for leadership. I hope these politically inclined men and women can resolve their personal dilemmas in a way that does justice both to their own talents and to the integrity of their religious commitments. I hope that, one way or another, their constituencies find worthy public representatives. But relevant as this controversy may be to the scores of individuals and local communities involved, against the backdrop of so many human problems this one does not loom large.

The fact is, this question has become a lightning rod for several other issues: the proper distribution of decision-making authority between Rome, local church authorities, and individual conscience; the rethinking of both priestly ministry and the traditional roles of religious orders; the attitude of the church toward social change and political activity. These are the questions that are important. It is because answers to them have often been implied in positions taken on the matter of priests and nuns in politics that the latter issue has justifiably stirred wider interest and strong feelings.

Yet it would be a mistake to assume that positions on the narrower question necessarily and inevitably entail positions on the wider ones. Someone could be passionately opposed to Vatican highhandedness in dealing with particular cases of politically active priests and nuns, or even hold that this question should not be in Rome's bailiwick generally—and still believe, on quite separate grounds, that political office is inappropriate for such religious figures. Someone could be completely open to rethinking ministry and traditional roles for religious orders—and yet, in his or her own rethinking, not conclude to the appropriateness of political office holding. Someone could be a fierce partisan of the church's concern for the political order and social change—and yet conclude that such concern is best served by a division of labor in which political careers fall to the laity. I mention these possibilities here not to defend them, but to remind us not to imagine that more is at stake in the immediate resolution of the narrower question than is necessarily the case.

Perhaps it is already clear that I approach this matter with more than a grain of skepticism, though I hope with not too much. Skepticism about politics, of course, but about priests also. Skepticism to a lesser extent—because they raise issues of a newer sort—about members of religious communities. Such skepticism may seem ungenerous. After all, a number of the leading cases in this controversy have involved individuals known for their labors on behalf of social justice, or certainly what I, at least, would define as social justice. Still, this very fact, I would suggest, militates in favor of my several grains of skepticism: they save us from moving too quickly and non-reflectively from our admiration for the individuals involved to a resolution of the general question that their activities have posed.

My skepticism, to begin with, is the offspring of history. I cannot help but recall that with only a few exceptions—Don Luigi Sturzo comes to mind—the history of clerical involvement in politics is a history of moral disaster. From Cardinal Richelieu to Father Tiso, the Slovakian premier who collaborated with the Nazis in the dismemberment and occupation of Czechoslovakia, priest-politicians have compiled a remarkable record of compromising the Gospel and the church. To be sure, the unsavory alliance of the church with political power went far deeper than an occasional coupling of priesthood and officeholder in a single individual. Prohibiting such a dual role is by no means a sufficient safeguard against all the potential abuses of church by state and state by church. Nonetheless, with all due allowance for possible exceptions and without resolving here and now exactly who should determine such exceptions, it seems that the presumption against priests holding political office is a sensible, small acknowledgment of the lessons we have learned, so belatedly and painfully, from the past. Alexis DeTocqueville had a keen sense of those lessons when he hailed the fact that, although religion was a formative influence on American political life, "American clergy in general . . . keep aloof from parties and from public affairs." On grounds of history alone, I would be tempted to say, "Let priests stay clear of political office for a century or so. Perhaps, then, we could evaluate the experiment and reopen the discussion."

If history feeds my skepticism about the advantages of priestly office holding, I am also impressed with the cogency of the theological argument. As liturgical presider, the priest, in some important sense, must represent the unity of the faithful. As political office holder, he is, in actual fact, the representative not only of a segment of the electorate but of particular interests and ideology. (To cloak this reality by speaking of a political role only in terms of representing or serving the "people" or the "community" or "justice" is to render political life in a dangerously naive and one-sided fashion.)

The priest's ritual responsibilities have given rise to a whole complicated system of education and conduct. Much of it is currently being questioned and revised. Some observers even contemplate the eventual reduction of "priestness" to simple function. It will imply no residue of character, outlook, psychological or symbolic cathexis of spiritual power that would not be shed with the vestments. For some Catholics such a development is unthinkable. For others, priests even more than lay people, it promises a kind of wonderful release from the burden of clericalism. I myself doubt that such a development is desirable or, even more to the point, humanly likely. As long as the church has a sacramental life that has not been stripped, like a Congregational church, to a bare minimum, its priests will be set apart. And this apartness will not cease to pose dangerous temptations.

It is clear to me that even the best-meaning priests active in politics get mileage from their clerical status. People may hold quite different judgments on the Sandinista regime in Nicaragua or on the arguments in favor of an "exception" that allowed priests to serve in the government of a small nation trying to enlist its best talent following a devastating revolutionary struggle. Yet whatever differing judgments may be held on those matters, it seems undeniable that the priesthood of these individuals has been repeatedly put forward—by the government, by its supporters, by others—as a guarantee of the regime's integrity, a kind of Seal of Good Housekeeping, as though ordination were a sure fire vaccination against complicity with authoritarianism.

Whenever any incompatibility between the priesthood and political office holding is suggested, two objections are immediately forthcoming. The first is that the priest is a citizen like any other citizen; he should not be deprived of a citizen's rights. Of course he should not be *deprived* of them—legally barred from seeking office, for instance. But priests are not alone in being asked to willingly refrain from what remains a right on the grounds that seeking office would conflict with a particular vocation. Journalists of the better sort have all kinds of scruples about how closely they should be involved in politics. Sometimes the inhibitions are a matter of a personal code; sometimes they are newspaper policy. Between business and government, military leaders and civilian officials, government workers and elected officials, there are a host of prohibitions to provide necessary distance between potentially conflicting vocations.

The second objection is more substantial. It is true that priests do not celebrate the Eucharist, preach, or conduct other sacramental rites forty hours a week. Many priests have therefore pursued other work, as professors, writers, editors, social workers, lawyers, physicians, psychologists, and administrators; more rarely, although perhaps with better Scriptural warrant, as fishermen, craftsmen, and manual laborers. Certainly many of these vocations present severe ethical challenges on a regular basis, perhaps comparable to the compromises and even illegalities constantly confronted in political life. So why is a political career any different?

It is, and for two reasons. To begin with, the priesthood and political office are not only different tasks, they are also, in striking ways, *similar* tasks. They both involve formal public representation, largely achieved through words and symbolic gestures. It is here that the possibilities for confusion and abuse arise in a way not ordinarily posed for the priest-professor or, say, the priest-steelworker.

The second reason distinguishing political office holding from other vocations is that the state is the ultimate repository of force in society; when necessary, it backs law with coercion; it uses deadly power to defend its place in what remains a largely anarchic international order. That this dimension of the state's life poses special problems for the priesthood has been recognized, at the extreme margin, in the prohibition against priests bearing arms.

From these two reasons, we can draw grounds for differentiating among different kinds of political office holding in regard to their possible incompatibility with the priestly calling. So far I have been using the term in the way it has largely been used in the recent controversies: to refer to elective office, especially above the local level. In such elective office, the element of public representation is to the fore. By contrast, many appointed offices, especially administrative ones, are filled not so much on a representative basis as on a technical one. Those posts, too, may present ethical dilemmas but essentially not very different ones than might be faced by the president of a private university, the administrator of a religiously-affiliated hospital, or the director of a diocesan social agency. One can easily contemplate priests in these roles. One can also contemplate a priest serving on the Civil Rights Commission or some other presidential or blue-ribbon investigating body. Here the particular capacity being sought is precisely a degree of sensitivity to moral issues—or at least a degree of compassionate disinterestedness—that one associates with a religious leader.

Yet even some appointed offices have important representative dimensions. Should a priest serve as Secretary of State, representing the nation in its international conflicts and bargaining? Or serve as White House press secretary, representing an administration's face to the world? I doubt it—not even if the individuals involved had high technical qualifications as diplomats or journalists.

In the same way, one can distinguish among a range of offices, both elective and appointive, in terms of their proximity to the coercive functions of government. A schoolboard member, the head of a local planning board, even a town council member stand at some distance from the state's direct use of force, even though these are elected positions and perhaps questionable on the grounds of their representative character. (Local offices, in addition, often present a reasonable ground for an "exceptional" role for a priest, namely the shortage of comparable talent that may exist within a restricted district; the same argument is far less convincing when advanced at the state or national level.) But a local sheriff's job or District Attorney's, whether appointed or elected, poses far greater problems. Here the state's ultimate recourse to force when needed to resolve conflicts appears to run up against the priest's responsibility to be a sign of reconciliation and unity. And offices like Secretary of Defense, head of the CIA or FBI, although appointed and in many respects "technical" rather than "representative", seem highly incompatible with the priesthood.

Obviously there exists no mechanical formula for resolving all the ambiguities in this area. Nevertheless, as a kind of mental aid, I find it helpful to imagine a graph in which points along the x axis indicate the greater degrees of representative function attaching to different political offices, while points along the y axis indicate increasing degrees of proximity to the state's employment of direct coercion. The further out that any political office might be located from the point where these two axes intersect at a right angle, the less appropriate it would be for a priest to hold that post. It also makes sense to me for the church to set down a few benchmarks along these continuums, e.g., no bearing arms, no elective office.

What if one moves away from the specific issue of political office and considers other highly visible roles in the political arena? Canon Law, for instance, now prohibits priests from holding offices in the trade union movement. I am not certain of the reasoning behind this. I can speculate that the ruling stems from the fact that historically the trade union movement in many nations has been highly politicized or oriented toward class conflict or both. All the considerations pertaining to political office may therefore be relevant in this case as well. But what about the panoply of lobbying organizations, including occupationally based ones, much more typical of American political life? Should a priest-professor serve as an official for the American Association of University Professors, or a priest-surgeon as an official of the AMA?

Perhaps I am mistaken, but the prospect does not really trouble me. I suppose—and this might depend all too much on the discretion of the priests involved—that it would be evident that such individuals were serving in their capacities as professor or physician rather than priest. Nor am I troubled by priests holding positions even as priests on behalf of groups for whom the church could reasonably be assumed to have a special concern—the poor, the afflicted, the excluded. (Nonetheless, the gray areas are obvious. Poor and excluded workers may eventually come to constitute a significant, organized interest group. This suggests the wisdom of priests' preferring an unofficial advisory role to formal office in such movements.)

I am in fact more troubled by the question of priests taking official leadership positions in general "public interest" lobbying organizations. The fact is that these bodies put themselves forward—quite sincerely—as representing the common good, and yet we know that their interpretations of that common good, like all of ours, will always be partial, will in truth reflect certain broader or narrower interests in society. Here, as in the case of elective state or national office, the different kinds of representation are all too apt to be confused—representation of a particular constituency, political ideology, or set of interests, on the one hand, and representation of a community of faith across political and geographical and even time boundaries (a moral *tradition*) on the other hand. I am, to be sure, far more sympathetic to the political agenda of Americans for Democratic Action than to that of the Moral Majority, but I am uncomfortable with the fact that both these lobbying groups are currently headed by clergymen.

Does what I have said about priests apply equally to those not ordained but in religious orders, especially to women religious? In regard to proximity to the state's exercise of violence, I think the answer is yes. In regard to the representative character of political office, I think the answer—in strict logic—is no. In actual practice, however, it is yes and no.

It is not very controversial to argue the inappropriateness for those in religious orders, whether ordained or not, of political positions directly related to the use of force. In the case of women religious, to be sure, the acceptability of this proposition—e.g., that a nun should not be appointed commander of the Marine Corps—may rest, in part, on established ideas about gender, that women are nurturers rather than hunters and fighters. But whatever the source of our predispositions, they also appear to suit the commitment of those in religious life to the fullest possible living of the evangelical counsels and, above all, to Jesus' example of emptying, non-resistant love.

But what about political office beyond this particular category of positions? The consecrated religious life, as the Second Vatican Council makes clear, is not some halfway state between the laity and the clergy. It is a form of life that includes both laity and clergy. It is also a form of life that includes contemplative and apostolic callings. Women religious are laity, and many of their orders, especially in the United States are apostolic—dedicated to actively bringing the message of God's kingdom to the world. Historically, their efforts have been directed toward special tasks and special groups in society—toward teaching the poor (or in some cases the rich), toward caring for orphans, or nursing the sick. They have never had the same "universal" liturgical role as priests, and there exist none of the corresponding reasons why, like other members of the laity, they should not add at least some political vocations to those they have traditionally exercised. It is not hard to understand how frustrating it must be for women religious to be constantly told that in regard to sacramental or ecclesiastical power they have no chance, on account of their sex, to be treated as anything but laity, while in regard to discipline, they are regularly treated as clergy.

So much for the logic, or rather the illogic, of the current situation. There is more to it than that, however. Madness has its method, illogic has its logic. The present extention to women religious of the restriction on priests' participation in partisan politics has some basis in actual practice. However unfounded in theory, it remains a fact that women religious have functioned up until the very recent past in exactly the kind of quasi-clerical middle state that the Second Vatican Council says they are not. In the minds of many ordinary Catholics, the nuns—or the "good sisters"—continue to be viewed as quasi-priests, indeed in some cases as super-priests.

It is not sufficient to decry this as a misunderstanding. This perception was based on the fact that women religious dressed distinctively; led lives set apart from the laity's; and, though they were often simultaneously exploited by the institutional church, they often demanded and frequently received special treatment. Ask any graduate of parochial schools over the age of thirty. Whatever the theological theory, in practice women religious did represent the church in a way quite beyond that characteristic of the rest of the laity. When critics of Agnes Mansour's position in Michigan seemed to base their objections on such a perception that women religious occupied a kind of quasi-clerical state, those who responded by simply insisting she was a lay-woman, and should be treated no differently than any other layperson in government service, ran the risk of relying on a legalism without regard to concrete historical cirumstances, in much the same manner as Vatican officialdom does so often.

The consecrated religious life, after all, is not a matter of individual perfection but of service within the church community—and *to some extent* that means taking the church the way it is at any given moment. For this orientation toward the church as a whole, there is a solid principled basis. Religious orders are not private associations; their vows, their constitutions, their particular charisms are recognized by the church. It is not right to say that the chosen tasks of different religious communities are their business alone, although it does make sense that such choices should be their business *initially* and *primarily*.

The preeminent reality in this area is that religious life is in a state of evolution. Slightly more than two decades ago when I was in college, the university newspaper I edited revealed that a venerable Catholic institution on university premises practiced racial segregation. The resulting picket line was joined by a number of Franciscan sisters. The time was pre-Vatican Council and pre-Selma civil rights march. The sisters were, of course, in habit. The media were fascinated. Pictures of the picketing Franciscans appeared on local TV, in all the city newspapers, even in *Time* magazine. Those sisters were not treated, believe me, like the rest of us picketing laypeople. Their presence was seen as indicative, in some sense, of a new attitude about racial justice in the institutional church, and I think rightly so. The Franciscans' habits are long gone (and so, alas, are many of the picket lines); but it would be naive to deny that such a representative character still attaches in a milder way to women religious.

Nonetheless, there have been exceptional changes. Those changes have radically diminished the visible distinctions between laity and religious. Gradually the world, Catholic and non-Catholic, is coming to recognize women religious as constituting a quasi-lay rather than a quasi-clerical group, which is at least somewhat closer to the truth. If the members of certain religious communities increasingly enter political careers, Catholics and others will grow accustomed to it. They will neither be scandalized nor impressed by this development, any more than they were by the fact that in the past certain women's orders concentrated on an apostolate to the poor while others concentrated on an apostolate to the rich. The fact that some politicians are members of religious orders may eventually be relegated to a minor item in their standard "bio's," like the fact that various governors have been physicians or some Cabinet members have been officials in the Mormon or Presbyterian churches. People will no doubt be shocked slightly more than usual when a woman religious in politics casts a blatantly opportunistic vote or is caught providing political favors. But people would have been similarly shocked a little more than normally if a woman religious heading a private hospital or university were found dipping into the institution's funds for private purposes. The only difference in political life is that the temptations may be a little more frequent, the rationalizations easier to come by, and the glare of publicity a lot greater. Still, one can reasonably hope that the instances will be rare.

The presence of non-ordained women and men religious in political careers may very well leaven both the world of politics and the world of peace-and-justice activists, the former with examples of altruistic dedication, the latter with a sense of concreteness and compromise. I think, however, that as members of religious orders reconsider their traditional roles, they may be lured into overestimating the value of political activities as an alternative. There is much to be said for the belief that politics does not change much, that government largely keeps the show on the road, that at best it consolidates and institutionalizes changes in society which begin initially with marginal movements nurtured into legitimacy only by women and men willing to make unusual sacrifices and lead radically different sorts of lives. I myself am too temperamentally attuned to politics to want to believe this, but I pray that the church never be short on "countercultural" holy men and women who make me think twice.

Part 4
THE DEBATE: YES, NO, MAYBE

The question of clergy and religious women and men serving in public office in the United States is a complex one that seems to exclude any absolute positions in the abstract. Nevertheless, from the perspective of past as well as contemporary experience, two of our contributors were willing to take opposing views on the question. Kenneth Himes argues in defense of occasional participation by clergy on the basis of the flexibility of the clerical role historically. He argues even more forcibly for the participation of religious men and women directly in politics on the grounds of the nature of religious vows and the charisms of individual congregations.

Robert Spaeth, on the other hand, takes a position against such participation, arguing from the wisdom of the separation of the roles of lay and ecclesial persons. More importantly, he proposes a prudential argument specific to the United States experience, suggesting that the direct participation of clergy and religious in political offices gives bishops and popes de facto the power to "intervene" in the political process through their canonical authority over priests and sisters.

Kenneth R. Himes, OFM

YES, PRIESTS AND RELIGIOUS SHOULD BE PERMITTED TO HOLD PUBLIC OFFICE

INTRODUCTION

The issue of clerics and religious in political office has come to the fore due to certain celebrated cases both here in the United States as well as in other countries. It would be a mistake, however, to think that specific cases are intelligible apart from a broader context that raises significant theological issues.

Anyone with even tangential knowledge of Roman Catholicism is aware that in the last twenty years or so the understanding of priesthood and religious life has become unsettled. What time has revealed to us since the close of Vatican II is not unarguably clear. Many of us surveying the post-conciliar scene admit much to bemoan and much to praise; the problem is that we do not agree on what merits our approval and what deserves our lamentation.

Given that fact I wish to stress that while I advance several theses in this essay I do so tentatively. As this volume attests, the topic of priests and religious in political office—I will suggest they are really two different topics—must be addressed from a number of perspectives. Other authors provide canonical, historical, political, biographical information. This essay is by a religious priest who has training in moral theology and a special interest in social ethics. Thus, my viewpoint is partial. I claim no compelling argument; rather I offer a perspective that makes the possibility of priests and religious in political office seem plausible.[1]

This approach is advisable because the fundamental divide between those who oppose and support such an option involves profound theological questions that are still very much under discussion. That in itself suggests to me that no hard and fast prohibition is wise. For when a topic like the relationship of church and world requires rethinking in our post-conciliar age it ought not to surprise us that the cleric-lay distinction, the charism of religious life, and the nature of ordained ministry should be called into question.

In what follows I will sketch the shifting context for posing the question of clerics in public office and discuss some objections to that idea. Finally, I will take up the matter of religious in political positions. My reason for distinguishing between clerics and non-clerical religious should become clear in the course of the essay.

I

The description of the laity found in the Dogmatic Constitution on the Church is one that most Catholics gladly accepted in 1965. It is a view that acknowledges the dignity of work in the secular arena and affirms such work as part of the church's mission.

> A secular quality is proper and special to laymen. It is true that those in holy orders can at times engage in secular activities, and even have a secular profession. But by reason of their particular vocation they are chiefly and professedly ordained to the sacred ministry. Similarly, by their state in life, religious give splendid and striking testimony that the world cannot be transfigured and offered to God without the spirit of the beatitudes.
> But the laity, by their vocation, seek the kingdom of God by engaging in temporal affairs and by ordering them according to the plan of God. They live in the world, that is, in each and in all of the secular professions and occupations. They live in the ordinary circumstances of family and social life, from which the very web of their existence is woven.
> They are called there by God so that by exercising their proper function and being led by the spirit of the gospel they can work for the sanctification of the world from within, in the manner of leaven. In this way they can make Christ known to others, especially by the testimony of a life resplendent in faith, hope, and charity. The layman is closely involved in temporal affairs of every sort. It is therefore his special task to illumine and organize these affairs in such a way that they may always start out, develop, and persist according to Christ's mind, to the praise of the Creator and the Redeemer.[2]

I use the word "description" purposefully in my portrayal of what the council fathers did in paragraph 31 since they looked upon this section as the customary way of understanding the laity's role. In other words, the conciliar text does not present an ontological definition of the lay state. There is no assertion that we have in this passage distilled the essence of what the ministry or calling of the lay person entails.[3]

At the council when the chapter containing paragraph 31 was introduced it was noted that what was intended to be presented was a "typological description" not an "ontological definition." As Joseph Komonchak has noted, the expression "typological description" seems "to be a terminological innovation in church documents, and the Relator offered no help in explaining it." Komonchak continues, "we are, it is clear, offered a description, and, it seems, a description of a type, that is, of what typifies a lay person's situation and activity. A lay person typically is married, has a job, lives in the world, etc."[4] In sum, we find in Lumen Gentium less a theological claim than a customary observation about the usual manner of a group's functioning.

If that is the case with the council's treatment of the laity in paragraph 31, might it not also be the case when there is reference to clerics and religious in the document? Customarily such persons are engaged in full-time church-related tasks. But there can always be exceptions to the customs especially when these customs are employed descriptively not prescriptively. Just as there are lay people involved in the internal affairs of the institutional church so too there can be clerics and religious concerned with secular tasks.[5]

There appear to be solid reasons for a reluctance to force either group, lay or cleric, into too strict a mold. Throughout history it is difficult to ascertain a uniform practice of ministry. In the first centuries of the christian community there was a less precise distinction between ordained and lay ministers. Certainly the typological descriptions of Vatican II would have been difficult to apply. Lay people had a role in the internal maintenance of the community and presbyters had few special duties, functioning mainly as elders assisting the bishop who was usually the only full-time minister within the christian assembly. For centuries clerics held all manner of secular positions—bankers, statesmen, bureaucrats at court or in civic government, tradesmen. In fact, as David Power has written, to be a cleric in the middle ages meant "preferment in access to certain secular functions."[6]

Our present way of thinking about cleric and lay has been influenced by a variety of factors over the centuries. In the early medieval period the rise of monasticism and adoption of certain monastic characteristics by priests helped to develop a spirituality for clerics. But once the idea of spiritual men being aloof from the world found its way into christian consciousness there emerged the danger of clerics losing their sense of unity with the laity.

Other sociological elements contributed to the emergence of a special class of clerics. On the level of self-understanding the secularizing trends of western society created a disengagement between church and world that forced a re-thinking of the clerical role. The church saw the need for distinguishing a sacred realm from the reaches of a state that was no longer avowedly christian or even religious. Clergy helped establish and control institutions through which the church operated in its own sphere, while encouraging the laity to bring the message to the world like so many emissaries from a religious preserve.

On the functional level the organization of such a burgeoning religious institution required the time and energy of clerics devoted full-time to the maintenance of religious practice. Not only sacramental tasks but jobs affiliated with running an institution—finance, buildings and grounds, administration, establishment of schools and hospitals, oversight of employees, and similar work—were considered clerical tasks because they had to do with ecclesiastical organization. Over the course of time the idea became predominant that clerics had full-time concern with internal affairs of the church and lay people found their ministry or apostolate in the secular world.[7]

What is crucial to see is that we are dealing here not with metaphysically determined roles but with historically conditioned role-expectations that evolve as conditions change. One of the great dangers for a theology of priesthood is to "ontologize" a particular cultural form of pastoral ministry as being of its essence. History reveals a proclivity to turn typological definitions into metaphysical ones.[8] Vatican II reflected the proper reluctance to "freeze" ministry into some eternal mold allowing as it did for considerable freedom in enfleshing the ordained ministerial role.

> . . .(T)he second Vatican Council in its constitution on the church and its decree on the priestly ministry describes the priest's functions in terms of the tripartite division between pastoral care, ministry of the word and ministry of the sacraments. This is certainly true, but when we scrutinize these documents we cannot but notice how little they clarify the questions we ask about what in practice a priest may be expected to do.[9]

The way Vatican II dealt with the cleric-lay distinction admits of some blurring of that divide when certain exceptional, that is, uncustomary, ministries are pursued by members of either group. But there is a more substantial point to be made and that is to challenge the common perception of the terms cleric and lay. It is possible to ask not only whether exceptions to the ideal-types of cleric and lay offered in Lumen Gentium are possible; but the more crucial question must be asked as well, whether these types have exhausted their usefulness? In the present era there is a growing diversification of ministry and profound reconceptualization of the mission of the church to the world. Just as clerics were led to define their role anew in a period of church-world disengagement, is it not plausible to consider re-definition in an age of renewed engagement? As we work out details of such a church-world relationship it must be kept in mind that the work of social transformation is a religious task intrinsic to the christian commitment.[10] How this is so and the reason why it will affect our understanding of ordained ministry calls for explanation.

In an article summarizing recent research on Catholic theology of ministry Herve Legrand argued for the "priority of the object of ministry over the person of the minister,"[11] his point being that the primary question we should ask with regard to ministry is not about proper roles and categories of ministers but rather the more fundamental inquiry is concerned with our understanding of the mission of the church. All subsequent issues of ministry flow from this basic matter of Christian ministry, what is the church's mission? Only after examining this question can we move on to problems that arise from differentiation of ministries according to clerical and lay states. Ordained pastoral ministry is but a specification and de-limitation of the duty shared by all the baptized to further the church's mission. This primary issue of mission is the starting point for thinking about ministry, not the lay-cleric distinction.

Clearly we are living in an age that is bringing about a re-thinking of the mission of the church in theology as well as in pastoral practice. While conciliar documents do not emerge from a vacuum it is legitimate to take the Pastoral Constitution of Vatican II as a point of departure for investigating the contemporary debate regarding church mission. Since the council there has been a distinct political turn in Roman Catholic ecclesiology. The church has embraced the political realm (*le politique*) as a field of mission. Despite some scattered criticism this has been widely accepted as not only appropriate but requisite for all christians. This ecclesial development, however, does not settle arguments about the manner of clerical involvement in more specifically partisan politics (*la politique*). This more focused level of engagement with the world continues to raise difficulties. The resolution of the problems will only be made more complicated when we realize that the larger issue of the church and *le politique* was not satisfactorily handled at the council or in the immediate post-conciliar theologies.

The claim that the council did not adequately treat the issue of church and world becomes more evident if we look at the Pastoral Constitution; specifically, at the process behind the formulation of the document at the council. What becomes clear is that the council laid out a broad position that required later efforts at achieving precision in theological expression. We are presently witnessing such efforts in the writing of a number of skillful theologians. Before explaining those recent formulations it is necessary to grasp just what was and was not accomplished at the council.

During Vatican II various drafts of Schema 13, as the Pastoral Constitution was then called, were produced. Many of these took a somewhat dualistic approach to the natural and supernatural, stressing the differences between the two orders of temporal and spiritual. This was manifested in the way the relation of Kingdom—therefore church as sign of the Kingdom—and world was construed. A revised draft, in direct reply, emphasized the unity of humanity's vocation; that is, the order of redemption was understood to include the order of creation. There is not a created world and some redeemed other realm of spirit but one redeemed world which is the home of human beings who are both spirit and flesh united. During the debates over this new draft some bishops expressed discomfort with the document. The episcopal reservation was that there was too close a correlation between human history and salvation history. The eventual result was the endorsement of a broadly sketched position in the final document. "Hence, while earthly progress must be carefully distinguished from the growth of Christ's Kingdom, to the extent that the former can contribute to the better ordering of human society, it is of vital concern to the Kingdom of God."[12]

In effect, the outcome of the conciliar debate was the production of a statement that avoided trying to settle disputed theological questions but asserted two fundamental beliefs: there is a close connection between the Kingdom and human history, but no simple equivalence. As a result there was a fair amount of room for theological investigation since the broad nature of the affirmations force no single opinion as to how one explains a close relationship—that is not a simple identification—between Kingdom and world. The council's position took us only so far in understanding the issue, and a great deal of attention has been given since 1965 to moving the question along to greater specificity and precision.[13]

Another way of appreciating the evolution of the issue is to recall the changes in theological method which have taken place within the last twenty years. Even during the council the thrust of Roman Catholic theology's turn to the *subject* was evident. By this I mean that contemporary theology takes seriously the movement of western philosophy from early Greek cosmological interest to modern anthropological emphasis. Anthropology becomes the starting point for theology since christian faith is the experience of divinity through humanity. This anthropocentric turn called attention to the human conditions necessary for the possibility of revelation. In this view, revelation is not a "stone thrown into the water" but a word spoken to those who are already predisposed to be hearers of the word. There is an inner relation between human self-understanding (our ability to receive revelation) and the correlative reality of revelation itself.

The theological turn to the subject explains why human experience is a hermeneutical principle for revelation. It is only by asking what it means to be human, and seeing how faith in God answers the question, that religious language will be grasped as something intrinsic to human existence and not a supernatural addition to an already complete natural creature. To be human is to be constituted as a questioner, a seeker for truth and meaning; and theology today strives to illustrate how religious questions are simply the most profoundly human questions. Thus, we cannot see revelation as supplying answers to unimportant questions, but rather revelation must be interpreted in light of the concerns that arise from human existence. In short, it is not only that the church has something to say to the world but it must be acknowledged that the world has something to say to the church and *that*, in turn, will affect how we understand what it is the church has to say.

More recent has been the political turn in contemporary theology which serves as a corrective but not a rejection of the anthropocentric turn. Political theology is not the same as a theology of politics. Political theology is first of all about method.[14] It extends anthropocentric theology's claim that one cannot understand revelation without asking "what does revelation mean in light of human experience" to include in that explanation of human experience a person's actual insertion into life in his/her particular world. We cannot allow theology to talk about the experience of some abstract person but only the concrete individual in his/her specific situation. Hence, the import of those skills of social analysis that enable one to reflect upon experience in a systematic way.[15] Once this step of integrating theology and social analysis is taken the question for a thinker like Gustavo Gutierrez becomes "what is the meaning of faith in a life committed to the struggle against injustice and alienation?"[16] This question shows the way for what Joseph Komonchak suggests is a mutually critical correlation between church and world.

In 1965 the correlation was incomplete; the council asked what does the church have to say to this or that aspect of human experience. The "signs of the times" were to be read in light of the gospel.[17] Thus, we could have a theology of politics. The political turn expands such a correlation of Word and world to the level of mutuality. For now we must ask what does the lived experience of a commitment to social justice and peace-making say to the community of faith? Now we must scrutinize the gospel in light of the signs of the times. Political resistance is perceived to be constitutive of religious self-understanding. Just as the anthropocentric turn enabled us to see that human experience poses questions for an understanding of revelation, so too the political turn reveals that our commitment to social change frames our understanding of church. This is a very important idea in our taking up the question of church mission for it casts into some doubt the wisdom of separating the question of church from the question of church-world relationship.

There is not first a moment of defining church apart from world, then a second moment defining church missioned to the world. We cannot take the first step in splendid ecclesial isolation for we must ask what does it mean to be church in light of the world we encounter; a world where political existence is problematic and constitutive of our existence. The church that speaks a message to the world is shaped by the world even before it speaks its message. To paraphrase Joseph Komonchak, we need both questions: what in light of the Word is the meaning of our socio-political existence? *and* what in light of our socio-political existence is the meaning of the Word (Church)? Because the council did not ask the second question, Gaudium et Spes does not specify the church-world relationship in a way which resolves matters satisfactorily. Post-conciliar theological writings are pointing us toward a resolution and it appears the eventual outcome will be to affirm that the struggle against injustice and for peace is constitutive of the church's mission.

What difference will such a mutual correlation make for our thinking about priests in politics? The answer can be seen if we consider what the lay-cleric distinction has meant and might mean in a renewed ecclesiology. According to the council, the laity typically live out the gospel in the world while clerics (and religious) typically involve themselves in ministries more related to the institutional church. But if we come to see that christian faith is constitutively political, then values and meanings which clergy embody and transmit are always politically significant, and one realizes the true distinction is between membership in the community gathered around Christ and society, not between lay and cleric. It may well be that in our liberal western culture we have not been as sensitive to the public significance of our faith as we should be but our ability to learn from the experience of some third-world christians has been a new source of stimulation and enlightenment on this matter.

The tendency of Euro-Americans to undervalue the public role of religion is of theological import for it has allowed us to separate talk about religious mission from our work for justice and peace as if this latter were not religious. First, we have a specific or christian mission and then we ask how to relate to the world. Thus, we can define the specifically christian, a cleric's realm, as devoid of political significance. Liberalism's bifurcation of religious and public life only reinforces a lay-cleric distinction which is rooted in a theological perspective that reveals

> . . . a tendency to locate the *specifium Christianum* primarily in a cultural opposition to a vaguely described "materialism" and a specifically described sexual morality. The political and economic structures and practices of the society tend to be taken for granted. A sign of this is that direct political action is typically assigned to the laity who remain in a world from which the Church, in the persons of the clergy and religious, has effectively and even on principle emigrated.[18]

The true distinction is not between some pre-political realm of religion inhabited by clerics and the autonomous world of politics inhabited by the laity. Political theology has helped us to see that since humans are necessarily political so too must any anthropological theology be correlated with the life of the *polis*. What is needed is the distinction between the church (made up of cleric/lay/religious) and the world so that entrance into the church could be seen as the political act it is. How the political significance of being christian gets acted out will then vary according to competencies which a priori we cannot assume will divide neatly into clerical and lay states. Training, experience, and interests may influence members of either group to seek direct political power.[19] In any event it cannot be claimed that there is a non-political sphere of religion which is populated by clerics.

At the same time no one need claim that socio-political ministry exhausts the mission of the church in order to say that it truly is an element of the church's mission and as fitting for clerical involvement as education, counseling, or administration of charitable institutions. The manner of clerical involvement in bringing about social change will look different in our time than in previous eras due to the expanding role played by the state in a welfare society. In our modern age the state has taken on a significant, even decisive, role in effecting societal transformation. It does not seem unreasonable that those who seek to be faithful to the church's mission will find in the task of holding public office—elected or appointed—an instrument for religious service. Traditional areas of institutional church engagement such as health care, refugee aid, education, and charity are increasingly topics of state concern in an era of welfare-state liberalism. It might be expected, therefore, that clerics who once worked in the private voluntary sector to address social questions will find political office a new avenue for expression of traditional concerns long affiliated with acceptable clerical behavior.

As Francis Meehan has pointed out there is a spirituality undergirding the administration and influencing of political institutions just as there is a spirituality of personal and interpersonal matters.[20] Our social institutions are carriers of value, they can enrich or denigrate the life of a people. Structures that enhance the sense of human dignity become a way of mediating God's goodness just as surely as the mutual love of a married couple mediates God's presence to the spouses. Every humanizing structure that supports the dignity of people, that brings forth food, justice, peace, health, is a participation in the restoration Christ seeks to bring to a world marred by sin. The creation of a society that respects human rights can be an epiphany of God for those who have been violated by that society's institutions.

Of course this is most dramatically seen in the case of highly oppressive societies where the movement to reform can be unambiguously recognized as a step away from social sin. In more just and representative democracies people of good will can disagree as to whether a given reform proposal is so starkly a moral imperative. But the modern welfare state of our nation provides its own challenge. Confronted by the large bureaucratic structures of our society a person can feel impotent to bring about change; a certain lack of imagination or conviction to become personally involved overtakes us. A priest holding power in such a setting can energize and direct the faith constituency in the pursuit of reform measures that witness to a constitutive element of the church's mission. This is not to say that the specifics of a cleric's political stance will necessarily be followed but the efficacy of active political engagement will be underscored so that not only the why of achieving social justice and peaceful reconciliation is highlighted, but people are reminded as to where such goals are to be sought.

What I have sought to do up to now is simply make a case for the church to remain open-minded on the issue of clerics in political office. While basic ideas like the mission of the church, the church's relationship to the world and the cleric-lay distinction are being rethought, it appears to be rash to definitively deny the possibility of priests in civil office.

Several questions remain as to whether this possibility should be acted upon, and I would like to touch on a few of them in this essay. One troubling factor that gives some people pause about approving priests in political office is talk of a "new clericalism." The idea that priests will seek to dominate the Catholic presence in political activity especially in the areas of social justice and peace-making is worrisome. While clericalism of any kind is to be deplored I doubt whether this is a real danger in the future of Catholic political life. Given the restrictions upon candidates for priesthood, in terms of gender and life-style, it seems probable that the ranks of ordained presbyters will remain quite depleted in the future. Add to that the issue of competence and training and it is likely that the priest in political office will remain an exceptional case. When such a man appears on the scene, however, it can be interpreted as a sign of support and encouragement for lay Catholic politicians who need to remember the tremendous opportunities for good that are available to those who exercise power for the welfare of a civil community. The priest in such a role serves as a dramatic witness to the religious mission of building justice and peace among peoples.

The claim of some that priests in politics will undermine the role of the laity is but one complaint on this score. Others argue the real danger is to the priesthood, for politics is "dirty business" that forces priests to identify with solutions, platforms, programs that are far short of the Kingdom of God to which they owe their allegiance. This is particularly so since in our form of government politics is often the art of compromise. However, unless we are to call for no Catholic support of the state and oppose any lay participation in political life, it remains unclear why priests cannot enter into politics. If electoral politics and bureaucratic governmental administration are unacceptable for priests because they require compromise, why is such activity open to non-ordained believers? Is there not a vestige of an old dualism—perfectionism for an elite and minimalism for the masses—latent in such a stance? Perhaps, consistency is achieved, however, by decrying lay Catholic participation in politics, too. The possibility of an anti-state stance exists in christian social thought and the strain of quasi-anarchism which rejects the political realm as a moral backwater should not be cavalierly dismissed. Still, this position cannot claim to be the only or even the most accepted position in Catholic tradition. Until the preponderant presumption in favor of active involvement by believers in the life of the state is weakened I do not think we can deny priests access to political office on the grounds that it is morally compromising.

Another complaint against the wisdom of priests in politics entails the harm which will be done to the religious community by one of its leaders assuming a partisan position. It is said that the priest should serve as a unifier and reconciler in the community and this role would be sacrificed if the priest were too closely affiliated with a particular political opinion. How could a cleric be a source of unity in the community of faith under the circumstances? Now, two points can be made here. First, the ministry of reconciliation while real does not consume all the functions of a presbyter, and it may well be that in the name of reconciliation we settle for a false peace because we deny true differences in our haste to acquire a semblance of unity in the christian assembly. Just as there are times when the Word divides and scandalizes so too there may be times when the ministry of the Word leads one to take sides in the quest for truth and justice which must undergird any meaningful reconciliation. A second matter should be raised. Why must the political stance of a priest necessarily be viewed as divisive even if it is partisan? That is, people are coming to see the distinction between endorsement of gospel values and concrete policy choices for implementing, protecting, and instilling values. Confidence in the ability of the community to distinguish value choices from policy proposals is presumed by the National Conference of Catholic Bishops in their recent pastoral letter on war and peace. It is not such a leap from bishops endorsing a halt to the testing, production, and deployment of nuclear weapons to a priest-congressman voting for the nuclear freeze. In both cases divisiveness is possible only if we do not differentiate between the gospel ideal of peace and the prudential policy choice of means. What the wider community can come to realize is that a priest's political strategy is not gospel approved even if gospel motivated, and the witness of the cleric may spur others to seek out the political means they judge best to translate their value commitment into public policy.[21] That is all to the good and achieves one of the precise aims of clerical involvement in politics—motivating other members of the faith community to work for justice and peace through the political institutions available.

In answering these objections to partisan involvement in politics by priests I am not dismissing the objections. I am merely trying to point out another side to the issue that also merits our consideration. It is not my intention to suggest the idea of clerics in political office raises no troubling questions. My only claim is that countervailing goods can be discerned which should allow us to state that under some circumstances, and given the present theological flux surrounding mission, ministry, and orders, it is possible for a priest to assume political office. Priesthood in the Catholic church is really a genus that admits of many species: pastors, teachers, writers, bureaucrats, scientists, poets, contemplatives, counselors, secretaries, chauffeurs, and more. Ordained ministry is really a grouping of ministries along a wide spectrum and the total exclusion of public office holders from such a diverse assemblage of men seems to be, on the face of it, unnecessary.

II

The question of non-clerical religious in political office is, I believe, of a different nature than what has been discussed up to now. My own view is that there is little or no problem with religious (non-clerical) holding political office. I recognize that this is not the way most church officials see the matter but what may be part of the difficulty is that the charism of religious life is not properly understood by a number of people. This sense is reinforced by the way religious men and women experience their place in the church. As has often been said by religious when discussing ecclesiastical officials, "when they talk about responsibilities and duties we're treated like clerics, but when they consider privileges and power we're treated like the laity." Whatever the validity of the observation, it indicates a perception held by a large number of lay religious men and women that they are neither fish nor fowl. The immediate response to such a statement might be to point out the modifier before "religious" in the preceding sentence. Religious life is not clerical but lay. Hence, why the confusion? The confusion arises because of the double standard that is evident when the church treats vowed religious different from other laity.

A case which illustrates the problem is the recent dispute surrounding Agnes Mary Mansour's dismissal from the Sisters of Mercy.

Sister Mansour was offered a position as director of the Michigan Department of Social Services. A part of her responsibility would be to administer the state of Michigan's medicaid funds including that portion of the funds used for assisting poor women to procure abortions if they so choose. Church officials judged this to be an unsuitable post for a religious woman and presented Mansour with the choice of resignation from her religious community or withdrawal from the governmental position.[22]

Several issues are involved in this dispute, not all of them relevant to the point I wish to make. The morality of abortion, the interplay of morality and public policy, and due process in church disciplinary procedures are some of the important items that any satisfactory analysis of the Mansour case must take into consideration. But I am not analyzing the Mansour case *per se*, only using it to illustrate the perplexity of lay religious in the church. How is it that a position held by a Catholic layman (Mansour's predecessor in the office) without opposition from church leaders can become a cause celebre when held by a woman religious? The reason must be that, although still a lay person, a vowed religious has special responsibilities or plays a special role that makes such a political office more problematic than for a married lay person.

What then is the basis for such a double standard? One possible way of expressing it is to explain that religious consecration entails entrance into a sacred realm that requires rejection of certain tasks open to others. The difficulty with this view is the assumption of a church-world distinction which is subject to dispute. I will not repeat arguments already made in the initial section of this essay; it is enough to state that the meaning of religious consecration is misinterpreted if it is understood as initiation into a non-secular existence of churchly life.

An even more important concern is to avoid explaining the double standard in such a way as to misconstrue the baptismal vows of every christian. I fear this error can be found in the text "Essential Elements in Church Teaching on Religious Life" issued by the Vatican Congregation for Religious and Secular Institutes.[23] There we read that religious life, in distinction from secular institutes and lay existence, entails a special role. "The very nature of religious vocation involves a public witness to the Christ and to the Church. Religious profession is made by vows which the Church receives as public."[24] The trouble with the above statement is that it distinguishes between religious and other laity on the basis of the public nature of the vows. That is to undercut our best theologies of baptism which stress the public meaning (and political significance) of church membership. In an era that is retrieving the public character of baptismal commitment there is the need to re-think the meaning of religious profession if, as in the Vatican statement, emphasis is placed on the public nature of religious profession as a distinctive quality. My claim is that the vows of religious add nothing new to a lay person's responsibility for public witness already incurred by virtue of one's earlier baptismal vows. Thus, it is a mistake to suggest that a vowed religious cannot hold political office because his/her vows require a public witness not also required of baptized laity. This viewpoint is, I think, a sound inference of contemporary theologies of baptism.

The theology behind the Rite of Christian Initiation of Adults (RCIA) assumes that faith requires free acceptance. Entrance into the community of faith, the Church, is the embodiment of that free acceptance. Adult baptism, therefore, is the norm for our understanding of christian initiation regardless of whether quantitatively it is normal or exceptional when compared to infant baptism.[25] Because by its very nature the church is called to public witness it is false to entertain the idea that one could be called to the church and yet not take on a public task. To do so would be to misconstrue the very nature of the church which is essentially public and does not admit of private membership. Initiation into the church is a public act. Any attempt to distinguish between vowed religious and other laity on the basis of the public nature of religious profession slights the rich meaning of baptismal commitment common to all.

Public vows made by religious men and women are not more public nor more free than the baptismal vows. Religious life is simply a particular way of living out one's baptismal commitment through a given style of life. I suggest the marriage vows of a christian couple are of the same standing, a specification and public commitment of how one will witness to the primary vows of baptism.

Further, I propose that religious life, like marriage, is best thought of as a commitment to live christianity in a given community. Just as the marriage vows are a covenanting of two individuals into a new familial community so too religious vows are a bonding with a group of people who constitute communities known as Augustinian, Carmelite, Trinitarian, etc. The traditional vows are specifications of what a communal life looks like but they are *per se* quite indeterminate. That is why there is not one set of constitutions for religious orders but many, for religious communities have distinctive ways of contextualizing and interpreting the vows. Poverty, chastity, and obedience may be normal elements of a communal religious life but they do not exhaust what religious life involves anymore than the marriage vows exhaust what it means to be in relationship to one's spouse. The emphasis on public vows is not the distinguishing mark of religious and I do not think such vows can be used as a rationale for prohibiting religious men and women from assuming public office.

It is the commitment to live a certain way of life, a certain manner of embodying the gospel as this is found with a particular group of people, that marks one as a member of a religious community. Only by taking seriously the actual history of a group does the plurality of religious life come into focus. A disadvantage of stressing the vows is that they do not distinguish Franciscans from Benedictines. If a community is to rediscover its charism it must stress the stories, the experiences, the classics that formed it.[26] Thus, if someone asks me what it means to be a Franciscan I do not begin by talking about the vows but by talking about Francis of Assisi and his vision of the gospel. Seeing religious life as a vow to community highlights that I am not some generically religious man but a Franciscan. It is that community with its understanding of the gospel formed by concrete persons, stories, experiences, classics that I have joined and to which I owe allegiance. That is why a person takes vows to specific religious superiors and to follow a particular rule of life. No one aspires to be some ideal type called a "religious," no one seeks to take three vows in the abstract; men and women aspire to be Franciscans, Dominicans, Benedictines, etc. It is the express historical embodiment of a vision of the gospel that attracts people. And an understanding of religious life that divorces itself from the historical reality for the sake of some abstraction called "religious life" simply does not do justice to the experience of persons.

To focus on the vows is an inexact way of grasping the essence of a religious vocation. Rather, the commitment to join a community with an approved way of life is more helpful in understanding religious life. Such a way of discussing the experience of those who are members of religious orders, centering on the concrete communal expression of gospel living rather than the abstraction of the vows, enables us to see how it is possible for religious men and women to hold political office. For if we take as our point of departure the charism of a community it will be difficult to issue universal norms that apply equally to the various groups who have ecclesiastically approved rules of life. For the charisms are quite diverse and what is true for some communities may not be true for others. To illustrate this point about diversity one need only look at how the topic of corporate mission in religious life confuses rather than clarifies the issue of religious as political office-holders.

In a recent declaration on religious life church leaders emphasized the importance of a corporate mission in the life of religious,
going so far as to call it an essential element in religious life.

> It is to the institute as a whole that the church commits that
> sharing in the mission of Christ which characterizes it and
> which is expressed in works inspired by the founding char-
> ism. This corporate mission does not mean that all members
> of the institute are doing the same thing or that the gifts and
> qualities of the individual are not respected. It does mean
> that the works of all the members are directly related to the
> common apostolate, which the church has recognized as ex-
> pressing concretely the purpose of the institute. This com-
> mon and constant apostolate is part of the institute's sound
> traditions. It is so closely related to identity that it cannot be
> changed without affecting the character of the institute it-
> self.[27]

The stress on corporate mission too easily leads to the confusion
of thinking of religious as quasi-officeholders in the church; that is,
people charged with a particular ministry by virtue of their religious
profession. But religious life is not an office in the church. The symbol
of religious commitment is often obscured due to its commonly perceived relationship to institutionalized ministries within the church.
This popular perception, evident in the church document just quoted,
is a misperception because religious life does not entail a corporate
mission as one of its essential elements. To show this to be the case I
appeal to the Franciscan tradition. I do so not only because this is my
own tradition but more importantly because the rule for First Order
Franciscans is followed by more male religious (OFM, OFM Cap.,
OFM Conv.) than any other ecclesiastically approved rule.

The Rule of 1223 begins "The rule and life of the Friars Minor is
this: to observe the holy Gospel of our Lord Jesus Christ by living in
obedience, without anything of their own, and in chastity."[28] Francis
began with this sentence in order to expressly state that friars are not
to seek guidance from anything that glosses over the gospel text itself.
At no point does the saint from Assisi restrict the idea of Franciscan
ministry and work. As long as it did not conflict with a life of prayer
and simplicity a friar's ministry was acceptable.

This spirit is reflected in the present constitutions of the Order of
Friars Minor.

. . .(I)t is becoming more frequent to find friars engaged in salaried trades and professions within enterprises and institutions which belong neither to the Order nor to the Church. *An orientation of this kind appears to us to be in line with our vocations; by it we are part of a society in a special way working for its upbuilding and we are brought closer to those who live by their work.* While placing us squarely on the road to the future, it brings us back to one of the institutions of our origins.

We believe therefore that the friars may work at any job or profession that is compatible with the Christian and Franciscan way of life.[29]

To put the point simply, the Franciscan tradition expressly denies it has any corporate mission beyond that of living the gospel and that mission is shared by all christians, lay or cleric, by virtue of baptism. Hence corporate mission cannot be characteristic of religious *qua* religious, and affiliation with institutional ministries of the church is not the earmark of a religious commitment.

All christians have the responsibility for ministry; some who are ordained are normally viewed as full-time workers in certain essential ministries. Those religious who are not ordained do not necessarily have such ministerial expectations by virtue of their role in the church. In this respect their situation is similar to other lay people who are single or married. They have a call to ministry by virtue of baptism; and they have by their marriage or religious vows chosen the manner in which they will live as they serve God's Kingdom. But the nature of religious life and the vows of religious do not determine the ministry of the person any more than does the nature of marriage or the vows of the married couple. Both sets of vows are concerned with a way of life not with ministry. The error is to presume that because one is a member of a religious order one has taken on responsibility for a corporate mission rather than taking on a commitment to live according to a given community's vision which may or may not include a corporate mission. Some religious communities may customarily be associated with certain ministries and that is quite obviously appropriate, but it is not that which defines them as religious.

What of such communities? Are the members of those institutes that are traditionally associated with certain apostolates therefore barred from political office because it would be to stray too far afield from the corporate mission which is part of their community's charism? Caution is called for here since I think each individual charism must be studied, as well as the wide variety of political offices available in a complex society such as ours, before concluding that the office and the religious commitment are incompatible. Again, I am opposing a universal rule that would be thought to be applicable in each case without first studying the individual circumstances. An example of the difficulty of the task is found in the Mansour incident.

Again, I am not interested in all the details of the Mansour case but only how it illuminates the matter of religious in political office. The Sisters of Mercy are a community of religious women with an outstanding record of service in health care and other church-related ministries. To my knowledge the role of public official is not, however, part of their long-standing tradition of service. When Agnes Mary Mansour was nominated as director of social services for the state of Michigan she sought the permission of her religious superiors. That permission was granted because "the mission of the Department of Social Services is very much in keeping with the mission of the church and very much in keeping with the special emphasis by the Sisters of Mercy on service to the poor."[30] In a later statement by her superiors, following Mansour's dispensation from religious community, the same theme is found: " . . . we will continue to support her service to the people of Michigan as consistent with the mission of the Sisters of Mercy."[31] Edmund Szoka, Archbishop of Detroit, never objected to Mansour's taking office in principle; his concern was that the abortion issue not be confused by her actions and "that the appointment conforms to the traditional service and ministry of the Sisters of Mercy . . ."[32] Apparent in all of this is that a religious community's charism is a living reality and cannot be reduced to "this is the way we have always done it around here."

The Sisters of Mercy take a fourth vow, that of service to the poor, sick, uneducated. In the modern welfare state numerous opportunities present themselves for precisely the kind of service that the fourth vow of Mercy sisters requires. From the above quotations it is evident that the community saw things that way as did Archbishop Szoka. In other words, just because the issue of political office is a fairly recent one in the life of a religious order it cannot simply be thought of as non-traditional. The expression of the charism evolves as new avenues of ministry open up, but the spirit of the community's charism perdures. This would seem to be one of the lessons of the Mansour case: political office is not incompatible, in principle, with a sense of corporate mission. What must be decided, almost on a case by case basis, is whether the corporate mission can be witnessed to in the forum of public service on a governmental level. To issue norms restricting all religious from political office is to overlook the variety of religious orders and their respective charisms and histories.

To sum up what I have proposed in this section of the essay let me offer several theses: 1) religious do not hold office in the church; 2) with regard to institutional ministries of the church, the public vows of religious men and women do not place them in a unique position any more than the public vows of married couples; 3) some communities by virtue of their charism are traditionally associated with one or more essential church ministries and the compatibility of such charisms with political office is open to discernment and further study. My tentative conclusion is that lay religious should have the freedom to hold political office unless it can be demonstrated that such a ministry is incompatible with the charism of the religious community a person has joined. That case may be possible to make in some instances but not in all.

A final consideration is the confusion that would result from my proposal due to the widespread assumption that religious life restricts one to certain ministries and/or makes one a church official. What is needed is pastoral sensitivity to those who are confused and susceptible to offense if they thought a religious was acting as a church official in the pursuit of political office. The remedy for that confusion is not prohibition of the rightful freedom of religious but education of people to the status of religious.

NOTES

1.   A comment should be made about a self-imposed limit to the ambition of this reflection. Several recent books on ministry suggest to me that we may need to drastically reconceptualize our understanding of priestly ministry. It is not all that evident to me that Vatican bureaucrats, chancery and provincialate officials, academics and others who have tenuous claims to presbyteral service in a local community are best thought of as priests, however useful their work. I abstain from such provocative questioning in this essay even though I find myself sympathetic with writing that performs just this service. For the purposes of this essay I accept that the presbyteral order admits of quite diverse ministries which, in an undifferentiated way, are called priestly. In this essay I simply ask whether political office can be one such priestly task.

For an example of a recent study that asks and answers some hard questions about ministry see the stimulating work by Thomas O'Meara, O.P., *A Theology of Ministry* (New York: Paulist Press, 1983).

2. Lumen Gentium, par. 31. Walter Abbott, ed., *Documents of Vatican II* (New York: American Press, 1966).

3. Edward Schillebeeckx, O.P., "The Typological Definition of the Christian Layman according to Vatican II," in *The Mission of the Church* (New York: Seabury Press, 1973) pp. 90-116. The article was brought to my attention by Joseph Komonchak's "Clergy, Laity, and the Church's Mission in the World" which originally appeared in *The Jurist* 41 (1981) and is reprinted in this volume. Komonchak's is an excellent essay which I draw upon heavily at various points in my reflections.

4. Komonchak, "Clergy, Laity and the Church's Mission," p. 175.

5. This seems to be admitted in both Lumen Gentium, par. 31 and Gaudium et Spes, par. 43.

6. David Power, *The Christian Priest: Elder and Prophet* (London: Sheed and Ward, 1973) p. 6.

7. Ibid., p. 7.

8. O'Meara, *Theology of Ministry*, esp. pp. 95-133.

9. Power, *The Christian Priest*, pp. 7-8.

10. 1971 Synod, Justice in the World, (Washington: United States Catholic Conference, 1972) p. 34.

11. Herve Legrand, "Ministries: Main Lines of Research in Catholic Theology," *Pro Mundi Vita* 50 (1974): 7-16 at 7.

12. Gaudium et Spes, par. 39 in Abbott, *Documents*.

13. The preceding two paragraphs are based on Gustavo Gutierrez, *A Theology of Liberation* (Maryknoll: Orbis Books, 1971) pp. 168-172.

14. An early statement of this position is J. B. Metz, "Religion and Society in the Light of a Political Theology," *Harvard Theological Review* 61 (1968): 507-532.

15. An accessible introduction to methods of social analysis is Peter Henriot and Joe Holland, *Social Analysis: Linking Faith and Justice* 2nd ed. (Maryknoll: Orbis Books, 1983). Examples of how such tools are integrated with theological reflection can be seen in James Hug, ed., *Tracing the Spirit* (New York: Paulist Press, 1983) esp. the essays by T. Clarke, J. Holland, L. Rasmussen, and J. Hug.

16. Gutierrez, *Theology of Liberation*, p. 135 as quoted in Komonchak, "Clergy, Laity, and the Church's Mission," p. 186.

17. Gaudium et Spes, par. 4.

18. Komonchak, "Clergy, Laity, and the Church's Mission," p. 192.

19. Ibid., pp. 192-193.

20. Francis Meehan, *A Contemporary Social Spirituality* (Maryknoll: Orbis Books, 1982) esp. pp. 1-33. I rely upon Meehan for the thoughts of the following paragraph.

21. It is ironic that Vatican officials who stressed this distinction at a Roman meeting called to discuss the war and peace pastoral had such difficulty in seeing the same distinction at work in the rationale of Agnes Mary Mansour.

22. The details of the Mansour case can be found in *Origins* 13 (1984): 33-36; 197-206, and also in a comprehensive article by Madonna Kolbenschlag in *Commonweal,* June 17, 1983.

23. Vatican Congregation for Religious and Secular Institutes, "Essential Elements in Church Teaching on Religious Life," *Origins* 13 (1984): 133-142.

24. Ibid., p. 134.

25. *Rite of Christian Initiation of Adults* (Washington, D.C.: United States Catholic Conference, 1974).

26. See the thoughtful remarks of David Tracy on the meaning of classic in *The Analogical Imagination* (New York: Crossroad Publishing, 1981) pp. 99-229.

27. "Essential Elements," p. 136.

28. Francis of Assisi, "Rule of 1223," in *Francis and Clare: the Complete Works* trans. and intro. by Regis Armstrong, OFM Cap. and Ignatius Brady, OFM (New York: Paulist Press, 1982) p. 137.

29. *The Plan for Franciscan Living* (Pulaski, WI: English Speaking Conference of Provincials, 1974) p. 104. Emphasis in original. On the same point it is useful to quote several other articles from the constitutions.

"Exercising the freedom which the Rule affords in selecting an apostolate, the friars should always choose those works which the signs of the time indicate are most in need of Franciscan witness in a given region. They should not meddle in affairs that are unrelated to the nature of the brotherhood." Art. 99.1

"The friars should not be attached to any kind of apostolate as if it were their own, even if it is a longstanding apostolate. As long as there is provision for the good of the faithful, they should be ready to leave to others the apostolates and places they have established and begin again in new apostolates which are needed more." Art. 99.2

"The friars, together and individually, should use whatever talents they have to undertake any kind of work whatever, always giving priority to service to the needy and those who have not yet received the message of salvation." Art. 102.1

"Mindful of their own call, the friars should be one with all people of good will in efforts of charity, social assistance and international 'solidarity' in which the possibility of human and economic growth is offered to individuals and nations caught in need and in which justice and peace are strengthened in the world." Art. 103

30. "Statement of Sr. Agnes Mary Mansour on Her Dispensation from the Sisters of Mercy of the Union." *Origins* 13 (1983): 35.

31. "Statement of the Central Administration of the Sisters of Mercy of the Union on the dispensation of Sister Agnes Mary Mansour." *Origins* 13 (1983): 36.

32. "A Chronology of Events in the Agnes Mary Mansour Case by the Administrative Team of the Mercy Sisters Detroit Province." *Origins* 13 (1983): 200.

Robert L. Spaeth

PRIESTS AND SISTERS SHOULD AVOID POLITICAL OFFICE

INTRODUCTION

It is interesting, perhaps instructive, to imagine a world in which priests and members of religious orders aspiring to political office would experience only the problems of other Catholic politicians. In this world—fantastic to some, desirable to others—the Code of Canon Law would place no obstacles in the path of those priests, brothers and sisters who feel the urge to attain elective or appointive office in local, state or federal government. No bishop would be asked to give his permission to any priest or sister seeking political office. Few bishops would attempt to remove a religious office-holder and none would succeed. In this imaginary world, priests, sisters and the Catholic faithful would suspend their traditional belief that the clerical and the lay apostolates differ substantially in their relation to political life. Priests and sisters would seek and hold political office in numbers proportionate to lay people, without giving evidence that they represent the authoritative part of the Catholic Church or that they are in some special way subject to ecclesiastical authority. In short, for political purposes and in political settings, lay persons and priests and sisters would be indistinguishable from one another.

But this is not the world Catholics live in. Such a world has never existed. It does not exist now in the United States. It is readily arguable that it never will exist as long as the U.S. Constitution and the Roman Catholic Church continue to function—a very long time indeed. The real Catholic world—the one containing popes, bishops, canon law and ecclesiastical authority—is a world in which priests and sisters will experience many special difficulties if they try to attain political office and even more difficulties if they succeed. The difficulties are rooted in a traditional Catholic understanding of the role of the clergy and of religious orders in the Church—still a powerful tradition—and in the relation of religious institutions to the polity of the United States.

It is my contention that prominent strands in American history, Catholic theology and current events converge to demonstrate that priests and sisters ought to avoid serving in elective or appointive political office. To reach such a conclusion gives no satisfaction, for no American ever advises any fellow American not to aspire to political office without feeling presumptuous. But I am as much a Catholic as an American; I know what my church expects from its clergy and religious as well as I know what my country needs from its citizens. I also know how unlikely it is that the Church will change those aspects of its theology and authority that cause trouble for political priests and sisters.

My argument, in brief, derives from a reading of history and theology—a debatable and controversial reading, to be sure. My argument is capped by an appeal to prudence; even if my history and theology are flawed, I say, it won't work, therefore don't do it. If I were a bishop, I would probably not interfere with the election or appointment of a priest or brother or sister to political office. But I have no such authority or office, nor will I ever have. So I reach a position compatible with the realities of Catholic institutional life.

HISTORY

Concern over the clergy in political office has been coextensive with the history of the nation. John Carroll, the first bishop of American Catholicism, issued a clear warning:

> I have observed that when the ministers of religion leave the duties of their profession to take a busy part in political matters they generally fall into contempt and sometimes even bring discredit to the cause in whose service they are engaged. (Quoted in John Cogley, *Catholic America*. Garden City, NY: Image Books, 1974, p. 20.)

Did Archbishop Carroll assume that a priest in political office would while serving in that capacity be a visible representative of the Church? No doubt contemporary priests—and, even more so, sisters—who are politically active would deny that they are representatives of the Church while serving in political office. But it is one thing to deny and another to escape identification with the Church in which one functions as a member of the clergy or a religious order.

When Alexis de Tocqueville visited the United States in the 1830s, he was at first surprised to discover that Catholic priests did not hold political office. He investigated the reasons:

> When I finally came to inquire into the attitudes of the clergy themselves, I found that most of them seemed voluntarily to steer clear of power and to take a sort of professional pride in claiming that it was no concern of theirs. (*Democracy in America*. Garden City, NY: Doubleday, 1969, p. 296.)

Tocqueville himself came to approve heartily of the "self-restraint" that induced the American Catholic clergy to remain "aloof from public business." (Ibid., p. 448) He made a firm judgment that the clergy's potential participation in politics posed serious dangers to religion itself:

> I am so deeply convinced of the almost inevitable dangers which face beliefs when their interpreters take part in public affairs, and so firmly persuaded that at all costs Christianity must be maintained among the new democracies that I would rather shut priests up within their sanctuaries than allow them to leave them. (pp. 545-46)

What are these dangers? Have they persisted into the 20th century and even into the 1980s?

Tocqueville argued first that religion in the United States influenced and partially controlled the habits and the thinking of the citizenry. This influence, he believed, was socially desirable because American political life was free. Liberty could readily be abused but, Tocqueville believed, "while the law allows the American people to do everything, there are things which religion prevents them from imagining and forbids them to dare." (p. 292) Because of this indirect action of religion on the social life of the polity, Tocqueville felt confident in deciding that religion "should therefore be considered as the first of (the Americans') political institutions." (p.292)

Secondly, Tocqueville argued that a source of the influence of religion in America was to be found in the constitutional separation of church and state. Religion exerted its influence because of, not in spite of, the fact that no religion could be established or favored in America. Of the Catholic priests he conversed with during his travels,

> all thought that the main reason for the quiet sway of religion over their country was the complete separation of church and state. I have no hesitation in stating that throughout my stay in America I met nobody, lay or cleric, who did not agree about that. (p. 295)

Finally, according to Tocqueville's analysis, it is the indirect but powerful moral influence of religion that the clergy places at risk when they enter active politics. This is Tocqueville's concern, but it must also be a concern for our time, for the need for moral influences to control the tempting abuses of liberty remains. Even if today the clergy are not unanimous about their "quiet sway," nevertheless they should not, in my opinion, minimize their indirect influence.

Tocqueville concluded that the rough-and-tumble of political life itself would diminish the moral influence of those members of the clergy holding political office:

> As long as a religion relies only upon the sentiments which are the consolation of every affliction, it can draw the heart of mankind to itself. When it is mingled with the bitter passions of this world, it is sometimes constrained to defend allies who are such from interest rather than from love; and it has to repulse as adversaries men who still love religion, although they are fighting against religion's allies. *Hence religion cannot share the material strength of the rulers without being burdened with some of the animosity roused against them.* (p. 297—emphasis mine)

This observation may be more true today than it was a century and a half ago. (Politics has levelled its practitioners; no one in a legislature, senate, city council, or school board today gets respect from citizens because of his or her status, including religious status.) Politicians have come to accept the popular animosity that Tocqueville called attention to. They trade respect for power. But the clergy still depend for much of their influence on the respect they are accorded.

Some of the clergy, it is true, no longer share the insight Tocqueville credited to the clergy he met, that they "saw they would have to give up religious influence if they wanted to acquire political power." (p. 298) And why has this insight begun to fade away? The answer to this question can be found on the same page of *Democracy in America*: "When governments seem so strong and laws so stable, men do not see the danger that religion may run by allying itself with power." (p. 298) Better, perhaps to anticipate the dangers of clergy in politics than to wait for the results.

A position based solely on Tocqueville's argument would run the risk of basing contemporary political judgments on the conditions of religious and political life of the 1830s. Several modifications in Tocqueville's analysis might, however, bring it up to date. For example, Tocqueville's assumption that clergy in politics would be gaining power and sharing "the material strength of the rulers" applies to some clerical politicians but not to others. Many clerical politicians today enter politics to challenge the powerful rather than to join them, even "to speak truth to power." A second modification might weaken Tocqueville's central assumption that religion—the clergy in particular—in fact has great political influence without political practice. There is evidence that the American Catholic hierarchy today believe their influence has decreased and see politics as the path to regaining the moral sway that Tocqueville observed. In 1981, the president of the National Conference of Catholic Bishops, John R. Roach, said, "As a church, we are political practitioners because we have to be" (*Origins*, 3 Sep. 1981, p. 180). His text suggests that by the "church" and by "we" he meant the bishops. Later in 1981, Roach said "the social vision of faith increasingly calls the church to a public theology and public witness on political questions" (*Origins*, 3 Dec. 1981, p. 391). Such modifications, in my opinion, do not seriously compromise Tocqueville's conclusion that political office-holding by priests is inadvisable in the United States. Tocqueville's cautions need to be taken seriously today as well as a century and a half ago.

Neither Carroll's nor Tocqueville's warnings would seem to apply to religious orders of sisters, since both authors wrote in times when women were excluded from political office and from most forms of political activity. Moreover, religious sisters (and brothers) fall into neither the clerical nor the lay classification. Nonetheless, Tocqueville's concerns about indirect vs. direct religious influences on the citizenry do apply to the work of religious sisters. Whether sisters are among the "interpreters" of religion—Tocqueville's word—in the same sense as priests needs clarification, to be sure. Church law and Church authorities have brought sisters under the canonical proscription against clerical participation in political office; many sisters think this is inappropriate, since sisters do not have clerical status or functions. Some of the laity see sisters and priests as together constituting official religious leadership, though this perception may be changing. Given the perception of sisters by most bishops and many lay people, sisters as well as priests may need to diminish their official standing—with the bishops and with the laity—in order to become accepted as politicians. This reduction in status was what Tocqueville warned against. But if priests and sisters cannot shed their religious status in political office, then they may run afoul of the situation Archbishop Carroll warned against—bringing "discredit to the cause in whose service they are engaged."

A superficial reading of Tocqueville's remarks on the influence of the clergy may mislead us into thinking that he would oppose the holding of political office by any religious believer, clerical or lay. When Tocqueville warns that "religion cannot share the material strength of the rulers without being burdened with some of the animosity roused against them," one could infer that Catholic lay persons are also being warned. After all, do not laity and clergy carry the same moral and religious beliefs into political life? My answer to this question is "Yes, but": Yes, but clergy and laity differ essentially in their relationship to the institutional Church. As Quentin L. Quade wrote in 1983, "the believer-as-citizen, Catholic or other, is not the agent of any church, but simply a value-informed citizen, politically identical to any other citizen informed by whatever values are dear to him" (*Catholicism in Crisis*, May 1983, p. 42). Clearly Tocqueville thought that clergy in politics continued in some sense to be agents of the Church.

If it remains true today that priests are agents—that is, representatives—of the Church and continue to be such while in political office, then Tocqueville's argument applies to them. It never applied to the laity, and it can be made to apply to members of religious orders who are not priests only with difficulty. What is clearer, however, is that priests, brothers and sisters are subject to the authority of the Catholic hierarchy in a way not applicable to lay people. It seems likely that as the American Catholic bishops make political judgments of more and more particularity—as they have been doing for about 15 years—they will enforce their judgments with as much firmness as they find feasible. Those over whom their authority will naturally extend—virtually automatically—will be priests, brothers and sisters. The laity in their political lives are not expected to subject themselves to the authority of bishops. Moreover, the laity can resist and have resisted efforts by the hierarchy to impose political judgments—this is the fact that allows Catholic lay people to function as free American citizens. Priests and sisters do not enjoy the same freedom.

Whether the use of episcopal authority in the political lives of priests and sisters is proper or an abuse remains problematic. Yet as long as bishops effectively exercise this authority, priests and sisters in political office will continue to be perceived as official or quasi-official representatives of the Church, with both the advantages and the disadvantages that such a status brings.

THEOLOGY

For the bishops of the Vatican Council II, reasons to advise priests to avoid active politics ran even deeper than the analysis of Tocqueville. Whether the conciliar theology shoring up this advice applies to religious sisters and brothers—directly or indirectly—as well as to priests remains unclear.

Vatican II spoke emphatically of the great differences between the functions of priests and lay people in the church. The role of the laity in "the temporal order" is addressed in the Decree on the Apostolate of Lay People, "Apostolicam Actuositatem":

> Laymen ought to take on themselves as their distinctive task (the) renewal of the temporal order. Guided by the light of the Gospel and the mind of the Church, prompted by Christian love, they should act in this domain in a direct way and in their own specific manner. ("Apostolicam Actuositatem," #7. Austin Flannery, ed., *Vatican Council II: The Conciliar and Post Conciliar Documents.* Collegeville, Minn.: Liturgical Press, 1975, p. 774.)

This passage not only offers a religious basis for a lay person's political action but also suggests that whoever is not a lay person has a different task in the Church, since the renewal of the temporal order is a "distinctive task," that is, a task characteristic of lay persons, one serving to identify them as lay persons.

Vatican II theology on the role of priests in the temporal order is defined in the Decree on the Ministry and Life of Priests, "Presbyterorum Ordinis":

> The priests of the New Testament are, it is true, by their vocation to ordination, set apart in some way in the midst of the People of God, but this is not in order that they should be separated from that people or from any man, but

that they should be completely consecrated to the task for which God chooses them. ("Presbyterorum Ordinis," #3. Ibid., p. 866.)

If the meaning of "set apart" in this passage does not seem to refer specifically to politics, a statement several pages later clarifies the ambiguity somewhat: "In building up a community of Christians, priests can never be the servants of any human ideology or party" (ibid., #6, p. 875).

Vatican II theology, it would seem, assigns the laity and the clergy sharply different tasks. How this distinction is to be applied to the manifold callings of a real society depends on one's understanding and interpretation of the conciliar documents. Whether the passages quoted here acccurately reflect the overall spirit of Vatican II is not obvious. The situation is complicated by the question of whether religious sisters and brothers are to be discussed in the same terms as the clergy, that is, whether with respect to the temporal order, they are subject to similar restrictions as the clergy. Certain passages in the Decree on the Up-to-date Renewal of Religious Life, "Perfectae Caritatis," imply that the Council fathers intended religious sisters and brothers—called "members of institutes"—to be "set apart" in much the same manner as priests:

The members of each institute should recall, first of all, that when they made professions of the evangelical counsels they were responding to a divine call, to the end that, not merely being dead to sin but renouncing the world also, they might live for God alone. ("Perfectae Caritatis," #5. Ibid., p. 614.)

The phrase "renouncing the world" shares some ambiguity with the term "set apart" applied to priests, but the meanings of the two can hardly differ in any important way. "Perfectae Caritatis" adds, "The members of each institute, therefore, ought to seek God before all else, and solely" (ibid.).

No Vatican II passage by itself demonstrates that priests and sisters ought to eschew the active political life. But taken together, the quotations I have presented here point to a conclusion—more than plausible, less than convincing—that priests and sisters ought to recognize that their special place in the Church separates them in an important way from the temporal order and that those not ordained or enrolled in the religious life are expected to enter that temporal order and to take on its renewal as their specific, distinctive task.

If it were not for the attractions of political life, such a simple understanding of Vatican II theology might carry the day, and we would once again find that priests and sisters, in Tocqueville's words, "voluntarily steer clear of power." But this understanding is not shared by all theologians, and certainly not by many politically-minded priests and religious—hence the contemporary theological disputes about the political activity undertaken by members of the clergy and religious orders. My own opinion is that any priest or sister who enters political office as a full-time profession could only with great difficulty claim to be a devoted follower of the prescriptions of Vatican II quoted above. Yet he or she may be acting in the spirit of Vatican II without special focus on the passages I have singled out. Interpretations of Vatican II theology vary greatly, as always, and my opinion is only one among many.

The strength of theological interpretations—whether for good or ill—depends in part on the status and authority of the interpreter. Whether certain priests or sisters find political office to be compatible with the mandates of Vatican II may matter less than whether a bishop or religious superior shares their judgment. Priests and sisters answer to clearly defined figures of authority; their roles in the church, unlike those of lay persons, become concretized in hierarchical relationships. These hierarchical relationships, moreover, are made into legal statutes by canon law. Priests and sisters cannot escape the translation of theological judgments into authority and law; in this sense they lack the freedom of action that lay persons enjoy in the Church—and freedom of action means a great deal in American political life.

The new Code of Canon Law, promulgated in 1983, is built on the theology of Vatican II, or perhaps on a particular understanding of that theology. On the question of priests in politics, the new Code is unambiguous: "Clerics are forbidden to assume public office whenever it means sharing in the exercise of civil power" (Can. 285, #3. *The Code of Canon Law*. London: Collins Liturgical Publications, 1983, p. 49). If it were not for the authority of bishops to make exceptions to such regulations, this proscription would have driven every political priest from public office around the world—and in practical terms the debate would be over.

Religious brothers and sisters according to the new canon law, are said to be in a state "neither clerical nor lay" (Can. 588, #1. Ibid., p. 107). However, with respect to authority, this third state is more like the clerical state:

Institutes of consecrated life, since they are dedicated in a special way to the service of God and of the whole Church, are in a particular manner subject to its supreme authority. (Can. 590, #1. Ibid., p. 107.)

And in Canon 672, members of religious orders are forbidden to hold public office: "Religious are bound by the provisions of Can. 277, 285, 286, 287 and 289" (Ibid., p. 122). (Canon 285 is quoted above.)

Canon law, in short, directly forbids priests and religious from occupying political office but in its recognition of episcopal discretion and authority makes exceptions possible for both.

The line of reasoning that begins with Vatican II and extends to Canon Law and ends with the authority of bishops over the political offices held by priests and sisters is coherent, logical, defensible—though hardly definitive. Whether the canonical restrictions are necessary or desirable or opportune constitute separate questions which would appear to have little practical significance, for alterations in the new code are highly unlikely for many years.

Simply forbidding priests and sisters to hold elective and appointive political offices may have been a better inference from the theology of Vatican II than allowing exceptions to the rule. It is the exceptions and the authority of bishops to make them that have caused much more difficulty for priests and sisters than the regulations themselves.

Religious authority and political activity do not mix well in American society. If a priest or sister holds political office, he or she holds it according to constitutional or statutory provisions, by election or appointment. For the political office-holder to be subject to the electorate's or the appointing officer's decision is the way of American politics. But for that office-holder to be subject also to the discretionary authority of a bishop removes the very freedom of action that allowed the office-holder to seek and hold office in the first place. In other words, if a priest or sister is to be free to seek public office at all, he or she deserves not to have that freedom compromised. By retaining authority over priests and sisters who have received permission to seek and hold political office, bishops take on a political authority—and political authority is something the American polity aims to deny to churches. In such a situation—played out in the cases of Father Robert Drinan, Sister Agnes Mary Mansour, and Father Robert Ogle, among others—religion and politics are mixed, to the detriment of the political freedom of certain priests and sisters. In short, the authority to make exceptions to canonical prohibitions on clerical political activity results in a *de facto* grant of political authority to Catholic bishops. This is the inevitable result of the reasoning that led from Vatican II to the 1983 Code of Canon Law. A further conclusion has not yet been drawn, but I would recommend it: Priests and sisters should avoid political activity even if they believe such activity to be in the spirit of Vatican II theology; if they insist on seeking political office, they will subject their political office to religious superiors and thus compromise the very political activity they believe in. They may also risk reducing or damaging their status as clergy or members of religious orders.

In the abstract, I admit, all of the above theological and legal argumentation is debatable and controversial. My conclusion—that Vatican II, Canon Law, etc., imply that priests and sisters ought to avoid political office—may not persuade many people. But my argument is not abstract—it has had real consequences for real people. If someone remains unconvinced by the history and the theology of priests and sisters in politics, events of recent years may be more persuasive.

CURRENT EVENTS

Hubert Humphrey used to say he learned more about economics from one South Dakota dust storm than he did from all his years in college (See Winthrop Griffith, *Humphrey: A Candid Biography*. New York: Morrow, 1965, p. 52). American Catholics had an opportunity for a similarly intense learning experience in 1980, when Father Robert F. Drinan, S.J., a fifth-term U.S. congressman, was ordered by the Vatican not to stand for re-election. The direct order—originating from Pope John Paul II and transmitted by the Jesuit superior general in Rome to Father Drinan's provincial superior in New England—and Drinan's immediate capitulation might have more to teach about priests in politics than all the history, theology, and canon law we might study on the subject.

If we didn't learn our lesson from the Drinan case, and if we thought religious sisters wouldn't suffer similar fates, three years later we had a second chance to learn, when Archbishop Edmund Szoka of Detroit revoked his permission for Sister Agnes Mary Mansour, R.S.M., to continue as the director of the Michigan Department of Social Services. Sister Mansour demurred, but within a few months was pressured into relinquishing her vows as a Sister of Mercy of the Union.

And in 1984, in Canada, Father Robert Ogle received a letter from the apostolic pro-nuncio, Archbishop Angelo Palmas, reminding him that canon law prohibits priests from holding political office. Ogle had been a member of the Canadian parliament for five years with the permission of his bishop, James P. Mahoney of Saskatoon. After receiving the letter Ogle announced he would not run for re-election.

Are three South Dakota dust storms sufficient?

The cases of Robert Drinan and Robert Ogle demonstrate the power of the Vatican over priests. They show that a Vatican decision can be made and will be made independent of the judgment of a priest's local superiors and bishop. The Jesuit provincial in New England, Father Edward M. O'Flaherty, was not consulted before he received the telephone call about Drinan from the Rome headquarters of the Jesuit order on April 27, 1980. That the filing deadline for candidates for Congress from Massachusetts was May 6 was seen as no obstacle by the Vatican; Flaherty was informed that the decision was final. That Drinan had been elected five times by his district's voters also was no obstacle. Father Ogle received his letter four months after Bishop Mahoney had consulted Cardinal Silvio Oddi, head of the Sacred Congregation for the Clergy; Cardinal Oddi had informed the bishop he could give Ogle permission to run for re-election.

The Drinan case taught American Catholics not to be misled by the fact that certain priests have entered public office and have remained there for a time. In 1977, in Drinan's fourth term, religious reporter Jim Castelli wrote confidently, but prematurely, "Drinan. . .seems about to become a fixture in the House" (*Commonweal*, 24 June 1977, p. 398). Castelli generalized: "the involvement of religious in politics is now fairly widely accepted" (ibid., p. 399). The repeated permissions to run for Congress that Drinan had received from his American superiors counted for naught in Rome. Nor did the Vatican find any reason to explain why its decision was made.

Fr. Flaherty has reported that the Vatican had not singled out Drinan for personal discipline:

> It has been stressed to me that Vatican and Jesuit authorities in Rome wish to underline the point that the principal reason for the order was the pope's convictions about the proper role of priests. Indeed, one highly placed Vatican official privately expressed the hope that it might be possible to persuade people that 'the pope was acting exclu-

sively out of principle. There was no intention of singling out Father Drinan for criticism.

(*Origins*, 22 May 1980, p. 16.)

But what if the pope had decided to issue the order because of something about Drinan's politics, his position on abortion legislation, for example? The order could have been given in exactly the same way and would have been defended on a different principle. Doubtless Drinan would also have obeyed in this hypothetical case. The authority of the Vatican over priests in politics is firm enough so that the Vatican's reasons for acting are of little or no consequence to those who must obey. The Vatican's power reveals the local bishop's permission for priests to be in politics as undependable.

When the Vatican intervenes in the American political process, fears of religious interference in American political life are revived. American politics suffers as well as the politician affected, since direct control over any politician by a religious organization contradicts the American principle of separation of church and state. But since the Vatican seems not to be moved by this notion, shouldn't priests eschew political office for the good of the nation and the integrity of its politics?

The case of Agnes Mary Mansour taught the same lesson as the Drinan and Ogle cases—and much more. Sister Mansour accepted an appointment as Director of Social Services from Michigan Governor James Blanchard on December 29, 1982. Detroit Archbishop Edmund Szoka approved her appointment "as long as she makes clear her opposition to abortion" (*Origins*,1 Sep. 1983, p. 205). By placing this condition on his permission, Archbishop Szoka taught us a special lesson: bishops when allowing priests or sisters to enter political office have the prerogative to impose conditions. A political office-holder who accepts conditions from a religious superior gives up some political liberty to a religious leader, the very political liberty that enables a politician to make decisions in the public interest.

As Sister Mansour bitterly discovered later, the Archbishop's conditions were more precise than they appeared at the outset. On Feb. 23, 1983, Szoka called for Mansour's resignation from her new office, reporting that he had "clearly told her that if she did not publicly oppose Medicaid payment for abortion, I would have to declare my objection and opposition to her appointment" (*Origins*, 26 May 1983, p. 35). Szoka thus demonstrated that conditions placed on a bishop's permission may change, and that his permission may be withdrawn at any time. The degree of control over a clerical or religious political office-holder thus claimed by a bishop is extraordinary in American political terms. Its potential for abuse is alarming.

That Agnes Mary Mansour was a sister and not a priest counted for naught in her case. That a bishop has authority over a sister entering politics was a settled fact in the case—settled in the bishop's mind and in the Vatican's. Early in the dispute, which lasted only three months, Sister Mansour expressed a view of episcopal authority that appears too mild in retrospect. In a statement at her confirmation hearing on March 8, she said of Archbishop Szoka:

> His demand of me and of my religious superiors that I resign. . .raised once again the suspicion that the church can intrude in state affairs and Catholics, much less a Catholic sister, are not free from church control. (*Origins*, 31 March 1983, p. 677.)

In a short time, the "suspicion" became a reality. Mansour was given the choice of resigning her political office or being dispensed from her religious vows. The Vatican sent its own representative— Auxiliary Bishop Anthony Bevilacqua of Brooklyn—to deliver this mandatory choice. Bishop Bevilacqua reminded Mansour of "her vows of obedience to the Holy Father" (*Origins*, 26 May 1983, p. 36). Her protestations had brought Mansour up against the hard rock of Church authority.

CONCLUSION

Sister Mansour lost after a brief period of protest. Father Drinan gave up without a fight. Father Ogle abandoned his bid for re-election within two weeks after hearing from the Vatican nuncio. Father Robert Cornell, a Norbertine priest and former congressman, capitulated to his bishop in the wake of the Drinan case and dropped out of his 1980 re-election campaign. In 1984, Elizabeth Morancy and Arlene Violet, Sisters of Mercy in Rhode Island, left their religious order because Bishop Louis E. Gelineau of Providence insisted they choose between their religious vows and political office. Morancy is a State Representative; Violet was a candidate for Rhode Island attorney general.

Need there be more cases to convince American priests and sisters that they cannot prevail against bishops and the Vatican? That their political ambitions likely will be controlled and then dashed by their religious superiors? That political office for them will always be subject to religious authority?

When the Vatican drove Robert Drinan from the U.S. Congress, the editors of *Commonweal* tried to react with moderation. "We believe," the editors wrote, "the ordained ministers should avoid political office but can see good grounds for exceptions" (*Commonweal*, 23 May 1980, p. 293). A similar judgment was expressed by Monsignor George G. Higgins, former director of the U.S. bishops' Social Action Department: "While, as a general rule, I can see no urgent need for priests to run for political office under partisan auspices, I would allow for exceptions" ("May Church Ministers Be Politicians?" *Concilium* #157, 1982, p. 85). Higgins added that he "would generally advise against" the involvement of the clergy in elected political office (ibid., p. 83). Neither Higgins nor the *Commonweal* editors, however, seemed to find any problems with the exceptions themselves.

A simple rule, whether canonical or not, that would exclude priests and sisters from political office without exceptions could with some difficulty be defended on theological and historical grounds. Probably such a blanket rule would be attacked as unreasonable by many American Catholics, lay and clerical, despite historical precedents and statements in documents of Vatican II. Such a rule does not exist, however, and arguments for and against it are only theoretical. The rule that does exist bars priests, brothers and sisters from political office *unless they receive permission from their bishop*. In other words, for priests and sisters to practice active politics in the United States, they must give over their right to decide on beginning and continuing in political office into the hands of their bishop, who may in turn be overruled by the Vatican. The bishops or the Vatican may impose conditions, change their minds, make decisions on grounds acceptable only to themselves, engage in dialogue or not, divulge their reasoning or not.

The history, theology and current events presented in this chapter lead to two practical conclusions. The first is that the seeking and holding of elective or appointive public office by Catholic priests and members of religious orders risks compromising the separation of church and state, risks a mixing of religion and politics that the U.S. Constitution in its First Amendment intends to avoid. The second is that sisters, brothers and priests who take the risk will probably have difficulties retaining their office—difficulties imposed by their bishop or the Vatican itself. Given this situation, does it make good sense for priests and sisters to aspire to political office? It might for some here and there, but in general it seems clear enough that priests and sisters ought to avoid political office.

Any discussion of the proper relationship of Catholic priests and religious to partisan politics and service in government posts must inevitably make reference to specific provisions in Canon Law concerning these matters. The situation of U.S. clergy and religious has been complicated by the differences in restrictiveness, emphasis and interpretation between the 1917 Code and the Revised Code of 1983. We have included both the Latin and English texts of key canons for ready reference.

In addition to the documents of Vatican II and several pastoral letters of the three most recent popes, one document has particular relevance to the subject of this volume, a publication of the Sacred Congregation for Religious and Secular Institutes titled, "Religious Life and Human Promotion," 1980.

In respect to the involvement of priests in politics, the most recent collective episcopal commentary is found in a few pertinent paragraphs in "The Ministerial Priesthood," a pastoral document issued by Pope Paul VI and the Bishops' Synod of 1971.

Also, a significant assessment of the experience of American religious vis a vis the socio-political sector was a joint report prepared for the Vatican by the Leadership Conference of Women Religious and the Conference of Major Superiors of Men in 1978 called, "U.S. Religious Orders Today."

Since no national organizations of priests of comparable scope and representation have taken a position on this issue, and since the U.S. Conference of Catholic Bishops has issued only general policy statements on religion and politics, we have included a position paper

413

on "The Priest and Politics," a policy statement developed by the Association of Pittsburgh Priests, as an example of the views of a significant number of U.S. clergy. This was the only collectively sponsored document we were able to locate on the subject.

CODE OF CANON LAW, 1917

Canon 139

§1. Clerics shall also avoid those occupations which, although not unbecoming, are alien to the clerical state.

§2. Without an apostolic indult, clerics shall not practice medicine or surgery, or act as public notaries, except in the ecclesiastical Curia; and they shall not accept public offices which involve the exercise of lay jurisdiction or administrative duties.

§3. Without permission of their ordinary, clerics shall not undertake the administration or the management of the goods or the property of lay persons, or secular offices which involve the obligation of rendering an account; nor shall they act as procurator or advocate, except in ecclesiastical court, or when their own interests or the interests of the Church are involved, in the secular court. Clerics shall not take any part, even as witnesses, without necessity, in secular criminal cases involving the possible infliction of grave personal punishment.

§4. Clerics shall not solicit or accept the office of senator or deputy, without the permission of the Holy See in those countries where it is required, or, in other places, the permission of their own ordinary as well as of the ordinary of the place where the election is to be held.

Canon 139

§1. Ea etiam, quae, licet non indecora, a clericali tamen statu aliena sunt, vitent.

§2. Sine apostolico indulto medicinam vel chirurgiam ne exerceant; tabelliones seu publicos notarios, nisi in Curia ecclesiastica, ne agant; officia publica, quae exercitium laicalis iurisdictionis vel administrationis secumferunt, ne assumant.

§3. Sine licentia sui Ordinarii ne ineant gestiones bonorum ad laicos pertinentium aut officia saecularia quae secumferant onus reddendarum rationum; procuratoris aut advocati munus ne exerceant,

nisi in tribunali ecclesiastico, aut in civili quando agitur de causa pro-
pria aut suae ecclesiae; in laicali iudicio criminali, gravem personalem
poenam prosequente, nullam partem habeant, ne testimonium qui-
dem sine necessitate ferentes.

§4. Senatorum aut oratorum legibus ferendis, quos *deputatos* vo-
cant, munus ne sollicitent neve accepent sine licentia Sanctae Sedis in
locis ubi pontificia prohibitio intercesserit; idem ne attentent aliis in
locis sine licentia tum sui Ordinarii, tum Ordinarii loci in quo electio
facienda est.

Canon 141

§1. Clerics are forbidden to volunteer for military service unless
they do so with the permission of their ordinary for the purpose of
freeing themselves the earlier from military obligations; nor should
they participate in civil conflict or disturbances of the public order.

§2. A cleric in minor orders who, contrary to the rule of §1, has
voluntarily entered military service, by that very fact forfeits the clerical state.

Canon 141

§1. Saecularem militiam ne capessant voluntarii, nisi cum sui Ordinarii licentia, ut citius liberi evadant, id fecerint; neve intestinis bellis
et ordinis publici perturbationibus opem quoquo modo ferant.

§2. Clericus minor qui contra praescriptum §1 sponte sua militiae
nomen dederit, ipso iure e statu clericali decidit.

Canon 592

All religious are bound to the common obligations of clerics
treated of in canons 124-142, except it appears otherwise from the
context or from the nature of the case.

Canon 592

Obligationibus communibus clericorum, de quibus in can. 124-
142, etiam religiosi omnes tenentur, nisi ex contextu sermonis vel ex
rei natura aliud constet.

CODE OF CANON LAW, 1983

Canon 285

§1. In accord with the prescriptions of particular law, clerics are to refrain completely from all those things which are unbecoming to their state.

§2. Clerics are to avoid those things which, although not unbecoming, are nevertheless alien to the clerical state.

§3. Clerics are forbidden to assume public offices which entail a participation in the exercise of civil power.

§4. Without the permission of their ordinary clerics are neither to become agents for goods belonging to laypersons nor assume secular offices which entail an obligation to render accounts; they are forbidden to act as surety, even on behalf of their own goods, without consultation with their proper ordinary; they are likewise to refrain from signing promissory notes whereby they undertake the obligation to pay an amount of money without any determined reason.

Canon 285

§1. Clerici ab iis omnibus, quae statum suum dedecent, prorsus abstineant, iuxta iuris particularis praescripta.

§2. Ea quae, licet non indecora, a clericali tamen statu aliena sunt, clerici vitent.

§3. Officia publica, quae participationem in exercitio civilis potestatis secumferunt, clerici assumere vetantur.

§4. Sine licentia sui Ordinarii, ne ineant gestiones bonorum ad laicos pertinentium aut officia saecularia, quae secumferunt onus reddendarum rationum; a fideiubendo, etiam de bonis propriis, inconsulto proprio Ordinario, prohibentur; item a subscribendis syngraphis, quibus nempe obligatio solvendae pecuniae, nulla definita causa, suscipitur, abstineant.

Canon 287

§1. Most especially, clerics are always to foster that peace and harmony based on justice which is to be observed among all persons.

§2. Clerics are not to have an active role in political parties and in the direction of labor unions unless the need to protect the rights of the Church or to promote the common good requires it in the judgment of the competent ecclesiastical authority.

Canon 287

§1. Clerici pacem et concordiam iustitia innixam inter homines servandam quam maxime semper foveant.

§2. In factionibus politicis atque in regendis consociationibus syndicalibus activam partem ne habeant, nisi iudicio competentis auctoritatis ecclesiasticae, Ecclesiae iura tuenda aut bonum commune promovendum id requirant.

Canon 672

Religious are bound by the prescriptions of cann. 277, 285, 286, 287, and 289, and, moreover, religious clerics are bound by the prescriptions of can. 279, §2; in lay institutes of pontifical right, the permission mentioned in can. 285, §4 can be granted by the proper major superior.

Canon 672

Religiosi adstringuntur praescriptis cann. 277, 285, 286, 287 et 289, et religiosi clerici insuper praescriptis can. 279 § 2; in institutis laicalibus iuris pontificii, licentia de qua in can. 285, § 4 concedi potest a proprio Superiore maiore.

Canon 739

Besides the obligations which they have as members according to the constitutions the members are bound by the common obligations of clerics, unless something else is evident from the nature of the matter or from the context.

Canon 739

Sodales, praeter obligationes quibus, uti sodales, obnoxii sunt secundum constitutiones, communibus obligationibus clericorum adstringuntur, nisi ex natura rei vel ex contextu sermonis aliud constet.

Canon 678

§1. Religious are subject to the authority of bishops, whom they are obliged to follow with devoted humility and respect, in those matters which involve the care of souls, the public exercise of divine worship and other works of the apostolate.

§2. In exercising an external apostolate, religious are also subject to their own superiors and must remain faithful to the discipline of the institute, which obligation bishops themselves should not fail to insist upon in cases which warrant it.

§3. In organizing the works of the apostolate of religious, it is necessary that diocesan bishops and religious superiors proceed after consultation with each other.

Canon 678

§1. Religiosi subsunt potestati Episcoporum, quos devoto obsequio ac reverentia prosequi tenentur, in iis quae curam animarum, exercitium publicum cultus divini et alia apostolatus opera respiciunt.

§2. In apostolatu externo exercendo religiosi propriis quoque Superioribus subsunt et disciplinae instituti fideles permanere debent; quam obligationem ipsi Episcopi, si casus ferat, urgere ne omittant.

§3. In operibus apostolatus religiosorum ordinandis Episcopi dioecesani et Superiores religiosi collatis consiliis procedant oportet.

A Document Published by the Vatican Congregation for Religious and for Secular Institutes, 1980

RELIGIOUS LIFE AND HUMAN PROMOTION

INTRODUCTION

Importance and urgency of appropriate involvement of religious in integral human promotion:

The evangelical demands of religious life find an incentive for renewal in the "signs of the times." The church, in her mission to contemporary society, needs to study carefully the emerging phenomena that characterize our times. These indicate the areas of choice for evangelization and human promotion.

The teaching of the magisterium, in fact, increasingly clarifies the profound links between the gospel requirements of the church's mission and the widespread commitment to the advancement of people and the creation of a worthy society.

Evangelization, for the church, means bringing the good news into all strata of humanity and through it transforming humanity itself from within: its criteria of discernment, its determinant values, its sources of inspiration, its designs for living, opening them up to a total vision of humanity.[1]

To accomplish this mission, the church must search out the signs of the times and interpret them in the light of the Gospel, thus responding to persistent human questions.[2]

—Religious are called to give singular witness to this prophetic dimension. The continuous conversion of heart and spiritual freedom which the Lord's counsels inspire and promote make them present to their contemporaries in such a way as to remind everyone that the building of the secular city must be founded on the Lord and have him as its goal.[3]

Since the profession of the counsels binds religious to the church in a special way,[4] it is they who are exhorted more insistently and trustingly to renew themselves wisely in openness to human needs, problems and searchings.[5]

—Over and above the social and political dramas, in fact, the church is conscious of her special mission to give a decisive answer to the profound questions of the human heart.[6]

For this reason, recent documents of the magisterium, wishing to integrate adequately evangelization and human promotion, stress how fruitful the relationship between evangelization and religious life is for the common mission of the church[7] and the extent to which the work of religious has contributed in every age to the human and spiritual promotion of humanity.[8]

—A radical change of mentality and attitudes[9] is needed to apply evangelical commitment to the concrete and often disturbing problems of human promotion.

This path of conversion, involving persons and preferential decisions in apostolic initiatives and works, was bound to have its moments of uncertainty and difficulty.

Besides, the doctrinal reassessment which, in various parts of the world, accompanied the praiseworthy endeavor to participate in the complex realities of the times, revealed positive and stimulating intuitions as well as narrow and ambiguous views.

The reflections of the synod on evangelization in the modern world (1974) and, later, the apostolic exhortation *Evangelii Nuntiandi,* gave important clarifications and guidelines.

—Religious faced particular problems and difficulties when they tried to intervene more decisively in the areas of greater injustice and oppression. Conflicting viewpoints within the ecclesial community and within the institutes themselves made the search for solutions still more difficult.

Furthermore, changed social and political contexts were creating new and unexpected situations. The traditional expressions of religious life were bound to face difficult challenges in their manner of presence and in their apostolic works. The need for greater solidarity with their contemporaries, especially the poor and the underprivileged, compelled religious men and women to become more actively involved, sometimes even in the working world and in politics.

—The importance and urgency of the appropriate involvement of religious in integral human promotion prompted the Sacred Congregation for Religious and for Secular Institutes to give special attention in this matter to the specific role of religious in the mission of the church.

The intention was to encourage a real search for renewal and, on the basis of circumstances and experience, to offer criteria for discernment inspired by the magisterium of the church, by the nature and mission of religious life and by the goals of an evangelization which is closely linked to human promotion in today's historical circumstances.

The plenary meeting of the sacred congregation April 25-28, 1978, therefore, studied a number of matters resulting from a wide-ranging international inquiry, in which the episcopal conferences, the pontifical representatives, numerous institutes of both men and women and the conferences of major superiors, men and women, collaborated.

—Four major concerns of utmost importance surfaced: a) the option for the poor and for justice in our time; b) social activities and works of religious; c) involvement in the working world; d) direct participation in politics.

—The resulting guidelines are intended to assist all those who are responsible for religious life in the church in their task of communication, formation and coordination. It is they who must approve criteria and choices which, while taking into account the principles and guidelines offered here, respond to the diversity and complexity of the situations, so that episcopal conferences and conferences of religious in the different countries may reinforce the specific role of religious life in the common task of evangelization and human promotion in whatever ways they deem most suitable.

—The pastoral teaching of John Paul II has, in the meantime, clarified and defined the presence and involvement of the church in the world, giving additional matter for reflection and inspiration. It highlights the present attention given both to human problems and to the irreplaceable encounter with Christ and with his Gospel.

We are encouraged, therefore, to clarify the direction of a path of evangelization and human promotion which, by a new and special title of consecration to God and to his purpose in human history, pertains to religious in the church.

I. FOUR MAIN CONCERNS

1. The desire to be increasingly involved and active in the present historical situations within which the church fulfills her mission seems to be a constant factor in religious renewal:

—in those places where, either through the works of their institutes or those of the local church, religious are called to carry out a social mission which is at the same time profoundly religious,

—and also, in those places where circumstances require new initiatives which are more pertinent to the life and problems of the people.

In every situation, however, careful reflection is needed to specify common criteria and options.

That is why, taking as our starting point the four main problems surfaced by the inquiry, we wish to indicate certain important points for evaluation and guidance. It will then be easier to point out the general principles of discernment.

A. *The Option for the Poor and for Justice*

2. The prophetic mission of Christ who was "sent to preach good news to the poor" (Lk. 4:18), finds a strong resonance in today's church.

Proof of this can be found in numerous pontifical statements and in the clear and enlightening words of the pastoral constitution *Gaudium et Spes,* which appeal for closer solidarity between the church and the lives of the people. The Synod of Bishops in 1971, in its document *Justice in the World,* pointed out the need for a conscientization in this dimension of the church's evangelizing mission.

The apostolic exhortation *Evangelii Nuntiandi* enlarged on these appeals, calling on every sector within the people of God to accept its responsibilities and to reach out to the life and conditions of "people engaged with all their energy in the effort and struggle to overcome everything which condemns them to remain on the margin of life."[10]

3. The themes of a gospel liberation founded on the kingdom of God[11] should therefore be very familiar to religious.

Indeed, the witness of religious who have courageously supported the lowly and the defense of human rights has been an effective echo of the Gospel and of the voice of the church. However, as we have already noted, the consequent interpretations and reactions within the local church and religious communities and even secular society have not always shown a similar sensitivity and concern.

4. Some guiding principles, therefore, seem desirable so that the preferential choice of the poor and concern for justice may correspond to the purpose and style proper to the church's mission and within it to religious life.

a) Religious often find themselves in a position to experience at close range the events that affect the people whom they serve. The prophetic nature of religious life requires that religious "embody the church in her desire to give herself completely to the radical demands of the Beatitudes."[12] They are "often to be found at the outposts of the mission, and they take the greatest of risks for their health and for their very lives."[13]

b) This sincere desire to serve the Gospel and work for integral human promotion demands that communion be at the core of every concern and that it be built up with patience and perseverance, seeking the truth in charity.

c) Conferences of religious, without prejudice to the charism of each institute, could have the important function of providing incentive and balance in this regard in coordination with episcopal conferences[14] and especially with the Justice and Peace Commission and with Cor Unum. It would be possible in this way to overcome positions of ambiguity taken either from a supposed and false neutrality or from group prejudice. Besides, different cultures and temperaments, as well as varying social and political contexts, would therein find an appropriate forum for mutual exchanges and for a communal consensus that would give security and surer effectiveness.

d) This presence for the defense and promotion of justice ought to manifest itself most actively and particularly in those persecuted sectors of "voiceless injustices" to which the synod of 1971 referred.[15]

In fact, while some social groups are able to form vigorous structures of protest and support, we see, on the other hand, much suffering and injustice which have little resonance in the hearts of so many of our contemporaries: the plight of refugees, those persecuted for their political views or their profession of the faith;[16] violations of the rights of the unborn; unjustified curtailment of human and religious liberty; lack of social assistance, which increases the trials of the elderly and marginalized . . .

It is for these, especially that the church wishes to be voice, conscience and commitment.[17]

e) The witness of religious for justice in the world, however, implies, for themselves in particular, a constant review of their life options, their use of goods and their manner of relating, because the one who dares to speak to others about justice must above all be just in the eyes of others.[18]

Here we see that life-giving relationship between evangelization and human promotion which comes from the "silent witness" which *Evangelii Nuntiandi,* 69, presents to us as the first and most effective challenge to the world and to the church itself.

From this point of view the "role played in evangelization by religious men and women consecrated to prayer, silence, penance and sacrifice"[19] is particularly effective in witness and in apostolic fruitfulness. Indeed, the contemplative dimension inherent in every form of religious life is especially strong in them. The contemplative dimension, then, shows that religious life in all its forms not only does not alienate religious from other human beings and make them useless for human society, but, on the contrary, permits them to be present to their brothers and sisters in a deeper way in the charity of Christ.[20]

B. Social Activities and Works of Religious

5. The various activities and works which, through a diversity of charisms, characterize the mission of religious are one of the most important means by which the church carries out its mission of evangelization and human promotion in the world.[21] Hence the importance of the renewal of religious for the renewal of the church and the world.[22]

This is why *Evangelii Nuntiandi,* 31, asks that there be an awareness of the profound links between evangelization and human promotion. To forget this would be to ignore "the gospel teaching on love for one's suffering and needy neighbor."

6. Open to the signs of the times, religious will be able to seek and implement a new manner of presence which is in keeping with their founder's creativity and the original purposes of their own institutes.[23]

In this context, a certain course of action in renewal emerges:

a) The activities and "social works" which were always part of the mission of religious bear witness to their constant commitment to integral human promotion. Schools, hospitals, charity centers and initiatives on behalf of the poor and for the cultural and spiritual improvement of people not only retain their relevance but, suitably updated, are often discovered to be privileged means of evangelization, of witness and of authentic human promotion.

In the evangelical service of so many and such urgent activities for human and social promotion, religious translate into a convincing "sign"[24] the gift of a life totally available to God, to the church and to others.

b) The Spirit, who constantly inspires new forms and institutions of consecrated life in answer to the needs of the times, also animates the already existing ones with a renewed capacity for involvement in keeping with changing ecclesial and social changes.

c) In the church's openness to ministries and in a continuous and orderly communal growth,[25] religious are able to discover new forms of active participation, involving the Christian community increasingly in their initiatives and works.

In this way they have the opportunity to show what their own particular charism brings to the promotion of ministries which correspond to the apostolic and social purposes of their own institutes.

d) The participation of the laity in the activities and works of religious assumes new proportions with the development of the ecclesial dimension of coresponsibility in a common mission. With adequate preparation, this participation could be extended even to works hitherto entrusted exclusively to religious.[26]

e) Present social conditions, on the other hand, require new forms of solidarity and involvement. Changes taking place in some areas in the civil sphere are beginning to develop responsibility on all levels of society through structures and means of participation. Thus, everyone is called to take an active role in solving problems relating to the building of the social order.

Side by side with the contribution of the laity, the witness and experience of religious can make an important contribution in this field toward solutions which are in line with the criteria of the Gospel and the pastoral directives of the magisterium.[27]

C. Involvement in the Working World

7. The pastoral concern of the church for the working world is shown in numerous pronouncements which the encyclical *Mater et Magistra* sums up, placing them within the context of the new economic and social conditions.

Faced with such a vast sector of humanity which insistently challenges the mission of the whole Christian community, religious experience a greater need for solidarity and participation. They feel that their choice of evangelical poverty already imposes on them the duty of recognizing the authentic values contained in the common law of work.[28]

8. The magisterium of the bishops described precisely, in the case

of priests, the reasons, objectives and conditions which should guide the more committed choices of involvement in the working world.[29]

Obviously, these directives apply to priest-religious also. But, given the specific nature of religious life, and its special bonds with the church's mission,[30] they are applicable analogously to other men and women religious as well.

In addition, the characteristics proper to the vocation and mission of religious suggest some criteria which could determine and direct their possible involvement in the work world:

a) dynamic fidelity to the purposes for which the Spirit brought their institutes into existence in the church;[31]

b) the desire to witness to gospel values which restore dignity to work and show its true purpose;[32]

c) a commitment to strengthen the religious dimensions which characterize their profession and demonstrate the attractiveness of the kingdom of God to which they have committed themselves radically;[33]

d) fraternal sharing, which the daily communal experience in religious life supports and nourishes and which manifests the newness of Christ's love in establishing solidarity among peoples.[34]

9. Specific criteria in choice and behavior are needed, also, in the actual ways of participating.

As a matter of fact, there are two possible forms of involvement in the working world, both of which have characteristics that deserve distinct consideration:

a)—The taking on of a secular profession carried out in the same social and economic conditions as civilians (in schools, hospitals . . .)

In some countries this is imposed by changed political circumstances, as in the case of nationalization when the state takes control of the services. Sometimes it is legislative reform or the internal needs of the religious institute which prompt religious to take on a position equivalent to that of lay people so as to continue their own apostolic activities. The search for new forms of involvement has also been responsible for participation in the ordinary social structures.

In all cases, concern for the general nature of religious life and for the specific goals of one's own institute requires that these new situations be faithful to community requirements and the commitment to obedience and religious poverty.

As a matter of fact, a civil profession commits religious at a more directly individual level, makes them more dependent on structures outside their institute and creates a new relationship between work and salary. These are some of the aspects that the authorities in the institute should take into account when considering these options. Indeed, these aspects require a capacity for discernment which safeguards and strengthens the religious purpose for which the options are undertaken.

b)—Involvement in a labor situation, along with the values it is meant to realize, presents special problems.

In fact, worker-religious enter a world which has its own laws, its tensions and, especially nowadays, its powerful pressures arising from prevailing ideologies and trade-union conflicts which are often disturbing and ambiguous.

For this reason, it could happen that, in sharing the condition of workers so as to bear witness to the church's pastoral concern,[35] religious might be caught up in a view of humanity, society, history and the working world itself which is not in harmony with the criteria for discernment and the directives for action contained in the social teaching of the magisterium. That is why such an undertaking requires special care and guarantees.[36]

10. Even more, involvement in trade-union activities demands a clear awareness of pastoral objectives as well as of the limitations and risks of exploitation that could result in the lives and activity of religious.

Certain principles should guide reflection on this matter.

a) In principle there does not seem to be any intrinsic incompatibility between religious life and social involvement even at trade-union level. At times, according to the different laws, involvement in trade-union activity might be a necessary part of participation in the world of labor; on the other hand, such involvement might be prompted by solidarity in the legitimate defense of human rights.[37]

b) Political involvement, however, often poses difficult problems. These situations should be evaluated according to the criteria given in the following section (cf. "D. Involvement in Politics"). Special care is needed in dealing with ideologies which promote class struggle. In this case, the teaching of *Octogesima Adveniens* (26-36) would be most necessary.

c) From experience up to the present, moreover, it is possible to deduce certain principles of behavior to direct the purpose and style of such choices. Within a body as influential in society as the world of labor, religious are the bearers of human and Christian values which will oblige them to repudiate certain methods of trade-union action or of political maneuvering which do not respond to the exact demands of justice which alone are the reason for their involvement.

Within their own communities also, these religious should know how to foster values of communion, avoiding undesirable polarizations. Such an attitude will help the communities to take balanced and credible options.

d) Another essential criterion which should determine the involvement of religious is the awareness that it is particularly to the laity by vocation and mission that the duty of promoting solidarity and justice within secular structures belongs.[38] Their role in complementarity, especially in this area, will be expressed above all by their witness and their contribution to an ever more adequate formation of the laity.

D. Involvement in Politics

11. Religious have shown, generally, that they are conscious of the fact that their involvement in human promotion is a service of the Gospel to humanity, not a preferential choice of ideologies or political parties.

On the contrary, in any such involvement, they see the risk of a loss of the identity proper to religious life and to the church's mission[39] as well as a dangerous tendency to absolutize ideas and methods and to become a prey to easy and selfish exploitation.

12. Some guiding principles, in harmony with the teaching of the magisterium, would then seem necessary to throw light on a subject which in itself is a matter of heated debate and is sometimes misleading.

a) Politics can be understood in the wider and more general sense as the dynamic organization of the whole life of society. In this respect, it constitutes a duty of responsible and active human participation for all citizens. Looked at in this way, the role of religious in activities and works is profoundly meaningful in its encouragement of and commitment to those cultural and social changes which contribute to human promotion.

b) But if politics means direct involvement with a political party, then certain reservations must be made in view of the vocation and mission of religious in the church and in society, so as to arrive at correct criteria governing a possible involvement.

1. Religious, aware of the worthwhile contribution that their gospel witness and the variety of their apostolic initiatives make, should not be deluded into thinking that they will have greater influence on the development of persons and peoples by substituting a political involvement in the strict sense for their own specific tasks.[40]

2. To establish the kingdom of God within the very structures of the world, insofar as this constitutes evangelical promotion in human history, is certainly a theme of great interest for the whole Christian

community, and therefore for religious also; but not in the sense that they allow themselves to become involved directly in politics. Through their scholastic institutes, the communications media, and multiple religious and education projects, they can actively contribute especially to the formation of the young, thus making them architects of human and social development. The repercussions of this apostolate will not fail to be felt in the political sphere also. This is not through a strategy of conquest but through that service to human society which is the mission mandated by Christ to the whole ecclesial community (Lk. 22:25-27)

3. It is from this point of view that the efforts of women religious to cooperate in the advancement of women are to be encouraged, so that women may succeed in being involved in those areas of public and ecclesial life which best correspond with their particular nature and the qualities that are proper to them.

4. In this way, religious will be credible gospel experts, and as such will be effective in healing and building up society, even when they stand apart from certain political options, being seen not as men and women who take sides, but as agents of peace and fraternal solidarity.

In fact, by the primacy of love of God which their options effectively manifest,[42] religious situate themselves as persons of the Absolute in the dynamism of the church, which is thirsty for the divine Absolute.[43] They are called to be in the midst of the people of God both sign and stimulant of this fundamental option which promotes and conditions all others.

5. Active involvement in politics remains an exception then, to be engaged in only by way of substitution and to be evaluated according to special criteria. If exceptional circumstances require it, the individual cases must be examined so that, with the approval of the authorities of the local church and the religious institutes, decisions can be made that are beneficial to the ecclesial and secular community. But the priority of the specific mission of the church and of religious life must always be kept in mind as well as the methods proper to it.[44]

II. GENERAL CRITERIA OF DISCERNMENT

13. Four great loyalties constitute the basic motivation and guide of the role of religious in human promotion, according to the conciliar principles for renewal[45] and taking into account the problems examined thus far:

—fidelity to humanity and to our times,
—fidelity to Christ and the Gospel,
—fidelity to the church and to its mission in the world,
—fidelity to religious life and to the charism of one's own institute.

A. *Present to Humanity and to Our Times*

14. The cultural, social and political changes which affect peoples and continents, not without distress, demand of the church an evangelical presence which is a response to the most widespread hopes and aspirations of humanity.[46]

This pressing pastoral concern, made more acute by the reflections and goals of the Second Vatican Council, has reappeared in the Synod of Bishops and in apostolic exhortations, appealing clearly and insistently to the Christian community to make courageous choices in the process of renewal so as to draw modern men and women to the Gospel, the source of all authentic human and social progress.[47]

15. The history of today's world, embodied in the concrete existence of every person, becomes an open book for serious meditation by the church and by all Christians.[48] It is a challenge to all vocations in the church, calling them to an exacting revision of life and commitment.

Religious, because of the radicality of their evangelical options, feel more profoundly challenged. They know that in the measure they themselves are converted to God's original plan for humanity as revealed in the new man Jesus[49] they will help accelerate in others that conversion of mentality and outlook which will make the reform of economic, social and political structures authentic and stable and place them in the service of a more just and peaceful coexistence.[50]

16.   To achieve this, in striving for renewal in their witness and mission, all religious institutes are exhorted to procure for their members "a proper understanding of humanity, of the conditions of the times and of the needs of the church, so that, making wise judgments about the contemporary world in the light of faith and burning with apostolic zeal, they may be able to help men and women more effectively."[51]

B. *By the Transforming Power of Christ and the Gospel*

17.   The Gospels bear witness to Christ and to the fidelity with which he fulfilled the mission for which he was consecrated by the Spirit.[52] It was a mission of evangelization and human redemption

which led him to live among his people, sharing their lot, but illuminating and directing it, preaching and witnessing to the Gospel of conversion to the kingdom of God.[53]

His startling proposal of the Beatitudes introduced a radical change of perspective in evaluating temporal reality and human and social relations which he wished to be centered on a justice-sanctity animated by the new law of love.[54]

His life options should be especially characteristic of religious, who make their own the "form of life which the Son of God embraced when he came into the world."[55]

18.   Faithful to this supreme norm,[56] religious know that they are caught up daily in a path of conversion to the kingdom of God, which makes them in the church and before the world a sign capable of attracting, thus inspiring a profound revision of life and values.[57]

This is, without doubt, the most needed and fruitful commitment to which they are called,[58] even in those areas where the Christian community works for human promotion and for the development of social relations inspired by principles of solidarity and fraternal communion.

In this way, they cooperate in "safeguarding the originality of Christian liberation and the energies that it is capable of developing—liberation in its full, profound sense, as Jesus proclaimed and accomplished it."[59]

19.   The power of transformation which is contained in the spirit of the Beatitudes and penetrates dynamically the life of religious, characterizes their vocation and mission.[60] For them the first Beatitude and primary liberation is the encounter with Christ, poor among the poor, testifying that they really believe in the pre-eminence of the kingdom of God above all earthly things and in its highest demands.[61]

By spreading in this way the Christian and profoundly human meaning of the realities of history, which finds its origin in the Beatitudes which have now become the criterion for life, religious show how close is the bond between the Gospel and human promotion in social coexistence. For this reason, the church can point to the evangelical witness of religious as a splendid and singular proof that the way of the Beatitudes is the only one capable of "transforming the world and offering it to God."[62]

C. In the Organic Ecclesial Communion

20.   The common vocation of Christians to union with God and union with each other for the salvation of the world[63] should be considered before diversity of gifts and ministries.

On this common vocation are based the relations of communion between the ecclesial components and, especially, with those whom the Holy Spirit has chosen as bishops to nourish the church of God.[64]

21. Religious, united more intimately to the church,[65] participate in a way altogether proper to them in the sacramental nature of the people of God,[66] and in the local churches they belong in a special way to the diocesan family.[67]

The conciliar decree on the pastoral office of bishops pays special attention to the role of religious. It places them among the cooperators with the bishop inasmuch as they attend to pastoral needs in conformity with the characteristic purposes, each of their own institute.[68]

22. The identity of religious life and of its specific role is further clarified by the pluriformity and complementarity of vocations and ministries in the church.

It is necessary, therefore, to know and appreciate the duties that pertain to each of the components: the hierarchical ministry, consecrated life in its various forms, the laity.

Thus the exercise of one's own function unfolds in a constant search for fraternal convergence and mutual complementarity, which is at once an affirmation of one's own identity and of ecclesial communion.

23. This is a general criterion of discernment, more obvious when there is a clear awareness of the roles of the various groups in the church and when their complementary aspects are taken into account.

It is the special function of the laity to seek the kingdom of God in dealing with temporal affairs and ordering them as God wishes.[69]

The secular nature of some institutes, among the various forms of consecrated life, permits a more direct presence and a fuller involvement in secular realities and structures. In these institutes, on this account called secular, the members individually exercise their specific apostolate in any appropriate context, thus strengthening the structures of the world.[70]

On the other hand, religious by their choice of life, limit their participation in secular structures, but do not alienate themselves from the actions of the other members of the church in building the secular city as a place capable of receiving the kingdom of God.[71] However, they are present to it in their own special way, not by substituting for other groups in the church either in duties or methods, but by becoming an increasingly radical sign of an evangelical way of life and of involvement through the public witness of their profession, which is carried out communally in all its dimensions.

If religious participate in the ministerial priesthood, they are, by this new title, exhorted to preside over and serve the ecclesial community, thus giving a more striking witness of communion.[72]

24.   Experts in communion, religious are, therefore, called to be an ecclesial community in the church and in the world, witnesses and architects of the plan for unity which is the crowning point of human history in God's design.[73]

Above all, by the profession of the evangelical counsels, which frees one from what might be an obstacle to the fervor of charity, religious are communally a prophetic sign of intimate union with God, who is loved above all things.[74]

Furthermore, through the daily experience of communion of life, prayer and apostolate—the essential and distinctive elements of their form of consecrated life[75]—they are a sign of fraternal fellowship. In fact, in a world frequently very deeply divided and before their brethren in the faith, they give witness to the possibility of a community of goods, of fraternal love, of a program of life and activity which is theirs because they have accepted the call to follow more closely and more freely Christ the Lord, who was sent by the Father so that, firstborn among many brothers and sisters, he might establish a new fraternal fellowship in the gift of his Spirit.[76]

25.   From their communitarian way of living flows that form of presence and involvement which should characterize them in the church's mission and which we now emphasize in view of the options concerning human promotion.

In speaking of the variety of gifts and ministries, it should be noted that the laity and members of secular institutes can take on apostolic, social and political responsibilities as individuals in accordance with the purpose assigned them by the Spirit.

This is not the case with religious. They have freely and consciously chosen to participate completely in their mission of witness, presence and apostolic activity in obedience to the common purpose and to the superiors of their institute. This participation expresses fraternity and support, especially when the apostolic mandate exposes religious to greater and more demanding responsibilities in the sphere of difficult social contexts.

26.   The imperative need for the fundamental criterion of communion is rendered more urgent by the diversity of situations in which Christians find themselves in the world, especially in the socio-political field.[77]

When it is a question of choices which, in an evangelization-human promotion context, necessarily involve both one's own community and the ecclesial community, there is the need always to bear in mind the directive of *Octogesima Adveniens*, 4.[78]

27. The characteristic of communion should permeate the very structures of the common life and activity of religious. In virtue of this characteristic, the profoundly ecclesial nature of religious life becomes a pre-eminent aspect of their mission within the church and within secular society itself.[79]

In this light, acknowledgement of the ministry of bishops as the center of unity in the organic ecclesial communion, and the encouragement of a similar acceptance by the other members of the people of God, is a specific requirement of the special role of religious in the Christian community.

Nor should religious fear any obstacle to the generosity and creativity of their projects[80] from the hierarchical nature of this ecclesial communion,[81] because every sacred authority is given for the purpose of harmoniously promoting charisms and ministries.[82] Indeed, on the contrary, religious are encouraged[83] to be "enterprising in their undertakings and initiatives"; this is in keeping with the charismatic and prophetic nature of religious life itself.

Through their mission, which is open to the universal church and carried out in the local churches,[84] religious are most favorably placed to strengthen those forms of suitable coordination which *Mutuae Relationes* presents as the path to an organic ecclesial communion.[85]

D. In Dynamic Fidelity to Their Own Consecration According to the Charism of the Founder

28. A renewed presence of religious in the church's mission of evangelization and human promotion would not be fully authentic if they were to renounce, even in part, the characteristics of religious life and the special nature of the individual institutes.[86] This requirement, which we have noted constantly, should be a serious obligation of religious communities.

29. It is a question of a dynamic fidelity which is open to the impulse of the Spirit, who speaks through ecclesial events, the signs of the times and through the constant exhortation of the magisterium.

Made more watchful by being better informed of the needs of humanity today, its problems, searchings and hopes,[87] religious communities are better able to discern the true signs of God's presence and designs in the happenings and expectations which they share with the other members of the church. Communal dialogue,[88] guided by faith, by reciprocal acceptance and respect for persons and by religious obe-

dience, is the best way of carrying on this discernment. Precisely because religious communities of their nature are built on faith, they
preserve and radiate the light which helps the whole people of God to
identify the intentions of the Lord regarding the integral human vocation and to discover fully human solutions to all problems.[89]

30. The burning question, which *Evangelii Nuntiandi*, 52 makes
the apex of the apostolic exhortation on the renewal of religious life,
rises like a cry from the heart, in which Paul VI expressed his intense
pastoral concern, his great love for humanity and today's world and
the confidence he placed in religious men and women.

It throws light on the concrete choices of renewal. Their urgency
appeals for a fidelity capable of restoring to the present life and mission of each institute the ardor with which the founders were inflamed
by the original inspirations of the Spirit.[90]

31. It is a constant reference to life in its dynamic profundity as
Pope John Paul II with enlightening words reaffirms:[91] "to life as it
presents itself to us today, bringing with it the riches of traditions of
the past, to offer us the possibility of using them today . . .

"We must be very searching in our discernment of how to help
the religious vocation today toward self-awareness, growth; how religious life should function in the ensemble of the church's life at the
present time. We are still seeking the answer to this question—and
rightly so. We can find it in the teaching of the Second Vatican Council; in the exhortation *Evangelii Nuntiandi*; and in the many statements
of the popes, the synods and episcopal conferences. This answer is
fundamental and many-sided."

The pope reaffirms his hopes for a religious life faithful to these
principles, which make it "an immense fund of generosity" without
which "the church would not be fully itself."

"In an ever renewed fidelity to the charism of the founders, congregations should strive to be responsive to the church's expectations,
to the commitments which the church and its pastors consider the most
urgent at this time, to implement a mission which has so much need
of well-prepared workers."[92]

III. FORMATION REQUIREMENTS

32. The problems facing religious life in its renewal so that there
may be a harmony between evangelization and human promotion
have repercussions on the formation level.

This might require a revision of formation programs and methods at the initial period as well as during the successive phases and during ongoing formation.

In this regard, a re-reading of the conciliar criteria for renewal[93] will show that it is not a question of simple adaptations of certain external forms. It is a deep education in attitude and in lifestyle which makes it possible to remain true to one's self even in new forms of presence. This presence will always be as consecrated persons who seek the full conversion of people and society to the ways of the Gospel through witness and services.[94]

33. In this regard, some aspects of formation seem to merit special attention.

a) There is need to assure an awareness of the profound nature and characteristics of religious life, both in itself and in its dynamic involvement in the mission of the ecclesial community in today's society. Fidelity to the charism of the institute and a creative involvement in a renewal of activities and work are also among the more important elements of initial and ongoing formation.

b) The profession of the evangelical counsels, in the context of religious life-church-modern world, may require new attitudes which are attentive to the value of prophetic sign as a power for the conversion and transformation of the world, of its mode of thinking and of its relationship.[95]

c) Life in common, seen especially as an experience and witness of communion, develops the capacity for adaptation[96] permitting a response to different forms of activity. These do not weaken fraternal bonds and sharing of the institute's specific service to the church. In fact, with this attitude, these bonds could be strengthened.

d) New forms of involvement, which have been described in examining the above problems, could possibly create unforeseen situations. This calls for a spiritual and human preparation in the formation programs of religious life which can help to achieve a mature presence on the part of consecrated persons capable of renewed relationships both within and outside their own communities.

Involvement in the life of the church and in its mission in an attitude of coresponsibility and complementarity, implies an up-to-date knowledge of its projects and the goals it hopes to attain.[97]

From the teaching of the Second Vatican Council and from the insistence with which the Synods of Bishops have referred to the matter it is clear that there can be no dichotomy between formation for the permanent gospel commitment and human promotion according to God's plan. Therefore, a program of formation and renewal in religious institutes would not be adequate and complete unless it took into account the church's thinking in this matter.[98]

This is even more necessary if religious are to be capable of their apostolic duty of reawakening consciences,[99] of forming other Christians, particularly the laity, in such a way that they will assume their proper role in this common mission of evangelization and human promotion with competence and security.[100]

Since the missionary dimension of the church depends especially on the generous availability of religious,[101] the formation of those called to this excellent form of evangelization and human promotion will need to be genuinely adaptable to the cultures, sensibilities and specific problems of the localities.[102]

34.   Chapters and general curias assume considerable importance in the programing and animation for this updating and renewal in fidelity to the Spirit and to history. It is their duty:

—to discern the options which best respond today to the original purposes of the institute;

—to guide the religious and communities by means of appropriate initiatives of information and formation.

—to promote, in thoughtful and substantive dialogue, a rethinking of works so as to motivate those who perhaps have done little updating and to encourage and direct the search for new and suitable approaches.

All this aims at encouraging a more attractive and clear discovery of the values of consecration and mission which are basic for a conscious and joyful membership and participation in one's own institute.

35.   Conferences of religious, because of their more immediate knowledge of ecclesial and social conditions, are in a better position to identify the problems of different countries and continents. Through an exchange of experiences and study meetings, they could, in collaboration with the episcopal conferences and respecting the various charisms, find solutions and means more in harmony with the hopes for integral human promotion. In all of this, let them always be inspired by the Gospel and guided constantly by the magisterium of the church.

Cardinal Edward Pironio
Prefect
Archbishop Augustin Mayer
Secretary

NOTES

1. *Evangelii Nuntiandi,* 18-19.
2. *Gaudium et Spes,* 4: "It is not, then through opportunism or a desire for novelty that the church, expert in humanity, defends human rights. It is through an authentic gospel commitment which, as Christ's case, cares for the most needy." (John Paul II, Puebla Address, III, 3)
3. *Lumen Gentium,* 46.
4. LG, 44; *Mutuae Relationes,* 8; 10.
5. *Evangelica Testificatio 52-53.*
6. GS, 10.
7. EN, 69.
8. *Populorum Progressio,* 12.
9. *ET,* 17; GS, 63; ET, 52.
10. EN, 30.
11. *Ibid.,* 33-34. In his inaugural address in Puebla (III, 4), John Paul II stated: "Christ was not indifferent to this great and demanding imperative of social morality. Neither can the church be. In the church's spirit, which is the Spirit of Christ, and supported by her vast and solid doctrine, let us get to work in this field."
12. EN, 69; LG, 31; MR, 14a.
13. EN, 69.
14. MR, 59-60 and f.
15. AAS 1971, pp. 928-932.
16. EN, 39.
17. "The pope wishes to speak for you, to be the voice of those who cannot speak and of those who have been silenced, so as to be a conscience for consciences, an appeal for action, to recover lost time, which is oftentime of prolonged suffering and unfulfilled hopes." (John Paul II to the *campesinos* of Latin America, Jan. 29, 1979).
18. Synod of 1971, p. 933.
19. EN, 69.
20. LG, 46.
21. *Perfectae Caritatis,* 1; LG, 46.
22. ET, 52.
23. MR, 19; 23f; 41.
24. EN, 69; Puebla document, nn. 733-734: Apostolic openness of ministries and a preferential choice of the poor are the most evident tendencies in religious life in Latin America. In fact, more and more, religious men and women are to be found in the difficult and under-

privileged areas. . . . This choice does not presuppose the exclusion of anyone, but it does mean a preference for and nearness to the poor. This has brought about a rethinking of traditional works so as to make a better response to the demands of evangelization . . .

25. LG, 9-12; 34-36; *Christus Dominus*, 33-35; EN, 13; 58; *Apostolicam Actuositatem*, 2, 6-10.

26. Cf. document of the Sacred Congregation for Catholic Education, on the Catholic school. (March 19, 1977), nn. 60-61: participation of the Christian community in the educative process of the Catholic school.

27. CD, 35; MR, 22-23.

28. PC, 13; ET, 20; cf. GS, 67-72 concerning the human and Christian elements of work.

29. *Presbyterorum Ordinis*, 8; *Octogesima Adveniens*, 48. The document of the Synod of Bishops which treats of the ministerial priesthood (cf. AAS 1971, p. 912-913, recalling *Presbyterorum Ordinis*, 8, states that the priestly ministry is to be considered a function which is valid in itself and, indeed, in the light of faith, is more excellent than others. If, in particular circumstances, other activities accompany this ministry, the criterion of suitability is to be sought in the resulting contribution to the pastoral ministry of the church. It is especially the bishop and his council of priests that must decide having consulted, when necessary, the episcopal conference.

30. MR, 10; LG, 44.

31. Cf. ET, 20: "But your activities cannot derogate from the vocation of your various institutes, nor habitually involve work such as would take the place of their specific tasks." Cf. also the document of the Sacred Congregation for Catholic Education on the school, n. 74-76.

32. ET, 20.

33. LG, 44; PC, 1; ET, 3.

34. PC, 15; ET, 21; 39.

35. OA, 48.

36. OA, 48 and 50.

37. Cf. Puebla doc., nos. 1162-1163 and 1244 (discourse of John Paul II to workers).

38. LG, 31; 33 - AA, 7; 13 - GS, 67; 68; 72.

39. GS, 42; 76; Synod 1971, AAS, p. 932: Puebla doc., nos. 558-559.

40. Cf. discourse of John Paul II to the Union of Superiors General, Nov. 24, 1978, in which he asked them to "interpret in the correct gospel sense the option for the poorer classes and for all victims of hu-

man selfishness, without giving way to socio-political radicalism . . . to draw close to the people without prejudice of their religious identity, and without dimming the specific originality of their own vocation." Cf. also Puebla doc., n. 528.

41. MR, 49-50.

42. ET, 1; PC, 6.

43. EN, 69; Puebla doc., nos. 527-529.

44. Cf. Synod 1971, AAS, p. 912-913: The criterion given for priests, as already mentioned for other forms of involvement in secular structures (no. 8), guides the behavior of religious also, due to the close links of religious life with the hierarchical apostolate (CD, 34) and the special relationship which binds it to the pastoral responsibility of the church (LG, 45-46). In *Mutuae Relationes,* (nos. 5-10-36) the theological reasons are dealt with more at length and practical conclusions are drawn for ecclesial obedience and appropriate arrangement. Cf. also the Puebla doc., n. 769, where the pope's words are quoted. "You are religious and priests; you are not social or political leaders or officials of a temporal power. Therefore I tell you again: Let us not be under the illusion that we are serving the Gospel if we try to dilute our charism by an exaggerated interest in the wide field of temporal problems." (AAS, LXXI, p. 193)

45. Cf. PC, 2.

46. GS, 9.

47. Cf. especially the synods of 1971 and 1974; the apostolic exhortation *Evangelii Nuntiandi,* which is complemented under the directly social and political aspects by *Octogesima Adveniens.*

48. Cf. *Redemptor Hominis,* 14; "The church cannot abandon man . . . Man in the full truth of his existence, of his personal being and also of his community and social being. This man is the primary route that the church must travel in fulfilling her mission."

49. GS, 22; RH, 8.

50. GS, 63.

51. PC, 2,d; MR, 26-32.

52. Is. 42:1-7; 61:1-4; Lk. 4:17-19; cf. Puebla doc., nos. 1130: "The evangelization of the poor was for Jesus one of the messianic signs, and for us too it will be a sign of gospel authenticity."

53. Mk. 1:15.

54. Mt. 5:3-12; 5:20,43-48.

55. LG, 44; PC, 1.

56. PC, 2,a.

57. LG, 44; EN, 69.

58. MR, 16; 26-28.

59. John Paul II, Puebla, inaugural dis. III, 6; EN, 9; 30-39; cf. also, in the same inaugural discourse, I, 2-5 the call to a solid Christology and the unique Gospel, without minimizing or deforming interpretations, as the basis for our capacity to "serve man, our people, to impregnate their culture with the Gospel, to transform hearts, to humanize systems and structures." Cf. RH, 11.

60. LG, 31.

61. *Ibid.*, 44.

62. LG, 31.

63. MR, 4.

64. Acts 20:28; MR, 5-9.

65. LG, 44.

66. MR. 10.

67. CD, 34; the theological principles and criteria of application are described at length in the document *Mutuae Relationes.*

68. CD, 33-35.

69. LG, 31.

70. Motu proprio *Primo Feliciter,* AAS, 1948, p. 285; PC, 11.

71. LG, 46.

72. LG, 28; GS, 43; MR, 36.

73. GS, 19; 32 - cf. Puebla doc., nos. 211-219; 721: "Consecrated life is evangelizing in itself in view of communion and participation."

74. LG, 44.

75. PC, 15; cf. Puebla doc., nos. 730-732.

76. GS, 32.

77. OA, 3.

78. "Confronted with such diverse situations, we read in *Octogesima Adveniens,* 4, it is difficult to sum it up in one word or to propose a universally valid solution. It is for the Christian communities to analyze objectively the situation in their own country, clarify it in the light of the unchanging words of the Gospel, draw principles for reflection, criteria for judging and directives for action from the church's social teaching. It is for the Christian community to discern, with the help of the Holy Spirit, in communion with the bishops concerned and in dialogue with the other Christian brethren and all men of good will, the choices and commitments that must be made to bring about the social, political and economic changes that are obviously needed in many cases. In looking for what changes ought to be made, Christians should first renew their trust in the power and originality of gospel demands." cf. Puebla doc., n. 473.

79. "Religious should not only accept, but they should loyally

strive for unbreakable unity of intention and action with the bishops. There cannot and must not be any lack of collaboration, which is at once responsible and active, but also docile and trusting, on the part of religious, whose charism makes them so much more suitable ministers in the service of the Gospel." (John Paul II, inaug. disc. Puebla, II).

80. MR, 5.

81. *Ibid.*, n. 19; 41.

82. LG, 10-12; 27; PO, 9; AA, 2.

83. EN, 69.

84. LG, 45-46; CD, 33-35; cf. discourse of John Paul II to superiors general, Nov. 24, 1978.

85. MR, no. 52 and f.

86. LG, Chapt. 6; PC, 2; MR, nos. 11-12.

87. GS, 1-10; ET, 25.

88. PC, 14; ET, 25.

89. GS, 11.

90. MR, 23f.

91. Discourse to superiors general, Nov. 24, 1978.

92. Discourse to International Union of Superiors General, Nov. 16, 1978.

93. PC, 2; 18; ES, II, 15-19; 33-38.

94. PC, 18.

95. ET, 13-29; cf. Puebla doc., no. 476: "Our social behavior is an integral part of our following of Christ."

96. PC, 3; 15.

97. PC, 2,c.

98. "With reference to this teaching, the church has a mission to carry out: It must preach, educate persons and groups, form public opinion, give guidance to public authorities. Draw, then, from these genuine sources. Speak with the voice of experience, of the sufferings and hopes of contemporary humanity." (John Paul II, Puebla, inaugural discourse, III, 4).

99. ET, 18.

100. *Justice in the World* (Synod 1971), AAS pp. 935-937), together with a synthesis of the church's principal doctrinal statements, also gives directives for a commitment to an "education for justice."

And again, John Paul II (Puebla, inaug. dis., III, 7): "Allow me then to recall the urgency of sensitizing the faithful to this social teaching of the church. Special attention should be given to the formation of a social conscience at all levels in all sectors. When injustices are on the increase and the gap between poor and rich is widening painfully, social teaching, creative and open to the wide fields of the church's presence, should be an invaluable instrument of formation and action."

101. EN, 69.
102. *Ad Gentes*, 18; 25-27.

A Document of the 1971 Bishops' Synod

THE MINISTERIAL PRIESTHOOD

I, 7: THE PRIEST AND TEMPORAL MATTERS

The proper mission entrusted by Christ to the priest, as to the Church, is not of the political, economic or social order, but of the religious order (cf. GS 42); yet, in the pursuit of his ministry, the priest can contribute greatly to the establishment of a more just secular order, especially in places where the human problems of injustice and oppression are more serious. He must always, however, preserve ecclesial communion and reject violence in words or deeds as not being in accordance with the Gospel.

II, 2: SECULAR AND POLITICAL ACTIVITY

(1) The priestly ministry, even if compared with other activities, not only is to be considered as a fully valid human activity but indeed as more excellent than other activities, though this great value can be fully understood only in the light of faith. Thus, as a general rule, the priestly ministry shall be a full-time occupation. Sharing in the secular activities of men is by no means to be considered the principal end nor can such participation suffice to give expression to priests' specific responsibility. Priests, without being of the world and without taking it as their model, must nevertheless live in the world (cf. PO 3, 17; Jn 17:14–16), as witnesses and stewards of another life (cf. PO 3).

In order to determine in concrete circumstances whether secular activity is in accord with the priestly ministry, inquiry should be made whether and in what way those duties and activities serve the mission of the Church, those who have not yet received the Gospel message and finally the Christian community. This is to be judged by the local bishop with his presbyterium, and if necessary in consultation with the episcopal conference.

When activities of this sort, which ordinarily pertain to the laity, are as it were demanded by the priest's very mission to evangelize, they must be harmonized with his other ministerial activities, in those circumstances where they can be considered as necessary forms of true ministry (cf. PO 8).

(b) Together with the entire Church, priests are obliged, to the utmost of their ability, to select a definite pattern of action, when it is a question of the defense of fundamental human rights, the promotion of the full development of persons and the pursuit of the cause of peace and justice; the means must indeed always be consonant with the Gospel. These principles are all valid not only in the individual sphere, but also in the social field; in this regard priests should help the laity to devote themselves to forming their consciences rightly.

In circumstances in which there legitimately exist different political, social and economic options, priests like all citizens have a right to select their personal options. But since political options are by nature contingent and never in an entirely adequate and perennial way interpret the Gospel, the priest, who is the witness of things to come, must keep a certain distance from any political office or involvement.

In order that he may remain a valid sign of unity and be able to preach the Gospel in its entirety, the priest can sometimes be obliged to abstain from the exercise of his own right in this matter. Moreover, care must be taken lest his option appear to Christians to be the only legitimate one or become a cause of division among the faithful. Let priests be mindful of the laity's maturity, which is to be valued highly when it is a question of their specific role.

Leadership or active militancy on behalf of any political party is to be excluded by every priest unless, in concrete and exceptional circumstances, this is truly required by the good of the community, and receives the consent of the bishop after consultation with the priests' council and, if circumstances call for it, with the episcopal conference.

The priority of the specific mission which pervades the entire priestly existence must therefore always be kept in mind so that, with great confidence, and having a renewed experience of the things of God, priests may be able to announce these things efficaciously and with joy to the men who await them.

REPORT TO THE VATICAN:
U.S. RELIGIOUS ORDERS TODAY

A Paper Forwarded to the Vatican Congregation for Religious and for Secular Institutes by the Leadership Conference of Women Religious and the Conference of Major Superiors of Men in the United States, 1978

I. POST-VATICAN II UNDERSTANDING OF RELIGIOUS LIFE

It is worth noting at the outset that in a post-Vatican II understanding of religious life emphasis falls on *life:* Life lived in community, life lived in the world, life lived with all other people—and in particular with the laity. Let us mention, without elaboration then, themes that are at the heart of this reflection.

A. *Citizenship.* Religious understand that through birth into a particular nation, ethnic group, culture, they are bearers of the human patrimony in its more universal manifestations but also in the particularity of their country. They are citizens of the world community. They are citizens of their land. As citizens, they understand their duty of furthering the common good with the inevitable implications this will have for the political. As Jesus loved his humanity and so sought the humanization of life, so religious believe they have the duty of sharing with all humanity the advancement of humankind.

B. *Baptism.* It is from baptism that religious, along with the laity and all others in the church, receive their commission to evangelize. And from this perspective, religious and laity alike are called to a life of evangelical, gospel, holiness.

Stemming in part from this consideration is the conviction that religious life should not be lived in separation from the laity. Indeed, many a bishop in the synods of '71 and '74 pointed out how congenial to the people (e.g. in Africa, Latin America) was the creation of communities in which all in the church shared and in which service of God was not separated from service of the human family, God's family.

C. *Religious life.* Religious life, once seen as a closed community of the vowed, now is seen by many as an intensified form of the announcing of the kingdom through the witness of a consecrated life. (It is understood that the witness of service is integral to the consecrated life.)

D. *Spirituality.* An earlier spirituality had wanted, insofar as religious are related to the world, to confine the function of religious almost exclusively to witness. By this was meant that the consecrated person through the vows stood as symbol of the true values of the Beatitudes. Unfortunately, this symbol has, at times, been used to emphasize the transcendent character of religious life and to negate or to minimize the incarnational character.

E. It might be added that other *theological strands* are interwoven in this main line of reflection; namely,

> —Today's religious are the children of Vatican II. Religious, in many instances, base their understanding of the church upon *Lumen Gentium.* In this understanding, church as "people of God" exacts significant roles of religious which are less distinguishable from those of the laity.
> —With *Gaudium et Spes* and *Evangelii Nuntiandi,* religious believe that easy separation of the religious from the world is foreign to the church's mission. A longing for a final home does not preclude, but reinforces, concern for a more human world on earth. (*GS*)
> —With the synod of '71, religious believe that love of God is inseparable from love of God's people, that the justice of God is willed for our world and that, as a consequence, one cannot be just before God if one is not just before people.

F. The religious' contemplation of Jesus has led to new understandings of religious life. If the following of the cross remains important, that very cross takes on new dimensions. The crucified Jesus went to his death because he dared to liberate from sin and death. But this was also a liberation from unjust structures—from a Torah that only burdened, from a priesthood that bound people in darkness. Christ identified with the poor and the powerless. He took sides and acted politically. And it was this that brought him to his trial and death.

G. Religious have everywhere become children of the theology of *reading the signs of the times*. They understand, with post-Vatican II theology, what significance aspirations of peoples, movements of our times, events have for the discovery of what God's kingdom demands. With the synod of '71's *Justice in the World*, religious reflect, under the guidance of the Spirit, on where people are, on what their needs are.

H. Vatican II and theological developments since Vatican II have awakened the consciousness and conscience of religious to justice as a constitutive element of holiness. Moreover, contemporary challenges which have demanded action on behalf of justice in solidarity with the poor and oppressed have energized religious to recapture the original charisms of their congregations. Action on behalf of justice has been a determining factor in the reassessment religious have been making of their own calling.

II. IMPLICATIONS FOR RELIGIOUS

As religious have reflected on various documents of the magisterium and on their actions on behalf of justice, they have been drawn to discernment based on difficult and careful analysis of the socio-economic and political realities of today. Through their commitment to the teachings of the church, to the poor and the oppressed, through their identity with the victims of injustice, they have come to a deeper, clearer realization that the prevailing situation of today's world for most people is one of unfreedom, of marginalization of masses of men and women, of severe poverty for millions of humans (even 20 percent of the people in the affluent United States), of starvation, of discrimination, of deprivation of opportunity, etc.

While in no way denying or doubting the reality and evil of personal sin, religious have come to realize that much of the injustice of today's world is structural. It exists in or is brought about by the very social, economic, political and military structures of our global society. And they are thus led to ask: How do we witness in this situation? How do we serve?

From this analytical base, they are motivated to speak out in witness of biblical values. They are led to restructure their own congregations and ministries to provide greater flexibility for response to injustice. They are led to simplify their own lifestyles, to dissociate from the powers of this world, to reject those "values" that mark a society as decadent, materialistic and unjust. Their doing so makes their witness not only more credible in itself, but also a more authentic public expression of that humanization which expressed the meaning of the Gospel of Jesus' own life, and of the teaching of the church.

But there is more. Religious today are, as a result of their prayer and discernment and in imitation of Jesus Christ, moving more and more into real identity of life with the poor and the powerless. They strive to share their condition, to support their efforts to cope with their situation and especially to change it. They strive to be a voice for the voiceless, to denounce—in word and action—the grave injustices which dehumanize today's poor majority.

III. POLITICAL PRAXIS

Religious, once again with surprising convergence from one continent to another, have found the following political actions fully compatible with the preceding reflection on religious life—indeed as flowing inexorably therefrom. This is the kingdom. This is where the Spirit guides.

A. *Denounce injustices.* From practices such as unjust detainment of political prisoners, torture, unfair trial, religious have learned that in many places political processes themselves are abused to marginalize whole classes of society. They see everywhere the intolerably excessive share that the rich and powerful are able to draw to themselves, depriving the poor and the weak of the benefits handed out by the state. Returning missionaries have made religious more generally conscious of the extent to which governments of the mission-sending country may be the exploiters. Religious are coming to see more that *we* are part of the problem—another cogent reason for believing that religious must play active roles proportionate to their complicity.

B. *Educate and conscientize.* Religious play a large part in the church's educational endeavor through their schools and other ministries of continuing education. If education is to be that described in *Justice in the World*, then it has powerful "political" implications: it will arouse consciousness to understanding the forces of injustice. It will evoke a critical sense with respect to values of society. It will challenge existing ethos. Such education is and will be considered by some as subversive.

C. *Announce*. *Octogesima Adveniens* invites all in the church to exercise that utopian vision which reaches beyond all existing forms of society and, in the light of the Gospel, to imagine a new earth. Those opposing the engagement of religious in education will equally reject their announcing a new society.

D. *Take sides with the poor and the oppressed*. Religious believe that if they are to have true *sign* value, they must be in the midst of the poor and oppressed. A number of activities in this respect are very familiar. Among them are:

—Giving talks in the local civic community;
—Supporting such reform legislation as tax, health benefits, unemployment aid;
—Signing letters of protest;
—Marching in favor of the exploited;
—Creating, among the abandoned, nuclear communities of witness and service, of community education to issues;
—Lobbying—but not as extraparliamentary opposition or political alternative.

E. *Denounce abuses by multinational corporations through stockholder suits*. U.S. religious have discovered and refined a creative tool for reaching the consciences of corporate executives and boards of trustees of large corporations: they initiate formal motions for disclosure of certain immoral or oppressive practices of such international companies and present such motions (with requisite signatures, etc.) at annual meetings of stockholders. The result has been a raising of consciousness both of ourselves and of larger publics.

F. *Guide movements*. Religious have played important roles in guiding organizations (trade unions, workers' movements, family centers, etc.) into channels supportive of the preceding lines of activity and away from more traditional emphasis on purely personal perfection.

G. *Creat communities*. In Latin America and elsewhere religious share in community building. Such new communities, where they grow in strength and take on a sense of direction, become a new political force—perhaps the only truly people's movement available in situations of oppression.

H. *Assume leadership roles*. With growing experience, religious in the United States have been able to undertake certain forms of direct political activity. They have endorsed candidates because of stands for justice. Certain individual religious have run for office in the hope of effecting change or, at least, of giving a new form of witness to concern.

I. *Accept a prophetic role.* U.S. religious congregations have in general been prepared to accept a varying degree of what has come to be called prophetic action. This may take the form of extralegal or paralegal or even illegal action, for example, denouncing through civil disobedience the Vietnam War, participating in strikes (in some countries considered illegal). Apropos of this latter (as many political actions enumerated earlier) religious often feel that staying out of the fray leaves the laity, lacking the freedom the religious possess, to bear the heat of the battle for justice.

J. *In summary*, from this view of their life as religious, congregation after congregation (and chapter after chapter) has declared its resolution to identify with the poor, to exercise solidarity with the victims of injustice, to serve them, to empower the powerless, to speak out for the voiceless, to enter into struggle for global justice precisely as an exercise of their faith and their commitment as religious.

IV. SOME FINAL REFLECTIONS TOWARD GUIDING PRINCIPLES

A. *Our method.* It will be evident that our method is not that of starting from definitions of either the religious or the political, but rather of starting where reflection in the light of the Spirit has brought religious. We would hope that the validity of this method would be appreciated in the light of post-Vatican II theology.

B. *Our Theology.* We need not repeat that we believe our reflections are solidly built on a post-Vatican II understanding of the gospel call. In particular, it is our belief that definitional division of laity and religious is unproductive for this purpose, however valid in other directions.

In particular it is our belief that the notion of religious assuming certain lay roles in "supplementary" capacity is less valuable than at first may appear. The simple fact is that all the political activities we ascribe to religious appear to be not supplementary, but normal.

C. *Collegiality.* It is the express directive of Paul VI in *Octogesima Adveniens* that discernment of political direction be undertaken by the entire ecclesial community. If we understand *Lumen Gentium* correctly, collegiality, if strictly operative only within the episcopal order, has implications for dialogue and openness with all others in the church.

In this connection might it not be pointed out that generals and provincials have legitimate ecclesial authority? These superiors have been exercising leadership within their communities on the question of socio-political involvement. This is generally done in close touch with local bishops. The situation has in no sense been one of freewheeling, independent decision on the part of religious.

Finally, many major superiors will attest that the critical problem is not too much socio-political involvement. Quite the contrary, it is the continuing indifference of religious to the call of Paul VI, Vatican II, and the synods to concern themselves with justice in the world—and in the specific political contexts in which alone justice can be achieved.

D. *Pluralism. Evangelii Nuntiandi*, among other documents, recognizes legitimate pluralism in evangelical activity, and this for several reasons: legitimate theological pluralism, diversity of charisms within religious families, above all, diversity of cultures. We would think that certain activities quite acceptable within our culture would possibly cause difficulty in acceptance in others. For one thing, partisan politics are not noticeably ideological in the United States. Second, freedom of expression by the individual is highly esteemed here.

E. *Discernment.* In the discernment of action, religious should not only follow the above-mentioned principle, but also seek the guidance of the Holy Spirit, continually reflect on their motivation, and respect the legitimate exercise of episcopal authority. Both religious and the hierarchy should recognize that religious are acting in the realm of what Aquinas called "political prudence," and his, or equivalent, rules for prudential behavior ought to be operative. (It is understood that "prudence" here means not pusilanimity but the art of making final, practical moral judgments).

Conclusion. In the making of judgments today about the appropriateness of religious in political activities, freedom to experiment, to learn and to grow through experience are indispensable for processes of discernment. In addition, because a discernment of local churches, inculturated and incarnated in their own peculiar situation, is necessarily different from that of some other local churches, there must be allowed and encouraged a genuine pluralism. Rigid universal norms are simply unreal in today's pluralistic world. Collaborative efforts on the part of national conferences of bishops and of major superiors will help assure that discernment and pluralism are directed toward realizing the mission of the church. Trust and encouragement on the part of hierarchies and Roman congregations will help to foster a life of consecration that witnesses to a faith that does justice and is a credible sign of God's love.

A Statement Issued by
The Association of Pittsburgh Priests, 1983

THE PRIEST AND POLITICS

"The priest's service is not that of a doctor, of a social worker, of a politician or of a trade unionist . . . The priest has his essential function to perform in the field of souls, of their relations with God and their interior relations with their fellows." *John Paul II, July 2, 1980, to Brazilian priests, Rio de Janeiro*

"Party politics are not for you." *John Paul II, February 13, 1983, to Nigerian priests, in Nigeria*

We wish to address an issue raised in these and other remarks of Pope John Paul II—the priest and politics.

We are fifty priests of the Pittsburgh Catholic diocese. We serve in a variety of pastoral positions in our diocese: in parishes (urban, suburban and rural), in campus ministry and in specialized ministry. We are deeply troubled by the repeated warnings from Pope John Paul II against "priests in politics". We believe his words and his actions are in this instance clearly inconsistent with our priestly tradition. We feel that his repeated statements against priests in politics may be interpreted as authority against any priestly involvement in the wider community.

The Pope gave dramatic form to his carefully phrased views when, during his recent visit to Nicaragua, he vigorously and publicly lectured Ernesto Cardenal, a Jesuit priest who is serving in the cabinet of that nation as Minister of Culture. This public rebuke, ill-timed and most ungracious, revealed for all the depth of the Pope's feelings on the issue of priests and politics.

454

In our own nation we have had the experience of a direct Papal order that prevented Robert Drinan, an American Jesuit priest, from running for reelection to Congress in 1980. The same order, never published, kept Robert Cornell, a religious priest from Wisconsin, from seeking his second term in Congress.

First, we wish to make several distinctions. In American usage, the phrase "priest in politics" has several meanings.

In our nation, and in other democratic nations, it can mean a priest who gains a position in government through popular election. He places himself before the people of a district, who send him to political office by a majority vote. It should be noted here that some priests seeking office have failed to win election. Robert Cornell, the Wisconsin priest, was defeated when seeking a second term in Congress. He was about to make another attempt when Pope John Paul's order to Robert Drinan was applied to him. Charles Owen Rice, a priest of our diocese nationally known as a "labor priest" was defeated when he sought election to Pittsburgh City Council in 1971.

Sometimes as in the case of Robert Drinan, the elected position is full time and salaried. It is inconsistent with any other pastoral or specialized position. Msgr. Rice had an agreement with the then bishop of Pittsburgh that he would resign his pastorate if he were to be elected.

In other instances, the elected position is part-time, with little or no salary and is consistent with a full-time pastoral ministry. John Powis, a priest of the Brooklyn diocese, was elected to a seat on a community school board in the Ocean Hill section of New York City during a period of turbulent change and conflict. He continued to serve on the staff of his local parish, also in Ocean Hill.

A second meaning of "priest in politics" is that of a priest holding an appointed position in a governmental agency or on a governmental committee. Here also the position may be full-time and salaried, or it may be part-time. Numerous American priests have served on committees or commissions, often without pay, sometimes receiving expenses, and usually while continuing a pastoral assignment. Bishop Joseph M. Sullivan of Brooklyn was only last month appointed by Governor Mario Cuomo as one of twenty-one members of a Council on Fiscal and Economic Priorities.

Geno Baroni, a priest of the Washington (D.C.) archdiocese, is the most recent and prominent example of this type of priestly involvement in government. Monsignor Baroni was Assistant Secretary for Housing and Community Development in the cabinet of President

Jimmy Carter, from 1976 through to 1980. Baroni subsequently resumed pastoral work in his archdiocese.

In our own diocese, Charles Owen Rice, mentioned already, served as director for the Office of Price Administration during the second world war here in the city of Pittsburgh. That was a full-time and salaried position for Monsignor Rice. Today he is serving on the Allegheny County Prison Board, a part-time and unsalaried position where he has been a strong advocate of decent treatment for prisoners. Rice is currently pastor in a suburban parish.

Words and phrases often have another meaning than what may appear in a dictionary. A third meaning of the phrase "priest in politics", and one far more common than the other two, is the intervention of a priest, alone or with others, in a community problem—local, regional or national. The priest may preach on moral aspects of the problem. He may visit public officials and speak with them, or speak out either before a public body or at a public meeting. Priests may join in forms of public protest, including non-violent civil disobedience. Beginning with the Freedom Marches in the South during the 1960's and extending to Vietnam War and now anti-nuclear arms protests, some American priests have been prominently identified with this type of political action.

It is this type of priestly involvement in politics that has been for us the occasion of the most controversy.

The history of the ethnically diverse priests of our own diocese, as elsewhere, is filled with instances of the parish priest speaking or acting on behalf of his people on what could well be called a political issue. Two examples are of particular pride to us as Pittsburgh priests.

Albert Kazincy, pastor of St. Michael's in Braddock, gave vigorous and dramatic support to the steelworkers in their unsuccessful strike of 1919. Thomas Bell pays eloquent tribute to Father Kazincy in his novel, *Out of This Furnace*.

In 1932, James Cox, pastor of old St. Patrick's in the heart of Pittsburgh, led a march of over twenty thousand unemployed workers to Washington, D.C. The goal of the march was legislation to put the millions of unemployed American workers back to work. President Herbert Hoover received Father Cox with courtesy but not with agreement. The enormous popularity of James Cox's leadership is shown in a turnout of fifty-five thousand persons for a rally at a local stadium after the marchers had returned to Pittsburgh. Cox proclaimed at this rally that the battle was against "Wall Street and Smithfield Street". Even today, fifty years later, old-timers remember him with respect and affection.

In more recent years, priests have taken an active role in many neighborhood organizations, echoing the involvement of the ethnic pastor in the early part of this century. Priests of our diocese have served frequently alongside their parishioners in fighting the indifference of elected officials and the neglect of some neighborhoods. Sometimes, as with Focus on Renewal in McKees Rocks and the Metropolitan Citizens Organization in Pittsburgh and McKeesport, priests have joined parishioners and neighbors to oppose private and public corruption. These priests have often been supported, but sometimes criticized, for their involvement in politics.

This tradition of priestly involvement in the community has had the tacit acceptance of the bishops of the diocese. Rare has been the instance where a priest was disciplined or removed from an assignment because of community involvement. Much more often, the priest received quiet, indirect but firm support from the Bishop of his time. Wisely, the Bishop did not back every word or deed by his priests— but he often rejected efforts by persons, sometimes very prominent and powerful, who sought the removal of a priest for his involvement in what they angrily called "politics". These critics asserted that a priest has no business in such matters, but by their consistent silence the Bishops of Pittsburgh have disagreed.

Nor is our history in Pittsburgh any different from the history of most of the American Catholic church. Priests serving in full-time elected office have been rare, as the Church by official policy intends it to be. Robert Drinan and Robert Cornell were the only American priests to serve in Congress during the twentieth century. We are not aware of a single priest who has held full-time elected office in our diocese in its entire history. Priests serving in full-time appointed positions in government have also been few ... but the history of the American church is full of priests who have involved themselves in the political problems of their time, and usually in a way that grew directly from their priestly ministry.

Indeed, it was a Bishop who in 1975 was found to be the natural choice to head the newly formed California Agricultural Labor Relations Board as full-time chairman. Auxiliary Bishop Roger Mahony had been serving as executive director of the California Catholic Conference, in which position he had been involved in negotiations on behalf of the U.S. Catholic bishops with both sides in an enduring grape strike.

At this point, two great priests of the nineteenth century come to mind. Damien de Veuster was a Belgian priest who came to serve as pastor to the lepers on Molokai in what were then called the Sandwich

Islands, now the Hawaiian Islands and one of our fifty states. Father Damien's priestly ministry to the lepers ended when he himself contracted the sickness and died from it.

Not as well known, however, is his political involvement. His leper parishioners depended in their isolated village on food and supplies sent by the Board of Health in Honolulu. This Board showed itself extremely insensitive to the needs of lepers, even failing to send supplies that had been voted by the island legislature. Damien frequently pressured the Board on behalf of his parishioners. He made trips to Honolulu to intercede. On one such trip he was told bluntly by the President of the Board of Health that his role was the spiritual care of the lepers and nothing more.

Pierre (Peter) de Smet has been called the best known American Jesuit priest of the nineteenth century. From 1823 he spent fifty years in priestly work among the Indians of the western plains and mountains. He played a central role in the peace commissions of 1867 and 1868, which brought an end to fighting between the U.S. Army and several Indian tribes. On a trip to Washington in 1861 he urged the Superintendent of Indian Affairs to release treaty monies to the Osage and Potawatomie tribes. He even suggested that the two tribes might side with the Confederacy if the payments were not forthcoming. The payments were released following his intervention.

Finally, one quick mention of priests elsewhere. In the twentieth century, the greatest example, and the most respected, of priestly involvement in politics is that of Luigi Sturzo. Don Sturzo was elected to office in Italy and even founded a political party that helped to hold back the thrust of the Communists. Luigi Sturzo was publicly recognized by at least two Popes as an outstanding priest.

We have given this history from our own diocese and from the American church because it is important for us all, and for John Paul II, to understand that there is an honored and tested tradition of priestly involvement in politics, in the several meanings of that phrase which we have sketched.

Just what is it that Pope John Paul asks of priests? To us it is evident that he is concerned about much more than the rare instance of a priest in full-time elected or appointed office. His order to remove Robert Drinan from Congress, an order we believe to have been unjust, is symptomatic of a deeper concern. He speaks on his trips not only to Ernesto Cardenal in his full-time cabinet position but to the priests of Brazil and Nigeria, none of whom hold any full-time elected office.

We believe that Pope John Paul has not understood the experience of the American priest in politics, in the several meanings of that phrase. In John Paul's native Poland, who would say that there have not been priests and bishops in recent years involved in political issues? Who would say that the late Cardinal Wyszinski was a spiritual man who never concerned himself with political matters?

In Poland, where the Catholic church has a unique position even under a Communist government, the bishop and priest can be involved in politics, so to speak, while remaining inside the church. In Poland, sermons, even religious processions, can have a strong political meaning. Polish bishops and priests have not marched in protest demonstrations, as have some American priests, but they have marshalled their people with telling effect to oppose unjust government policies.

In Poland, a Marian procession can be a political event. In the United States and other western nations where Catholicism is not the predominant religion, and where the practice of religion is free from government restrictions, priestly involvement in political matters is quite different.

We salute the brave priests of Poland who have supported and encouraged the working people of the outlawed union, Solidarity. We salute the bishops and priests who have spoken from Polish pulpits for human rights and religious freedom. We honor the memory of the Polish priests who died in Nazi concentration camps during World War II. They worked and died for justice in one particular set of circumstances. Polish priests and bishops today work for religious freedom and human rights in another set of circumstances. Priests in the United States (and other western nations) work for justice in another set of circumstances.

Like the bishops of Pittsburgh who gave support to priests who worked for justice in political matters (and who did not constantly put down the work of these priests), so should John Paul as a good pastor support his priests in their work for justice, decency and human dignity.

We have been deeply moved by many of the words of Pope John Paul II. Who could not be affected by such an address as that he gave at Yankee Stadium (New York) on October 2, 1979? The very title of the talk, "Do Not Leave to the Poor the Crumbs of Your Feast," bespeaks the power of the message.

We intend this statement as a dialogue with the Pope, with our priestly colleagues and with all our brothers and sisters in the church. "As a church we are political practitioners because we have to be. It is important to understand what is appropriate in that position and what is not. It is even more important to understand why it is essential that the church use the methods available to it to influence public policy, because it is by that policy that the moral order is frequently established." (Archbishop John Roach, president, National Conference of Catholic Bishops, speaking to the Knights of Columbus, supreme convention, August 12, 1982).

The priest cannot love the poor in the abstract but must love them in the flesh. The priest cannot seek justice and righteousness in a theoretical way but in the circumstances of the time and place where he fulfills his ministry. Work for justice is an essential part of the priestly ministry, as it is essential for every Christian man and woman. This work for justice takes different forms in different societies. We suggest that when Pope John Paul better understands the traditions of American priests and of other nations, then we will have a better, more constructive, less negative dialogue on how the quest for peace and justice is worked out in priestly ministry.

CONTRIBUTORS

MSGR. GENO CHARLES BARONI was ordained for the diocese of Johnstown-Altoona, Pennsylvania in 1956. After several years as an assistant pastor in Altoona and at Sts. Paul and Augustine parish in Washington, D.C., he was appointed chair of the urban task force for the U.S. Catholic Conference. In 1970 he founded the National Center for Urban Ethnic Affairs and served as the first president of that organization. When Jimmy Carter was elected President in 1976, Baroni was appointed assistant secretary for Housing and Urban Development, the highest Federal position ever held by an active clergyman. In 1981 Baroni resigned from HUD and became a special assistant for Urban Affairs to Archbishop James Hickey of Washington, D.C. He died at the age of 53 in August 1984 after a long illness, a few weeks after approving this memoir for publication in this volume.

HON. RICHARD F. CELESTE, a Democrat, was elected as Ohio's 64th governor in 1982. From 1979 to 1981 he served as director of the Peace Corps, after a term as lieutenant governor of Ohio, 1974-1978. A Rhodes Scholar and Carnegie teaching fellow at Yale, Governor Celeste also served as assistant to the U.S. Ambassador to India in New Delhi during the 1960's. As governor of Ohio, his administration has been distinguished by fiscal realism and progressive social policy. Since his inauguration, he has appointed several members of religious orders to positions in state government.

CAROL COSTON, OP, is the founding director of NETWORK, a Catholic social justice lobby in Washington, D.C. Coston met Clare Dunn, CSJ, in 1972 and in the intervening years they collaborated on several political ministry projects. Prior to her NETWORK experience Coston worked as an educator in Michigan, Puerto Rico and Florida; later she served as administrator of a

461

high school dropout program and in a low-income housing project. Currently she chairs the Adrian Dominican Corporate Investment Board and is engaged in a project to study worker-owned cooperatives and organic farming.

AGNES CUNNINGHAM, SSCM, S.T.D., is a professor of Patristic Theology and Early Christianity and director of the Department of Church History at Saint Mary of the Lake Seminary, Mundelein, Illinois. She was the first woman to be president of the Catholic Theological Society of America, 1977-78. Currently she is theological consultant to the NCCB Ad Hoc Committee on Women in Church and Society and executive director of the Chicago Theological Institute, the north side cluster of seminary and theological schools in the Chicago area. She is a member of the Servants of the Holy Heart of Mary congregation; co-author of *Human Sexuality* (Paulist Press), editor of *The Early Church and the State* volume in the Sources of Early Christian Thought series (Fortress Press), and author of several other monographs.

HON. JOHN C. DANFORTH, a Republican, is an ordained Episcopal priest and a two-term senator from the State of Missouri. A former attorney general of Missouri, he serves on the U.S. Senate Committees on Finance, Commerce, and Budget. A graduate of Princeton (his senior thesis was on "The Christology of Reinhold Niebuhr"), Yale Divinity School and Yale Law School, he is an associate of St. Alban's Church in Washington, D.C., and a member of the governing board of the National Cathedral. Every Tuesday morning, he conducts his regular weekly communion service before he begins his day in the U.S. Senate.

ROBERT F. DRINAN, SJ, was elected to the U.S. House of Representatives from the Fourth District of Massachusetts in 1970. As a member of the House Judiciary Committee he was an influential voice in the resolution for impeachment that led to President Nixon's resignation, as well as an advocate of reforms in human and civil rights policies and in the Federal Code. When the Vatican intervened in 1980, he withdrew his name as a candidate for re-election. An attorney and formerly dean of the Boston College Law School, subsequent to his tenure in Congress he served as chairman of the Americans for Democratic Action and is currently a professor in the Georgetown Law School in Washington.

CLARE DUNN, CSJ, a sister of St. Joseph of Carondelet, was the first nun elected to a state legislature in the United States. Elected to the Arizona state legislature in 1974, she was serving her fourth term when she was killed in a head-on collision on July 31, 1981, while returning to Tucson from a special session of the legislature. The accident occurred when some undocumented workers inadvertently entered the highway going the wrong way.

MARY EWENS, OP, is the president of Edgewood College in Madison, Wisconsin. She holds a doctorate in American Studies and has written extensively on the American nun. She is the author of *The Role of the Nun in Nineteenth-Century America*, (Arno Press, 1978) and is a Dominican sister of Sinsinawa, Wisconsin.

CAROLYN FARRELL, BVM, was the first woman to be elected to city council and to serve as mayor of the city of Dubuque, Iowa. A Sister of Charity of the Blessed Virgin Mary, and formerly a school principal and director of Continuing Education at Clarke College, Dubuque, she became a city council member in 1978 and was elected mayor in 1980. Currently she is regional representative for her religious community and vice-chair of the Campaign Finance Disclosure Commission for the State of Iowa.

GERALD FOGARTY, SJ, is an associate professor in the Department of Religious Studies at the University of Virginia, Charlottesville, Virginia. He received his doctorate in church history from Yale and is the author of two books in his field: *The Vatican and the American Hierarchy from 1870 to 1965* (Stuttgart: Anton Hiersemann, 1982) and *The Vatican and the Americanist Crisis* (Rome: Gregorian Univ. Press, 1974). In addition he has authored many articles on historical aspects of religion and politics, including an article on "Private Religion and Public Patriotism," in the *U.S. Catholic Historian*, Fall, 1984.

THOMAS M. GANNON, a former Jesuit and editor of *America* magazine, is an attorney in Washington, D.C.

EMILY GEORGE, RSM, was assistant administrator general of the Sisters of Mercy of the Union from 1980-1984, during the time when the involvement of several Sisters of Mercy in politics became an issue with church authorities. Formerly provincial of the Detroit province and president of Mercy College in Detroit, George holds a doctorate in American history and has several publications in her field. As an educator she has been on the faculty of several institutions and had a brief stint as an associate director of a shelter for battered women in Detroit. Sister Emily George was on a research leave at the University of Notre Dame when she was killed in an auto accident in December 1984.

DR. ALAN GEYER is executive director of the Churches' Center for Theology and Public Policy in Washington, D.C. A political scientist and ethicist, he formerly served as editor of the *Christian Century* and Dag Hammarskjöld Professor of Peace Studies at Colgate University. He is president of the Society of Christian Ethics.

THEODORE M. HESBURGH, CSC, a priest of the Congregation of Holy Cross, has headed the University of Notre Dame since 1952. Father Hesburgh has held 14 Presidential appointments over the years, and they have involved him in virtually all the major social issues—civil rights, peaceful uses of atomic energy, campus unrest, amnesty for Vietnam offenders, Third World development, and immigration reform, to mention only a few. In addition to his unique record of public service for which he was awarded the Medal of Freedom, he has continued to be a major influence in American higher education. As chair of the International Federation of Catholic Universities from 1963 to 1970, he was instrumental in redefining the nature and mission of the contemporary Catholic university. His work off campus has also included service to four popes, three of them as permanent Holy See representative to the International Atomic Energy Agency in Vienna from 1956 to 1970. He is currently a member of Pope John Paul II's Pontifical Council for Culture.

KENNETH HIMES, OFM, is an assistant professor of moral theology and social ethics at Washington Theological Union in Washington, D.C. He is a priest of the Order of Friars Minor, New York province, and received his doctorate in religion from Duke University. He has published articles on questions of social ethics, including an article on "Local Church as Mediating Structure in Public Policy," forthcoming in *Social Thought*. This year he is engaged in a research project to study "Social Sin and Personal Culpability."

MADONNA KOLBENSCHLAG, HM, is a fellow of the Woodstock Theological Center in Washington, D.C., and a Sister of the Humility of Mary. She has published and lectured widely on a variety of subjects including women's development and spirituality, public policy and religious affairs. She has been active in politics since the 1970's when she was a delegate to the Indiana State Democratic Convention; she was also a mayoral appointee to the South Bend Commission on the Status of Women, and later served as a legislative assistant to Congresswoman Mary Rose Oakar (Dem-OH) in the U.S. House of Representatives. She was formerly a professor of American Studies at the University of

Notre Dame and is best known for her book, *Kiss Sleeping Beauty Good-Bye* (Bantam, 1982).

JOSEPH A. KOMONCHAK is a priest of the Archdiocese of New York and an associate professor of theology in the Department of Religion and Religious Education at the Catholic University of America. He is the author of numerous articles on ecclesiology, ministry and the Church's mission in the world. This past year he has been a fellow at the Woodrow Wilson International Center for Scholars in Washington, D.C.

JOHN LANGAN, SJ, has been a fellow of the Woodstock Theological Center in Washington, D.C. since 1975. He also serves as a lecturer in the philosophy and government departments at Georgetown University and has been a visiting professor in the Yale Divinity School. He has contributed articles to many journals on human rights, just war theory, and Catholic social teaching.

AGNES MARY MANSOUR, a sister of Mercy of the Union for 30 years, is currently director of social services for the State of Michigan, an office that administrates the second largest welfare budget in the United States. Prior to accepting the state post, Mansour was president of Mercy College in Detroit and a candidate for the congressional primary in 1982. When her responsibility for administrating Medicaid funding became an issue, Archbishop Edmund Skoza withdrew his permission for her to serve in the state post, and she was subsequently forced by the Vatican to leave her religious congregation in 1983.

ELIZABETH MORANCY is now in her fourth term as a state representative in the Rhode Island General Assembly (she was unopposed in the 1984 election). Morancy had been a Sister of Mercy of the Union for 25 years when Bishop Gelineau of Providence reversed his position on her candidacy for public office, forcing her to seek dispensation from her vows. Active for many years in inner-city social work, for the past four years she has worked especially with the Hmong refugees and other marginated groups in her district, one of the poorest in the state. In addition to her legislative duties, she is Director of the Rhode Island Protection and Advocacy System.

MARY SEAN O'REILLY is an attorney and Judge-Court Master for the Family Law Courts of Tarrant County, Texas. Her appointment as judge followed several years of service as legal counsel to women and children affected by family violence and other crises in the Fort Worth area. A Sister of St. Mary of Namur for

16 years, she recently sought a dispensation subsequent to a community discernment process concerning corporate directions.

LAWRENCE M. O'ROURKE is the White House correspondent for the *St. Louis Post-Dispatch*, an attorney and former deputy assistant secretary in the U.S. Department of Education in the Carter administration. He has traveled extensively in the Soviet Union as well as in the People's Republic of China, and has been a chronicler of Geno Baroni for many years. He is currently working on a biography of Baroni.

ARDETH PLATTE, OP, is a Grand Rapids Dominican sister now in her third term as councilwoman in Saginaw, Michigan. Her service in city government has been distinguished by her work and interventions on numerous social and human rights issues: housing, education, family violence, racial and sex discrimination, employment, substance abuse, pollution control, resistance to nuclear weapons and a local nuclear power plant. She serves on the Michigan Advisory Committee to the U.S. Civil Rights Commission and has served on the board of the Michigan Catholic Conference. She has received numerous awards and citations from the Michigan House and Senate for her civic service. She is a co-director of the Saginaw Home for Peace and Justice and currently serves as Mayor pro-tem of the city of Saginaw.

JAMES H. PROVOST, J.C.D., is a priest of the diocese of Helena, Montana, and an associate professor of canon law at the Catholic University of America in Washington, D.C., where he has been on the faculty since 1979. He is also executive coordinator of the Canon Law Society of America and managing editor of *The Jurist*, a canon law journal. Provost earned his doctorate in canon law at the Lateran University in Rome in 1967, and served as Chancellor and Officialis for the diocese of Helena from 1967 to 1979. He has published articles in various canonical and theological journals and has edited several books on canonical subjects.

JOSEPH D. SIMON, SVD, is a priest of the Society of the Divine Word and academic dean and vice president of Divine Word College in Iowa. He received his licentiate in church history from Gregorian University in Rome and has been an elected member of the Epworth, Iowa city council since 1976. Fr. Simon also serves on the Eastern Iowa Regional Planning Board, on the Regional Housing Authority and on several other civic commissions and organizational boards.

JACQUELINE SLATER, CSJ, is a sister of St. Joseph of Carondelet who served three terms as alderman for the 6th Ward of Minneapolis, Minnesota, from 1978 to 1984. As an elected member of the city council she chaired the Government Operations and Intergovernmental Relations Committees. She was active on the community development, planning and transportation commissions and became a voice for the "independent view" in city politics. Prior to her political career, she was a science teacher and involved in urban renewal projects. Sister Jacqueline Slater died unexpectedly in November 1984 following open heart surgery.

ROSEMARY SMITH, SC, J.C.D., is a Sister of Charity of New Jersey, a canon lawyer and Judge and Defender of the Bond in the Marriage Tribunal of the diocese of Little Rock, Ark. She has been a consultant to many religious congregations and dioceses regarding constitutions revision, chapters and other canonical issues. Formerly an educator and past provincial councilor for her congregation, she also serves as Delegate for Religious in the diocese.

ROBERT L. SPAETH is dean of the College of Arts and Sciences at St. John's University, Collegeville, Minnesota, and author of *No Easy Answers: Christians Debate Nuclear Arms* (Minneapolis: Winston Press, 1983). Spaeth has been a contributor to several publications on issues surrounding the subject of religion and politics, including an article entitled "A Dangerous Game: The Catholic Clergy Enter Political Life," in *Catholicism and Crisis*, December, 1983. His new book, *The Church and a Catholic's Conscience,* will be published by Winston Press in 1985.

PETER STEINFELS is the editor of *Commonweal* magazine and the author of a critical study, *The Neoconservatives: The Men Who Are Changing America's Politics* (Simon and Schuster, 1979). From 1972 to 1977 he was Associate for the Humanities at the Hastings Institute of Society, Ethics and Life Sciences in Hastings-on-Hudson, N.Y., where he edited the Hastings Center Report. Steinfels is the author of numerous articles, reviews and commentaries on religious and political affairs.

ROLAND H. ST. PIERRE, OMI, is a priest of the Oblates of Mary Immaculate of New England, the first Catholic priest elected mayor of a city in the United States. While serving three terms as the chief executive of Plattsburgh, N.Y., from 1971-1977, he worked to eradicate the patronage system in city politics, strengthened civil service regulations and introduced sound financial management practice into city government. Prior to his tenure as mayor he was a pastor and at one time edited the French and English magazines published by his order. In 1984 he became the Catholic chaplain at the new State prison in Altona, N.Y., where he ministers to inmate and staff needs today.

NANCY SYLVESTER, IHM, is the national coordinator of NETWORK, a Catholic social justice lobby based in Washington, D.C. She also served as the co-chair of the Coalition for a New Foreign and Military Policy and has lectured widely on social justice and the political process. She is a sister of the Immaculate Heart of Mary of Monroe, Michigan.

BISHOP KENNETH E. UNTENER was ordained to the priesthood in 1963 by Cardinal Dearden of Detroit. In 1965 Untener was appointed assistant chancellor for the Archdiocese of Detroit and for several years co-hosted a weekly interfaith television program called "Dialogue." Bishop Untener holds a doctorate in theology from the Gregorian University in Rome and served as the Rector of St. John's Seminary from 1977 to 1980, when he was appointed Bishop of Saginaw, Michigan. Currently, Bishop Untener serves as a member of several committees of the National Conference of Catholic Bishops: on Liturgy, on the Laity, on Pastoral Research and Practices, and on the follow-up committee for the bishops' pastoral on war and peace. He is the author of several articles, including an essay on local church theology, "Local Church and Universal Church," *America*, October 13, 1984.

PAUL J. WEBER is a professor in the Department of Political Science and chairman of the Social Science division at the University of Louisville. He is co-author of *Private Churches and Public Money* (Greenwood, 1981). His articles on church, state and politics have appeared in several scholarly and legal journals.